UNREASONABLE HISTORIES

: A BOOK IN THE SERIES :

Radical Perspectives: A Radical History Review book series

SERIES EDITORS: Daniel J. Walkowitz, New York University

Barbara Weinstein, New York University

History, as radical historians have long observed, cannot be severed from autho-
rial subjectivity, indeed from politics. Political concerns animate the questions we
ask, the subjects on which we write. For over thirty years the *Radical History Review*
has led in nurturing and advancing politically engaged historical research. Radical
Perspectives seeks to further the journal's mission: any author wishing to be in the
series makes a self-conscious decision to associate her or his work with a radical
perspective. To be sure, many of us are currently struggling with the issue of what
it means to be a radical historian in the early twenty-first century, and this series is
intended to provide some signposts for what we would judge to be radical history.
It will offer innovative ways of telling stories from multiple perspectives; comparative, transnational, and global histories that transcend conventional boundaries
of region and nation; works that elaborate on the implications of the postcolonial
move to "provincialize Europe"; studies of the public in and of the past, including
those that consider the commodification of the past; histories that explore the
intersection of identities such as gender, race, class, and sexuality with an eye to
their political implications and complications. Above all, this book series seeks to
create an important intellectual space and discursive community to explore the
very issue of what constitutes radical history. Within this context, some of the
books published in the series may privilege alternative and oppositional political
cultures, but all will be concerned with the way power is constituted, contested,
used, and abused.

UNREASONABLE HISTORIES

:::

**NATIVISM, MULTIRACIAL LIVES, AND
THE GENEALOGICAL IMAGINATION
IN BRITISH AFRICA**

::

Christopher J. Lee

Duke University Press
DURHAM AND LONDON
2014

:::

Designed by Kristina Kachele
Typeset in Chaparral Pro by Tseng Information Systems, Inc.

Library of Congress Cataloging-in-Publication Data
Lee, Christopher J.
Unreasonable histories : nativism, multiracial lives, and the
genealogical imagination in British Africa / Christopher J. Lee.
pages cm — (Radical perspectives)
Includes bibliographical references and index.
ISBN 978-0-8223-5713-1 (cloth : alk. paper)
ISBN 978-0-8223-5725-4 (pbk. : alk. paper)
1. Great Britain—Colonies—Africa—Administration.
2. Great Britain—Colonies—Race relations.
3. Racially mixed people—Africa—History.
I. Title. II. Series: Radical perspectives.
DT32.5.L44 2015
968.9004′05—dc23   2014020690

ISBN 978-0-8223-7637-8 (e-book)

Cover art: Guy Tillim, *Petros Village, Malawi, #27*, 2006 (top);
Petros Village, Malawi, #9, 2006 (bottom). Courtesy of the artist.

CONTENTS

::

A NOTE ON ILLUSTRATIONS

∷

This book contains a number of photographs as illustrations, many of which are from the National Archives of the United Kingdom. I have also taken photographs of various colonial-era documents from the National Archives of Malawi, the National Archives of Zimbabwe, and the National Archives of Zambia. Although many illustrations are images of people and places discussed in the narrative, a select number are intended for evocative purposes—to capture the appearance, atmosphere, and attitudes of a certain time and place, thus providing ways of seeing from the past. This book consequently uses photographs as a unique and serious source for scholars to situate historical narratives visually. (The work of W. G. Sebald is also an influence.) However, given their origin, some images may be considered Eurocentric in perspective. I utilize these illustrations with this caveat in mind. Although I offer commentary with each illustration, I anticipate that readers will be sensitive to both the explicit and suggestive uses of these images and will bear in mind the critical acknowledgment of their limitations as stated here, without my having to repeat this position throughout the text.

A NOTE ON TERMINOLOGY

::

This book addresses the histories of multiracial people in British Central Africa. The term *multiracial* (designating more than one race) is commonly employed by sociologists and other scholars today instead of more dated expressions such as *mulatto* and *mixed race*. I consequently use *multiracial* in preference over the other two terms. When I do apply the ambiguous descriptions *mixed* or *mixed race*, I often place the words in quotes to highlight my critical view of these overused and analytically unhelpful adjectives, which tend to obscure both personal and social histories as argued in this book. I similarly place pejorative expressions such as *half-caste* in quotes. In the context of southern Africa, the term *Coloured* is often utilized. I use it as well, though with caution and specificity, since this book seeks to develop a broader comparative conversation between experiences found in southern Africa, elsewhere in Africa, and other parts of the world. The term *Coloured* is controversial in some quarters—particularly in South Africa, where it is viewed as part of an apartheid-era terminology. Provisional solutions by other scholars have included placing the term in quotes ("Coloured"), making it lower-case (coloured), and qualifying it with prefatory language (so-called Coloured), all which attempt to unsettle a strict racial meaning. Though I am deeply sympathetic to such politics, this book exercises the term in capitalized form, given its common historical use in this way and due to the fact that lower-case and quoted forms do not necessarily safeguard it from more problematic practices and understandings.

Most significantly, this book emphasizes regionally specific historical terms such as *Anglo-African*, *Euro-African*, *Eur-African*, and *Eurafrican* when appropriate. These self-fashioned expressions found in the Rhodesias and Nyasaland during the colonial period are qualitatively different from the more generic, state-sanctioned *Coloured*, as addressed in the chapters that follow. Many regional intellectuals and organizations criticized this latter expression, and I have taken these local views seriously. This book therefore works against the idea that *Coloured, Anglo-African*, and *Eurafrican* are interchangeable, synonymous terms. They instead reflect different sets of politics and layered historical experiences marked by particular familial, cultural, and imperial claims indicated through the prefixes of *Eur* and *Anglo* as well as the base word *African*. In sum, this book employs when appropriate a distinct historical terminology to emphasize local and regional forms of self-construction and creative agency as a provisional subterfuge for the predicament of uncritically reproducing colonial state categories and the political effects they can have.

ACKNOWLEDGMENTS

::

This book is, in part, about ways of thinking and the consequent ways of being that follow from them. From the vantage point of the present, it is about the histories left behind by such experiences. Writing this book has also been an experience, and this book also has a history. I have benefited from a range of teachers, friends, colleagues, and family members who have taught me both how to think and how to be. While the word *acknowledgment* does not quite capture the size of the debt I owe, or the sense of humility I feel, it is a pleasure to have the opportunity to thank so many people.

This book took its earliest form as a doctoral dissertation at Stanford University, where I had the good fortune to study with a number of excellent scholars, above all Richard Roberts, George M. Fredrickson, and Richard White. At Stanford and the University of California, Berkeley, I also profited from working with and receiving assistance from Christine Capper-Sullivan, Lynn Eden, Karen Fung, Tabitha Kanogo, Sam Mchombo, Donald Moore, Valentin Mudimbe, Gary Mukai, and Martha Saavedra. I hold particular gratitude for Kennell Jackson, who initiated me into Stanford life with lunches at Branner Hall and conversations about a diverse range of topics. My greatest debt is to Richard Roberts—for his instruction, for his persistent advocacy and generosity, and for his general guidance on having a productive, meaningful career. Everything I know about African social history—its range, its possibilities, and its importance—originates with his teaching. While I conducted fieldwork, I received support from various scholars in Malawi and South Africa. At Chancellor College, the University of Malawi, Kings Phiri hosted my stays in Zomba on several occasions. I thank him and Wiseman Chirwa for conversation and making my visits possible. Rob Jamieson and his family also accommodated me in Malawi, for which I am grateful. Staff members at the National Archives of Malawi met all my research needs. At the University of Cape Town, I thank

Brenda Cooper, Harry Garuba, Bill Nasson, and Chris Saunders for arranging concurrent residencies at the Department of Historical Studies and at the Centre for African Studies. Zimitri Erasmus took an early interest in my research, and her questions and comments have informed my thinking. I owe special thanks to Mohamed Adhikari for providing an essential first audience as an authority on South African Coloured history, as well as presenting an opportunity to publish as my work matured.

Since completing my doctorate, I have continued to receive support from a range of people. Emmanuel Akyeampong did a rare thing by giving me my first job. I extend my gratitude to him and Caroline Elkins for a productive year at Harvard University. I spent a similarly indispensable year at Dalhousie University with Phil Zachernuk and Gary Kynoch, who granted me the benefit of their time and critical engagement with early versions of the ideas explored here. Jocelyn Alexander, Brian Raftopoulos, Gemma Rodrigues, and Graham and Annia Stewart provided invaluable help and support during two research trips to Zimbabwe. David Gordon and Marja Hinfelaar provided essential assistance in Zambia. The staff at the National Archives of Zimbabwe and the National Archives of Zambia offered persistent guidance, as did the staff at the National Archives of the United Kingdom. Much of my career thus far has been spent at the University of North Carolina (UNC) at Chapel Hill, where I gained from the company, insights, and support from a range of colleagues. At UNC and neighboring Duke and North Carolina State Universities, I thank Barbara Anderson, Ed Balleisen, Paul Berliner, Kathryn Burns, Bruce Hall, Engseng Ho, Jerma Jackson, Owen Kalinga, Charles Kurzman, Michael Lambert, Lisa Lindsay, Terence McIntosh, Louise Meintjes, Susan Pennybacker, Eunice Sahle, Bereket Selassie, Karin Shapiro, Sarah Shields, and Ken Vickery for taking interest in my work and, more significantly, standing by through periods of thick and thin.

A number of foundations, universities, and programs offered financial support for research and writing. The history departments at Stanford, Harvard, Dalhousie, and UNC provided grants that aided my research. The School of Humanities and Sciences and the Institute for International Studies, both at Stanford, and the University Research Council, the Center for Global Initiatives, and the African Studies Center, all at UNC, provided different forms of summer and travel funding. The Foreign Language and Area Studies program and the Fulbright-Hays program at the U.S. Department of Education provided major support for initial fieldwork. The

Mellon, MacArthur, and Woodrow Wilson Foundations sustained periods of writing. The American Historical Association and the American Philosophical Society provided smaller grants that nevertheless were important. I also benefited from two residential fellowships while trying to find permanent employment. A Mellon-Sawyer program at Stanford and an Izaak Walton Killam fellowship at Dalhousie helped during this early period. At UNC, I held the D. Earl Pardue Fellowship at the Institute for the Arts and Humanities; I thank John McGowan for his support. A visiting fellowship at the Centre for Humanities Research at the University of the Western Cape, funded by the Ford and Mellon Foundations, introduced me to an inspiring intellectual community. I thank Premesh Lalu for his generosity in hosting my visit. Finally, I would like to thank Julie Hardwick and the Institute for Historical Studies at the University of Texas at Austin for space and time at a penultimate stage of writing and revision.

Money sustains research, but friends and colleagues sustain the researcher. Over the past decade (and earlier), I have gained much from the company of many through graduate school, conferences, fieldwork, and places in between. For taking interest in my work, asking questions, providing stimulating thought, and supplying answers, I thank (beyond those already mentioned) Kathryn Barrett-Gaines, Maria-Benedita Basto, Gillian Berchowitz, Christiaan Beyers, Jim Brennan, Gary Burgess, Jerry Buttrey, Enver Casimir, Augustine Chan, Sharad Chari, Ruramisai Charumbira, Mhoze Chikowero, John Comaroff, Alice Conklin, Wayne Dooling, Sabrina Drill, Sarah Emily Duff, Harri Englund, Steve Fabian, Toyin Falola, Kathleen Foody, Ellie Gamble, Abosede George, Sally and Jim Gilliatt, Sandra Greene, Zoe Groves, Sean Hanretta, Barbara Harlow, Walter Hawthorne, Jean Hay, Stacey Hynd, Sean Jacobs, Rachel Jean-Baptiste, Hilary Jones, Nancy Kendall, Dane Kennedy, Tom Killion, Martin Klein, Ben Lawrance, Dan Magaziner, Minkah Makalani, Ibbo Mandaza, John Mason, Ian McDonald, Juliette Milner-Thornton, Helen Moffett, Jamie Monson, Andrew Offenburger, Emily Osborn, Marty Otañez, Mel Page, Jane Parpart, Derek Peterson, Rachel Petrocelli, Jeremy Prestholdt, Carina Ray, Claire Robertson, Shira Robinson, Macha Roesink, Lynn Schler, Pamela Scully, Ahmad Sikainga, Jon Soske, Erika Stevens, Jim Sweet, Ruth Watson, Luise White, Christian Williams, Daniel Yon, and Clemens Zobel. Former students such as Randy Brown, Ryan Brown, Diana Gergel, Will Hayles, Toussaint Losier, Laura Premack, and Rob Rouphail have taught me as much as I have taught them. Zach Smith and Dasa Mortensen provided astute comments on an earlier version of this manuscript, as only graduate students can. I met Emily Burrill shortly after I returned from my initial fieldwork, and I had the privilege to spend the next seven years with her. I thank her for her care, support, and intellect during that time, which shaped my thinking and benefited this book at an early stage in innumerable ways.

Regarding previous publication, a version of chapter 1 appeared as "Do Colonial People Exist? Rethinking Ethno-Genesis and Peoplehood through the *Longue Durée* in South-East Central Africa," *Social History* 36, no. 2 (2011): 169–91. A version of chapter 2 appeared as "Gender without Groups: Confession, Resistance, and Selfhood in the Colonial Archive," *Gender and History* 24, no. 3 (2012): 701–17. A version of chapter 3 appeared as "Children in the Archives: Epistolary Evidence, Youth Agency, and the Social Meanings of 'Coming of Age' in Interwar Nyasaland," *Journal of Family History* 35, no. 1 (2010): 24–47. Versions of chapter 4 appeared as "*Jus Soli* and *Jus Sanguinis* in the Colonies: The Interwar Politics of Race, Culture, and Multi-Racial Legal Status in British Africa," *Law and History Review* 29, no. 2 (2011): 497–522 and "The 'Native' Undefined: Colonial Categories, Anglo-African Status, and the Politics of Kinship in British Central Africa, 1929–1938," *Journal of African History* 46, no. 3 (2005): 455–78. Some of the research presented in chapter 6 appeared in "'A Generous Dream, but Difficult to Realize': The Anglo-African Community of Nyasaland, 1929–1940," *Society of Malawi Journal* 61, no. 2 (2008): 19–41.

This book was completed during a difficult period, personally and professionally, over the past five years. A particular set of people sustained me. I am indebted to Antoinette Burton, Philippa Levine, and Richard Roberts, once more, for their immediate assistance and meaningful words during moments of crisis and uncertainty. Fred Cooper, Pier Larson, Kenda Mutongi, Susan Pennybacker, and Vijay Prashad similarly provided support when I needed it most. Isabel Hofmeyr, Owen Kalinga, Paul Landau, Dilip Menon, Pauline Peters, Joey Power, Brian Raftopoulos, Tim Scarnecchia, and Karin Shapiro read penultimate drafts of the manuscript, for which I am immensely grateful. Miriam Angress at Duke University Press has been an ideal editor, guiding this project with patience, clarity, and wisdom. I thank her, Radical Perspectives series editors Barbara Weinstein and Daniel Walkowitz, as well as the peer review readers for their assistance and cogent insights. Clifton Crais, Jonathon Glassman, Jason Parker, Bereket Selassie, Helen Tilley, Megan Vaughan, and Karin (again) offered help, perspective, and encouragement at different times, which I will continue to remember. Many have traveled to Johannesburg during the past century to seek their fortune, and I have made a similar journey. I am indebted to Dilip and Isabel (once more) for opening a door of opportunity. Matt Andrews, Mike Huner, and Josh Nadel used to distract me with beer, pool, and UNC basketball to great effect, which I miss. Peter Hallett and Nathan Wentworth have consistently reminded me of my roots and given me the kind of reassurance that only childhood friends can. They are my brothers. My sister, Jennifer, and her family have offered similar support throughout. Jennifer Bartlett above all sustained me during an extremely difficult time, when much of what I had worked toward I felt I had lost. She gave me the confidence to keep going. This book would not have appeared without her being there and her understanding of what it has meant to me.

This book is dedicated to three people, who have been less involved in its making but who nevertheless informed its inception. My parents have supported me throughout my life, this project being no exception. More significantly, many of the questions explored in this book have their early origins in their personal history. I thank them for their unwavering care and enduring patience with a son who has more often than not been unreasonable in his pursuits. François Manchuelle first taught me about Africa's past. He is the reason I decided to pursue a career in this field. Among many lessons I remember, the most important was to have a sense of historical imagination, to develop a sense of understanding and empathy that generates feelings of connection, not difference. This basic principle has guided my teaching, research, and writing. I still have an undergraduate paper on Mongo Beti's *Mission to Kala*, on which he wrote, "I can imagine you publishing a version of this someday." I wish I could share the publication of this book with him. With appreciation, I hope it fulfills, in small measure, the early promise he sought to cultivate.

Johannesburg, December 2013

INTRODUCTION

:::

COLONIALISM, NATIVISM, AND THE
GENEALOGICAL IMAGINATION

::

On the eve of 1964, the British Central African Federation (1953–63) that had united Northern Rhodesia, Southern Rhodesia, and Nyasaland for ten years ended. By July 6, 1964, Nyasaland achieved its independence to become Malawi, with Zambia following suit on October 24, 1964. Southern Rhodesia would pursue an entirely different political path through the white-led Rhodesian Front's Unilateral Declaration of Independence on November 11, 1965. A prolonged armed struggle would result, lasting until 1980 with the founding of Zimbabwe. However, the official collapse of the federation on December 31, 1963, virtually guaranteed eventual change across the region. British control and influence—even among Southern Rhodesia's white community—would decline dramatically in a span of less than two years. To mark the occasion, a symbolic funeral procession took place on New Year's Day, 1964, at the headquarters of the Malawi Congress Party (MCP) in Limbe, Nyasaland, with a coffin provocatively labeled "Federation Corpse" burned as an effigy of imperial failure. Hastings Kamuzu Banda (1898–1997), leader of the MCP and future president of Malawi (figure I.1), prefaced this emblematic gesture with a short speech in which he affirmed, with pointed refrain, "Now at last, the Federation is dissolved, dissolved, dissolved."[1] In a similar spirit of disenchantment, Kenneth Kaunda, president of Zambia and leader of the United National Independence Party, commented several years later that the federation had been a doomed effort to counter African nationalism, presenting "a brake upon African advancement in the North." In his view, whites throughout the region had been "blinding themselves to the signs writ large in the skies over post-war Africa," a case of "shouting against the wind."[2] In these ways, the

FIGURE I.1. President Hastings Kamuzu Banda of Malawi (left) with President Julius
Nyerere of Tanzania (right), early 1960s. Used by permission of the National Archives
of the United Kingdom (CO 1069/165/9).

federation seemed fated to fail in the minds of its most public critics—a
last imperial experiment—being a mere transition phase on the way to
complete decolonization.[3]

Yet this regional political change in British-ruled central Africa did not
reflect a universal consensus of popular opinion. Other voices supported
the continuation of British governance that had been established in the
late nineteenth century, evincing a politics of imperial identity and belonging that dissolved amid the racial revolutions of the 1960s. On a different evening in 1964, a car filled with several young men, assumed to be
members of the MCP's paramilitary Young Pioneers, pulled into the drive-
way of Henry Ascroft (born in 1904) on Chileka Road near the outskirts
of Blantyre, Malawi. Ascroft had been a founding member of the Anglo-
African Association during the late 1920s and spent much of his political
life as an advocate for Nyasaland's "Anglo-African" community—people of
multiracial background who claimed African, British, and Indian heritage.[4]
The visit was a surprise and, given the time of day, unwelcome. The young

men left only after Ascroft had been physically beaten with their message firmly delivered: the Banda government did not approve of Ascroft's political views or sympathize with what remained of Anglo-African interests. The MCP stridently objected to a politics espoused by Ascroft that elevated European ancestry and entitlement over African interests, a colonial-era loyalism out of step with the transition then occurring.

This episode proved to be a turning point. Ascroft's health quickly deteriorated, leading to his death in 1965. In recounting these details to me over thirty years later, his daughters, Jessica and Ann, spoke with a mix of reverence and distance, relating their father's activities and politics as part of a different era of time, silenced by decades of autocratic rule under the Banda regime (1964–94) yet still held in family memory.[5] In retrospect this event appears as a minor incident in Malawi's postcolonial history, more personal than public in nature. There were others like Ascroft who did not meet a similar fate. Ismail K. Surtee, an Indo-African man committed to the MCP, became Speaker of the National Assembly of Malawi shortly after independence.[6] Yet Ascroft's treatment fell within an established pattern. State power under Banda often intervened in the affairs of perceived political opponents, brutally suppressing contrary political outlooks, social identities, and historical experiences.[7] As another informant told me regarding Ascroft's views toward Banda and Malawi's independence, Ascroft was "not sure as to what the changes would bring in this country [for Anglo-Africans], what their fate would be, so they tried to resist."[8]

This book returns to the colonial period to examine the perspectives and histories of individuals like Ascroft—people of multiracial background who cultivated connections with regional colonial states and the British Empire more generally. It is concerned with those who lost—politically, socially, and culturally—with the end of colonialism, whose histories have since been marginalized by the politics of African nationalism during the postcolonial period. Indeed, despite Malawi's diverse and extensive historiography, my first encounter with Ascroft and the Anglo-African community was not through an existing published account but the result of sifting through documents at the National Archives of Malawi in Zomba while researching a different topic. The Anglo-African Association merited enough attention to receive a subject heading within an index compiled by a colonial archivist, an unusual inclusion amid more predictable listings of tobacco production, missionary activities, and annual fishing quotas from Lake Nyasa. My agenda soon changed. Although Ascroft's perspectives were ones I resolutely rejected—exhibiting strident forms of racism and imperial patriotism in equal measure—they were also difficult to ignore, possessing an unvarnished honesty and even intellectual sophistication. They disclosed an unconventional worldview involving notions of kinship and racial heritage that not only articulated what it meant to be "Anglo-African," but also argued for a politics of colonial loyalty and entitlement that sharply contrasted with the politics of anticolonial resistance common in many postcolonial social histories. Although descent and genealogy have played key roles in defining racial difference, their uses in this context were intriguingly inventive, clearly motivated by self-interest, and forcefully grounded in sentiments of family and lived personal experience rather than sociological abstraction—a kind of folk racism that only oppression could conceive. This surreptitious genealogical imagination was at once eccentric yet accessible, organic and local in orientation yet connected to broader patterns of cultural knowledge and historical experience. Above all, it suggested a history that had not been accounted for, a story waiting to be told, and a new set of possibilities about how histories of race and colonialism might be written.[9]

This book is about this genealogical imagination—its origins, its diverse morphologies and instrumental uses, and its historical demise. This socially constructed imagination was and remains a form of critical practice. It is essential to understanding how multiracial people negotiated a colonial world defined by racial difference and, more specifically, distinctions between *native* and *non-native*—to revisit the terminology of the time.[10] It reveals an alternative social and political outlook that challenges assumptions about ethical life during the colonial period by introducing a critical vocabulary of connection, rather than resistance. Through this focus, this book contributes to an expanding literature on the varied political cultures that appeared under colonial rule, particularly those articulated by subaltern communities whose marginalization produced exceptional perspectives that challenge postcolonial nationalism and its versions of the past. But neither is it about restoring a set of moribund ideas that are ultimately of little consequence. Larger themes emerge regarding the catalysts, rationales, and limitations of such imaginative practices. At its core, this book is a study of racial thought under colonialism in British Central Africa from the early to the mid-twentieth century and the ways in which it informed a cluster of issues—sexual behavior, social identification, political arguments, legal status, urban planning, poverty, and colonial common sense. It does not settle on any single aspect but traces the causal interplay among them, affecting the different realms in which multiracial Africans lived and the ways in which they negotiated these matters. This plural format captured in the chapters that follow draws attention to how people made strategic sense of a complex world infused with distinctions that could both provide and limit opportunity. Indeed, though intellectual origins are touched upon, this book is more concerned with constitutive practices.[11] Race is understood to be a marker, as well as a phenomenological schema—a structure of thought for explaining the world. Race is irreducible to any single context or explanation—what Ann Laura Stoler has called its polyvalent mobility—with each of the aforementioned issues carrying historical and pedagogical significance.[12] The forthcoming chapters consequently argue for the importance of racial minorities and their layered histories under colonial rule. They challenge conventional narratives of state formation, the establishment of colonial legal systems, and the composition and support of national liberation struggles.[13] This book foregrounds the meaning of unfamiliar views like Ascroft's—what E. S. Atieno Odhiambo and David William Cohen have referred to as "knowledge from the shadows"—that indicate the emergence of colonial political imaginations that were uncommon, even enigmatic, and tell us new stories as a result.[14]

: NATIVISM AND ITS HIDDEN HISTORIES :

Race and racism are widely addressed problems that have fundamentally defined our past and present. They demand attention, requiring both historical understanding and methodical vigilance that resists revalidating them uncritically.[15] Race as a biological concept is a fiction. It is a sociohistorical construction as so many scholars have underscored. But racism is not a fabrication, as varied histories of slavery, imperialism, and violence attest.[16] Yet, despite the urgency of these issues, geographic, temporal, and analytic imbalances exist that raise vital questions about the universal definition, application, and meaning of *race* as a useful category for historical analysis. This situation particularly applies to African studies. *Race*—customarily defined by false notions of biological descent and intrinsic aptitude corresponding to physical type—and *racism*—the act of using race as a basis for social and political discrimination—were central aspects of modern colonialism, a fact widely accepted yet treated unevenly.[17] One explanation is the reductive quality that a racial framework can impart. Given the demography of most African societies, *ethnicity*— also informed by ideas of descent, though complemented by learned, historically rooted cultural practices—has been perceived as providing a more textured view of social relations and history stretching across time periods.[18] An ethnic paradigm has dominated African studies as a result. Indeed, this paradigm has been positioned as antiracist in orientation—a critical stance derived from the cultural relativism pioneered by scholars such as Franz Boas and his student Melville Herskovits.[19] But imperatives of historical method have also played a decisive role in the undervaluation of this issue. Given concerns for enduring dynamics of history and identification internal to the African continent, racial thought has typically been perceived as fixed to the colonial era—a system of intellectual belief introduced by European contact—having no deep or meaningful history prior to this period.[20] This problem is compounded by scholarship that has congregated in certain parts of the continent, particularly those with high densities of white settlement—South Africa being the prime example. Yet South Africa cannot remain a stand-in for the rest of the continent.[21]

This book addresses these predicaments. It is positioned within a recent turn in scholarship that has sought to rethink histories of race and racism beyond accustomed places and time periods.[22] This new scholarship has not only underscored the racial diversity of colonial societies. It has also enabled more complex understandings of colonialism and racism to emerge by outlining the multiple origins and outcomes of racial thought and difference. This book expands the geography of current research by undertaking a regional approach that accounts for the politics of racialization in British Central Africa (map I.1).[23] Its primary setting is the Nyasaland Protectorate (first established as the British Central Africa Protectorate from 1891 to 1907)—a classic out-of-the-way place in many respects, particularly with regard to the topic at hand.[24] But racial difference and discrimination did have meaning in this ostensibly peripheral context— seen most evocatively in the Chilembwe Uprising of 1915—and the set of histories here examine how such vivid local experiences formed part of a regional political scene that extended to Southern Rhodesia (chartered in 1889) and Northern Rhodesia (1911).[25] Before race and nationalism intersected to herald political change as they did in Malawi and Zambia in 1964 and Southern Rhodesia in 1965, race took legal, intellectual, and cultural shape in an imperial context. The regional framework of this book there-

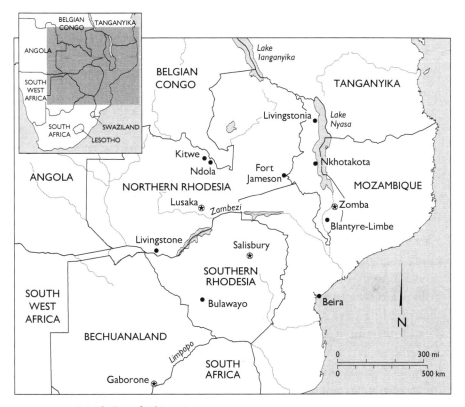

MAP I.1. British Central Africa, circa 1950.

fore intends to unfasten race and nation from each other — denaturalizing a relationship that has placed racial formation within narratives of anti-colonial activism, postcolonial nationalism, and group conflict more generally — to consider instead different social uses and political geographies.[26] Racial distinction was a consummate form of colonial reason, a central rationale that validated a rule of difference extending to realms of culture, class, land, and gender.[27] As such, it presented a means of organizing the world that neither states nor colonial subjects could avoid. In contrast to African nationalists and pan-Africanists who mobilized the experience of racial discrimination as a basis for anticolonial solidarity, it rationalized for multiracial people senses of legal and political entitlement on the basis of European racial descent, encouraging the evolution of a political language of imperial loyalty and reciprocity expressed through vernacular idioms of kinship and genealogy. For Ascroft and others like him, being multiracial offered degrees of social proximity to white settler and African communities alike. Being "Anglo-African" reflected a deeply felt, yet instrumental, intersection of relationships—familial, racial, and political in scope. The liminal status of Anglo-Africans consequently posed challenges to conventional categories of rule, with implications that still have meaning in the present.[28]

This book is critically minded as a result. It addresses the crucial question why histories of the kind observed here have been habitually marginalized by scholars. An understanding of "nativism" in its colonial and postcolonial forms is essential in this regard. Although *race* serves as a useful translation term, permitting historical comparisons between different temporal and geographic contexts, it can obscure the specific discursive practices that have inhibited recognition of and critical thinking about these communities in the past and present. In contrast, the terms *native* and *non-native* that marked basic distinctions of rights and rule in British Africa fundamentally affected their social and political status.[29] These locutions of dominance possess interactive elements of race, culture, and territory, and, given their historical use, it is more accurate and constructive to engage with them than with race alone. Revising our terms of analysis in this fashion, we gain a clearer sense why the subaltern histories described here were slighted during the colonial period and have remained underexamined since the historiographical turn that decolonization ultimately initiated. Colonial nativism—defined by an orientation toward black African communities, customary authorities, and local cultural tradition—not only structured colonial rule. It also produced an enduring *episteme*, to use an expression of V. Y. Mudimbe's—a regime of rationality that has organized the intellectual conditions of possibility for understanding Africa.[30] African studies as a field has been fundamentally shaped by this colonial order of knowledge. "Africanism" emerged from the colonial native question, broadly construed, being deeply racialized in the first instance and firmly entrenched in the ethnic politics of the customary in the second—to the exclusion of non-native and interstitial forms of historical experience.[31] Postcolonial scholarship has largely inhabited this intellectual trajectory of the black African subject established by colonialism. As Achille Mbembe has written, a prose of nativism has fixed race and geography such that the "idea of an Africanity that is not black is simply unthinkable."[32]

This provocation is not to say that a legacy of colonial thought has been received uncritically.[33] Ethnic identities and customary practices are still indispensable—and evolving—features of African life. But this shared epistemology continues to raise significant questions regarding the accepted parameters of academic inquiry and the choice of legitimate subject matter. It requires persistent engagement, a task that has been periodically undertaken by scholars.[34] Indeed, a distinct critical tradition can be located to southern Africa. During the early to mid-twentieth century, anthropologists A. R. Radcliffe-Brown, Isaac Schapera, and Max Gluckman called into question the uncomfortable rapport between scholarship and the South African native "problem"—specifically how the latter political discourse had structured and at times conscripted academic research to rationalize segregation, which they opposed.[35] They were not alone. The historian William Macmillan published an early, pathbreaking study of South Africa's Coloured population, citing this social group's national relevance given insistent questions concerning its political and legal status between the two world wars.[36] His study took a comprehensive approach, venturing into issues of slavery and frontier settlement during the preceding centuries to examine how interracial encounters and relationships generated multiple communities that would later be classified as "Coloured."[37] This holistic method, which embraced, rather than simplified, demographic complexity, presented layered histories of interaction that posed distinct challenges to the discrete boundaries of the native question. Macmillan argued for a more unified historical analysis of South Africa as a "common society"—a stance informed by his anti-segregationist politics.[38] This approach, along with Radcliffe-Brown and Schapera's idea of a single social system, influenced Gluckman's proposal of situational analysis to gain a more complete and accurate view of group relations in South Africa.[39] Archie Mafeje further refined this line of critical assessment two decades later, suggesting that an ideology of "tribalism" among scholars, inherited from colonialism, continued to oversimplify and obscure "the real nature of economic and power relations between Africans themselves, and between Africa and the capitalist world," drawing "an invidious and highly suspect distinction between Africans and other peoples."[40]

Despite the esteem granted to these scholars of the past and present, the effects of these recurrent arguments against colonial racial and ethnic typologies have remained more marginal than mainstream in African studies—a condition explained by politics. This book confronts this issue. The preceding critical tradition against hermetic understandings of identity, society, and history serves as a backdrop to the approach undertaken here. Andrew Apter has usefully summarized attempts to decolonize African anthropology before and after Mudimbe's important intervention, citing at once the methodological creativity of scholars to circumvent the legacies of colonial reason, yet the unrelenting dissatisfaction held by some like Mafeje.[41] This book proposes that decolonizing enduring epistemologies requires not simply theoretical innovation, but a concurrent empirical expansion—a reconsideration of how certain historical experiences can unsettle assumptions and enlarge expectations of what African history has been and could be.[42] Political protocols in turn must be reassessed. African nationalism before and after decolonization consolidated the power of black communities, resulting not only in the positive decline of racial distinction as a statutory method for organizing political order, but also making scholarship on local ethnic groups a renewed priority. Postcolonial nativism as an intellectual project emerged from this political transformation. Promoting indigenous identities, languages, and cultures formed a critical response to colonialism, as well as a means of authenticating and stabilizing manifold national identities. But such writing for the nation often did so to the exclusion—even active repression—of other unofficial histories.[43] Nativism that has taken various forms in both colonial and postcolonial scholarship has created invisible histories by generating hierarchies of credibility that have diminished experiences which did not fit into either native policies of the past or present definitions of postcolonial autochthony.[44] Scrutinizing such tacit continuities of knowledge and power is needed. Alluding to the connections between colonial and postcolonial reason, Edward Said has called nativism a regular "misfortune" of nationalism, a "besetting hobble of most post-colonial work" that has often reinforced colonial distinctions even while reevaluating the views and agency of local communities.[45]

This book consequently belongs to a recent literature that has started to critique the historiographical effects of African nationalism. This scholarship has challenged a pervasive ideological and teleological framing of African history—national liberation and the nation-state being the universal end to colonialism with a historical meaning shared by all—by addressing marginalized racial minorities as part of a postnational research agenda.[46] These alter-*native* subjectivities provide a more heterogeneous view of colonialism and thus enable a more expansive interpretation of Africa's past. Colonial societies were remarkably diverse. Yet this demo-

FIGURE I.2. A depiction of demographic diversity and domestic life near Mount Mulanje, in southern Nyasaland, including a white settler family (upper right corner), an African man (bottom center), and a Sikh man (top center), circa 1877. Used by permission of the National Archives of the United Kingdom (CO 1069/109/22).

graphic complexity remains understudied, particularly the question of how this colonial multitude reflected and informed the making of African history under imperial conditions. Imperialism generated extraordinary mobility within and between continents that resulted in the creation of new sociocultural communities in bustling metropoles such as Cape Town and Dar es Salaam, but equally in less cosmopolitan settings like Nyasaland (figure I.2). The presence of Lebanese and Omani neighborhoods in West and East Africa, Arab communities along the Saharan Sahel, Indian and Chinese populations across eastern and southern Africa, and a variety of European settlements throughout the continent—themselves ethnically heterogeneous—underscores how Africa underwent fundamental demographic change, rendering imperialism as much a project in sociocultural management as it was an economic venture.[47] Yet these alternative communities have frequently been judged as having only superficial histories on the continent, with origins elsewhere—beyond the geographic dictates of colonial and postcolonial nativism. The chronological depth, wide-ranging spatial distribution, and historical meaning of these experiences have frequently been disregarded, making scant impression on how the term *African* is defined and understood.

Multiracial communities have been a casualty of this pattern of occlusion. Across time and place, multiracial people have often occupied the shifting "middle ground" between empires and local societies—representing the widespread occurrence of interpersonal relationships between foreigners and indigenous societies, but also serving as pivotal brokers in the creation of trade and political influence, typically gaining status and power as a result.[48] Eurafrican, Luso-African, and métis populations emerged as early as the seventeenth century along the coast of West Africa, with the rise of the transatlantic slave trade.[49] On the East African coast, people of Afro-Arabian background appeared even earlier through networks of the Indian Ocean economy and the settlement of traders from the Persian and Omani Gulf regions.[50] Further south, among the *prazo* plantation estates of the Zambezi River valley established in the sixteenth century, the "Portuguese" community was primarily Afro-Portuguese.[51] In contrast to many of these earlier groups, the Coloured population in South Africa remains distinctive, albeit with controversy due to the employment of *Coloured* (*kleurling*, in Afrikaans) as an apartheid state category.[52] Other identity groups and terms materialized earlier on the frontier. The Griqua and the *Bastaards* (or *basters* and *bastervolk*) emerged in the eighteenth century and were equally inscribed with interracial histories.[53] Paul Landau has applied the French colonial expressions *métis* (a person of "mixed" racial background) and *métissage* ("mixing") to capture the broad dynamics of the South African frontier up through the early twentieth century.[54] Hermann Giliomee has further noted that the term *Afrikaner*—an identity strongly associated with racial purity and white supremacy—originated in the late nineteenth century to refer to "the half-bred offspring of slaves" and, more generally, people of "mixed descent."[55] Overall, these histories point to the extensive presence of multiracial Africans across the continent in the past and present.

The relative neglect in mainstream scholarship toward this spectrum of historical experience is therefore not for lack of acknowledgment, but for lack of historical imagination—a disciplinary reason that can be attributed to an entrenched nativism and the ethnic paradigm it has produced. The subaltern status of multiracial Africans is rendered not solely by postcolonial nationalism or elite historiographies as such, but by this inherited colonial epistemology that has privileged the claims of black autochthony over other "subject races."[56] This condition of exclusion has been enhanced by the racially "transgressive" origins of multiracial people that defied the conventional logics of colonial taxonomy.[57] Multiracial communities have inhabited the shadows of this enduring structure of knowledge, occupying a space beyond native questions, policies, and histories. They have been treated as "people without history" in both senses of the expression—being beyond history as conventionally defined, and thus having no history.[58] Colonialism actively created this situation, with states, officials, and settler communities choosing to look away to maintain a semblance of racial order. Such colonial contempt has informed postcolonial disregard—a situation of empirical precarity and scholarly inattention that demands a different historical methodology and a more expansive political horizon regarding the dimensions and meanings of moral life under colonial rule.

: COLONIAL KINSHIPS :

Nativism is not only a structure of knowledge. It is also a political formation as mentioned. To work critically against nativism is therefore to rethink the political—to consider the different ways in which colonial and postcolonial histories might be rewritten. It requires historical engagement beyond customary politics, beyond the anticolonial liberation paradigm, beyond the territorial contours of the nation-state-colony, and hence beyond political narratives as conventionally understood. This book consequently seeks to contribute to a set of arguments put forward over the past two decades about the need to reassess historical agency in order to circumvent established analytic conformities of colonial domination and African resistance.[59] By inscribing the experiences discussed here into our postcolonial historiography, a rereading of colonialism is made possible that marks a return to a less discrete, more entangled sense of the past from demographic, political, and cultural vantage points. Terminology is important to this book, as highlighted earlier. Regional practices of self-naming provide a textured sense of the social pluralism that existed and the intertwined politics involved. Not only do Anglo-African, Eurafrican, and similar communities indicate new forms of peoplehood, but the genealogical imagination that emerged concurrently underscores the innovative ways in which local activist intellectuals defined what it meant to be simultaneously African and a subject of the British Empire—an invented

Afro-Britishness that has often been neglected and at times forgotten due to the priorities of postcolonial historical writing.[60] These liminal identities signify critical subjectivities that actively engaged with the opportunities and constraints of the period, as well as provoke consideration in the present toward experiences that have exceeded our intellectual grasp.

These observations underline the risk of narrowly applying a racial lens to these histories—an approach that can oversimplify the cultural markers and political sensibilities involved. Racial terminology can conceal, rather than reveal, historical experience. The commonly used, albeit weak, descriptive expression *mixed race* conveys imprecision, obscurity, and disregard for the personal and community histories of people who placed a strong emphasis on familial kinship and genealogy, as examined in forthcoming chapters. In southern Africa, the term *Coloured* has been used in synonymous ways, being transformed from a British imperial term referring to anyone who was not white, particularly during the nineteenth century, to anyone who was perceived as having a racially mixed background, especially during the twentieth century. Given the word's flexibility, mobility, and evolution in meaning over time, a consistent need exists to historicize this category to render it more precise—not only historically, but also geographically, and politically.

With the establishment of the Union of South Africa in 1910, which united the British Cape and Natal colonies with the defeated Orange Free State and South African Republic following the South African War (1899–1902), only the Cape had used the term *Coloured* in a statutory manner, with its 1904 census employing this category. This usage contrasted with that of the 1904 Native Affairs Commission, which defined *native* as including Coloured persons.[61] But the identification of a separate tertiary "race" soon followed. "Some half a million people of many varying shades, the descendants of Hottentots, Malays, negro slaves, and many others, with a strong admixture of European blood, are comprehensively spoken of as 'the Coloured People,'" wrote William Macmillan in 1927, indicating the haphazard differentiation internal to the term as understood in South Africa.[62] The term *Coloured* entered the region of British Central Africa quite literally with the 1896 arrival of the Cape Boys Corps, which consisted of Coloured military recruits, in Southern Rhodesia from the Western Cape as part of the British South Africa Company's initial colonial incursion.[63] But it was not the only referent in the decades that followed. The expressions *Anglo-African*, *Euro-African*, *Indo-African*, and *Eurafrican*—as well as *Cape Afrikander*, in Southern Rhodesia—appeared across the region beginning in the 1920s, pointing to a diversity of self-naming practices that sought to articulate familial origins, cultural attachments, and political affiliations.[64] The application of the expression *Coloured* in instrumental fashion by regional states, schools, and missions was actively criticized by local communities and the political organizations they founded, given its occlusion of their connections with European communities, its overt and exclusively racial content, and its consequent discriminatory function in law.[65] As a sign of its centrality as a standard state category, it nonetheless became the principal term used in official censuses.[66] In Southern Rhodesia the category included people from the Cape Coloured community and first-generation people of mixed-race background, in addition to immigrants from Goa in India, St. Helena, and Mozambique—anyone whose racial background was perceptibly ambiguous in some fashion.[67]

This colonial practice still lingers in postcolonial scholarship and must be denaturalized. The term *Coloured* should be understood as having specific geographic and historical origins—an encroachment from the south, literally and figuratively—that belongs to a constellation of self-crafted expressions that people strategically employed to describe themselves. Restoring this diversity of locutions uncovers regionally situated patterns of history that challenge the reductive uniformities of a colonial racial lexicon. This book therefore complements a growing literature on this topic by extending beyond the Cape Coloured paradigm, while also expanding its analytic range and meaning by engaging broader debates in African studies.[68] In the same way that the terms *black* or *white* can homogenize social experience, the uncritical use of this category can overwhelm historical subtleties, suggesting a false sense of monolithic consistency— a singular experience—that streamlines an otherwise diverse set of histories.[69] This argument against standardization consequently goes further than semantics or simple factual accuracy. Locally self-fashioned subjectivities tell particular stories. Their formations highlight complex intersections of race, culture, and politics based on sentiments of familial connection that work against abstract essentialization. These compound terms gestured to an imperial context—*Anglo-African* echoing *Anglo-Indian*, for example—as did pejorative expressions such as *half-caste*, which also referenced India.[70] Although the population figures of these communities were small (table I.1), these intermediate categories demonstrated local views that were critical toward colonial practices of stark racial categori-

Census year	Nyasaland	Southern Rhodesia	Northern Rhodesia	Total (estimated)
1911	481	2,042	No data	2,523 (incomplete data)
1921	563	1,998	145	2,706
1926	850	2,158	No data	3,008 (incomplete data)
1931	1,591	2,402	425	4,418
1936	No data	3,187	No data	Insufficient data
1941	No data	3,974	No data	Insufficient data
1946	455 (1945 estimate)	4,559	804	5,818
1951	No data	5,991	1,112	7,103 (incomplete data)
1956	1,199	8,079	1,577	10,855

TABLE I.1. Official population statistics for "Coloured Persons" by colony in British Central Africa, drawn from a 1956 census. It should be noted that population figures for Nyasaland during the period 1911–31 included both "Asian" (Indian) and "Coloured" people. Numbers were often speculative and even lowered by colonial officials, given the illicit origins of this demographic group. On problems of clarity, S. S. Murray, for example, cites the 1,591 figure from the 1931 census as being solely "Indians" (S. S. Murray, *A Handbook of Nyasaland*, 57). In contrast, the 1956 census lists the 1931 census figure as consisting of both "Asian" and "Coloured" people, which could explain the high number for that year (Rhodesia and Nyasaland, *Federation of Rhodesia and Nyasaland*, 3). Unlisted in this chart are 1961 figures for Southern Rhodesia, which had the largest Coloured community among the three territories, that recorded 10,559 Coloured people compared to 7,253 Asians, 221,504 whites, and 3,550,000 Africans (estimated) (Southern Rhodesia, *1961 Census of the European, Asian and Coloured Population*, 3). It is significant to observe that, when white and Coloured numbers are totaled each year for the years 1946 and 1956, Nyasaland's Coloured population was proportionally larger than the Coloured populations in the other two colonies. In 1956, for example, the Coloured population in Nyasaland represented 15.1% of the white-Coloured population combined, compared to 4.4% in Southern Rhodesia and 2.4% in Northern Rhodesia (see Table 1.1). This factor could explain the level of activism there, despite smaller total numbers.

zation, indicating how socially marginal communities engaged with racial marking and mediated racial difference. Indeed, these histories not only reconfirm the active construction of identities under colonial rule. They demonstrate the sophistication of such self-constituting measures that resorted to different sources of knowledge—local and imperial, traditional and modern—to reconfigure these distinctions, their textured meanings, and their ensuing utility. Above all, these terms reveal the steadfast desire among multiracial Africans for social and political legitimacy. The boundaries of nativism and non-nativism appeared surmountable through the deployment of this invented terminology. Elevating these amalgamated self-locutions, rather than subsuming them beneath the colonial rubric of *Coloured*, ultimately enhances our comprehension of the past by indicating day-to-day phenomenologies, conciliatory interactions between states and communities, and how colonial people—even those on the periphery—exercised a range of techniques to define their place and status in Africa and the British Empire.[71]

Kinship and genealogy were essential to this repertoire. Actively embedded in these regional hyphenated terms, they presented structures of feeling that defined political and intellectual agency.[72] Although colonial histories of race and racism have tended to focus on conflict, these histories argue for the importance of socially constructed connections—the ways people engaged in new forms of collective identification through understandings of racial affiliation.[73] Kinship and genealogy were vital idioms for these actual, assumed, and putative communal bonds.[74] *Kinship*— defined by its horizontal nature, working across a shared temporal frame inhabited by one or more generations—and *genealogy*—typified by its vertical character, citing relations of descent between successive generations over time—symbolized affective ties that were close and often deeply felt. Serving as conceptual tools, they furnished templates for interpretation— a means for recognizing social and political opportunity through webs of personal relationships. This realm of vernacular connection that informed and structured possibilities of social action is captured in the expression *colonial kinships*—a phrase I use to describe this phenomenon of historical bonds developed under colonial rule that were familial, racial, and political in scope. This expression equally denotes a certain cosmology—a genealogical imagination—based on these connections, an outlook articulated by Ascroft and others that perceived a world of relationships, patronage, and obligation rather than incontrovertible differences. It emerged from archival work, conversations with different informants, and my own reflections about what to call this set of experiences that did not fit into discrete narratives and remained unnamed. This study does not reconstruct actual kinship trees or genealogical lineages as such. Rather, kinship and genealogy provided a language for social and political membership. The use of these terms in this book is therefore not about incontrovertible family bloodlines, primordial determinism, or the structuration of societies as hierarchical and unchanging over time. They represent instead social and contractual relationships substantiated through everyday interactions involving family, race, and political belonging. These claims and actions created colonial cultures of relatedness. Despite their small populations, these subaltern communities engaged in the production of racial knowledge, identity formation, and even empire making—often in surprising ways.[75]

: UNREASONABLE HISTORIES :

Against this backdrop of issues and arguments, a set of paradoxes appears—using, for example, a regional lens to understand a numerically minor set of communities or, similarly, examining the microhistories of a demographically marginal group to address issues as significant as racism and nativism. This book consequently draws on a diverse library of preceding scholarship that has offered timely critical interventions by placing confidence in the empiricism of small-scale events, incidental occasions, and the forgotten cultural element to illuminate everyday *mentalités* and the conditions of broader social transformation.[76] The forthcoming chapters explore how people peripheral to power lived through certain contexts of change and uncertainty with particular ideas. Evidence is treated both ethnographically and historically in order to move beyond chronology and causality and understand how certain experiences created forms of social knowledge—what Emmanuel Eze has called "ordinary reason"— that reveal insights interred by time.[77] These histories tell us about the personal effects—the details—of empire. As suggested above, these subaltern histories fall within the contours of definition originally outlined by Antonio Gramsci, being "fragmentary" and "episodic," as well as "intertwined" with "the history of States and groups of States."[78] But the historical technique that this book utilizes is a genealogical one. While all histories are provisional, this work is also experimental. The expression *genealogical imagination* in the title refers to both the political imagination uncovered and the alternative historical imagination demanded to assemble and think through this particular set of histories. As defined by Michel Foucault, a genealogical approach seeks to historicize phenomena that appear to be "without history."[79] In contrast to linear histories that presuppose the existence of cohesive identity groups, this genre favors a "complex course of descent" that highlights contingency and irregularity.[80] It is anti-teleological by definition, even when progressing from the past to the present.[81] A genealogical approach is further defined by its concern for subjugated forms of knowledge—knowledge that is not simply ignored, but actively disqualified.[82] Genealogical histories are ultimately counter-histories that critically resist dominant views and practices of conformity.

This book is therefore titled *Unreasonable Histories* with specific purpose in mind. The concept of unreasonable histories serves as a methodological tool with the term *unreasonable* employed in three ways, reflected in the book's tripartite structure. First, it refers to modes of evidence and the difficulty involved in restoring these subaltern histories. The challenges in dealing with a minority group based on historical contingencies rather than established practices of social reproduction include fragmented archives; a cultural memory that is diffuse rather than collectively held; and ephemeral knowledge about personal, family, and community origins more generally, given persistent perceptions of racial "transgression" and social illegitimacy.[83] This unstable situation of knowledge that resists easy historical generalizations has been shaped by colonial and postcolonial power and the relative disregard for livelihoods beyond native questions. Part I explores this theme with three chapters that examine historical beginnings in the 1910s and 1920s, a set of accounts under the rubric "Histories without Groups." Parts II and III attend to political emergence from the 1920s through the 1950s, posing two additional meanings of unreasonable. Part II, "Non-Native Questions," looks at the legal and policy realms that affected regional community development through matters of status, education, employment, and poverty. These communities introduced problems of native and non-native categorical definition by posing uneasy questions about racial descent and privilege that generated political and statutory uncertainties. Part III examines how Anglo-African, Euro-African, and Eurafrican people mobilized on this basis, creating communities of sentiment that used the affective ties of blood, kinship, and genealogy to create racial bonds of agnatic affiliation and patrilateral loyalty to regional colonial states and, more generally, the British Empire. Part III depicts how colonial kinship ties were transformed from a familial phenomenon (as discussed in part I) to an articulated genealogical imagination that sought political connection and entitlement. Yet these emergent politics had a specific cost. The form of unreason inhabiting this last section of the book is the racism employed to rationalize non-native status—an uncustomary form of politics that proved detrimental with decolonization.[84]

These forms of unreasonableness—methodological, categorical, and sociopolitical—are qualitatively different from one another, but they are also interrelated. They underscore the effects of power—colonial and postcolonial alike. The histories in this book reveal and critically address the limits of a colonial reason centered on racial difference expressed through discourses of nativism and non-nativism. But the relative disregard these communities have received in the postcolonial present suggests more. Such indifference is not due to their marginal demographic status alone. It discloses tacit forms of colonial-era nativist reasoning that continue to inform postcolonial scholarship. It is unsurprising that the racist imperial politics these communities espoused would, in turn, contribute to their social and political demise in the wake of decolonization—a fate captured with immediacy in the case of Henry Ascroft. Less understandable are the reasons these regional communities and their histories have been marginalized by scholars. Indeed, to return to the opening anecdote, this kind of archival moment, I am sure, is familiar to many historians. But rather than being an instance of pure serendipity, such symptomatic events signal a working set of spoken and unspoken academic rationales and political ideologies defining what is and is not suitable for study. Understanding the life of these communities has an uncertain utility when a predominant ethos is to explain the origins of the postcolonial nation-state. These histories do not fit programmatically into either imperial ambitions of the time or postindependence historiographies of the nation-state-colony—a fact explaining how and why these histories have been viewed, treated, and archived as they have.

Yet this unreasonableness is the precise quality that can productively challenge existing approaches regarding what counts as a usable past. It evinces limitations in contemporary scholarship that are empirical, political, and epistemological in scope. These histories that stand apart from mainstream scholarship reveal a fundamental shift in moral and political values between the colonial and postcolonial periods, from a time when racial hierarchies and imperial loyalty appeared rational and accepted to a period when such conventions and forms of intellection vanished, for all practical purposes. As stated, this book embraces a challenge issued by Achille Mbembe, that scholars should work beyond the contours of liberation histories that reduce political life to modular forms of "Afro-radicalism" and beyond narratives anchored in nativism that continue to promote the colonial idea of African identity as based on membership in "the black race."[85]

These communities have not entirely disappeared. But terms like *Anglo-African* and *Euro-African* have fallen into disuse, undergoing a type of social death. Their histories have largely been rendered invisible, highlighting the potential for patterns of identification and peoplehood to weaken over time. Identities are not about origins alone. They are equally about destinations: their long-term viability and status are shaped and determined by the contingencies of politics and the priorities of history. This book works through these observations regarding the precarity of empiricism and subjectivity, to think critically about the relationships between imperial experience, postcolonial scholarship, and the different forms of reason that have influenced them. Reason itself must be historicized. A renewal of awareness toward the intellectual and political rationales that motivate current research can result in productive shifts in method and subject, illuminating a more complex view of the past—even, and perhaps especially, aspects that we find disagreeable, are critical of, and wish to overlook.

PART I

HISTORIES WITHOUT GROUPS

Lower-Strata Lives, Enduring Regional Practices,
and the Prose of Colonial Nativism

::

The first part of this book addresses historical foundations. It is concerned with genre and evidence. The fragmented and temporally shallow histories of Anglo-African, Euro-African, and Eurafrican communities challenge a routine practice in the field of African history—namely, the organization of historical narratives around cohesive identity groups with a precolonial past. This analytic approach has served to legitimate historical patterns as enduring and uniquely African, beyond Western origin or influence.[1] This first section works beyond this principle. Ephemeral histories also have value. They still give shape and meaning to Africa's past. This part is consequently called "histories without groups" for three reasons: to underscore the individual, rather than group, experiences that inhabit these chapters; to position these experiences as a priori in relationship to active community formation; and to argue for historical experiences that critically challenge forms of categorization introduced by colonialism. The logic of groups was indispensable to colonial rule. Imperialism of the late nineteenth and early twentieth centuries commenced an age of taxonomy aided by modes of scientific, cultural, and political reason. The practice of clarifying identities and organizing communities spatially, culturally, and politically has left enduring legacies. Archives are acutely racialized and ethnicized, with colonial routines of legibility obscuring complex patterns of affiliation and identity—a condition not only detrimental to historical understanding, but one that caused extensive political harm, from Native Reserves in British Central Africa to Group Areas in South Africa.[2]

The uncustomary communities addressed in this book provide an opportunity to think beyond these colonial and postcolonial conformities. They invite a rethinking of method. The genre of histories without groups proposed here captures liminal experiences that evaded taxonomic practices. Not only do these elusive histories identify a microhistorical interplay of race, gender, and family — ontologies of intimacy — that affected later community formation, but they also present a critical position against a prose of colonial nativism centered on discrete social groupings.[3] Deconstructing nativism in its colonial and postcolonial versions requires disassembling the historical genres it has produced — to take identity groups and ethnohistories not as pre-given facts to be uncovered and rewritten, but to understand them as shaped and at times fabricated by colonialism.[4] This experimental genre has particular resonance for the people of this book, who faced persistent questions of group belonging. The chapters in this part, therefore, seek to avoid the anachronism of group analysis when collective sentiment and cohesion may not be present. To do so requires confronting a central impulse of mainstream social history to organize meaning around groups. When we perceive a "people without history," in Eric Wolf's expression, we aspire to restore that people to history as a recognized community.[5] This section examines the converse of Wolf's phrase — to consider the uses of histories without "people," in the sense of an organized, identifiable social group. These histories mark conditions of preemergence, to paraphrase Raymond Williams, which signal "active and pressing but not yet fully articulated" forms and practices, in order to underline the contingent nature of community formations new and uniquely fixed to the colonial period.[6]

This rethinking of historical beginnings through a provisional genre is vitally informed by questions of evidence. Social status and historical status are connected. The archives — oral and written alike — of socially marginal communities can be dispersed and are often thin. Time and ritual are crucial factors in the creation of custom and identity. The communities in this book had chronologically shallow histories of only a generation or two by the

1950s, pointing to the difficulties of working on subaltern people who lack collective practices of social reproduction and other formalized attributes of established community—initiation rites, marriage protocols, and similar cultural traditions. This temporal limitation for crafting social cohesion, which reveals the often unexamined potential for weak, even precarious, forms of peoplehood, is compounded by a discourse of colonial nativism that disregarded these experiences in favor of longstanding ethnic communities. Modes of evidence are an effect of power. The irregular presence of these uncustomary histories in the archival record reflects colonial contempt for these stories of perceived illegitimacy that defied boundaries of race and law. To uncover them requires sifting through the lower strata of bureaucratic native administration files—the very materiality of colonial discourse—to find forgotten events hidden among the debris of quotidian paperwork with headings elusive about what resides within.[7]

But this predicament can be a source of innovation. The colonial archive is not merely the autobiography of the colonial state. It presents a tension between the public and the private, sources of colonial power and duress as well as Freudian slips of state limitation and failing.[8] These histories are unreasonable insofar that they underscore methodological challenges. Yet, once reassembled, they tacitly critique the colonial politics of nativism that have rendered them so. Histories without groups provide a tentative solution, evincing social and political conditions of risk, exclusion, and suppression. Rather than ignore or despair over a fragmented archival record, scholars should actively posit these experiences as a critical contrast to prevalent notions of social wholeness structured by states, to open instead an alternative horizon for historical thinking, analysis, and writing.[9] Though this first part does not pinpoint specific foundational moments shared by all—a suggestion that would impart a retroactive sense of collective history—its chapters identify different sociocultural sites (from household spaces to regional geographies) and thematic realms of experience (from adult intimacies to displaced childhoods) that informed the strategies of collective identification discussed in part III. The genealogical imagination that appears later begins with these preliminary histories. These chapters, which inhabit a space between the public and the private, trace historical conditions that tested ruling mentalities framed by homogeneous categorical groups, as well as illuminate the intimate familial grounds for the emergence of colonial kinship relations as a historical phenomenon.

CHAPTER 1

: :

IDIOMS OF PLACE AND HISTORY

: :

Historical insights present themselves when you least expect them — often beyond the appointed rooms of dust-filled archives and tranquil libraries. In 1999 I walked up to the home of an informant located on the outskirts of Blantyre, Malawi. The daughter of a person whose life I had been researching at the national archives in Zomba, she had provided useful personal details and background about his life and politics and the colonial period generally. Though cellular telephones are ubiquitous today, they were not then, and my visit, after two long minibus rides, was unannounced. As I approached her thatch-and-concrete house, with several scattered dogs reporting my arrival, a man came out and asked who I was with some degree of suspicion. I answered that I was doing historical research about which my informant had been quite helpful, since it related to her father. The man briefly explained that he was her son and that she was away for the afternoon. To break the awkward silence that followed, I said that I was interested in the Anglo-African community and asked if he identified himself as "Anglo-African." No, he replied, he did not. After a moment's pause, he said he considered himself instead "philosophically Jewish," insisting that the genealogical portions of the Old Testament explained his views. Conjuring a secular interpretation and use, the sense of identity he embraced could be paraphrased prosaically as who-I-am-is-who-I-am-related-to. Nothing mattered to him in terms of social categories, to put it in academic terms. As I listened, his conversational views that afternoon gradually emerged as an example of how certain global forms of knowledge could be reconfigured into local, common-sense notions — an observation that intersected with the archival work I was pursuing at the time.

His grandfather was none other than Henry Ascroft, one of the founders and past presidents of the Anglo-African Association of Nyasaland, whose intriguing ideas had set me down this path toward the past. Ascroft's speeches to the association, his occasional articles in the *Rhodesian Tribune* published in Salisbury, Southern Rhodesia, and his petitions to the Nyasaland government conveyed a similar sensibility of kinship and identification, reflecting defiance toward conventional colonial categories of racial difference. It is unclear whether Ascroft directly influenced the perspectives of his grandson, or if his grandson's rationale confirmed a truth about Ascroft's colonial-era thinking. Kinship as a social idiom is not unique. Indeed, its use signaled a set of practices shared by this ephemeral social group and other African communities in the region. The biblical folk sociology his grandson imparted to me was unsurprising, given the pervasive influence of Christian missions in the region since the late nineteenth century. Yet it demonstrated continuity across generations. This occasion created an early dialogue between the archival documents I had been reading and the remaining legacies of colonialism I encountered through family memory. A genealogical imagination was at work in both instances despite the passage of time, suggesting the ongoing, transformative ways that local traditions converged with outside forms of social knowledge—whether racial or religious thought—to meet the needs of individual people and communities.[1]

This chapter departs from this fieldwork moment to consider interrelated questions of memory, generation, and historical beginnings. In doing so, it presents three contexts for situating these subaltern histories—precolonial, colonial, and postcolonial—with the purpose of outlining the different meanings these consecutive periods bestowed on these issues. Each context underscores shifting senses of transgression and normality vis-à-vis interracial sexual relations, dependent on time, place, and perspective—a critical intervention against colonial views that classified such relations as always illicit. Colonialism for multiracial people was a family experience. It provided an origin story. It formed an integral part of personal histories with genealogical connections that extended regionally from Malawi to Mozambique, Zimbabwe, and South Africa, and beyond to Europe and South Asia. The habitation of colonialism within family histories signals its persistence beyond moments of decolonization and, more generally, its different temporalities. But these intimate ontologies also raise fundamental questions about a social group with no perceptible precolonial history. Not only is the Anglo-African community subaltern in a classic postcolonial sense—numerically marginal, excluded from nationalist politics, and virtually absent from Malawi's postcolonial historiography—but this status is reinforced by the backdrop of the *longue durée*, having no deep history prior to Western colonial intrusion. The *Anglo* prefix in the term *Anglo-African* indicated a distinct chronological beginning. This predicament of historical shallowness challenges key presumptions about doing African history—namely, the importance of histories prior to colonial rule and the role of social reproduction in anchoring historical dynamics internal to the continent. This community approximates Eric Wolf's definition of "people without history"—in the sense of not being written about, of being left out of history—but this expression also appeared to apply in a more literal sense.[2] This experiential unlikeness, compared to established ethnic communities, has contributed to its marginalization. This chapter consequently introduces the question of weak forms of peoplehood—their emergence, role, and decline within certain contexts of power over time.

: INDIGENOUS EPISTEMOLOGIES AND RACIAL FRONTIERS :

God made white men, and God made black men, but the devil made half-castes.
—David Livingstone and Charles Livingstone, *Narrative of an Expedition to the Zambesi and Its Tributaries*

Though sexuality has become an influential theme for addressing the gendered effects of colonialism, scholarship in this area has rarely ventured into precolonial practices to understand colonial-era trends.[3] Intergroup contact, relations, and marriage were central dynamics of this earlier period. The region of British Central Africa was no exception. Nineteenth-century figures such as David Livingstone and Sir Harry Johnston noted the presence of "half-castes" and "mongrel races" in central Africa.[4] These observations attracted only fleeting attention at the time, being a mere complication in the matter of identifying cohesive ethnic groups or, in Livingstone's case, explaining the degenerative nature of those who participated in the East African slave trade during his travels (figure 1.1). "Half-castes" actively participated in this commerce from the Zambezi interior to the coast, at times accruing significant wealth as a result.[5] But passing acknowledgment of social and cultural mixture would continue. In his au-

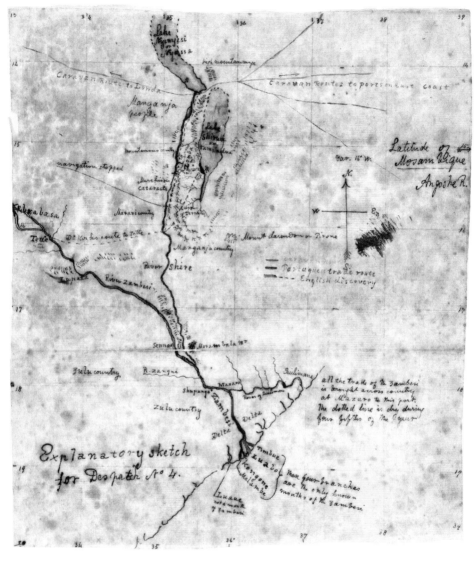

FIGURE 1.1. David Livingstone's 1859 map of exploration in the region of Malawi, which identified the names and geographic placement of different ethnic groups, in addition to noting natural features of lakes, rivers, and the Indian Ocean coastline. Used by permission of the National Archives of the United Kingdom (FO 63/871).

thoritative 1950 survey of British colonial rule in Africa, Lord Hailey cited the Nyasaland Protectorate as posing distinct challenges for the demographer, despite its small size. "Any study of the tribal distribution in Nyasaland is confused by the tendency to intermarriage," reported a 1945 government census, included in Hailey's summary. "This is especially true in the Shire Highlands [in southern Nyasaland], where the Anyanja, Yao, Angoni, Alomwe and Achikunda live side by side in the same villages. Patriarchal and matriarchal tribes in this area mix and intermarry in a way that is probably unique in East Central Africa. . . . On more than one occasion parents who claimed to belong to different tribes, the one patriarchal and the other matriarchal, were unable to agree as to which tribe their children should belong." The 1945 census concluded that the "sociological structure of the Protectorate is going through a most interesting period of adjustment to new conditions."[6]

Yet this process of intermarriage was hardly new. The British were not the first to colonize the region, being outnumbered compared to African immigrants of the nineteenth century.[7] The region of Malawi experienced the arrival, settlement, and cohabitation of a number of different ethnic groups—the Ngoni, Chewa, Mang'anja, and Yao among them. Indeed, these identities should be used cautiously, given their capacity to obscure patterns of demographic commingling and cultural creolization. The Mfecane—a period of state expansion and conflict during the first decades of the nineteenth century in what is today South Africa—sparked a social exodus across southeast Africa, one that converged with regional instability produced by the East African slave trade in the Lake Nyasa area after 1810.[8] The impact of these changes was not only political, but cultural. Ngoni settlers were part of the former dynamic of migration, introducing patrilineal cultural practices to indigenous Chewa communities in central and southern Malawi that had followed matrilineal uxorilocality (the practice of a husband residing with his wife's family) and avunculate (maternal uncle, or *nkhoswe*) customs. Patrilineal traditions that asserted the authority of the husband and father were similarly introduced by the Chikunda from the Zambezi River valley and Muslim traders under the command of Salim bin Abdallah (known as the first *jumbe*, a term for ruler) from the East African coast.[9] Both groups were involved in slave raiding. This trade that generated upheaval across the southern portion of the Lake Nyasa area not only affected structures of kinship through

the introduction of new practices, but it encouraged growth in slaveholding, which provided an alternative means for gaining kin apart from marriage. These changes did not automatically displace uxorilocal marriage
customs with virilocality (the practice of a wife living with her husband's
kin). The cultural imprint of intermarriage worked in multifaceted ways.
The Ngoni adopted local matrilineal traditions like *mzinda* (initiation rites)
in some cases, while the matrilineal Chewa paid *lobola* (bride price), an
agnatic custom, in others. Still, major transformations like the spread of
Christianity and Islam, particularly among the matrilineal Yao, introduced
patrilineal ideals that reinforced the authority of the husband and father.
These and other elements of historical change—especially labor migration
to the Rhodesias and South Africa—altered households and communities
to such an extent that the prevalence of uxorilocality, which centered on
wealth accumulated through small-scale landholding, had been modified,
if not entirely diminished, by the postcolonial period.[10]

Changing kin relations and practices consequently tell a history. These
overlapping historical trends generated a demographic complexity that re-
sisted state attempts to create legible ethnic groups. They challenged popular efforts as well. The production of ethnographic knowledge in Nyasaland as elsewhere was an activity pursued by a range of people—colonial
officials, missionaries, anthropologists, and educated Africans alike.
Nineteenth-century missionaries through their efforts to translate Christian gospel reported that they encountered "a Babel of linguistic confusion, the heritage of decades of movement by thousands of refugees and
captives."[11] Amid the later establishment of colonial indirect rule, intellectuals such as Y. B. Abdullah, George Simeon Mwase, and Kenneth Mdala
sought to apply a native perspective to such matters. Pursuing inventive
ethnohistorical work during the period between the two world wars, they
positioned themselves as experts on local history in order to claim political authority.[12] Sifting through this situation was not necessarily easier
for trained social scientists. Mary Douglas (née Tew) produced one of the
first comprehensive overviews of the Nyasaland region in 1950, in which
she remarked that "its inhabitants have been confused by the raids and
migrations of the last 100 years."[13] Anthropologists based at the Rhodes-
Livingstone Institute in Northern Rhodesia faced similar problems in
seeking ethnic clarity.[14] An "unexciting prospect" is how J. Clyde Mitchell
characterized the lakeside Tonga, with their "considerable tribal admixture
in the past."[15]

These latter anxieties found in the forewords, introductions, and addenda of colonial-era scholarship—a prose of colonial nativism—did not overrule state motivations to define and rule. But they highlight the risk of projecting group clarity onto the past from a postcolonial vantage point—the reproduction of a colonial-era mistake in the present—that can distort or conceal enduring patterns of intergroup conjugality. Reflecting on the Zomba History Project founded at Chancellor College at the University of Malawi in 1977, Megan Vaughan has pointed to this problem and the general challenge of a historically layered precolonial past—what Jean-Loup Amselle has called an originary syncretism.[16] As part of a team seeking to uncover ethnic histories, Vaughan describes how they were essentially reversing historical processes of intermingling and assimilation. Intergroup marriage formed a central part of social and political life, with exogamy between groups providing crucial access to new sources of land, labor, and social knowledge. Autochthons—such as Chewa and Mang'anja communities—had the advantage of controlling land and could offer settlers like the Ngoni and Yao territorial accommodation in exchange for material needs or political status, resulting in strategic alliances. The potential decline of such connections after a generation favored maximizing the diversity of such arrangements.[17] Negotiating this complexity embedded in local histories raised significant questions for Vaughan as to which was more important: reconstructing a presumed precolonial ethnohistory or understanding these processes that blurred distinctions. "In the nineteenth century Nyanja had become Yao," she writes, "in modern Malawi, historians appear capable of turning Yao into Nyanja." This continuity with past colonial efforts generated an uncomfortable self-consciousness about research intent and historical meaning. Indeed, Vaughan lamented the fact that her opening question to informants was the same as her colonial predecessors: "Who are you?"[18]

This social history of regional intergroup relations provides a vital backdrop for interracial relationships during the colonial period. It provides an indigenous epistemology for colonialism's racial frontiers.[19] Though the term *marriage* may not capture the full dimensions of colonial-era situations, the asymmetry of autochthon-settler power and the element of precarity involved propose continuities. These later experiences that are often perceived as deviant or exceptional were but newer versions of a preexisting tradition, based on reasoned motivations of exchange and building rapport. A strict focus on race and colonial social mores can obscure this normative perspective and the pragmatic meaning of strategic social experimentation among local communities. The Anglo-African community itself argued for this continuity to assert their social legitimacy. "There is no such thing as 'illegal miscegenation of races' in us whatsoever. What, and who, is halfcaste?" asked one member of the Anglo-African Association during the 1930s. "Is it a person born between white and black? Does the word halfcaste in its true sense not mean a person born between two persons each of whom belongs to a different nationality or race or tribe?"[20] These rhetorical questions suggest a compelling interpretation of their own history. Although it is important to position Anglo-Africans as distinctive to the colonial period, situating this history within a deeper past underlines their affinity with other communities, underscoring persistent regional histories of sexuality. Multiracial Africans were not an aberration, but a twentieth-century variation of an enduring regional process.

: COLONIAL PREDICAMENTS :

Adultery is extremely common and in very few parts of British Central Africa is looked upon as a very serious matter, as a wrong which cannot be compensated by a small payment. Yet in a way the natives are jealous of their women; they are not at all anxious to encourage intercourse between their wives and white men, though they seem to be much more jealous about the white man than their brother negro. As a general rule it may be said that illicit intercourse with women on the part of Europeans causes great dissatisfaction in the native mind and invariably gives rise to acts of revenge on their part and even to serious risings. On the other hand if the European tries to obtain a wife in a legitimate manner by negotiation and purchase they are not at all unwilling to treat and no ill humour whatever results from his inter-marrying with them. In their eyes it is simply a matter of justice.
—Sir Harry Johnston, *British Central Africa*

If precolonial intergroup marriage practices offered social opportunities, status, and gain, relationships between African women and European men met with a different reception during the colonial period. Precolonial opportunities transformed into colonial-era predicaments, at least from a state perspective. Johnston's views are both characteristic and perceptive in this regard, given his role as the first commissioner (1891–99) of the British Central Africa Protectorate (the name preceding Nyasaland) and his active interests in native types and local ethnology as found in his encyclopedic account, *British Central Africa* (1897). Yet even in this latter instance of colonial taxonomic reasoning, one finds open recognition and discussion of "intercourse" between white men and African women, if only in passing. Local customs did not end with the advent of colonial rule. Fears of disease and racial degeneration circulated, but the factor of race arguably made little difference in practice when sexual opportunity presented itself.[21] Ideologies of racial difference could take latent forms. Indeed, the Rhodesias and Nyasaland never passed antimiscegenation legislation as such.[22] But states still had concerns, both political and legal in scope. Although sexual permissiveness did exist, to transgress racial differences publicly risked undermining political legitimacy and power. As Dane Kennedy has written, colonial anxieties about interracial sex and political rebellion occupied the same spectrum, revolving as much around concerns for the stability and contentment of African communities as the security of white settlers.[23]

In contrast to its southern neighbors, racial prejudice in Nyasaland was more often articulated in unregulated fashion, rather than legally codified extensively. Everyday practices of labor exploitation through the threat of corporal punishment represented the most notorious form of discrimination. Private land ownership and native reserves similarly marked unequal treatment. *Thangata*—an expression for the system of rent paid through labor by African tenants on white-owned land—combined these two kinds of injustice.[24] But strict laws toward personal conduct were weakly enforced, if and when they existed. Interracial sexual relations disclosed this context of informality. "Black peril" scares—social panics based on the fear of black men sexually violating white women—never occurred in Nyasaland on the same scale as they did in Southern Rhodesia and South Africa, a reflection of the smaller presence of white settlement (table 1.1).[25] Still, periodic moral panics and interracial relationships were occasionally reported in the *Nyasaland Times*. Moreover, population figures suggest a hidden history. A 1934 protectorate-wide census listed the Anglo-African population at 1,202. A further numerical breakdown indicates that a third of this figure was under the age of five, signaling that interracial relationships were common and arguably increasing during the 1920s. George Mwase, displaying the views of educated African men from the period, observed the emergence of this issue and the questions of responsibility it raised. "A Mulatto is a child born by a whiteman [sic] out of black woman or African woman, who is now roughly called a half-caste," he wrote matter-

	Nyasaland population		S. Rhodesia population		N. Rhodesia population	
CENSUS YEAR	WHITE	AFRICAN	WHITE	AFRICAN	WHITE	AFRICAN
1911	766	960,000	23,606	740,000	1,497	820,000
1921	1,486	1,175,000	33,620	860,000	3,634	980,000
1926	1,656	1,245,000	39,174	930,000	No data	No data
1931	1,975	1,545,000	49,910	1,080,000	13,846	1,330,000
1936	No data	No data	55,408	1,260,000	No data	No data
1941	No data	No data	68,954	1,400,000	No data	No data
1946	1,948 (1945 estimate)	2,044,707 (1945 estimate)	82,386	1,770,000	21,907	1,660,000
1951	No data	No data	135,596	2,170,000	37,079	1,890,000
1956	6,732	2,570,000	177,124	2,540,000	65,277	2,100,000

TABLE 1.1. African and white population figures by colony in British Central Africa. Drawn from Rhodesia and Nyasaland, *Federation of Rhodesia and Nyasaland: Census of Population, 1956,* 3.

of-factly. "This person has a lot of his comrades in the country. I want to know who is responsible of [*sic*] this person in the country?"[26] The founding of the Anglo-African Association in 1929, the organization that instigated the 1934 census, attempted to provide an answer to this question in the years that followed.[27]

Yet little direct documentation accounts for this trend. Sexuality could create silences. Official power had a choice of what to record, but when it came to private issues, such power could be limited, even feeble.[28] Racism, even if latent, compounded this absence. Although concubinage was considered a "norm for bachelors" in the "lonelier districts" of the British Empire such as Nyasaland, this local archival gap indicates a likely desire to have such relationships undocumented, a position reflecting the influence of the 1909 Crewe Circular, which prohibited colonial officers from having sexual relationships with native women.[29] As one Nyasaland official commented in 1934, this policy was "the most historic circular in the Colonial Service."[30] If a bit flippant in tone, this remark nevertheless underscored common knowledge, with such discouragement deterring documentation.

Intentional silence avoided any accidental impressions of complicity.[31] In addition to the threat of sexually transmitted disease, a white man's sexual involvement with an African woman could only result in lowering him "in the eyes of the natives and diminishing his authority over them."[32] Similar views extended beyond government service. In a case from 1901, Albert James Storey of Blantyre sought to marry an African woman, Alice Ndumei of Kuligowe's village in southern Angoniland. Storey was unable to obtain a marriage license—not for legal reasons, since nothing prevented inter-marriage in the Foreign Marriage Act (1892) or in the Order in Council (1892), but for the stated rationale that Ndumei was "a native woman of the most ordinary type . . . known to be excessively stupid," and she could not comprehend the contractual agreement that Storey wanted to make with her.[33] This precedent with such transparent racism and the implication of degeneracy undoubtedly discouraged interracial marriage—either through a Christian service or by colonial law—and reinforced secrecy.

With fewer white settlers, particularly women, in Nyasaland, which reduced the fear of black peril, state concern centered on local communities. The reverse problem of "white peril"—white men posing a sexual threat to African women—became an issue in 1920 and 1921, as it did elsewhere in the region during the interwar period.[34] Anxiety did not reach the same magnitude as with black peril scares in Southern Rhodesia between 1902 and 1916, but they reflected a similar tightening of social control.[35] In Southern Rhodesia relationships between white men and black women were considered "a hundredth part as serious as the cohabitation between a native male and a white woman," though it remained "a scandal and disgrace that Europeans should allow the prestige of our race to be so lowered in the eyes of the natives with impunity."[36] Districts across the colony varied in how widespread the practice of concubinage was, with some noting the relative decline of "this evil" due to the "class of settler" now immigrating to the colony after the First World War.[37] But it had not disappeared. Innuendo and anecdotal knowledge were abundant. "One or two white men living outside keep native women but the practice does not amount to an open scandal," a native commissioner in Rusapi observed. "One of the white men in question contemplates marrying his woman as he has children by her and wishes to legitimize these children."[38] During the same period, the native commissioner in Umtali remarked: "In view of the number of half castes one sees it would be idle to deny that a good deal of promiscuous intercourse does take place, chiefly in the township of

Umtali and at the various mining centres, but I am not prepared to admit that the intermixture between white and black in this district amounts to a public scandal."³⁹ Interracial sex therefore appeared as a prosaic part of colonial life—a topic of gossip, which, as a mode of communication, could generate bonds of social intimacy and tentative moral agreement that in turn could regulate personal behavior before it erupted into scandal.⁴⁰

Local gossip did not always succeed in this fashion. Still, it conveyed apprehensions over social respectability, how the latter was understood and maintained, and the ways in which it was thwarted.⁴¹ Differences emerged regarding time, formality, and the type of men involved. "A District of this kind with a large white farming population, the majority of whom are married, is naturally fairly free from the particular evil mentioned," noted the native commissioner in Mazoe. "There are, however, certain European foreign storekeepers who are known to have illicit sexual intercourse with native alien women, without actually harbouring such women. . . . The foreign Storekeepers [sic] are practically a class apart and looked down upon by the people of British or Dutch descent: this being so I think that the immoral relationship between such storekeepers and foreign native women can hardly be called a public scandal, however reprehensible their conduct may be from the point of view of private morality."⁴² Children also figured intermittently in these reports as cited before, another subject of gossip that communicated disgrace and irresponsibility. "About 10 years ago, men made no secret about it, but today the majority makes every effort to conceal it. It is a well known fact that on the Mines [sic] there are always a number of native women prostitutes and that white men do cohabit with them, but very seldom live with them for any length of time," wrote the native commissioner at Inyati. "There are approximately 51 half-caste children in this district as a result of this practice. The father in many instances being unknown, some of these children are now marrying natives, and in time will be absorbed."⁴³

These attitudes in Southern Rhodesia approached those in Nyasaland, pointing to regional anxieties not entirely dependent on settler demography. Indeed, the situation after World War I presented a different context from earlier black peril scares, which were defined by early white migration and unformed social boundaries. Increasing mobility among African women intersected with the gradual establishment of indirect rule, contributing to the emergence of a new set of legal concerns to secure racial boundaries and reestablish patriarchal control. This climate of transition could translate idle gossip into more charged forms of rumor that sought forms of truth.[44] On September 25, 1920, the local magistrate of the Ncheu District—a district to the northwest of the Nyasaland colonial capital of Zomba—reported several instances of "Europeans appropriating and keeping the wives of natives." He expressed fear that "such acts are sure to lead to resentment on the part of the natives," incensing "the natives [to act] against Europeans."[45] He asked if the existing law offered protection or compensation to the injured African husband, an inversion of assumed priority that nonetheless reflected the unease of the time.[46] The opinions of chiefs and African well-being more generally had become important. Although indirect rule would not be fully established in Nyasaland until the passage of the Native Authorities Courts Ordinance and Native Authorities Treasuries Ordinance of 1933, measures beginning in 1912 had initiated this gradual process of incorporating customary leaders and law into the colonial ruling structure.[47] More significant, the 1915 Chilembwe Uprising—a brief moment of rebellion that generated distinct political anxieties for British officials—pushed state attention toward African, rather than solely settler, interests across the spectrum.

Disagreement emerged, however, as to how to respond to these legal and political demands. The attorney general of Nyasaland argued that if the 1902 Marriage Ordinance or the 1902 Christian Native Marriage Ordinance recognized an African marriage, the husband could not sue a white man who committed adultery with his wife but could only seek a divorce from his wife and obtain compensation for reasons of adultery, leaving the white man unpunished.[48] This approach appeared inadequate to officials at Ncheu, who, echoing Johnston, stressed that the Ngoni considered "adultery as a very grave offence and their punishments for adultery in the old days were extremely severe. . . . As the influx of settlers into the Protectorate increases such offenses will probably become more numerous and it seems advisable that some provision should be made for dealing with such matters"[49] (see figures 1.2 and 1.3). White settlers should pay the same compensation as an African adulterer, thus giving customary protocol a higher priority than asserting white privilege.[50] A similar tactic had been discussed among officials in Southern Rhodesia regarding the Native Adultery Punishment Ordinance, an act initially proposed by chiefs who were "losing the control of their women and girls who were running away with alien natives to the Mines and Towns."[51] Native commissioners were hesitant to extend this law to white men since "it would place every isolated Trader, Pros-

FIGURE 1.2. Ngoni chiefs, 1886, taken by Consul A. G. H. Hawes. Used by permission of the National Archives of the United Kingdom (CO 1069/108/59).

pector or person in danger of blackmail."[52] Furthermore, this statute applied only to married African women. "There is but little doubt . . . that the morals of the younger generation of native women are not improving, and that promiscuous sexual intercourse exists to a considerable extent," commented one official in Southern Rhodesia. "I am of [the] opinion that if the provisions of the Natives Adultery Ordinance, governing the native *married* women, were applied to the unmarried girls the natives would benefit greatly, and this regulation would be appreciated by the natives generally and particularly by the older natives."[53] Even so, it failed to account for interracial relationships. As a native commissioner in Chilimanzi, Southern Rhodesia, noted, "a native married woman is subjected to a severe penalty if she commits adultery with a native yet the law allows her to commit this social offence with any European without punishment. There are numbers of low, unscrupulous white men in the country who think nothing of inducing a native married woman to leave her husband for the purpose of illicit sexual intercourse and yet the law winks at this offence."[54]

Group of Angoni Women.

FIGURE 1.3. Ngoni women, adolescent girls, and children, 1886, taken by Consul A. G. H. Hawes. Used by permission of the National Archives of the United Kingdom (CO 1069/108/93).

These legal discrepancies encouraged criminal punishment for white men, even if their interracial promiscuities did not amount to "a public scandal owing to the fact that the majority of illicit intercourses take place in out of the way places. . . . If these practices prevailed in towns it certainly would amount to a public scandal."[55] Idle gossip and innuendo were therefore transformed into active rumor by colonial officials motivated by fear due to legal uncertainties. Concern centered on appeasing African authorities. A decade later in Bechuanaland (present day Botswana), Tshekedi Khama, regent of the Bangwato and uncle of the future Botswana president Seretse Khama, famously punished a young white man, Phinehas McIntosh, by flogging him for repeated acts of social misconduct, among them having several African women as concubines. Tshekedi Khama told McIntosh that he disciplined him in this manner since "he did not live the life of a white man [and] neither that of [a] Native."[56] Similar criticism surfaced earlier in Nyasaland with a pervasive unease that unruly white men could become "a menace to the tranquility of the native population" even if, in the words of one official, African women were "proverbially lax in their morals." It would be "undesirable" if "natives should fail in litigation against Europeans when 20 years of experience of hundreds of similar cases show that they would succeed against a native defendant."[57] Yet concubinage appeared to be passively handled. At Fort Johnston on the southern shore of Lake Nyasa, an official reported that incidents "of married native women being taken to live with Europeans have occurred in this District as in many others, but few cases have been brought to my notice in which the European seduced the woman knowing her to be married and none in which the compensation demanded was refused."[58] Officials in the tea estate district of Mlanje, south of Zomba, reported that "no such cases have occurred in this District; they have however in others; almost invariably compensation has been at once paid, and the case settled out of Court, by arrangement in order to avoid public scandal."[59] An official at Mzimba, in the northern part of the protectorate, similarly had "dealt with such cases in the past, but the legal difficulty has not arisen as the European, by the time he came before me, was always willing to pay at once what was demanded." Even so, a legal measure should be in place when "the European's sense of shame fails."[60]

Though official testimony was individual, the gossip it drew on hinted at a broader social history. Regional responses outlined different local attitudes. In Karonga in the far north, where there were few whites, no cases were recorded, yet some stories circulated given the temporary military presence during World War I. The "many half-educated natives (especially the members of the North Nyasa Native Association)" who were "very conscious of their colour and would be easily inflamed by any wrong of the kind under consideration" provided one potential deterrent.[61] Another official elsewhere noted that it was "unlikely that such a case would occur because the Atonga are so sensitive on the subject that a woman of their tribe would fear the disgrace of an attachment of this kind."[62] "Concubinage between Europeans and native women undoubtedly exists in the country but I should say that there are very few cases of native women married under the provisions of the Marriage Ordinance who are living with Europeans," wrote still another official. "The majority of cases are those in which Europeans cohabit with unmarried native women, the matter is usually arranged between the European and the father of the girl, and the woman then becomes the property of the European."[63] In some cases "the woman had been given to him by the headman of a village who informed him that she was unmarried." It was also believed that "some husbands were not above encouraging their wives to go to Europeans in order to obtain compensation afterwards."[64] "I certainly think that cases of native women being induced to leave their husbands and reside with Europeans is a matter which might lead to trouble," wrote an official at Liwonde, "but it happens that more often than not the husband is a consenting party."[65]

Rumors of such arrangements not only fed colonial anxieties over loss of control. They also suggest a sense of continuity with earlier practices of intergroup marriage as a social opportunity. Although colonial officials worried that ignoring "the injured husband's just claim" could "incite him to overt acts of retaliation such as arson" and provoke "the native mind against Europeans in general," an alternative perspective on agency emerges through this anecdotal knowledge.[66] The desire "to protect the native family" against a certain "class of European" reflected a prevalent reluctance to stoke African grievances.[67] But this broad concern concealed more complex kinds of social interaction. Official recognition for two types of customary marriage in the protectorate—"the Manganja type" (matrilineal) in which "the Husband pays for his Wife by a partial surrender of his own liberty, building a hut for her in her people's village & to some extent becoming 'their man'" and a second "Angoni type" (patrilineal) in which "cattle or cash or goods are, in effect, paid for the woman"—schematized native marriage practices as unchanging, essentialized forms, rather than granting consideration to individual circumstances and incentive.[68] Though respect for such customs marked an attempt at cultural sensitivity, the prevalent notion that these acts constituted "a gross interference with native life," with white adulterers to be treated "in like manner as a native in a similar case," offers only one interpretation, which granted agency only to the white men involved.[69] When agency is granted to African men, it is only to prevent their resistance or attempted blackmail. "In dealing with these cases, great care should be taken to prove that the husband of a good looking woman has not sent his wife to seduce the man, in order to obtain compensation; a very common procedure among natives, especially Yaos," cautioned one official.[70] Since discussion centered on conflicts between men, women are, moreover, completely marginalized—a silence that raises further questions about individual agency and about the possible roles of *nkhoswe* and matrilineal custom. Such biases embedded in this colonial prose conceal the possibility of alternative forms of social interaction offering status and material gain.

Thus, what appears in this fragmented testimony is an incomplete, if suggestive, record of the diverse origins of the Anglo-African community and its regional counterparts. A predictable pattern of ethnogenesis did not exist, with the occurrence of interracial relationships at least partly dependent on population densities and the scale of day-to-day contact between white and local communities. But this archival predicament tells a history regarding the precarious conditions and apprehensive views that informed the production of this documentation—a record shaped by local gossip and official rumor that in turn distorted and often obscured, if not entirely quieted, historical patterns for the sake of legal priorities and social respectability. A pragmatic vision took hold, telling in the first instance a story of repression and in the second instance a story of how men, colonial and colonized, sought legal reconciliation when relationships violated marital, not simply racial, bounds. Anxieties surfaced about cultural deference, legal protocol, and patriarchal order—not just race. But beyond this unease, many of the personal histories involved remained unclear. As Luise White has written, rumors arise from ambiguous situations. They mark attempts at explanation with incomplete information.[71] As for the silence that surrounds rumor and its protoform of local gossip, it too signals a negotiation between what is known and unknown, what to tell and what to leave unspoken for reasons of active evasion or simple uncertainty.[72] Such ambiguities did not dissipate. These conditions of anecdotal knowledge that generated legal complexities in the short term also produced enduring questions of illegitimacy that multiracial people would persistently confront.

: SOCIAL HISTORY, FAMILY HISTORY, PERSONAL HISTORY :

In my case, I in particular was very curious, that probably one day I maybe may go and try to dig roots, you know? Find out. But you see, coming from a very poor family—you see he [my father] was really struggling to even feed us, even for us to go to school—it was like, that was a multimillion-dollar question, you see? I just sort of gave up and said, no, history is "the father of so-and-so."
—interview with Eunice Mussa

As discussed at the start of this chapter, an elusive social memory of Anglo-African identity still exists, but it has been so transformed by postcolonial politics that the use of the category has declined. The identity is fixed to the colonial period. Family histories, however, illuminate its personal meaning. They provide context for and evidence of the practices described above, working against colonial rumor and gossip. These histories also contrast with — and critique — interpretations of interracial relationships as transgressive. Although such perspectives reflect common public attitudes, these relationships involved ordinary people who had their own stories to tell. As a result, this evidence reveals the difference between local personal meaning and colonial state prerogatives. The people I talked to recognized categories of race and gender that were involved, though they often spoke in a family vernacular that came more naturally to them — the roles of father, mother, grandfather, and grandmother. The use of personal language is perhaps unsurprising. Nevertheless, it should be treated as a challenge to academic scholarship. Social categories of difference were secondary. A genealogical imagination came through that drew people together, rather than apart, underscoring the ways in which interracial relationships were not perceived as universally illicit but were often rendered normative through family and by time.

These family stories occupy a particular place in the genre of oral history, consisting of life histories rather than statist or political narratives.[73] The chronologically shallow histories of these regional communities, combined with genealogical origins both local and foreign, produced uneven qualities of depth and recollection. The history of postcolonial Malawi under the Banda regime also undoubtedly contributed to the suppression of certain memories.[74] Genealogy and kinship are what shaped and sustained these personal histories and bound them together. Many family stories were anchored by arrivals and settlement, the coming of a European or Indian man (a grandfather or great-grandfather) and his putative marriage to an African woman (a grandmother or great-grandmother). One person reported: "Both grandfathers were Europeans. One was of Scotch descent. One was English. Both grandmothers were Africans. One was Ngoni, that's my mother's mother, who was from Ncheu. But my father's mother was Yao on Chief Kapeni's side"[75] (see figures 1.4 and 1.5). These ethnic identities not only add another layer to attachments, they genuflect toward preexisting patterns of interethnic relations, as discussed previously. The inclusion of Kapeni in this history offers a vital detail, given his status as one of five principal Yao chiefs who established themselves in southern Malawi during the 1860s.[76] Kapeni's position near Blantyre and Limbe guaranteed

Chief Kapeni.   *Yao Tribe.*

FIGURE 1.4. Chief Kapeni of the Yao, 1886, taken by Consul A. G. H. Hawes. His head covering indicates his Islamic faith, and his rifle is a symbol of wealth, resulting from Yao involvement in the East African slave trade. Used by permission of the National Archives of the United Kingdom (CO 1069/108/131).

Group of Yao Women.

FIGURE 1.5. Yao women, adolescent girls, and children, 1886, taken by Consul
A. G. H. Hawes. Used by permission of the National Archives of the United Kingdom
(CO 1069/108/111).

his involvement with settlers and colonial officials over matters of land—
factors that likely played a role in this family's history.[77]

It was not always clear in conversation how these "marriages" were arranged and recognized, though the people I spoke to frequently insisted
on their validity. Such claims were important, given persistent questions
of illegitimacy. In the case of conjugal relationships, some were recognized
by customary law if not by colonial law. However, notions of customary
protocol could be difficult to discern with specificity, with direct questions
often resulting in equally firm answers that revealed results rather than
processes of intention and negotiation. In one interview, I asked Henry
Ascroft's daughter Jessica, "So they were married according to African customary law?" To which she simply replied, "According to African customary
law." When I asked if her grandparents also married under British law or
with a Christian decree, she answered, "I don't think they ever did." Elabo-

Chief Kapeni's Village.

Mount Sochi

FIGURE 1.6. Chief Kapeni's village, 1886, taken by Consul A. G. H. Hawes. Used by permission of the National Archives of the United Kingdom (CO 1069/108/135).

rating the circumstances of her grandparents' relationship, Ascroft said: "In those days the way they used to marry, it was what they called African customary law: they go and they ask the chief, they say 'I want a wife, can you find a wife for me?' The chief says, 'All right, I think you can marry this one, if the person agrees.'" This testimony supports evidence discussed in the previous section regarding the active arrangement of relationships. Ascroft depicted the agreement reached by Chief Kapeni in her family's history as a practice common among customary authorities. "He was the chief that received the Europeans and gave them wives," she remarked. "They were the ones who gave the Europeans wives when they first came into this country."[78] But such interpretations, even if taken as generally accurate, disclosed little about the involvement of other relatives beyond the local authority of the chief (figure 1.6). The role of Kapeni arguably indicates the complex shift toward patrilineal custom among the Yao discussed earlier and the low, possibly slave, status of the women involved. If these unanswered questions leave our view of the past opaque, it is clear that these stories often sought to provide legitimation in the face of such mnemonic uncertainties. They sought alignment with local norms. Telling these histories did not simply restore the past; they validated the family.

Even so, other people I spoke to expressed less confidence about the formality of such arrangements, especially since uncles and brothers, not chiefs per se, typically played prominent roles in brokering marriages under matrilineal custom. One informant admitted that she knew her grandfather had a wife in Scotland and that no formal marriage existed between him and her grandmother. In her words, they were "living together, let's put it that way."[79] These personal contingencies were reinforced by childhood memories that recalled differences between European and Indian fathers and how such factors affected family life. Yusuf Ismael, who was Indo-African and a founding member of the Anglo-African Association, captured this distinction: "Those with Indian fathers were much happier all the time because the fathers took them as their children and lived with them openly. Lived in their homes, the father's home openly, while our [Anglo-African] friends didn't live openly . . . they [the white fathers] had to hide them. . . . Those Europeans who still had African women, the women had to be behind the houses . . . the children lived with their mothers behind the houses."[80] These recollections of familial attachment and racial difference in its quotidian forms—with domestic segregation depicted through vivid spatial details—indicate the fluid nature of these relationships and the mutable character of racial hierarchies that resist generalization, in addition to suggesting how such childhood experiences could shape future patterns of identification. The connections between Indian men and African women imply a shared sense of colonial subjectivity, later reflected in the ways the Indian community supported African nationalism under the Malawi Congress Party.[81]

But given the nature and sensitivity of family history, such matters of race were debated, shaping what Victor Turner once referred to as genealogical recall.[82] The past, with its finite qualities and social value, was negotiated and governed by norms of authentication, authority, and establishing continuity.[83] Other informants stressed the overriding importance of kinship and genealogy as a means of mitigating discrimination and enabling the formation of adaptive elective affinities, even in cases where formal marriages were infrequent.[84] In contrast to Ismael's account, Robert Jamieson, a Malawian of Anglo-African descent, said that when "British engineers, missionaries, or businessmen came into this country they actually took their African women into their homes and recognized their children. . . . The European Coloureds tended to recognize what their parentage was." Jamieson emphasized that "generally you will find that British settlers took upon themselves their children from the village. Sometimes they didn't even look after the women, but they looked after the children."[85] What is significant is that Ismael and Jamieson both seek to amplify meaning from personal experience, to legitimate their family histories through the remembrance of affection and care.

Overall, a number of European and Indian men who arrived to work as planters, for the Nyasaland Railway, for the British Central Africa Company, and as soldiers during World War I became involved in relationships with local women. They inadvertently participated in and promoted a regional process of intergroup conjugality that began during the precolonial era. At the same time, these personal memories point to an experience unique to the colonial period. Colonialism was a family experience for multiracial Africans, providing an origin story for many that marked a difference in status from surrounding native communities, even if their own status was not entirely non-native. In Jamieson's view, Anglo-Africans had been "removed from the culture of their mothers" and "brought into the culture of their fathers," so that "when change [decolonization] came, we tended to line up with our British parentage."[86] These colonial kinship alignments oriented around paternal descent paralleled the spread of agnatic customs introduced during the nineteenth century. These histories can therefore be seen both as individual and as contributing to a broader regional process.

As with archival documents, it was likewise less easy to recover through interviews the experiences and perspectives of the African women involved, even though many of my informants were women. But the reasons in this context were different. Asking specific questions about these relationships—how they happened, how they were experienced, how they ended—frequently resulted once more in broad, objective replies but not intimate personal details. The public stereotype of these relationships as illicit and racially degenerate may have prompted reluctance and silence. Yet perhaps this situation is no surprise. Who but the participants would remember such intimate exchanges? This condition reflects who my informants were—the children and grandchildren from such relationships—and the priorities of memory. Origins that established identity and stability were discussed, whereas tensions and conflict that undermined senses of family, legitimacy, and belonging were less often mentioned or perhaps even remembered—what Jaap van Velsen once called genealogical amnesia.[87] The tense and tender ties that constitute domestic relations possess their own forms of intention—in this case, genealogical histories whose primary purpose was to preserve a sense of personal history and identity for family members.[88] Such is the postcolonial condition of memory for these families, for whom *Anglo-African* and *Indo-African* had no permanent value as public identities. Yet it is also vital to recognize the continuities between such terms and their postcolonial remains.[89] These self-descriptions sought to impose normality on relationships otherwise seen as socially transgressive in the public eye, employing for political purposes a genealogical imagination that materialized from these family histories.

These private practices of the present therefore illuminate how individuals used modalities of kinship and family to critique and negotiate everyday forms of social difference across time periods. Their recollections point to different scales of meaning between personal histories, the emergence of community histories, and broader patterns of regional social change.[90] Their insights on origins, marriage, childhood, and later identification disrupt and reshape the contours of these discrete genres, pointing to experiences before, during, and after active community formation.[91] Experience is mediated by experience, with the present ineluctably shaping the structure and meaning of the past.[92] These collected postcolonial memories consequently underscore the broad rubric of this first part of the book, depicting mutable experiences that unsettle categorical naming and elude social groupings that once existed and have since dissolved. They mark a different temporality—a genealogical time, to borrow an expression from Michael D. Jackson—that captured enduring personal bonds that mattered. But neither should this situation be construed as unusual or esoteric. Another informant condensed the significance of family and social relationships in a more ordinary fashion, saying: "In those days I believe they were like family. Once they knew each other they were always mixing together, you know?"[93]

: INTIMATE ONTOLOGIES AND COLONIAL HAUNTOLOGIES :

This chapter has examined different idioms of history—gossip, rumor, and memory among them—encountered through fieldwork and archival research. It has addressed the ways in which variable temporalities—

precolonial and colonial, colonial and postcolonial, social and personal—
can shape interpretations of the past. Colonialism was a family experience.
But European colonization of the late nineteenth century was not the first
process of this kind. In the *longue durée*, these histories form part of an
ongoing historical pattern. The racial frontiers of colonial societies were a
new variation on preexisting social frontiers. They were not only spaces of
difference and tension, but also zones of interaction and creation.[94] This
perspective highlights the risk of dwelling on European attitudes at the
expense of silencing local viewpoints and custom, as well as long-term
patterns of historical change. This argument is particularly pertinent for
colonies such as Nyasaland, where white settlement was less dense and
indigenous practices and moral economies persisted. Though social anxieties were not absent, it is important to recognize ongoing elements of
active experimentation. The idea of endogamy as a social norm is a political and historical construction. Yet an emphasis on the *longue durée* should
not undervalue the contingencies and social vulnerabilities that emerged
in the colonial era. Anglo-African identity was an expression of resilient
trends of intergroup relationships, but it remained fixed to the colonial
period. These intimate ontologies transformed into colonial hauntologies—beginnings that still inhabit moments of reminiscence, despite the
passage of time.[95] Residual family memories recall the significance of colonial kinship ties, but only through a present that both draws on and com-
partmentalizes that past. The ultimate precarity and postcolonial social
death of Anglo-African identity is balanced with the endurance of a con-
jured genealogical imagination, relegated to the personal care and memory
of those who continue to live with such pasts.

CHAPTER 2

::

ADAIMA'S STORY

::

As indicated at the end of the previous chapter, the stories people tell about the past are not exclusively about community history or categorical origins. Instead, they are often about personal and family beginnings. By addressing interracial relationships as a formative experience, the preceding chapter breaks a frequent silence in the existing literature—a silence that tacitly reflects the charged status such histories of dissident sexuality could have.[1] As Patrick Wolfe has written, colonial officials—and even scholars—have too often treated such people as if they were immaculately conceived.[2] Such histories matter. They were not merely the sometime subject of local gossip and colonial rumor but, more significantly, became ethically constitutive stories through personal retelling that provided a basis for family memory and identification.[3] They established forms of self-worth. Yet if one initial conclusion can be made, it is that the domestic turn found in oral histories implicitly underscored the diminished vitality of Anglo-African as a mode of public identification, even when people who ostensibly fit that category were directly asked about it. Indeed, the most common answer I received when I interviewed people about how they identified themselves was "Malawian"—undoubtedly a sign of the conformities of a postcolonial nationalism and its nativist underpinnings. This situation speaks to the potential decline of certain types of colonial peoplehood, as I have argued previously, but it equally highlights the enduring habitation of such histories within private realms beyond social consensus and group activity. Such recollections locate the importance of family and the ability to speak about family with a sense of authority, in contrast to broader social histories. The domestic settings in which these conversations took place—

on a front stoop, at a dinner table, in a living room, and, on one occasion, in a bedroom, where my informant preferred to talk lying down because of his age and infirmity—added contextual shape and influence to these stories—not only introducing themes of everyday life, but also providing a secure place to negotiate the past and present. Yet social and political matters were never far. The oral testimony I collected was certainly domesticated in its way, but it did not entirely depart from the effects of colonial and postcolonial state power.[4]

This chapter continues examination of the domestic and the permeable boundaries between the public and private. Rather than foregrounding the social, it attends to the individual. The histories described in the preceding chapter pointed to patterns of social change and the involvement of individuals in articulating regional histories—whether chiefs, district officials, or descendants of the Anglo-African community. This chapter focuses on a single case study—the story of a woman named Adaima. Her history is told through a single document produced by an unnamed white man, an archival fragment that is limited in scope but vivid in detail. Written in pencil, this text takes the form of a long letter, although the intended recipient, like the author, is unknown. Presumably the audience was a colonial official, given the legal request made in the document. But its most immediate quality is its sheer existence—a piece of evidence that offers a firsthand account of an interracial relationship, a small miracle of description both idiosyncratic and isolated. Given its singularity, this chapter extends the genre of histories without groups to engage with fragmented evidence of this kind.[5] While the experience of Adaima and her master (or lover, or benefactor, or abuser?) was not unique, this incidental story of a relationship turned wrong tells a history beyond gossip, rumor, and memory.

Foregrounding Adaima's imperfectly preserved life, my method here is similar to the previous chapter's juxtaposition of oral recollections against written material. This fleeting "world on paper" provides crucial insight on sexual relationships that my informants could not.[6] Despite distinct limitations, it offers firsthand detail that I was unable to retrieve otherwise. Its violent content in particular works against more benign impressions of the past as shaped by family memory. Furthermore, it presents an important critical intervention against "black peril" scares (or "black perils" for short)—social phenomena that have adversely dominated existing historical narratives of interracial sex in southern Africa. A sharp distinction must be drawn between such perils and the more ubiquitous practice of

At Her Majesty's Consulate — Nyassa January 1886.

FIGURE 2.1. An 1886 portrait of settlers before the Nyasaland Protectorate was formally established, taken by Consul A. G. H. Hawes. Used by permission of the National Archives of the United Kingdom (CO 1069/108/85).

white men having intimate relations with African women. This minor historical drama consequently underscores how individual experiences, even those contained in ephemeral forms of documentation, can serve as a foundation for reconsidering patterns of personal and collective meaning.

: **PERILS OF DISTRACTION** :

As the preceding chapter addressed, intergroup relationships emerged in contexts of social mobility—precolonial and colonial alike. White settlers formed one part of this broader pattern of migration and settlement over the course of the nineteenth and twentieth centuries. Their lives converged with this preexisting history, shaping it and being shaped by it. From the 1880s to the 1950s, European immigration to British Central Africa (see figure 2.1) overlapped with the simultaneous regional movement of African men and women. Both sets of people sought financial gain and social opportunity introduced by colonial rule. Mining in Southern and Northern Rhodesia centered on gold and copper, respectively, presented new finan-

FIGURE 2.2. Agricultural production—probably tea or coffee—in Nyasaland, circa 1877. Used by permission of the National Archives of the United Kingdom (CO 1069/109/15).

cial incentives, as did cultivating cash crops such as cotton, tobacco, coffee, and tea in Nyasaland (see figures 2.2 and 2.3).[7] Regional colonial states encouraged African labor migration for the benefit of regional economies but also sought to control the social and political lives of African workers such that they did not interfere with either economic priorities or the community life of white settlers. It is in this context of labor and mobility that sexual apprehension toward African men appeared during the early twentieth century, intermittently surfacing as "black peril" scares.

These heightened moments of social panic reflect the complex intersection of race, sexuality, and politics under colonial rule. Indeed, these episodes concerning the purported sexual predation of African men have drawn too much attention, obscuring more ordinary occurrences of white men having relationships with African women. Black perils, particularly in Southern Rhodesia between 1902 and 1916, remain among the most vivid public manifestations of sexual attitudes and control during the colonial period in southern Africa.[8] Approximately two hundred African men were imprisoned in Southern Rhodesia, with twenty executed. But

Coffee Plantation at Zomba.

FIGURE 2.3. Coffee production in Zomba, Nyasaland, 1886, taken by Consul A. G. H. Hawes. Used by permission of the National Archives of the United Kingdom (CO 1069/108/119).

these cases obscure a deeper history. Black perils were decidedly modern. Settler-African relationships had occurred in southern Africa since the seventeenth century, a practice that shifted in meaning with emergent strands of scientific racism during the late nineteenth century. Panics in Natal during the 1870s provide one marker of this transition from a permissive frontier context to the establishment of firm racial boundaries. By the early twentieth century, this transformation appeared complete, with Johannesburg experiencing periodic scares from the 1890s through the 1910s—a time of rapid urbanization involving many people of different racial backgrounds and little state control.[9] The peak panic years of 1908, 1910, and 1911 in Southern Rhodesia have similarly been linked to increases in white immigration, which increased anxieties rather than reducing them. Yet racial demographic figures alone cannot explain these episodes: gender was nearly as important as race. The Criminal Law Amendment Ordinance of 1903 carried a death penalty not only for rape, but also for attempted rape. Other measures included the Immorality Suppression Ordinance No. 9 of 1903 and its later extension, the Immorality and Indecency Suppression Ordinance No. 1 of 1916—both of which targeted white women and black men. White men, in contrast, were not held accountable for relationships with African women. Legislation was consequently directed toward a particular equation of race and gender—one that protected white male entitlement.[10]

Black perils therefore distracted, and continue to distract, consideration from a wider social history of relationships between white men and African women. A distinction must be drawn between black perils (involving African men sexually threatening white women) and more regular occurrences of miscegenation (typically involving white men having sexual relationships with African women).[11] Based on perceived rather than actual threats, these perils diverted attention by producing social "noise" that camouflaged more common practices.[12] Though white peril did surface as a regional issue during the 1920s, as discussed in the previous chapter, it received far quieter treatment than its black counterpart—more often than not being the subject of local gossip and innuendo instead of politically charged rumor and outright scandal.[13] In 1921 and 1930 the Southern Rhodesian Legislative Council considered legal restrictions on the practice of concubinage but failed to pass any measures because such practices were believed to be in decline.[14] Nevertheless, black intellectuals across the region like George Simeon Mwase and Solomon Plaatje noted this problem. In an essay pointedly titled "The Mote and the Beam" (1921), after the biblical maxim warning of hypocritical judgment, Plaatje criticized the paradox of white attitudes in South Africa, in particular the "one-sided" laws that allowed white men "to flood the country with illegitimate half-castes" despite public pronouncements against interracial sex.[15] But this apparent contradiction signals once more the attention of colonial power, with its silence on the matter of white men indicating who was in charge—black men were tightly regulated, but white men were not. Furthermore, black perils were part of a broader set of concerns about African polygamy, prostitution, and perceived immorality more generally. Although these perils coincided with spikes in white immigration and economic downturns, they still reflected ongoing attempts to manage the place and mobility of settlers and natives alike when the law failed to establish control and stability.[16]

Adaima's story provides an opportunity to understand personal experience against the distortions of social discourse. It provides a significant counterpoint, indicating how white male behavior was supervised; how African women could be far more vulnerable than white women; and how more common practices of colonial concubinage can decenter the black peril phenomenon, with its disjointed correspondence between actual incidents of crime and the incitement of social concern. This alternative focus therefore moves beyond repeating the function of black peril outbursts to shore up white solidarity—a point that has been well established, but often leaves aside the circumstances of individual experience. The document containing Adaima's history is reproduced here in full (see figure 2.4). Though restoring marginalized persons to history can be a challenging task, her story provides an example of how histories without groups can reveal the texture and complexity of personal experiences, ones that articulate the choices and views of individual people, even if they left only fragmentary details in their wake.

: **THE COMPLETE DOCUMENT** :

Adaima, daughter of Nanseta, formerly residing at Chingwalawalu's village but now removed to Ndenga, came to Zomba about five years ago in guest of custom—one of my houseboys (Hamisi) came across her and brought her to my house. She stayed at my place for about 3 or 4 months and unfortunately became pregnant. While pregnant she left my house and went over to the Camp and took up her abode with a K. A. R. [King's African Rifles] Askari of the name Salima. Out of sentiment I sent for her father (Nanseta) and got him after some difficulty to persuade her to return to my place, pointing out that she was pregnant and that I did not wish the child that was to be born to be left to the mercy of a man who was not its father.

The child was born early in 1914, and is now nearly 4 years old—a boy who goes by the name of "James." I have had absolutely no connection with his mother from the time she first became pregnant, but owing to my strong attachment to this child James, I have tolerated the mother's presence here since his birth. The mother noticing my attachment to this child has been blackmailing me for the past 4 years during which period I have paid her considerably over £80 in cash. In addition to this money payment she has helped herself freely to my stores—pots and pans, jugs, basins, soap, tobacco, sugar, rice, chickens, etc. etc.

Her behavior since the birth of this child has been somewhat as follows:—Every few *days* or *weeks* she gets extremely violent, smashing

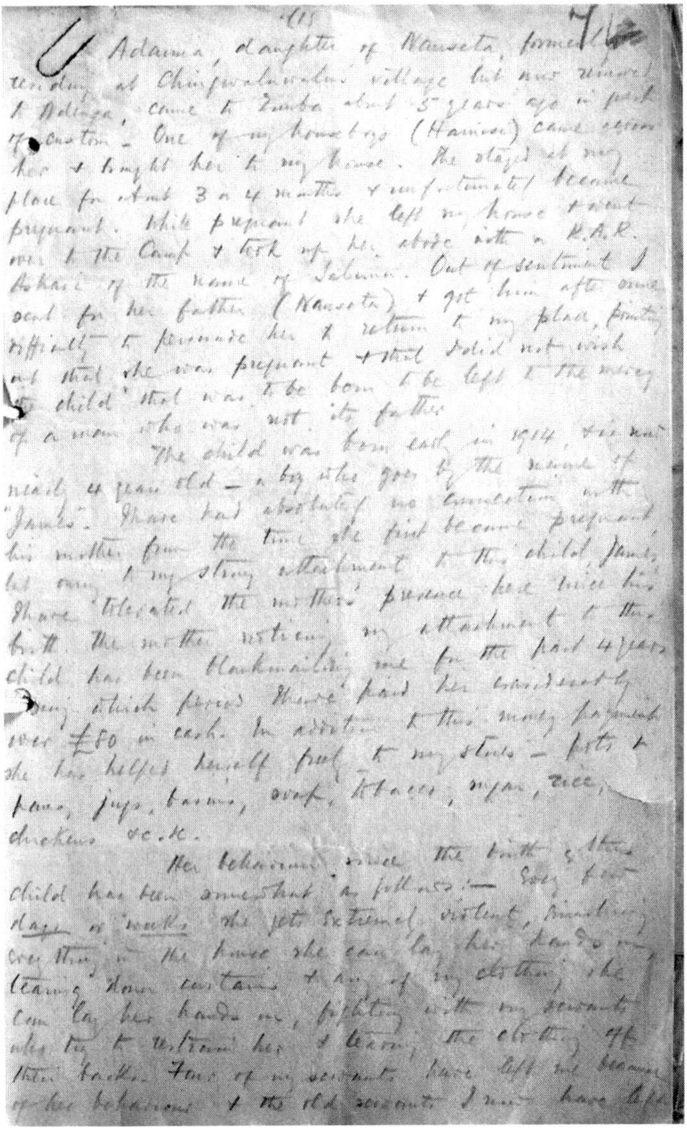

FIGURE 2.4. A photograph of part of the handwritten archival document regarding Adaima, undated (NS 1/35/3). Permission to photograph courtesy of the National Archives of Malawi.

everything in the house she can lay her hands on, tearing down curtains and any of my clothing she can lay her hands on, fighting with my servants who try to restrain her and tearing the clothing off their backs. Four of my servants have left me because of her behaviour and the old servants I now have [have] left me at their wits['] end to know what to do and implore me to take the action I am now taking. She has repeatedly struck at me with rackets, sticks, etc. but owing to my strong attachment to this child James I have gone on putting up with it. In addition to smashing everything she can lay her hands on she has done away with such things as my boots . . . scissors, pen knives, etc. etc. and no doubt given them to her admirers. Her blackmail lies in this that she has demanded to be paid 50/- [shillings] a month failing which she has threatened to take this child James to the Resident here so as to make the matter public.

I now come to a very important point. I have already said that I have had no connection with her, ever since she first became pregnant about 5 years ago. But my servant knows she has been cohabiting with others, and the proof of this lies in the fact that she now has another child which she has cunningly handed over to her mother to look after as there was no mistaking its paternity. As a matter of fact I know that the father of this child is one of my servants, Bwanali, whom I discharged some time ago. I suppose that even from the native point of view this fact of her becoming pregnant by another would justify her being sent away by me. And knowing my attachment to James she says she will not go without taking this child James with her. She knows I will not consent to this and she therefore remains in here making a nuisance of herself, smashing things in the house, fighting with my servants, and threatening to go to the Resident. This as I say has been going on for the past 4 years. When I tell her to go away she says she won't go without taking this child James with her. James has been brought up by me with the same care as a white child would receive—clothed, fed, and looked after by a specially paid servant. She has repeatedly been very cruel to this child and for the past 3 years has done nothing for him.

One of her commonest forms of annoyance is that when I am going anywhere she walks round the rooms and takes away my razors, brushes, and all the things one needs in . . . and when asked to . . . then becomes violent and starts smashing and tearing things in the house and fighting the servants. The whole house bears evidence of her deprevations [sic]—panes smashed, pictures beaten down, mosquito curtains and table cloths ripped up with knives, curtains torn down, etc. etc. All my servants and even her brothers and sisters who from time to time have stayed with her will bear out all I have said if evidence is wanted. She has frequently left the house awake at nights, shouting and yelling, fighting with the servants who try to restrain her, and smashing things right and left.

I don't know what the law will permit I am to do in this case, but as you can understand I want to be free of this woman. She was not acquired by me in the customary way from her parents, but as I have said was "picked up" by one of my houseboys and brought here—her home being in the Liwonde district. I want this child James to remain with me as I want him properly looked after and *educated*. I certainly don't want him to drift to her village and suffer from every form of neglect. The woman can go back to her second child by me of my ex-servant (Bwanali).

This morning, because I did not catch what sum of money she demanded, she broke several things in the house and ripped off two cushion covers.

I don't know what character her Headman Ndenga would give her, but the Principal Headman, Chingwalawalu, says that it is a "bad family" and that if it were not for the presence of muzungus [whites] he would with his own hands lop off her father's head for his truculent behavior.[17]

: TEXT, CONTEXT, AND EPHEMERAL KNOWLEDGE :

This document clearly describes the relationship between an unnamed European man and an African woman named Adaima. It narrates a custody battle over their son, James, a key dimension that explains the purpose of this testimony and its inclusion in a colonial archive. The document is undated, though we can assume that it was written around 1918, given the age of James as described in the document as well as supplementary, though unrelated, papers that surround it in the archival file labeled "Native Secretariat (NS) 1/35/3" in the National Archives of Malawi. Indeed, the surprise that I felt when I discovered this document was in part due to its archival placement—the only connection it had with the other documents in this file being colonial state concern for "half-caste" children. None of the other documents approached the same level of detail. The writer's confession and the relationship he describes is, therefore, an example of the extraordinary historical incidents haphazardly deposited and preserved in colonial archives. As Ann Laura Stoler has argued, archives are replete with contingent documents that do not concern the causes or outcomes of major events—or even events as such—but that instead chart tensions and anxieties materialized through everyday occasions of colonial life.[18] As a consequence, colonial repositories do not always reflect official state views but can offer what Antoinette Burton calls "fugitive traces of subjectivity," which illuminate what it meant to live under certain historical conditions.[19] Such traces constitute ephemeral forms of knowledge, presenting histories that are individual, even eccentric, in scope but that speak to broader patterns of experience.[20]

Given these parameters, one initial point to be made is that there were no notable black peril scares in Nyasaland, a reflection of its lower density of white settlement. For example, there were only 1,486 whites in Nyasaland in 1921 compared to 33,620 whites in Southern Rhodesia during the same year (see table 1.1). In contrast, an estimated 1,175,000 Africans lived in Nyasaland at the time. Yet interracial relationships were not uncommon, as demonstrated by the existence of colonial files on "half-caste" children. A 1934 government census conducted at the urging of the Anglo-African Association placed their total population at 1,202 people, as mentioned in the previous chapter—a not insignificant number, given that the European community numbered 1,975 people in a 1931 census.[21] Indeed, by 1935 the Nyasaland administration began to consider what its policy should be regarding "half-caste" children, referring to the 1934 Foggin Commission's report on Southern Rhodesia that addressed questions of status and education for such children.[22] The fragmented history of Adaima, James, and the document's author can thus be seen as both unique and ordinary, its evidence of experience providing a transcript valuable for its rare private detail in contrast to the public transcripts of black peril cases farther south. It can be contextualized within a pattern of domestic life in the region at the time, but its specific circumstances remain firmly individual.[23]

Of primary importance is the fact that this relationship involved a white man and an African woman. Although it consists of a monologue by the unnamed European—it is probable, though not certain, that he is British—the document itself is polyphonic to a degree, in that Adaima and James have a clear presence and even speak through their actions, as described by the writer. It is next to impossible to determine who Adaima was precisely, but the inclusion of her name, her son's name, her family relations, and the contrasting absence of the narrator's personal information reinforce her agency and historical presence. We can glean some information that can help us imagine her status and life. The name *Adaima* could be Yao in origin, a variation of the Muslim Swahili name *Daima* meaning "always" or "forever." It could also be an adopted nickname, drawn from the Chichewa verb *-ima* meaning "to stop." Applied colloquially, *Adaima* could refer to a woman who has stopped menstruating and is pregnant (i.e., "the pregnant one").[24] She was furthermore the daughter of Nanseta, which suggests that she may have been the kin of a chief of that name residing in the tea-growing Cholo District.[25] The likelihood that she had status is compromised in part, however, by the narrator's references to other headmen and the concluding comment that, according to another chief, she came from a "bad family," a judgment referring to her father's "truculent behavior." Liwonde is also mentioned as her home, indicating that she had resided to the north of Zomba on the opposite side from the Cholo District, which was located toward the far south of the protectorate. An enigmatic sense of mobility on her part is therefore present throughout the document. Indeed, it is possible that the writer is employing self-protective euphemisms when using the terms "daughter" and "father" with Adaima being a slave in status under the control of Chief Nanseta.[26] This condition could explain her inexact origins and uncertain movement, while also relating to discussions of concubinage in the previous chapter. The narrator says she was brought to his household by a servant and that she came and went thereafter. He had some contact with Adaima's purported father after she left his household pregnant, but the relationship between him and her father does not appear to be a close, or even familiar, one. Though African authorities often orchestrated such arrangements, these passing observations in the document tell us about both the informality of this relationship as well as the impermanence of domestic working relations more generally.[27]

The biography of the document's author is equally elusive. Though the document is written in pencil and may be an unfinished draft, his relative anonymity is presumably a self-protective choice given the small white community and the shame he could feel if the matter were made public. This unsigned concealment is an act of agency.[28] He undoubtedly had wealth of some kind, being able to maintain a household with a number of servants as well as to provide Adaima at least £80, a considerable sum at that time, over a period of four years. The chance of owning land and growing profitable cash crops had been an incentive for single men to migrate to the colony since the late nineteenth century. Furthermore, it is clear from the nature of the document and its apparent audience that the author had personal connections with the government, a status likely accrued through long-term residence. The archival placement of this letter in the Native Secretariat section implies that it reached a high level of attention.[29] But the threat of scandal remained—the document's intimation that this situation could affect the status of the writer, thus explaining his financial payments and endurance over a period of several years. A secret has been kept—at least from some eyes—until now.[30] The 1901 case of Albert James Storey mentioned in the previous chapter indicates that men in such relationships risked being perceived as "lacking in commonsense or in racial self-respect," even though such cases were "unfortunately frequent in this country."[31]

A sense of urgency nevertheless emerges. The author seeks a form of separation from Adaima as well as custody of their son, James, indicating not only a domestic arrangement but a matter of family. The author requests an official audience—with a district commissioner or the native commissioner—but hopes the handling of the matter will be private. Though his illicit relationship with Adaima may already have been a subject of gossip, given the peripheral presence of the writer's servants, it does not appear to have become a charged rumor, let alone a scandal. The writer ultimately wants "to be free of this woman" and have James "remain with me as I want him properly looked after and *educated*."[32] This desire for custody clearly expresses a sense of responsibility for and identification with James, who "has been brought up by me with the same care as a white child would receive—clothed, fed, and looked after by a specially paid servant."[33] The writer's aspiration for control of his son is therefore informed by broader notions of racial and cultural difference, reinforced by the disparaging view of the possibility of James staying with his mother: "I certainly don't want him to drift to her village and suffer from every form of neglect."[34] In short, the document reveals a complex boundary between public norms of respectability and the entanglements of private situations, between accepted social discourse regarding racial degeneracy and the sentimental bonds of family.

This sense of difference and the perceived threat it presents to James in the writer's view raises additional questions and ambiguities about the relationship between the writer and Adaima. He writes in passing that Adaima was "picked up" and that she was "not acquired by me in the customary way from her parents," indicating a situation of contingency.[35] Although the narrator describes Adaima's violent behavior, it is entirely plausible that she was a victim of violence or rape by him. Female domestic servants could undoubtedly be vulnerable to the desires of white men (figure 2.5).[36] The ambivalence of the narrator is among the most striking characteristics of this document, captured in his initial comment that Adaima "unfortunately became pregnant."[37] His wording and tone imply that the pregnancy was unexpected, unintended, and embarrassing. This perspective is further underscored by his attempt to downplay any sexual intimacy, despite the obvious fact it occurred. "I have had absolutely no connection with his mother from the time she first became pregnant," he writes early on in the letter, "but owing to my strong attachment to this child James, I have tolerated the mother's presence here since his birth."[38] He repeats this point later, insisting that "I have had no connection with her, ever since she first became pregnant about 5 years ago."[39] A sense of regret recurrently surfaces, shot through with formality. Coding his illicit relationship with Adaima through euphemisms like "connection" occludes their sexual intimacy and expresses a latent white anxiety over racial boundaries and their transgression. Yet the domestic scene the author details through description of possessions, "houseboys," and so forth provides a vivid sense of the intimate context of this situation and how such private spaces could destabilize colonial social boundaries on an everyday basis.[40]

The inherent tension expressed through the physically violent behavior of Adaima exemplifies the pervasiveness of this threat. It is important to reemphasize that she has no conventional voice in this document, and this point raises immediate questions of narrative bias. The writer seeks custody of James, so portraying Adaima negatively works to his benefit. Indeed, his pejorative characterization of her falls into a gendered trope of the irrational, hysterical woman.[41] A litany of descriptive comments about her—being "a nuisance," "smashing things," "fighting," "threatening," "tearing things," and "shouting and yelling" to the point where "the whole house bears evidence of her deprevations [sic]"—proves this attempt at defamation.[42] The author repeatedly validates his thumbnail psychological portrait by noting its routine—"every few *days* or *weeks* she gets extremely violent"—as well as the public nature and impact of her alleged character: "Four of my servants have left me because of her behaviour and the old servants I now have [have] left me at their wits['] end to know what to do and implore me to take the action I am now taking."[43] The inclusion of his servants is an attempt to suggest that his view is not an isolated one

The Laundress.

FIGURE 2.5. A female domestic worker—"The Laundress"—in Nyasaland, 1886, taken by Consul A. G. H. Hawes. Used by permission of the National Archives of the United Kingdom (CO 1069/108/67).

informed by racial or cultural difference; instead, a consensus purportedly exists regarding the negative effects of her conduct.

Nonetheless, despite the intrinsic limitations of this document, Adaima's actions indicate agency and even emotion, through bold feelings of anger and frustration that can be understood in different ways. The document reveals an economic dimension to the relationship, with the theft of items reflecting not only a form of resistance—a standard weapon of the weak—but also suggesting material incentives for her to sustain their relationship.[44] Indeed, the writer's description that their relationship and his attachment to James have created a situation where she "has been blackmailing me for the past 4 years during which period I have paid her considerably over £80 in cash" indicates that her actions likely consisted of ways to achieve strategic advantage rather than blank hysteria or irrationality—a tactic perhaps encouraged by her father, who persuaded her to return to the writer after she had left his household.[45] This furtive sense of agency extends to other relationships described in the document. Not only did Adaima have a relationship with the author, but she also had relationships with a soldier of the King's African Rifles as well as with one of the author's servants.[46] These actions threatened the narrator's authority and his sense of control. His fears that "the child that was to be born" could "be left to the mercy of a man who was not its father" and that Adaima's second pregnancy could "even from the native point of view . . . justify her being sent away by me" are both portrayed as events that undermine his power.[47] He faced humiliation on several fronts due to her actions: from her lovers, from his other servants, potentially from other whites and the colonial state, and from Adaima herself. Yet, despite these displays of resistance and agency on her part, his paternal feelings compelled him to follow a course of tolerance in the face of vulnerability, initially to "persuade her to return to my place" and later to tolerate her disruptive behavior, despite his statement that she was "making a nuisance of herself."[48]

Against this backdrop, the document can be read not only as a confession by a white man of his relationship with an African woman for the purpose of gaining custody of a child. It can also be understood as a gendered narrative of one woman's agency and willful action in the face of one man's authority. Indeed, Adaima's power emerges in this narrative through her challenge of the writer's paternal control specifically and his colonial power more generally. An inversion occurs. The writer expresses his intimidation and the awareness of it on Adaima's part when he writes that "*knowing* my attachment to James she says she will not go without taking this child James with her. She *knows* I will not consent to this and she therefore remains in here making a nuisance of herself, smashing things in the house, fighting with my servants, and threatening to go to the Resident."[49] This active sensibility is finally displayed in her threat of making their sexual relationship and James's existence wider public knowledge.[50] Adaima clearly understands the social ramifications of their relationship and is willing to use blackmail in order to empower herself, even if her ultimate motivations are not known. Taken as a whole, the type of awareness and self-consciousness that the writer describes Adaima as having reveals a recognition of her power, demonstrating that she is acting deliberately although her voice does not appear directly in the document.

Agency and resistance like Adaima's are not uncommon in many colonial histories and return us to questions of general interpretation. To what extent is Adaima's story typical? Does placing her against a broader historical backdrop enhance or reduce her individual experience as being one among many? Can we conclude that this is simply one woman's attempt to keep the custody of her child, or does it speak to a general history of women under colonial rule, or both? These questions are related to the degree to which individual experiences should be scaled up to represent comprehensive historical meaning. The document analyzed here contains an abundance of detail about a specific situation. But beyond Adaima's relationship with the writer, her son, and her places of habitation, little biographical information about her appears in this narrative fragment. Indeed, what is still unclear about Adaima's life includes the ways in which her social position and agency may have been further circumscribed by other men (her father, headmen, brothers, or maternal uncles, as was customary among matrilineal societies in the region) or women (her mother, aunts, or sisters). It is uncertain whether Adaima came from a matrilineal society or a patrilineal one. The writer's insistence on the role of her father suggests the latter was the case, though this could be a misinterpretation or euphemism on his part. In addition to these questions are affective considerations regarding her relationship with James and her intimate partners, including the document's author. Did she have a strong affection for James? Was her relationship with the author initially desired by her, or was it entirely arranged? Was it materially motivated, as the author suggests? Was her aggressive behavior a reaction against a violent form of traumatic, physical assault on his part? Furthermore, does the narrator's struggle for the custody of James substantiate the paternal claims of responsibility discussed in the previous chapter, or is this case too individual to reach this broader conclusion? Such questions are difficult to answer. Still, despite such limitations, this document reveals a more immediate sense of what interracial relationships could be like, beyond the discourse of gossip, rumor, and memory discussed earlier. All four modes of evidence are foundations for history. All four indicate the need for combining different sources of empirical knowledge.[51]

: HISTORIES WITHOUT GROUPS :

This chapter has interrogated claims of evidence and experience by juxtaposing black perils in southern Africa and the case of one relationship between an unnamed white man and an African woman named Adaima. Through this approach, it has highlighted the contrasting perspectives that emerge, with the general purpose of critiquing black peril phenomena as a distraction from the nature and precarity of individual histories. These social panics concealed far more common situations of concubinage that could have a profound impact on the personal lives of those involved. But, given the personal details presented in the document about Adaima, I hesitate to call this situation emblematic of the experiences of other African women—it is a history without a group. Isolated documents of this kind, which offer insights into the everyday lives of people we might not otherwise have, pose distinct challenges. It would be easy to pass over this archived story, to consider it exceptional and therefore disregard it. Adaima's story could similarly be dissolved into an aggregated social history of resistance and agency, albeit at the risk of losing a clear sense of her personal history. This chapter has sought to preserve the power of her story by reproducing it in whole. This approach is not simply a restorative gesture, but an attempt at representing an individual articulation of power along gendered and racial lines. This anonymous document depicts two respective attempts to escape from a situation of power and exploitation by Adaima and the author alike. The fact that this turbulent situation lasted for nearly five years suggests the degree to which resolution was sought beyond state scrutiny. This confession discloses a secret, and, as a result, it tells a particular story to a targeted audience.[52] This document reveals the personal, not simply the social and public, dimensions of such situations that reflect individual choice and action based on a specific horizon of possibilities.

This document ultimately depicts more textured senses of agency than might be conveyed through moral panics. Despite limitations of voice, it provides a level of detail and emotional immediacy unavailable through gossip, rumor, or personal memory. Echoing her own resistance to the nameless author, Adaima's story resists a colonial prose of nativism that would have her be yet another African woman whose life experience conforms to the history of a local ethnic community, if written about at all. The act of reproducing it here builds on previous scholarship by Shula Marks and Marcia Wright that has restored marginalized women to historical narratives of the region, demonstrating the value of reproducing primary sources as a means of amplifying the agency and voices of women, as well as the predicaments and challenges of their lives.[53] Without question, this document reflects the intersectional nature of many historical situations — exhibiting different views, struggles, and claims — whether or not this narrative fragment is tilted toward absolute fact or fictional fantasy.[54] It also reveals a tense juncture between individual lives and group politics and identities. The perspectives and actions that emerge bear the imprint of group histories and concerns, and historical agency should never be construed as purely individual. Keeping it personal, however, enables one to retain a sense of the people involved and their active roles in shaping and defining thematic experiences like gender, race, and interracial relationships — or, to quote Joan Scott, to understand "how difference is established, how it operates, how and in what ways it constitutes subjects who see and act in the world."[55] Narrating histories without groups can restore marginal lives to history without prescriptively subsuming them into larger social categories and meanings. Social groups — colonial and otherwise — are not the final, or even the most meaningful, resort. Another option is to reconsider the ways in which individual lives — even those, like Adaima's, that are limited to single documents — can be empirically sufficient in and of themselves.

CHAPTER 3

COMING OF AGE

::

An unanswered question from the preceding chapter is what became of Adaima's son, James. His fate remains unknown. But his case was not isolated, as shown by the native affairs file on "half-caste" children that included his brief presence in the colonial record. Questions of custody and responsibility formed a common theme. "Half-caste" children and youth occupied an uncertain social position between African and European communities, a vulnerability that drew the attention of colonial officials. The Nyasaland administration demonstrated concern for their welfare by debating financial support, schooling, and parental obligation. It pursued absent fathers from the 1910s through the 1930s. But children also took initiative in surprising ways. They at times wrote mission officials and colonial administrators and then, just as contingently, disappeared from the historical record. These written claims indicate the cultivation of a politics of kinship, a nascent genealogical imagination with intentions that were familial and financial in scope. These epistolary moments signaled the possibility of mobilizing genealogical descent as a means of making claims on fathers and colonial states. Children seized on these affective coordinates of birth.[1] However, they also faced conditions of social exclusion, displacement, and powerlessness that balanced their aspirations for connection and status. They fled their home villages only to become vagrants at different colonial outposts. At times they escaped the protectorate entirely, merely to return with few places to go. They could also fall under the control of relatives and guardians, with their interests filtered through the prism of these relationships.[2]

This chapter examines these forms of agency. Cases of vulnerable children reveal a world not often seen. In the same way that addressing interracial relationships breaks a silence generated by colonialism, examining childhood experiences can illuminate how such unsettled beginnings were negotiated and carried into adulthood, influencing later forms of social and political identification. Though the at-risk status of children may suggest parameters that limit agency, it is exactly these conditions that encouraged action. Existing correspondence from and about these children reveals a realm of communication indicating the interpersonal ways in which colonialism was perceived and engaged.[3] This epistolary evidence, similar to Adaima's story, offers glimmers of the past that oral histories do not fully provide. While I was conducting fieldwork on this issue of colonial childhood, an informant made a plain, but pragmatic, comment in passing that I needed to speak to "old people." This cogent observation pointed to the ongoing challenge of retrieving a receding colonial past, but also the difficulty in capturing the perspective of a certain age of life and its view of a particular period of time, not just an elderly adult's memory of that age and time.[4] Oral histories revealed this disjuncture between present age and past life stages in the formation of memory, often resulting in retrospective qualitative assessments by informants—on family matters, friendships made, and the nature of schooling in Blantyre and Southern Rhodesia, for example—rather than age-informed, event-oriented accounts reflective of the period in question. Enhancing this predicament of anachronism was the disconnection between letters found in the National Archives of Malawi and these oral histories, none of which were from people who had written letters or descendants of those who had. As discussed in the preceding chapters, these different sources of history created a false choice between oral and written documentation, both of which have strengths and weaknesses. This chapter explores how voices can be recovered from written material, thus allowing us to elude temporal barriers to childhood. It in turn demonstrates how children and youth attempted to make their own history, if not under conditions of their choosing. They are not people without history, even if they are not typically considered "people" as such: historical agents are tacitly assumed to be adults. Indeed, a different sense of historical subjectivity and action can appear—a coming of age marked by claiming social membership through an emergent genealogical imagination.[5]

: LETTERED LIVES CIRCA WORLD WAR I :

Correspondence that has survived in the archives can be brief, inconsistent, and one-sided, leaving the reader uncertain about the writer's lived experience between letters. But letter writing was a practice that many adopted in innovative, imaginative, and self-constituting ways. Letters provide highly personal perspectives that illuminate social constraints and opportunity. They are an ephemeral form of knowledge that contain voices otherwise often unrecorded and that challenge the placid surfaces of social consensus, to paraphrase E. P. Thompson.[6] Among children in particular, they can challenge notions of "ideal" group behavior that would have children acculturate and conform to social values in routine ways.[7]

This chapter interprets the archival existence of letters by and about children in both empirical and symptomatic ways, to provide insight and meaning that extends beyond the information individual letters contain. Consider this case from the First World War. In a letter dated October 26, 1917, Alfred Swann, a boy of African and British background, made a plea for assistance to a local official at Fort Johnston, on the southern shore of Lake Nyasa. Written in creolized form—primarily in the lakeside language of ChiNyanja, but also containing some English—his letter, excerpted here, reads:

> Dear Father Ambrostra,
>   My father how are you? If you are well, I am also well. When are you coming here, sir, to Kota Kota? If you come I will be happy.
>   The main aim of writing this letter is to ask if you can send us money, now I and Chamazani Swan [sic] go to school and we are in Standard 3 and we know a little how to speak English.
>   My mother is fine and we are coming to Fort Johnston in March 1918, but we are very, very poor. We have no money. We have no clothes. Why are you not writing letters to my father Swan in England to send us money? At our post office of Kota Kota, can you send us money, care of Alfred and Chamazani Swan, sir?[8]

It is unclear whether this letter reached the intended official, presumably at a mission.[9] What is certain is that it had found its way into the office of the acting superintendent of native affairs by March 1918 (see figure 3.1).

This office followed up by contacting Swann's alleged father, Alfred J. Swann of Sussex, England. In a confidential letter written roughly five

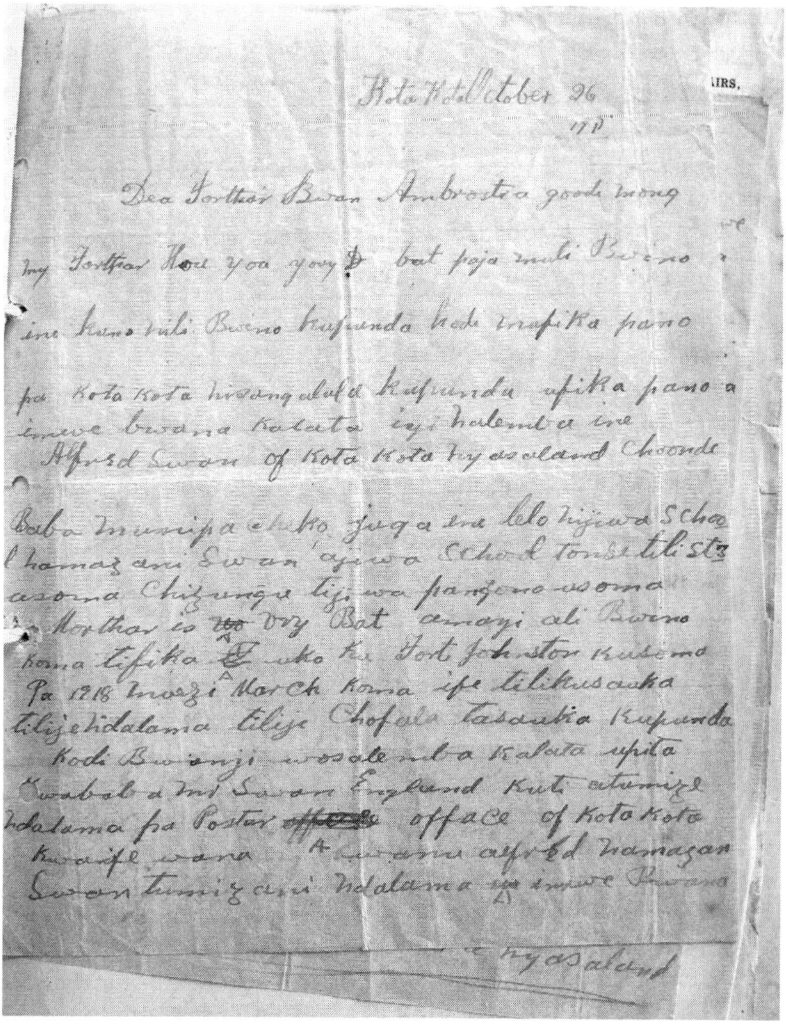
Kota Kota October 26
1917

Dea Forther Bwan Ambrosia good morng
my Forthar How you gowy bat paja muli Bwano
ine kuno vili Bwano kufunda kodi mafika pano
pa Kota Kota kusangalala kufunda ufika pano a
inwe bwana kalata iyi ndalemba ine
Alfred Swan of Kota Kota Nyasaland Chironde
Baba mwanipa chiko juga ine lelo nijiwa Schoo
l hamazani Swan ajiwa School tonse tili st
asoma Chizungu tiji wa panjowo usoma
Morthar is vry Bat amayi ali Bwino
koma tifika uko ku Fort Johnston kusoma
pa 1918 mwezi March koma ife tilikusaaka
tilije ndalama tilije Chofala tasauka kufunda
kodi Bwanji wosalemba kalata upita
kwabab a mr Swan England kuti atumize
ndalama pa Postar offace of Kota Kota
kwaife wana Swan alfred mamazan
Swan tumizani ndalama inwe Bwana
Nyasaland

FIGURE 3.1. Letter from Alfred Swann, October 26, 1917 (NS 1/35/3). Permission to photograph courtesy of the National Archives of Malawi.

months after his purported son's request, Swann was reminded of his obligation to his two "half caste children" in Nkhotakota, an indication that awareness of this situation had developed prior to the arrival of the younger Swann's letter.[10] Indeed, the older Swann had been contacted a year earlier to provide £100 for his children to attend a school in Beira, Portuguese East Africa (present-day Mozambique). This school could "take in half caste children, teach them trades, and bear all expenses until they are fit to go out into the world and make their own living."[11] No reply had been received from the senior Swann, so this request was now repeated. His children — "approximately 14 and 12 years old respectively" — could not remain "uneducated waifs and strays." Concluding his letter, the superintendent pointedly remarked: "Nor can you, surely, conscientiously ignore your responsibility in the matter."[12] The archival record is silent as to what happened in the months that followed. Approximately a year later, however, a new correspondence appeared, involving the Universities' Mission to Central Africa (UMCA) station at Nkhotakota, the native affairs office, and St. Augustine's Mission in Penhalonga, Southern Rhodesia. The UMCA had been in correspondence with the elder Swann, who, with the Nyasaland administration's encouragement, sought to place the two boys at St. Augustine's.[13] The Rhodesian mission expressed some reluctance, stating that "the natives of this country are backward intellectually as compared with the Nyanja races generally and we are afraid that we should have done less than justice to the boys . . . if we had dared to undertake them."[14] With this unpromising assessment, the correspondence ended after two years.

Such fragmentary evidence presents challenges similar to the preceding chapters. Action and documentation alike were intermittent. At its most transparent, the younger Swann's initial letter seeks monetary assistance. But a second set of issues appears through this appeal and the correspondence it generates. Despite being written primarily in ChiNyanja, the letter clearly constitutes an invocation of paternal affiliation to the older Swann — a gesture that had familial, racial, and cultural repercussions. Drawing on his surname, the younger Swann made a written kinship claim, and in this sense his letter constitutes a moment of identification. Yet this act still bears uncertainties. The extent to which the younger Swann knew his father is unclear, and the depth of his identification with his father is difficult to measure, given his financial need. The immediate circumstances of individual and social pressures beyond the written page elude the historian's grasp, even if the letter is provoked by a general condition of impoverishment. A third set of topics materializes regarding the state. Through the actions of the Nyasaland administration, the secondary correspondence generated by Swann's inquiry reveals a sense of colonial responsibility—a moral economy of the state—even if it is tentative and informal in nature. Although ideas of responsibility have frequently characterized colonial paternalism, such accountability has often been observed at the ideological, rather than interpersonal, level. This alternative scale of recognition and interaction is presented here, demonstrating the ways in which these broader ideas shaped individual actions of administrators as well as private interpretations of colonialism, as in the case of the younger Swann.[15]

His case was not isolated. As suggested in the correspondence, such children had been sent to Beira before. In January 1917 the native affairs office had contacted the Roman Catholic Montfort Marist Fathers mission at Nguludi—the oldest Catholic mission in the Blantyre District and one of the oldest missions in the protectorate—expressing the development of an unforeseen social issue. "There are in Nyasaland a certain number of half caste (European-Native) children," an official wrote, "varying from 8 to 14 years of age, whom it is desired should, if possible, be sent to a Mission for education and in fact handed over completely to the Mission."[16] Contacting Nguludi in contrast to the Anglican missions that predominated Nyasaland was perhaps unusual. But Roman Catholic missionaries were perceived as better equipped, with orphanages for "the illegitimate children of planters and Government officials" being a feature of mission stations.[17] Elaborating a set of intentions, the letter added: "The Government would prefer, if possible, that they should go to some Mission some distance outside the Nyasaland Protectorate and where they would be gradually taught to forget Nyasaland and eventually obtain work and settle down outside the Protectorate." Nguludi officials should recommend missionaries "in some other part of Africa who would be willing to accept [these] children from time to time." The Nyasaland administration hoped that such an arrangement could be formalized so that "one fixed sum could be paid to the Mission for each child when it first went and afterwards the Mission would take over complete responsibility."[18]

This correspondence therefore contained elements of an improvised policy toward "half-caste" children. These aspects included a sense of official responsibility for their welfare, but also an overt desire to handle the issue confidentially and preferably through informal means. Indeed, if the social position of these children appears ambiguous in hindsight, the creation of this status rests in part with this ambivalent contingency plan. Nguludi officials recommended a mission in Beira, and by March arrangements had been made to send children there.[19] The native affairs office expressed gratitude for the mission's willingness to undertake "complete control of the half caste children for the sum of £50."[20] At least one and possibly two children between the ages of eight and fourteen were sent to Beira immediately. More children were expected to go "as soon as arrangements for the payments have been made with the fathers who have retired from the country and are now living in England."[21] By September 1917, four children had been dispatched: "Moses age 13 years, Mpete age 10, John age 10, and Harrison age 8."[22] Officials requested confirmation of their arrival since "the children belong to two different parents," and receipts were to be sent to them.[23] Parental complicity therefore existed at some level, at least in the case of the fathers.[24] The correspondence repeated that "these children should loose [sic] all touch with Nyasaland" and, furthermore, that the government "would be very much obliged if you would, as far as possible, keep them out of touch with any Nyasaland natives and when their education is completed endeavor to obtain work for them in South Africa."[25] More children were sent between 1918 and 1920, with officials wanting to send children as young as three and as old as fifteen years, although the mission in Beira ultimately declined to accept children younger than seven.[26]

A significant obstacle was receiving financial support from fathers. In March 1917, for example, the government instructed officials at Fort Johnston to pay "the sum of 5/- a month [£3 a year], starting on the 1st April, 1917, to a woman named Biti Kalanje of Mchisa Village" in order to support "two children of Mr. H. Woodard by this woman."[27] Woodard, who was then living in Essex, England, had been told that Kalanje was "constantly bothering various officials in Zomba for money."[28] The government informed him that it had been investigating "the whole question of half caste children, your case being amongst others," and that his initial support was insufficient, "barely enough to keep them properly clothed, etc. from the period it was paid up till now." Although he had "done a good deal for these children" and it was understood that "the woman has no further claim" on him, "the children certainly have [a claim] until such time as they are able to earn their own living."[29] The children were eventually sent to Beira, with Woodard writing: "I hope at last the matter is settled for good."[30]

The Livingstonia Mission - The Mause at Livingstonia

FIGURE 3.2. The Livingstonia Mission, 1886, taken by Consul A. G. H. Hawes. It should be noted that the mission moved location twice, with this photograph depicting its second site in Bandawe along the western lakeshore. Used by permission of the National Archives of the United Kingdom (CO 1069/108/77).

But responsibility could also be unclear. A separate case involving Mary Percival, the "adopted daughter" of an A. J. Mallet Veale of Zomba, raised questions of guardianship.[31] Veale wanted Percival to be educated at the Livingstonia Mission on the northern lakeshore (figures 3.2 and 3.3).[32] This initial arrangement was breached, however, by the institution's decision to employ Percival as a nanny.[33] Although mission officials refunded her tuition and board, uncertainty emerged over whether Veale had custody. "As I grasp this matter Mary is the illegitimate and unacknowledged daughter of a European father since deceased and a Native mother also since deceased or hopelessly unknown," the Nyasaland assistant attorney general wrote. "I gather that the child is now upwards of 14 years old." Veale apparently received custody through officials at Fort Johnston in July 1915. He was "to maintain and educate the child and subject to the stipulation that she must report once a year to the Boma, Fort Johnston."[34] Despite this agreement, it became clear that Veale had not fulfilled his obligations. Her employment at Livingstonia was interpreted as a result of his neglect.

FIGURE 3.3. Children at the Livingstonia Mission, 1886, taken by Consul A. G. H. Hawes. Used by permission of the National Archives of the United Kingdom (CO 1069/108/29).

His custody rights were subsequently revoked on January 1, 1918.[35] Veale stated in his defense: "I took Mary from her village, where she was being badly treated. . . . She was twice sold by her people to a Portuguese."[36] Officials ultimately determined that she was "the daughter of the late Capt. Percival (killed in Flanders) and a native woman of Mingoche, but who is now somewhere in Portuguese territory."[37]

This evidence taken as a whole indicates a realm of precarious interpersonal relationships prompted by hesitant concern for children who found themselves vulnerably situated between European and African communities. The government attempted a confidential ad hoc policy to address these situations "without having to refer the matter to the Colonial Office."[38] Thus, an ambiguous situation existed, in which the government claimed responsibility while relinquishing it as expeditiously as possible — a British parallel to the paradox of "abandonment and intervention" in the case of métis children in French West Africa.[39] Counterposed to these perspectives is the question of local African views. One can assume that

African families absorbed children into their households for reasons of affection and value. The general scarcity of evidence referring to children seeking help suggests that many such children were assimilated into local communities, at least until they reached adulthood. But questions remain as to why children would go to the effort of writing. The likelihood of absorption does not account for the precarity or opportunism demonstrated in these letters. Indeed, given the informality of many African-European relationships, vulnerability and even abandonment presented possibilities.[40] During a meeting with Governor Hubert Young at Mzimba in 1934, African authorities raised the issue of relationships between African women and settlers, stating that they wished for such "marriages" to stop since "the offspring introduced a foreign element into the tribe. These offspring were ill prepared to follow the customs of the land and other disturbing complications were bound to follow if these unions were not forbidden."[41] It is therefore plausible that multiracial children faced acute insecurity because of the potential risks and instability of interracial relationships. Apprehension and criticism toward them did not solely reside with white settlers. Kinship and corporate belonging could be fragile.[42] Particularly striking is the fact that almost all the documented cases involve boys—a gendered dimension reflecting greater access to mission education and literacy for boys than for girls.[43] Western education undoubtedly changed cultural views and practices, perhaps especially among children.[44] But girls could also be valued more highly than boys for their labor and their crucial role in maintaining matrilineal relations. Further mitigating factors include a 1916 famine due to conditions of regional drought and successive food shortages, particularly in 1917 and 1918, when Alfred Swann first wrote. A number of children reportedly died from hunger.[45] These conditions could have encouraged both child abandonment and letters for state assistance.[46]

It is unclear why colonial officials responded in some cases but not others, developing a pattern of concern that was uneven and, at times, ineffective. Personal knowledge may be one factor.[47] The senior Swann was a noted official of the London Missionary Society who had had a high-profile career as an abolitionist and Christian missionary that he described in his memoir, *Fighting the Slave-Hunters in Central Africa* (1910). After 1894 he served as a colonial administrator in Nyasaland, retiring sometime before 1910 and dying in Britain in 1928.[48] Government officials no doubt knew him. A similar case in 1917 involved a boy named Carlos Wiese, who was left destitute and whose assumed father, Carl Wiese, was also a notable figure. The senior Wiese was German but spent most of his life in Mozambique, writing a memoir entitled *Expedition in East-Central Africa, 1888–1891, A Report* (1889).[49] The memoir makes no mention of children, though Sir Harry Johnston, the first commissioner of Nyasaland, "condemned Wiese's living with a black *muzungu* [white] woman."[50] Wiese married an Afro-Portuguese woman named Donna Romana of a prominent Zambezi River valley family and had two other African wives.[51] World War I and the movement of colonial personnel provide another possible explanation for child abandonment. The war effort had made liaisons between white men and African women probable, with the King's African Rifles and the South African Cape Corps having camps around Blantyre and Limbe, along the southern lakeshore near Fort Johnston, and in the north. Local communities got along particularly well with South African soldiers, who were known locally as *majoni*, since they "also worked for the British; they were slaves like us."[52] The reassignment of soldiers after the war likely separated some fathers from their children. In similar fashion, abandoned children of departed German residents also appeared.[53] Such exposure demanded political action and innovation from both sides—state and individual alike.

: THE GREAT DEPRESSION :

A second set of cases comes into view during the 1930s. Evidence from this time—another period of social and economic pressure—reinforces earlier themes, in addition to introducing new ones.[54] During the late 1920s and 1930s, the exploitation of children and youth for agricultural labor had become an issue. In 1927 the *Nyasaland Times* reported that 23,812 juveniles were employed, roughly 19,000 of whom were boys. The working conditions were frequently poor, and children received only half of what adults were paid. As a result, young workers were difficult to control.[55] This backdrop helps explain the selection of archived letters from the 1930s, many concerning youth older than those who were the subjects of official correspondence during the 1910s. In July 1931, for example, the superintendent of police for the Mlanje District, in southern Nyasaland, contacted the immigration department in Zomba about a "half-caste" youth named Adam Cox. "According to his own account he left this country about 1924 to go to Tanganyika Territory," the superintendent wrote. After his return, Cox was "unable to find his brothers Billie and Frank," although he wished to resettle in Nyasaland. His father had lived in Mlanje and "apparently went bankrupt . . . living for some time in native villages" there during World War I.[56] The younger Cox had no identity papers. He was "destitute as he is unable to find anywhere to live or work in this District."[57] A district commissioner asked whether Cox's father or the Tanganyika government might be contacted for assistance. "Beyond being able to read a little English and write Swahili and Chinyanja he has no attainments which would justify his employment," the commissioner wrote, "even if I was able to find a vacancy for him."[58] Cox's language skills suggest a strong sense of affiliation with his African background. However, he appears to have had little, if any, support from local relatives or community. His inability "to find anywhere to live" underscores this point.[59] A year later, the district commissioner at Fort Johnston reported that "Half-caste Adam Cox" had fallen into vagrancy.[60] After being denied admittance to Tanganyika, he was "now destitute and in rags" and had "been staying at the Native Shelter, Fort Johnston."[61] Furthermore, Cox refused to be vaccinated during "an outbreak of smallpox," since it had been "ruled that a half-caste is not a native, no action can be taken against him, apparently on that account, nor apparently is there any power to remove him [back] to Mlanje District." There was "little doubt that shortly he may be expected to get into trouble."[62] Intriguingly, though his father had been located, he refused "to have anything more to do with his half caste son."[63]

This correspondence reveals once more the distinct sense of vulnerability experienced by children of white fathers and African mothers, some of whom even felt a kinlessness without any recourse for support—a social limbo reminiscent of previous cases, extending further into early adulthood. The young Cox's refusal of "all offers of manual labor" is suggestive of labor conditions at the time. He may have regarded such work as beneath him, indicating a stronger association with his white father. But other children took alternative paths to avoid abject poverty—undoubtedly one of the worst possible outcomes. Education, for example, could prevent one from falling into dire circumstances. In a case similar to that of Alfred Swann, a youth named Anderson Bishop wrote to the government in August 1934 seeking assistance from his father. Handwritten in ChiYao and sent from the UMCA station at Fort Johnston, his letter stated that he had received support up to 1922 but not since. "I was at school from 1924 to 1932," Bishop wrote. "I have failed to proceed with my education because I have no money. . . . And I am asking you to tell me where my father is. Maybe he can send money for school fees."[64] He added: "I am told that you

The Scotch Mission Station Blantyre.
The Church

FIGURE 3.4. The Blantyre Mission, 1886, taken by Consul A. G. H. Hawes. Used by permission of the National Archives of the United Kingdom (CO 1069/108/57).

were friends with my father."[65] At twenty, Bishop was older than Swann when he wrote a request for help.[66] Nevertheless, given the fact that Bishop was still a son, if no longer a child, of a British subject, the administration handled his case in similar fashion. His father was Capt. P. D. Bishop, a member of the King's African Rifles during World War I and later a clerk and storekeeper.[67] Initial efforts to trace him were unsuccessful.[68] But after Bishop sent a second letter almost a year later in July 1935, officials made another attempt in January 1936.[69] By this time, they had a better sense of where his father was. A translation of Bishop's letter was sent to his presumed father in Bermuda, with a copy sent to the son as well, though the older Bishop's address was not included.[70] The son inquired in September if there had been any response, but there had not.[71]

Correspondence from another youth, Christopher H. Findler, expresses a similar request for aid so he could obtain an education. Of particular interest is the connection Findler still had with his African family. Writing from the Blantyre Mission (figure 3.4), Findler reported that his father had been a planter near Liwonde, in southern Nyasaland, where Findler had been born. His father "left the place when I was . . . two years old," and his African uncle subsequently raised him. Findler understood that his father was now at Fort Manning and asked if the government could help in contacting him.[72] Government officials made the usual inquiries and discovered that Findler's mother was "said to be in S. Rhodesia [but] it is not known where." Only one child was known to have been born to the couple.[73] Findler's uncle, the Reverend Clement K. Msamu at the Domasi Mission, later contacted the senior provincial commissioner in Blantyre, adding another layer of interest and perspective:

> I beg to inform Bwana that this boy Christopher H. Findler is my nephew. My sister the mother of this nephew was once residing at Chibwana's village, near Chindusi hill in Liwonde's District. Bwana Findler who was working as a planter in this District at Chindusi place was staying with my sister. During this time a male child was born. I do not know when or what time was that, but one thing I know is that in 1920 the sister brought this child to me that I should train the child. She could not do [it] herself, because the Bwana left her alone. She herself left the country for Southern Rhodesia many years ago. All this I had responsibility of sending the boy to school at Domasi Mission, and I paid myself school fees. In November 1933 I sent him to Blantyre for more education again. I can understand that the boy after he has learned from some friends whom I do not know that Bwana Findler is still alive, and now at Fort Manning, he wants that he should help him in this matter of education, not that the Senior P. Commissioner should fetch the said Bwana in.[74]

Unlike previous letters, this correspondence provides greater insight into the connections that could exist in such situations. In contrast to Cox, for example, Findler had a relationship with his African family and status within a matrilineal situation, given his maternal uncle's involvement. Unclear is Reverend Msamu's immediate role in this situation: whether he encouraged Findler to find his father to aid in paying his school fees, or if he sought to stop his nephew. In their efforts to track down Findler's father, officials at Fort Manning sent word to Blantyre that the elder Findler had "left the district about the middle of 1934."[75] The case was never resolved and was eventually closed in 1936.[76]

Expanding the parameters of this issue, Indo-African children were also a concern, if less frequently than those born of African-European relationships. In January 1922 the *Nyasaland Times* published a letter signed only by "An Indian" that noted "irregular unions between Indians and native women do exist in certain cases in the country," but the "'half caste' children" from such relationships "are, in almost every case, sent to India to be educated and brought up as civilized beings, nor are they likely to return to this country later and become a 'disturbing element.'"[77] Complementing oral evidence such as that discussed in the first chapter, such a view could explain the relative absence of Indo-African children as cases in official records. However, among those cases that do exist in the archive, earlier themes of absent fathers, custody, and support reemerge, suggesting that colonial concern was not sparked only by personal acquaintance or a sense of responsibility for children of British fathers.

The initiative of sons, rather than daughters, also appeared once more. One case during the 1930s regarded an Indo-African youth named Mussa Omar Mahomed in the Mzimba District, in the north. In 1932 the district commissioner there contacted the colonial administration with a report that "a half caste son (aged 12 years) of an Indian trader Khatry Omar Mahomed who was recently trading here with the firm Hussein and Omar has applied to me for maintenance." The firm had dissolved, and "the father of this boy has returned to India without making any arrangements for maintenance." The district commissioner requested that British officials in Kathiawar, India, be contacted, and that arrangements for the boy be made with the Livingstonia Mission since this mission had "a school for such children," as mentioned earlier. The commissioner remarked that "the mother who was a native woman is dead."[78] Based on the suggestion that the Indian community in Blantyre might be approached for support, a local community leader, M. G. Dharap, was contacted in early April.[79] Dharap replied that little help would be forthcoming. "I told Omar Mahomed's partner that it was his duty to give some job to the boy and maintain him," he wrote, "but he said that he had tried him in the store before, and found that he did not behave well."[80]

Given Mussa Omar Mahomed's location in northern Nyasaland, it is perhaps unsurprising that the Indian community in Blantyre and Limbe felt uncompelled to help him. Dharap suggested that his father be contacted in India, though he expressed doubt that this approach would succeed: "I do not think he will agree to give anything to the boy."[81] Officials requested that Dharap contact them if he received a reply from India, meanwhile reaching out to British authorities there.[82] Dharap wrote in August that he had not received a reply, and by October there was doubt that help would come.[83] However, in April 1933 Indian officials sent the Nyasaland administration a memo from the office of the governor general for the States of Western India.[84] Omar Mahomed had been in touch with Dharap in Blantyre and requested that he make arrangements for the boy.[85] Mahomed reported that the police commissioner of Junagadh—a city in Gujarat, in western India—had contacted him in January regarding his "12 year old son by a native woman." However, in his reply, he explained that the boy's African "grandfather and uncle took [him] away from me, as if they wished me to have no connection with him, immediately after the death of his mother, and did not allow the boy to stay with me at all." He also stated: "Sometimes he came to me and took from me some clothing and went back to his uncle's house and refused to stay with me when I asked him to do it. He gave to his uncle whatever clothing he took from me." The father additionally reported that the boy was then eighteen years old, not twelve, and "quite capable of earning his livelihood as a tailor in any store as he knows tailor's work quite well." The father asserted that the boy's desire for assistance was due to "bad advice" and recommended that he be made to "understand that he is not a child."[86]

Mussa Omar Mahomed was therefore not only connected to, but under the influence and possible coercion of his African family, particularly his maternal uncle and grandfather—a situation comparable to that of Christopher Findler. A second letter from Mussa's father to Dharap described how the police had contacted him again and how he responded by stating that he was in touch with Dharap about making financial arrangements, though he also had his own family of nine in India to consider.[87] In a third letter in April, he requested that Dharap help him collect a debt still owed him in Nyasaland.[88] His son could draw on these funds.[89] However, his father also suggested that if the boy was eighteen, he could support himself.[90] Officials attempted to confirm his age and status, and in early November 1933 the district commissioner for Mzimba reported that he had spoken with the boy's maternal aunt, who had said he "is now in the care of Latib (a Portuguese Indian half-caste) driver of Hussein Hassam at Lilongwe."[91] The commissioner described the boy as "now well cared for though to a considerable extent dependent upon the support of the maternal aunt, Maggie Nya Chavula[, a] nurse in the Mzimba Hospital . . . the father makes no provision for the support of the child."[92] By late November 1933 Mussa was "under the care of Mahomed Shah, the Mahomedan priest in charge of the mosque at Lilongwe. He is at present employed in the Mosque studying the Mohamedan [*sic*] language and learning the tenets of Islam. He receives 8/- a month [in] wages and rations."[93] Given this report, his father was not further obligated to support him.[94]

A final illustration involves the intriguing case of an Indo-African girl. Similar to the instance of Mary Percival, custody forms a central component of this story. In 1931 the district commissioner at Fort Johnston reported that an African woman was seeking custody of her child: "A woman [named] Jandika of Mponda, formerly the 'wife' of Allimahomed Abba of Fort Johnston, deceased, has approached me with regard to the return of her daughter, *Jileka*, who she states was taken to India ten years ago by the deceased, and has not returned."[95] Dharap also figured in this case.[96] In February 1931 Dharap contacted officials at Fort Johnston to state that he had attempted to contact Abba's relations in India and that, as far as he knew, "Allimahomed Abba took Jileka to India about 10 years ago, where she is being brought up in his house along with his legitimate children."[97] In a June letter from Bombay, a man named Kassam Ismail wrote that Jileka had been in India for eleven years and that she was to be "married shortly to a respectable man." He added: "I do not want to send her there [to Nyasaland] as she does not wish to go there. Her desire is to stay in India."[98] Ismail, as a subsequent letter revealed, was the father-in-law of Allimahomed Abba and the person "in whose charge Jileka was left by Allimahomed Abba."[99] Dharap additionally wrote: "I am informed that she was about seven years old when she went to India and therefore her present age should be about 18."[100]

This response from India further complicated matters. When Jandika understood that her daughter Jileka did not plan to return to Africa, she alleged that the family of Allimahomed Abba—who only "wished to show her [Jileka] to his mother"—was preventing her from returning. She further requested assistance for the four other children she had had with Abba, and said that "if Jileka will not return her prospective husband should pay a dowry" for her, which the mother "would use for the benefit of the four small children."[101] Officials immediately expressed doubt that these requests could be granted. The provincial commissioner said that it was unlikely the government could "take any action with a view to bringing Jileka back to Nyasaland."[102] The chief secretary agreed, writing that he was "unable to interfere in this matter, as Jileka has become absorbed in her father's family, and Indians living in India cannot be expected to pay a bride price which is not even customary among the matrilocal peoples of

Nyasaland."[103] Subsequent correspondence ensued as to whether to provide for Jandika's other four children "apart from any question of dowry,"
though it became unclear whether the trustees of Abba's remaining estate
would be "legally obliged to give assistance to the illegitimate half caste
children of Abba."[104] Dharap responded that, due to business losses, Abba
had "left no estate at all" and that he was even "unable to send anything
to his wife and legitimate children in India."[105] In this imperfect fashion,
similar to the other situations described, the case ended.

: ANECDOTAL KNOWLEDGE AND THE POLITICS OF BIRTH :

The welfare of multiracial children did not go unnoticed by the local settler
community. The Nyasaland Council of Women in particular brought the
matter to the government's attention in 1933. The council's members felt
that "half-caste girls were suffering economically and morally by being educated as natives," further indicating that girls were being assimilated into
local communities, as epistolary evidence tacitly suggested. The council
asked the government to clarify how it was handling this situation and its
general policy toward "the half-caste problem . . . in order that any efforts
the Council may make towards the employment of half-caste women and
girls may not conflict with it."[106] The official reply stated that the government was unaware that girls especially were suffering, though it understood the council's concerns. The possibility existed of "suitable education for them as hospital nurses and teachers." As for a general policy, the
government believed their status should depend on lifestyle. Noting that
separate status could be a "mixed blessing," given the fact that the majority
of "half-castes" lived in villages, officials said "that no obstacle should be
placed in the way of native half-castes being classed among members of a
higher civilization where their standard and manner of life justified such
classification. In particular, no obstacle should be raised to children, legitimate or illegitimate, of European or Indian fathers and native mothers
being treated in accordance with the status of their fathers where they
have been brought up in a manner suited to that status."[107]

This chapter has sought to move beyond this perspective of such children as a "problem" by recounting the dimensions and actions of individual lives. It has examined childhood and adolescence through limited,
but detailed, epistolary evidence that periodically presents the views of
children directly. These forms of written agency that emerge through let-

ters constitute a unique and valuable source of firsthand experience whose existence circumvents some of the difficulties of historicizing childhood. The nascent writers of these letters drew on kinship networks, expressing their self-interest with relatively little personal risk and much to gain. Even when their initiative is more elusively documented—through correspondence about, rather than by, children—the state response generated by their presence can be read as producing history. Similar to Adaima's story, their actions speak with a particular voice, if at times more faintly than we wish. Multiracial children and youth consequently participated in the making of colonial social orders, at times placing distinct claims on the state and, as a result, actively shaping notions of welfare and responsibility. Indeed, children have constituted a frequent trope in the existing secondary literature, but often representing a generalized condition rather than a specific period of life.[108] This chapter has sought to work against this perspective. The children and youth discussed here did reside on an imperial divide, drawing attention due to their liminal status, which crossed colonial boundaries. Ann Laura Stoler has written that the colonial archive on children is dense with the "charged vocabulary of distress, neglect, dismay, and disorder."[109]

The same view can be found here. However, equal attention must be paid to local African perspectives and to the actions of children and youth. Being interracial in background presented possibilities of both assimilation and vulnerability on local spectrums of belonging. Though interracial relationships should be situated as part of a regional pattern of social entanglement as argued before, such practices did not always guarantee security. Experimentation, even if a normative feature over time, could produce conditions of acute precarity. But dire circumstances of bare life could also provide motivation. These children became agents of opportunism. Their experiences evade group conformities. The surviving correspondence by and about them often remains unresolved, leaving narratives incomplete and thus elusive, but full of tantalizing details. Still, the letters reveal nascent forms of identification through claims of kinship—a surreptitious genealogical imagination founded on familial relations and produced by the pressures of colonialism, a dynamic that would persist into adulthood and the decades ahead.

PART II

NON-NATIVE QUESTIONS
Genealogical States and Colonial Bare Life

::

As outlined in part I, the beginnings of these histories had individual and family meaning that have persisted to the present, in addition to receiving occasional state attention as shown in the archival record. Part II examines how the social histories following these scattered events generated regional and imperial repercussions. It is concerned with colonial discourses of nativism and non-nativism and how they structured political opportunities and constraints. The scale of British territorial control did mark a difference in state formation and behavior in the *longue durée*. If part I explored a provisional genre of histories without groups to think through modes of fragmented evidence, forms of subjugated knowledge, and the contingent preconditions for active community formation, parts II and III consider the civil pathways toward and state challenges to self-conscious group making and colonial peoplehood. Part II marks a specific shift from archival preoccupations to legal and political considerations. Moving from questions of illicit private life under colonial rule to a different set of illegalities in the purview of colonial states, this section consequently departs from introductory matters of interracial relationships and the politics of birth to address their enduring social effects — namely, emergent forms of racial, cultural, and political identification centered on idioms of kinship and genealogy. These forms did not materialize ex nihilo. They were constructed under specific historical conditions determined by states and colonial policy. Historical agency in part I was enmeshed in relations of family, but in this section action is entangled in matters of law and social policy—a transition from bare life to politics.

This transition revolves around what can be called the non-native question—a recurrent political discussion regarding the definition and meaning of being non-native. It is the underdeveloped historical negative to the more frequently addressed native question. Part II argues for the importance of engaging with this issue. Indeed, the relative silence regarding non-nativeness should not be understood as a form of repression but as a result of a basic assumption: black Africans were natives and white Europeans were non-natives, as established and so often repeated in popular and historical imaginations. Furthermore, it is axiomatic that this kind of colonial racialization occurred from above as well as below. But this biopolitical process was directed in particular ways, primarily through idioms of the customary for native communities. In contrast to members of ethnic communities whose authorities and legal codes were incorporated into state structures, multiracial people inhabited an uncertain position as a colonized subject race—a place between native and non-native realms that transcended the customary and denaturalized these distinctions, producing political and social vulnerability. This interstitial situation challenged a world of law and bureaucratic reason that depended on taxonomic clarity. The mere presence of colonial kinship ties that multiracial people fostered undermined categorical definitions, producing an unreasonableness from a statutory angle through complex histories of racial descent that confronted a colonial *raison d'état* dependent on group legibility. But these impossible colonial subjects further unsettled hegemonic ruling boundaries of nativism and non-nativism by seeking the latter's higher status, generating an enduring dilemma for colonial states about classification and permissibility—as well as a constant wariness about multiracial people. Given their small numbers and the legal and political questions they presented, these people found themselves persistently between social worlds and often existentially displaced—at times publicly recognized, on other occasions disregarded.[1]

Therefore, moving from private spaces to state perspectives does not signal a complete departure from intimate matters and carnal knowledge. Attitudes against interracial liaisons left durable legacies that multiracial people had to negotiate. Perceptions of such social illegitimacy mediated through gossip and rumor contributed to perceptions of political and legal illegitimacy. State ambivalence continued, inverting a common stereotype of "mixed-race" people: Anglo-Africans and their regional counterparts were not ambiguous, states were. Unlike French and Portuguese colonies, formalized routes to assimilation did not exist, even in the abstract.[2] Colonial nativism marked a set of limits—racial, political, and cultural. Paralleling African initiatives during the same period, these communities continually challenged colonial prerogatives as a result, albeit through alternative means. Not only were regional governments unsure how to fit multiracial people into legal typologies, but they also remained unclear how to involve these communities in programs of colonial development. Debates occurred, and provisional plans were drawn up. But rather than resolution, part II illustrates the limits of state formation and, more generally, British imperial liberalism, revealing boundaries of inclusion and exclusion when the factor of racial descent surfaced.[3] A moral economy of concern and responsibility reappeared, but in this case it was suffused with notions of racial difference rather than familial sentiment alone. The term *genealogical* in this part's subtitle accordingly refers to the role descent played in categories of rule and the furtive sense of accountability held by officials—a genealogical imagination on the part of the state. It also signals the interconnected politics of Nyasaland, Southern Rhodesia, and Northern Rhodesia and the importance of region for understanding this history. The status and well-being of these interstitial communities were not local issues. They demanded wide attention over time. This emergent politics of recognition delineate a set of regional networks and biopolitical discourses that ultimately attempted to define and control multiracial communities against their own active intentions.[4]

CHAPTER 4

::

THE NATIVE UNDEFINED

::

This is a young country and problems will arise in the near future which
will have to be dealt with, and the more these problems can be foreseen and
provided for the less trouble there will be later on. . . . [G]reat care should be
expended on the expression "native of Africa." This is defined as meaning
a person "born in Africa who is not of European or Asiatic race or origin."
This would mean that those who have European or Asiatic blood in them,
however little, could come under the heading European or Asiatic. Take a
Cape boy, for example, is he a native of Africa or is he, if of partial European
descent a European, or if of partial Malay descent is he an Asiatic? This
thorny question is bound to arise in the near future and it would appear
as if this lack of clear definition opens the door to a lot of argument.
—"Immigration," *Nyasaland Times*, October 6, 1922

In April 1929 an unremarkable man—a local entrepreneur and the defendant in a minor lawsuit—entered the High Court of Nyasaland and made a
remarkable gesture. The son of an Indian immigrant and an African woman,
Suleman Abdul Karim declared himself a non-native and insisted that he
be tried as such. The lawsuit brought against him concerned the ownership
of a Ford truck for which he failed to complete payment. Approximately
ten months earlier, on June 28, 1928, Ernest Carr of Blantyre—an auction-
eer and businessman who frequently ran advertisements in the *Nyasaland
Times* during the 1920s—had sold the Ford to Karim, who signed a written
agreement that it would be paid for in installments: £30 as a down payment,
£20 on July 31, 1928, and five monthly payments of £10 starting August 31,
1928.[1] All told, this business transaction was intended to be resolved expeditiously by 1929. However, the minor historical expectation that this con-

tract had promised was not fulfilled. Karim made two payments, an initial one of £30 on the day of sale and a second of £8 on November 16. He defaulted on the rest. Furthermore, he failed to pay an insurance premium of £10 to the African Guarantee and Indemnity Company, for which Carr was a local agent. Despite these actions, Karim had not returned the Ford. Consequently, after several more months of unfulfilled waiting, a claim against Karim came before the High Court on April 11, 1929.[2]

The verdict in this case not only decided the fate of a Ford truck but also generated a broader official discussion regarding the legal status of multiracial people — specifically, whether they should be designated as native or non-native. This chapter addresses this categorical challenge that persons of multiracial background presented. The decade-long, and ultimately inconclusive, debate that ensued raised fundamental questions about how to define the categories of native and non-native, with concerns focused on whether a cultural criterion would apply or a classification based on racial descent — a distinction that revealed the shifting boundaries of imperial liberalism.[3] As in many cases involving the adjudication of identity, the details of this case appeared minor. Karim's decision to assert his non-native status seemed counterintuitive, rendering him more vulnerable to the prosecution's claim against him. Citing native status could have legally protected him under the guidelines set forth by the Credit Trade with Natives Ordinance of 1926, a law intended to protect African subjects from financial exploitation through unfair lending practices, particularly by whites. Although there is no clear evidence, Karim likely risked punishment as a means of maintaining good relations in a small business community — a gesture to build his reputation — even if it meant a financial penalty in the short term. But his decision had long-term implications. In his ruling, Judge Haythorne Reed noted that the defendant did "not wish to take the defense that he is a native" and that the court "must consider this." Citing the credit trade ordinance, Reed stated that "a native is defined as a native of Africa not being of European or Asiatic race or origin; accordingly . . . all others are non-natives."[4] He summarily ruled that the defendant held non-native status, due to his Indian father. "A person's race or origin does not depend on where he or she is born, just as being born in a manger does not make a person a cow, or a child of European parents being born in India or China is not therefore an Indian or a Chinaman," Reed wrote, to clarify his legal position. "Race depends on the blood in one's veins, and the words used 'race or origin' seem to have been chosen to include half-castes; otherwise I do not know why the word origin was used, or what sense I can give it additional to the word race."[5] Karim was subsequently deemed a "half-caste Indian . . . of Indian origin."[6] Karim accepted the ruling and requested time to pay off his debt.[7]

Although Karim exited the historical stage at this point, Reed's ruling in *Carr v. Karim* had repercussions beyond the Nyasaland court, reaching British colonial administrations across east and southern Africa and eventually the Colonial Office in London. It became an unanticipated catalyst for assessing questions of race, legal status, and statutory uniformity in British colonial Africa—a legal judgment that revealed unresolved issues in the administrative mind. Furthermore, it highlighted how the colonial kinship relations discussed in part I could generate legal and political problems that challenged the core terminology of colonial rule. A genealogical imagination not only took hold among multiracial people as they interpreted their social status and argued for their political rights. A similar one also inhabited colonial legal thought. The debate over descent that encompassed exchanges among officials and political organizations founded in the wake of the Reed ruling illuminate a broader predicament of entitlement and its boundaries in the face of escalating trends of Western cultural assimilation, the growing transparency of state racism, and, ultimately, the potential dissolution of the categories of native and non-native that underpinned colonial rule. These terms had structured political engagement across much of the British Empire. Indeed, the interwar period proved to be a crucial time, when colonial states sought to mitigate the political effects of World War I—particularly emerging forms of anticolonial self-determination that intersected with patterns of "detribalization" resulting in the further entrenchment of indirect rule.[8] *Carr v. Karim* occurred at a moment of political flux, highlighting a shifting ground of racial and cultural interaction that presented legal uncertainties and future political possibilities in equal measure. It evinced complex and unsettled state mentalities toward race and culture that underpinned the placid surface distinctions of native and non-native.[9]

: RACIAL STATES AND ETHNIC STATES :

Colonial states were variations of the modern racial state. European colonialism and racism went hand in hand. But the racial state model has arguably had minimal influence beyond South Africa until recently, despite the ubiquity of white minority regimes during the colonial period.[10] Indeed, conventional approaches to colonial state formation in Africa have often embraced an ethnic perspective, reflecting a model of indirect rule that incorporated traditional authorities and customary law into colonial state structures. This ethnic state model partly signals a concern for the perspectives of local communities, drawing attention to how states were shaped and understood on the ground. But Mahmood Mamdani has gone further to explain the working rationale of this approach by citing the plain disadvantages that outright racial rule had—namely, the creation of black majorities and a consequent political solidarity along racial lines.[11] The strategic uses of ethnic difference therefore explain the persistence of colonial hegemony through division and local collaboration. Indeed, the ethnic state model has informed understandings of an archetypal racial state: apartheid-era South Africa. Apartheid was not simply based on an argument of racial superiority; it was driven by notions of ethnic cultural relativism.[12]

However, an ethnic state model can occlude other practices of rule and forms of political imagination, particularly the more latent roles of race and racism. If there is value in applying the ethnic state model to South Africa, there is equal value in exploring the different ways the concept of the racial state might apply elsewhere on the continent. David Theo Goldberg has argued that the racial state is not defined solely by the identity of its governing personnel. It is the consequence of a state's method of "population definition, determination, and structuration." Such practices are racist when they "operate to exclude or privilege in or on racial terms, and in so far as they circulate in and reproduce a world whose meanings and effects are racist."[13] Colonial states were culpable in both instances. Yet, as *Carr v. Karim* demonstrates, the terms of rule could often be ill defined— based on general principles and shared assumptions rather than the complexity of lived experience. The term *native* was a key organizing principle of colonization, constituting an idea and a representation to be used for purposes of policy as well as a practical term of everyday use. Though its ubiquity suggests common agreement and acceptance, its meanings were inevitably multiplied through diverse local conditions.[14] A key basis for its universality in British Africa was the tacit understanding that it referred to a person who was black. It served as euphemistic shorthand for organizing the vast social heterogeneity that colonial states encountered. It offered a form of demographic legibility—or "definition, determination, and structuration," to repeat Goldberg's criteria—that enabled and ratio-nalized political exclusion through ideas of racial superiority, cultural dif-ference, and territorial origin. All three criteria mattered. Indeed, as the Reed ruling indicated, racial descent, culture, and geography each played vital roles in determining the definition of *native*, reflecting the involve-ment of the legal principles of *jus soli* (the right of soil, or territory) and *jus sanguinis* (the right of blood, or descent) in defining a person's status under colonial rule.[15]

: *JUS SOLI* AND *JUS SANGUINIS* IN THE COLONIES :

The adjudication of racial identity in courtroom settings has become a prevalent subgenre of sociological and legal research on race. The key contribution of this scholarship has been to underscore the contingent and fluid construction of racial identities and, as a result, the fictitious attributes of racial categories. It has highlighted the legal agency that indi-viduals have had in making claims that go against prevailing social ex-pectations or legal norms.[16] The case of *Carr v. Karim* fits into this area of research. However, beyond arguments for racial construction, which is no longer in dispute, questions remain regarding the specific rationales at work. Of interest here is the extent to which *jus soli* and *jus sanguinis*, which had gained widespread use in Europe during the nineteenth century, ap-plied to colonies and the issue of nativism. Ideas of descent and territory of birth both emerged in the High Court of Nyasaland. Reed's biblical alle-gory of the manger clearly intended to convey the naturalness of descent in contrast to relying on place of birth. Given that non-native status typically applied to European settlers who originated elsewhere, his judgment could be interpreted as a pragmatic move within an imperial context. However, Reed's privileging of descent created a distinct opening for claims to non-native status by multiracial people as it did white settler children born out-side of Britain. Seizing this opportunity came immediately.

In July 1929 the Anglo-African Association of Nyasaland was formed "at the suggestion of the Blantyre District Commissioner," who observed that due to the Reed ruling the status of multiracial people had been "entirely changed."[17] Given this legal opening, the association sought to determine what new prospects might have arisen.[18] Nineteen men were present at its inaugural meeting on July 28, less than four months after the Reed ruling. Status quickly emerged as "the most important question above all," with particular criticism directed toward the "painful designation" of "half-caste."[19] The association argued that "millions of similar people" existed elsewhere, "domiciled in various countries," and that positive recognition of them through access to education, higher wages, and other forms of social welfare would aid their community. Initially the government expressed support. Their requests were "reasonable," and the association could prove "useful." Noting that they were "not popular amongst the natives from whom they keep aloof," one official remarked that, although "circumstances have cut them off from Europeans," they were "very loyal to the British Government" and possessed an admirable aim "to raise themselves and prove worthy of the citizenship they have inherited."[20] The question of legal status through their "inherited" citizenship subsequently underpinned the activities and hopes of this organization and the community it represented. Indeed, the association was not unique. Though population numbers of multiracial people were similarly small in other colonies, regional organizations emerged during the interwar period, particularly in Southern Rhodesia — among them the Rhodesia Eurafrican Vigilance Association (established in 1925), the Rhodesia Cape Afrikander Association of Bulawayo (1928), the Cape Afrikander Population of Salisbury (1929), and the Coloured Community Service League of Southern Rhodesia (1931).[21]

Administrative difficulties were soon encountered. Even though the Nyasaland government perceived Anglo-Africans as a "clean, law abiding, respectful community" that deserved legislative consideration as "a separate class," opinion had shifted by April 1930 such that the colonial secretary, who ran day-to-day operations, commented to the attorney general: "I think this is likely to be a very difficult problem."[22] At the center of this predicament was not the decision of how to classify multiracial people, but how to define the categories of native and non-native more generally. Beyond specific mention in local laws and ordinances, no routine protocol existed. This absence reflected the broad character of British colonial law, which was "at once various and unitary" due to the shifting legal interface of English common law and indigenous customary law.[23] Colonial judges such as Reed in particular faced a balancing act of managing the boundaries between these two legal realms. These officials were often left to their own devices.[24] But given the ramifications in this case, the question of definition took on a regional perspective, with officials in British colonies throughout Africa consulted. The Colonial Office in London also played a vital role.[25] This imperial outlook was particularly salient in the wake of the Hilton Young Commission of 1928, which explored the possibility of closer association among Britain's East African colonies but also addressed Nyasaland and the Rhodesias.

The key question concerned descent. It was unclear if a "half-caste" with a British or European father automatically inherited the father's status.[26] British subjecthood—a widely held status that preceded modern British citizenship—remained determined by a *jus soli* rationale, but ideas of British citizenship gradually shifted during the early decades of the twentieth century to stress the principle of *jus sanguinis*. This transition reflected both the increasing mobility of people within and beyond the British Empire, as well as a desire to restrict alien residents of Britain and its territories from gaining national citizenship. The British Nationality and Status of Aliens Act of 1914, which went into effect in 1915, marked one key moment in this change, conferring citizenship on first-generation children with a British father.[27] Reflecting this context, the Nyasaland attorney general did not find fault with the Reed ruling. But he did argue that questions of race and origin should also be understood as separate from political status. "Origin and race are wholly distinct matters from Nationality," he stated. "All persons born in a country which is under British rule are natural-born British Subjects but the acquisition of such Nationality has no bearing on their race or origin. A European, Indian, Half-caste and native are alike British Subjects[,] but their race or origin is not influenced by the fact."[28] This initial opinion pointed to unanswered questions of how these imperial legal understandings corresponded to the locally used ruling categories of non-native and native that largely rested on racial difference.[29] It hinted at the legal and political complications introduced by the factor of race.[30] The descent clause of the 1914 act, which Reed likely drew on in his ruling, unsettled matters. Those who held the status of non-native—typically, though not exclusively, British settlers—gained the benefits of British common law, whereas natives were accountable to local customary law. Many Anglo-Africans were viewed as born out of wedlock, undermining at one level the issue of whether non-native status could be conferred on them.[31]

Still, legislation for defining the boundaries of these categories was deemed necessary—with the approval of the Colonial Office.[32] Governor Shenton Thomas of Nyasaland wrote a confidential letter to Lord Passfield, Secretary of State for the Colonies, in November 1930 to offer the view that "children born in lawful wedlock of the union of Europeans and Indians with native women [should] acquire the nationality of the father." But the status of illegitimate children was unclear, unless "under the ruling of the Judge the illegitimate offspring of such unions are merely non-natives under the Protection of the Crown."[33] In practice, given existing marriage codes that separated customary and English law, illegitimate children were more common, simply because interracial marriages recognized by English law were extremely rare. Thomas further noted that "Anglo-Africans" were "not regarded by the natives as belonging to the native community." But creating an entirely new intermediate status or including them as non-natives seemed impractical. "However much one may sympathise with the plight of these unfortunate people," Thomas argued, "it cannot [be] gainsaid that they are to be found in most, if not all, tropical African Dependencies and, so far as my information goes, they are everywhere regarded as natives."[34]

This perception was not entirely correct. In the Colonial Office's deliberations, several contexts were considered to resolve the issue, some of which emphasized the criterion of non-native descent as the Reed ruling had. But culture emerged as an added criterion as well. The definition of *native* as it pertained to the South African Native Administration Act of 1927—a central act of segregation—did not include persons of "Coloured" background as long as they did not "live as natives."[35] Under the Natives Urban Areas Act of 1923, the expression *Coloured person* was defined as "any person of mixed European and Native descent and shall include any person belonging to the class called Cape Malays."[36] Coloured South Africans were therefore not accountable to this law, nor were they subject to the Natives Taxation and Development Act of 1925, which excluded any persons of European descent unless they were living in a manner deemed to be "native."[37] Overall, Coloured South Africans were not defined as native under the law but were regarded a tertiary social group.[38] In Southern Rhodesia a similar situation existed, with the definition of *native* as it applied to the Native Urban Locations Ordinance of 1906 and the Native Pass Ordinance of 1913 requiring that both parents be African.[39] Concerning land tenure, the Land Apportionment Act of 1929—a key act of segregation later passed in 1930—defined *native* as a person who had "the blood of such tribes or races" and lived "after the manner of natives."[40] Local tax laws also followed both descent and culture.[41] Southern Rhodesia subsequently paralleled South Africa in the use of varying degrees of descent and lifestyle, a situation also found in Bechuanaland (present day Botswana) and Swaziland. Racial demographic differences among these locales meant that the importance of definition was relative to the degree of white settlement and the rigidity of racial boundaries sought. Culture added both another boundary and a potential opening. These preexisting measures consequently offered a template and semblance of regional uniformity to draw on for making policy.[42]

In January 1931 the Colonial Office held a meeting in London to address the issue of definition conclusively.[43] There was general agreement that the logic of the Reed ruling about the significance of descent was correct, though because of the criteria in existing legislation, debate ensued as to the additional role of culture. A Southern Rhodesia law—the Arms and Ammunitions Ordinance No. 2 of 1891—was proposed as an example of a strict descent argument—anyone with native blood was a native. It was criticized on those grounds, however, since it "followed very closely the American definition whereby it is impossible for anyone who has any aboriginal blood—however little it may be—in his veins to be considered a non-native."[44] Equally deliberated was a Northern Rhodesian definition that underscored a distinct cultural component. This approach was interpreted as potentially inadequate since it would not cover groups such as Swahili-speaking communities on the East African coast who were conventionally viewed as "native," though, from a cultural standpoint, were not always classified as "aboriginals of Africa."[45] The demographic and cultural heterogeneity across British Africa therefore confounded any easy generalization. The final recommendation was that status would be decided by local courts through an application process, rather than general legislation for a separate class. This approach was cited as already existing in New Zealand in cases of "half-caste Maori," and in the United States in the case of Native Americans.[46] Final adjudication would primarily be through a lifestyle measure—that is, non-native status would be conferred on the basis of a combination of descent and culture.[47] My use of the term *lifestyle* is intentional. The day-to-day surface characteristics it suggests points to the contingent visual nature of determining native cultural status captured in commonly used legal phrases such as "in the manner of," "after the manner of," and "live as natives." Culture proved to be as fluid and potentially fictive as race. As one official halfheartedly quipped, the situation and the potential opportunities it presented "may be regarded in some quarters as the thin end of the wedge, and even as opening a serious door—that of the railway dining car."[48]

With this outcome in London, the question of definition and its legal process moved to regional administrations, particularly in East Africa, which was preparing for a law conference.[49] As indicated before, understandings of citizenship and subjecthood continued to evolve during the interwar period. The issue of native classification and status converged with increasing autonomy on the part of British dominions to draw up their own citizenship rules following a series of imperial conferences during the 1920s. Though Nyasaland and other British colonies in east and central Africa did not have dominion status—only South Africa did in the context of Africa—their debates occurred within this context of tension between imperial uniformity and legal pluralism.[50] "The status of native half-castes is . . . a question which raises more than local issues," a circulated letter stated, and "it is desirable that the whole question should be considered in relation to East Africa generally before it assumes a more serious and urgent character."[51] The letter underscored that a person's legal status should depend primarily on descent, with a cultural standard playing a secondary role, and that "no obstacle should be placed in the way of native half-castes being classed among members of a higher civilisation where their standard and manner of life justifies such classification."[52]

The main question was whether the Reed ruling, which relied on descent alone, should be legalized universally, an approach that London was clearly leaning against. To this end, the letter outlined three options based on existing laws. The Arms and Ammunition Ordinance No. 2 of 1891 from Southern Rhodesia was one model which, as discussed previously, defined as native any individual who was a descendant of "any aboriginal native of Africa"—essentially, a one-drop rule in approach. The Interpretation Ordinance No. 55 of 1929 from Northern Rhodesia provided a second model, which stressed a cultural component: it excluded from non-native status anyone who was "living among and after the manner of any such tribe or race."[53] A third possibility was defining as native anyone "who is or whose father or mother was an aboriginal native of Africa," thus employing a strong descent rule, but—unlike the Southern Rhodesian ordinance—only for first-generation persons.[54] In practice, however, this measure could result in a similar form of strict hypodescent: a second-generation person would be unable to claim non-native status if his or her father or mother were defined as native. It appeared generationally limited in application, but the results could be the same. Overall, a persistent tension existed between racial descent and culture. Lord Passfield emphasized his desire that the governments of East Africa consider a standard protocol that would make non-native status depend primarily on a cultural standard.[55] However, this position raised the question of whether Western-acculturated Africans could circumvent classification. An emphasis on "mode of life" generated uncertainties due to widespread cultural change involving secular education, conversion to Christianity, new habits of dress and language, and other forms of assimilation to Western practices.[56] If culture became the primary criterion, a Western-educated African could ostensibly qualify for non-native status.

This question rested at the heart of the regional debate that followed. Furthermore, it pushed the racial underpinnings of native and non-native status to the surface. Noting the ensuing complications, the response from Nyasaland was one of frustration. In August 1931 the attorney general suggested that before the issue had been raised, "all half-castes were living as natives and wished to be treated as natives" and that the origins of the debate, in reference to the Anglo-African Association, were the result of "a few better educated half-castes, who are protesting against being classified as natives." In contrast to an earlier position, he argued: "The vast majority of half-castes in Nyasaland live in exactly the same manner as natives and would be completely lost and unhappy if by stroke of a pen, they were debarred from taking their place in the political life of a native village and I very much doubt whether a village Headman would permit a half-caste to remain in his village if he were considered by law to be outside his jurisdiction."[57] The view that "the majority [were] . . . living under native conditions" was reiterated elsewhere.[58] Northern Rhodesia, for example, expressed the desire to avoid "the establishment of a class neither European nor Indian on the one side, nor African on the other, which might separate itself from both, be despised by the one and despise the other."[59] African opinions mattered, particularly during this period against the backdrop of regionwide transitions to indirect rule. Zanzibar officials wrote that, although "Euro-Africans" and "Indo-Africans" were marginal, "Arab-Africans" were numerically significant and considered "non-Africans."[60] To create a separate class was seen as "politically undesirable."[61] Ugandan officials also said that the issue was not pressing and that many people were "content to accept the status of natives . . . since the advantages which, as natives, they enjoy in such matters as the holding of land and the provision of education are likely to outweigh in the minds of the majority any benefits they might derive from their being regarded as non-natives."[62] On the criterion of cultural lifestyle, the officials remarked, in reference to the level of African education, that there already existed "an increasing number of natives whose standard of living is in every way superior to that of a large number of non-natives."[63] Non-native descent was further seen as inadequate: "a bastard, in law, is a 'stranger in blood' to his father," and a "native" should be "any person whose parents were members of any tribe or tribes."[64]

As a result of this variety of opinions, the final report, published in January 1932, from the Office of the Conference of East African Governors included a statement that no consensus existed.[65] The Conference of Law Officers held in 1933 issued a separate statement, titled the "Status of Half Castes."[66] This document proposed that a legal position from Tanganyika (present-day Tanzania) be taken as a general model. It captured the pre-existing approaches of many regional administrations as well as the Colonial Office's emphasis on lifestyle. But, reflecting Tanganyika's status as a League of Nations trustee territory and the league's mandate to protect the rights and interests of native communities, the position of Tanganyika also sought to avoid "any word implying inherent inferiority of social status" by arriving at a definition of native.[67] The statement of the Conference of Law Officers directly specified, if with a transparent qualification, that "racial discrimination in law is objectionable in principle although in certain exceptional cases it can be justified."[68] The position of Tanganyika asserted that "the expression 'African' might be construed to include French citizens in Algeria, Egyptians, South Africans, and others, with inconvenient consequences" and that a definition of native was needed to clarify matters. "No different legal status is intended," it argued, "but only the adoption of a convenient term for use when the provisions of any particular enactment are required to be applied to a certain section of the community, generally described as 'the natives.'"[69]

It was recommended that a multiracial person could apply for non-native status provided these criteria were met: "(a) that he is partly of non-native descent. This is a definite condition not within the power of the individual to change in any way; (b) that he is not occupying land in accordance with native tenure or customary law; and (c) that he is not living among the members of any African tribe or community in accordance with their customary mode of life."[70] Debate still ensued about the expression "customary mode of life," with one perspective suggesting that "a well-to-do

Muganda might live in a brick house, use tables and chairs, drive about in a car, wear European clothes, etc., and this might be called 'the manner of' at least considerable numbers of Baganda; but it could certainly not be called 'in accordance with the customary mode of life' of the Baganda generally."[71] Static conceptions of native culture combined with provisional, ad hoc visual measurements of a person's lifestyle meant that ascertaining native or non-native status remained a persistent problem. Furthermore, notions of cultural lifestyle remained closely tied to racial identity, despite efforts to work against this impression. Non-native status was not officially seen as "superior" to "an inferior native status."[72] Yet the goal of defining categorical difference in principle without creating a transparent sense of legal and racial hierarchy continued to be a predicament.

The final version of the proposed law titled "The Interpretation (Definition of 'Native') Ordinance, 1933" defined *native* as "any person who is a member of or any one of whose parents is or was a member of an indigenous African tribe or community" and used the criteria set forth by Tanganyika to define the term *non-native*.[73] It contained specifics such as the inclusion of members of coastal Swahili-speaking black communities as natives, but not of Arabs, Somalis, Madagascans, Comoro Islanders, or Baluchis "born in Africa."[74] Such details pointed to the demographic diversity of certain locales—particularly along coastal Kenya, Tanganyika, and Zanzibar, where racial and cultural intermixture was especially robust due to the Indian Ocean trade.[75] These definitions also underscored the fact that the term *native* was not defined by race, culture, or geographic origin alone, but by a combination of all three. This cluster of determining factors reflected local issues related to land use and the legal status of resident colonial foreigners, such as Arab colonial subjects. But it also signaled interconnected sensibilities of racial and cultural difference. Culture was clearly a key deciding factor, after racial descent. The criterion "partly of non-native descent" preserved an opening for persons of multiracial background. But equally so, a person "any one of whose parents is or was a member of an indigenous African tribe or community" was still a native until proven otherwise. A formal court application process was required, through which a person could receive a certificate declaring "for all purposes" that he or she was "to be of the race of his non-native parent."[76] The application itself constituted a simple, one-page form of declaration on which the candidate, in addition to meeting the basic qualifications mentioned, needing to submit his or her occupation and parents' names and their "descriptions," to be accompanied by a photograph of the applicant.[77] Visual criteria retained an important role.

These provisional recommendations for the region soon met with a series of local reservations.[78] The Kenyan government feared the legal ambiguities vis-à-vis land rights, expressing concern that "considerable difficulties" could be posed by "the acquisition by persons only partly of non-native descent of land in the Highlands."[79] The issue of safeguarding land for white settlers was of key importance to Kenyan officials.[80] In April 1934 an official in Nairobi argued that "each Colony had its own peculiar difficulties" and that legal measures on the issue "must of necessity differ," with laws "on the general lines of the Tanganyika Bill adapted to each Colony" offering "the best hope of a solution."[81] Northern and Southern Rhodesia also embraced an increasingly passive attitude toward the issue.[82] In December 1935 the Northern Rhodesian administration indicated that it had not reached a decision on the matter.[83] Southern Rhodesia reported that a definition incorporating both race and culture had been discussed and was to be raised in the Rhodesian Parliament. No firm commitment to the 1933 proposal, however, had been made.[84] In Nyasaland, a discussion emerged about whether the ruling of *Carr v. Karim* should simply be followed, rather than enacting a separate bill defining the term *native*.[85] By 1938 Nyasaland officials sought to resolve this impasse by asking if other administrations had taken any action.[86] Kenya had enacted a 1934 definition that approximated the Tanganyika bill but addressed local issues; however, no additional steps had been undertaken by Northern Rhodesia, Zanzibar, Uganda, or Tanganyika itself.[87] With this failure of regional consensus, Nyasaland made no further moves to enact legislation.[88]

: COLONIAL *HOMO SACER* :

On the eve of World War II, British administrations across Africa had embraced and applied the indirect rule system, thus establishing customary rule to reinforce colonial hegemony in the face of growing trends of Western acculturation. Political recognition and incorporation of African leaders and law were intended to be stopgap measures against patterns of change that threatened "detribalization" and colonial control. Yet this system of governance simply put an ethnic exterior on racial rule, as described in this chapter. The question of definition that emerged through *Carr v.*

Karim highlighted tacit assumptions influencing native and non-native categories that underpinned colonial authority. Racial descent powerfully informed the contours and content of this colonial typology. Following the Reed ruling, a colonial version of *jus sanguinis* remained a crucial criterion in defining the enclosure of these categories, despite efforts to include a cultural component. The extent of debate and the resulting lack of consensus demonstrated the tensions over what Virginia Domínguez has called the "properties of blood," which were at the center of these legal classifications.[89] To specify a person's standing on the basis of cultural lifestyle could create a wide path from native to non-native status, threatening to undermine legal distinctions and thereby the very structure of indirect rule. However, to have categorical status depend strictly on racial descent would render transparent the racial assumptions of these categories and the fundamental discrimination of colonial rule—a fact that colonial administrations wished to avoid. Thus, the lack of consensus did not signal administrative ineptness or weakness, but a practical recognition that legal enclosure was best handled at the local level. Achieving universal applicability created more problems than solutions. By leaving definition open, states could accommodate contingencies that defied legal and social norms—as was the case with multiracial people. The ethnic state model with its political orientation privileging the customary can obscure these ruling predicaments and other forms of political imagination crafted by states and local communities. But the racial state is not a decisive alternative either. A more accurate model would combine the two—a native state paradigm that accounts for the complex intersectionality of race, culture, and geographic origin embedded in colonial nativism that defined the ruling politics of difference.[90]

The construction of colonial nativism and non-nativism must consequently be understood as an ongoing process, rather than a *fait accompli*. These expressions were at once universal and locally defined, underscoring a set of boundaries that could apply legally and politically in a variety of immediate contexts as well as signaling a broader set of distinctions that unified the imperial endeavor and could be translated to contexts elsewhere in Africa, Asia, and the Middle East. But colonial legal orders were neither total nor absolute, often remaining incomplete. Multiracial people continued to fall beyond the legal distinctions of native and non-native. They occupied a legal space between customary law and non-native entitlement, yet often remaining beholden to the power of each. This extralegal status—a colonial *homo sacer*—tested the categorical limits of rule.[91] The Reed ruling continued to circulate throughout the region of British Central Africa among multiracial communities as an acclaimed symbolic moment and popular rationale for political and social advantage. The doctrine of *jus sanguinis*—a form of reasoning with blood—held a particular grip, given its potential to grant access to non-native political entitlements, advantages that were racially determined and ultimately more restricted. The legal construction of nativism and non-nativism through this and other rationales set requirements for political membership, establishing limits and incentives that would continue to be embraced and challenged by a diverse colonial multitude.

CHAPTER 5

COMMISSIONS AND CIRCUMVENTION

: :

The legal debates of the interwar period left unanswered questions beyond those related to statutory definition. Basic facts of population size, geographic location, and economic standing drew the attention of colonial governments in British Central Africa before and after the Second World War—a cluster of issues that informed state action and inaction. Racial descent and cultural practice remained central features for determining native and non-native legal status. But such categorical distinctions were arguably less important for states than pressing social matters of employment, poverty, housing, education, and public health that affected day-to-day livelihoods. Indeed, although these two sets of concern were entangled, addressing social welfare served as a political subterfuge to avoid any firm legal decision regarding definition, locally or regionally. From the 1930s through the 1950s, administrations in Southern and Northern Rhodesia addressed these dilemmas through a series of commissions (see figure 5.1), building on an established twentieth-century tradition in southern Africa. South Africa's Native Affairs Commission (1903–5) was the first to make the native problem a central topic of government policy, with the Carnegie Foundation–funded commission (1929–32) and the Wilcocks Commission (1934–38) examining white poverty and the status of Coloured South Africans, respectively.[1] The most significant effort in Southern Rhodesia had been the Land Commission of 1925, created after the transition to self-government in 1923, which resulted in the Land Apportionment Act of 1930—a key measure of territorial segregation that regulated land claims and property rights on a racial basis across the colony.[2] For Northern Rhodesia, the 1935 Russell Commission regarding labor unrest along

House in "Straw" Compound.   (Livingstone)

FIGURE 5.1. Members of the 1950 Kreft Commission inspect Coloured housing in Livingstone, Northern Rhodesia. Used by permission of the National Archives of the United Kingdom (CO 795/170/13).

the Copperbelt reflected the significance of the mining industry to that colony's economic and political future. Commissions had become a prosaic feature of regional state formation by World War II.

This chapter asserts the importance of commissions and the value of reading their reports closely for understanding state interest in and response to the activities and needs of multiracial communities in Southern and Northern Rhodesia. Though a number of lesser commissions and minor inquiries were conducted, three major ones are focused on here: the 1933 Foggin Commission and the 1945 Beadle Commission, both held in Southern Rhodesia, and the 1950 Kreft Commission in Northern Rhodesia. Pressing social issues existed, poverty and education among them. These commissions collected information and formed part of an ethnographic state apparatus as a result.[3] But, as such, they also served instrumental purposes for interpellating identity.[4] This chapter argues that commissions provided states with an auxiliary means of constructing a de facto intermediate status for multiracial people without passing decisive legal measures, thus circumventing pointed statutory complications that could unsettle the native and non-native terms of rule. A technocratic, rather than legal or political, agenda took shape.[5] The emergence of regional policy commissions beginning in 1933, therefore, counterposed the existing legal impasse by demonstrating *prima facie* an active state concern—but at an eventual cost. These commissions naturalized the use of the expression *Coloured* as a routine state category, thus formalizing a tertiary racial classification that could blunt any legal claims that might ensue through racial descent.[6] This form of state racialization, which can be interpreted as part of a broader pattern of bureaucratic modernization north and south of the Limpopo River, would face scrutiny from local communities due to its obfuscation of connections with white settler communities.[7]

The resulting commission reports subsequently illustrate a distinct set of political calculations on the part of regional states. Although their chronological spacing and territorial coverage outline regional patterns of experience that underscore links between communities, they also reveal a genealogy of administrative thought. These reports sketch a politics of recognition that not only contrasted with concurrent legal uncertainties but also demonstrated how states sought to legitimate their authority in the eyes of subject communities, while in the same stroke delegitimating legal and political claims of non-native descent and entitlement—a type of colonial bad faith (see figure 5.2). State ambivalence toward the latter possibility still persisted. Though these commission reports present an intersection of official views, the opinions of civic organizations, and individual testimony by community members, they also indicate how colonial states attempted to structure regional debates, categorically and politically, over the status and welfare of multiracial people—communities that appeared beyond the law, if not beyond colonial power as such.

: BIRTH OF A "PROBLEM" :

"State commissions of inquiry are curious beasts," writes Ann Laura Stoler. "They are both of the state and authorized by notables outside their jurisdiction, forms of inquiry whose 'solutions' were often preordained and agreed upon before they were carried out."[8] Yet people of the time could have a far more sanguine perception of commissions, given surface promises of social opportunity and improvement that such inquiries held. Colonial commissions were about accountability—reporting to local communities as well as to political audiences in the metropole. They reflected a turn

House in "Straw" Compound. (Livingstone)

FIGURE 5.2. A Coloured household inspected by the 1950 Kreft Commission in Livingstone, Northern Rhodesia. Used by permission of the National Archives of the United Kingdom (CO 795/170/13).

toward social reform that emerged during the nineteenth century, identifying problems and proposing solutions that suggested state awareness and concern. Commissions therefore formed a central aspect of colonial legitimation. In 1945 G. Thomas Thornicroft, of the Euro-African Patriotic Society of Salisbury, viewed the conclusion of the recent Beadle Commission to be such an occasion, "a practical indication of a desire on the part of the State to place the [Coloured] community in its right place as part of the Citizenship of the Colony of Southern Rhodesia. This could and will be achieved if the community is granted full economic status and privileges as those applicable to European citizens."[9] Commissions thus contributed to the popular notion that officials listened to local opinions and public grievances and would act on issues raised if properly heard. It was accepted that commissions ventured into social, and at times private, spaces to understand specific subjects. Their reports consequently provide public transcripts of colonial power and its attention, demonstrating the reach of state interest into people's everyday lives. They represent and record attempts at defining social problems, but they also demonstrate the logistical obstacles and political predicaments involved in gaining control over such matters.

Limitations could prove useful. Unlike people, states could live with the difference between policy recommendations and political inaction, if fulfillment of the former generated more unreasonable problems than solutions—a typical outcome for the commissions discussed in this chapter. The 1933 Foggin Commission was the first, issuing a report titled *Report of the Committee appointed by the Government of Southern Rhodesia to Enquire into Questions Concerning the Education of Coloured and Half-Caste Children in the Colony* (1934). Headed by Southern Rhodesia's director of education, Lancelot Middleton Foggin, the primary mandate of this commission was to assess educational opportunities for Coloured Rhodesians, though it also addressed their status and development more generally.[10] Popular pressure had played a role, with local organizations such as the Rhodesia Eurafrican Vigilance Association (founded in 1925) and the related Rhodesia Cape Afrikander Association (1928) promoting a local Cape Coloured identity. In contrast, the Rhodesia Coloured Society (1929) had been established to represent the interests of first-generation Eurafricans. The Rhodesia Teachers' League, a professional trade organization, and the Coloured Community Service League were also started in 1931. All sought to promote their members' interests as non-native in orientation. The Native Registration Amendment Act of 1930 in particular stirred discontent with its employment of a cultural criterion to adjudicate status, which increased the risk that multiracial people would be classified as native.[11]

The commission's investigation lasted approximately nine months, from July 1933 to March 1934, and involved thirteen different locales, both rural and urban—including Salisbury, Bulawayo, Gwelo, and Umtali. Sixty-three witnesses from different racial communities provided testimony, representing employers, religious leaders, heads of organizations, members of the Coloured community, and parents of "half-caste" children. Further experience and policy expertise were collected from the South African government, the South African Institute of Race Relations, attendees of the Joint Coloured-European Conference of June 1933 that was held in Cape Town, and the report of the commission on Coloured education for 1925–26 in the Western Cape, demonstrating that a regional network of knowledge was drawn on. The information that shaped the Foggin Commission report published in 1934 reflected a diversity of knowledge from academics, community leaders, civic organizations, and government officials scattered across Southern Rhodesia and South Africa. South Africa's inclusion in particular accented the state's role in further universalizing the locution *Coloured*. Indeed, the Foggin Commission chronologically paralleled the Wilcocks Commission in South Africa, with shared concerns about the present and future status of multiracial people in the foreground.[12]

In Southern Rhodesia these broad issues were starkly framed by a general question regarding the removal of "half-caste children from purely Native surroundings in order to secure their status as members of a separate community neither European nor Native," an effort supported by local advocacy organizations.[13] A 1930 estimate of 1,138 such children was given, with 379 recognized by their fathers.[14] But, despite this popular pressure and the legal precedent of the Reed ruling, the government remained ambivalent about creating a new community between native and non-native categories. The timing was not inconsequential. In contrast to Nyasaland and Northern Rhodesia, Southern Rhodesia faced more direct challenges of race and segregation. First established as a commercial territory under the oversight of the British South Africa Company, white settlement in Southern Rhodesia started in 1890, with the company ceding control by 1907, and the establishment of limited self-government achieved in 1923 — a decisive assertion of settler rule. Space and land became persistent political difficulties. The 1930 Land Apportionment Act formalized territorial segregation, protecting white farming interests and relegating African land tenure to native reserves.[15] Two impulses coexisted with the implementation of segregation. On the one hand, the African reserve system was perceived as accommodating African interests, even protecting them from white encroachment. On the other hand, plans were made to develop African communities through education and employment. But Southern Rhodesia's system of segregation did not allow for assimilation per se. Similar to the situation in South Africa, a policy of separate development was established in Southern Rhodesia, a turn that informed the proceedings of the Foggin Commission, particularly with the arrival of a new government in 1933 led by Prime Minister Godfrey Huggins, who took a hardline segregationist stance.[16]

Indeed, recalling Stoler's observation, this political position foreclosed certain options at the outset. Regarding the foregrounded issue of education, a range of demands was tackled—access and purpose being the most important. But the implications of racial definition and community formation through educational institutions proved unavoidable, raising questions that remained difficult to answer. Seven primary schools that focused on Coloured education were in operation—a significant number, though "considerable numbers of Coloured children" were "out of reach of any facilities."[17] Educating these children could be accomplished by opening new schools or by providing boarding facilities at existing institutions like the Bulawayo Coloured School and two Roman Catholic sisterhoods, one at Avondale in Salisbury and the other in Embakwe.[18] But this issue raised hesitations regarding who qualified as "Coloured." Some people in the community identified with family origins that extended to South Africa, while others were born from local African-European relationships. Different educational treatment for "various types of Coloured children" was proposed, though ultimately viewed as unnecessary, "whether they are descended from the old Cape or St. Helena stocks, or are the mixed progeny of Eur-African, Indo-African, or Indo-European unions."[19] More telling, the commission allowed for children to attend native schools if supported by parents and local school officials.[20] All told, support for active government intervention in the removal of children to boarding schools appeared slight.

Yet an explicit sense of responsibility balanced this inaction. "It can hardly be denied that the State has definite obligations towards its Coloured citizens," the report stated. A number of measures established a standard future protocol, including provisions for schools when there were at least fifteen Coloured students in one place and bursaries for boarding at existing institutions when there were fewer than fifteen.[21] Compulsory education would be in force for children between the ages of seven and fifteen. Moreover, no difference would be made in the curriculum between Coloured and European children, though additional technical training, including possible teacher training in the Western Cape, should be provided for the former so that "the generation of young Coloured persons now growing up" would find a "proper place in the social and economic structure of the Colony." Without "a useful function in the community . . . they will be indignant, restless and dissatisfied."[22] Community development could achieve a more stable sense of status and security since Coloured Rhodesians were not integrated into the native reserves system or the African economy more generally. Various solutions were considered, including making land available for purchase within reach of towns, which could help control urban drift.[23] But broadly speaking, the report characterized the Coloured population as a "'depressed' one, suffering from a low standard of living and what it is now fashionable to describe as an 'inferiority complex.'"[24] One Coloured Rhodesian testified that this condition was due to "deliberate repression by Europeans," while another felt that it was a result of "the urban environment of Coloured families who in the towns are living in premises which are usually dilapidated and frequently have been left derelict by Europeans." A white Rhodesian argued that there was "a lack of race consciousness on the part of the Coloured people themselves."[25]

The commission ultimately perceived education as a remedy. School activities could enable community development, with Coloured teachers attaining leadership roles.[26] But support for "race consciousness" and uplift raised once more the controversy of state intervention in local households.[27] "Half-castes" were only a generation from an African lifestyle and livelihood. This proximity generated a range of opinion. "We were assured by many witnesses that there was no place for the half-caste in Native life," the commission reported. "As a child he was treated with scorn and loathing by his elders, bullied and unmercifully teased by those of his own age, and even sadly neglected by his own mother."[28] But testimony also surfaced that "in various instances the half-caste was regarded by pure-blooded Natives as in some way superior to themselves, that the half-caste man rose comparatively easily to a position of influence in Native life, and that the half-caste girl was eagerly sought in marriage by Natives of the highest standing in tribal life."[29] Recalling evidence in part I of this book, attitudes toward first-generation people varied. A general anxiety centered on the dilemma that "considerable numbers of half-castes [were] scattered throughout Native reserves in all parts of the Colony who have no other home than a Native kraal, no knowledge of any other than a Native language, and no experience of any other than a Native society."[30] But intervention remained a difficult option. Coloured and Eurafrican witnesses argued that without government help, the community's status "suffered in the eyes of Europeans, of Natives, and of the Government" through the existence of impoverished "half-caste" children.[31] Yet African opinion also took priority. Maternal consent was necessary, as well as consideration of the age of the child, since "it can hardly be conceived that the breaking of natural ties of kinship and dependence could be undertaken in the case of either infants and small children too young to be sent to school, or of those who had passed the school age and were settled in Native life."[32] Fiscal questions proved to be a final factor, because separating Coloured children from their native relatives was likely to increase the number of Coloured Rhodesians eventually seeking jobs. With unemployment high, such an increase could ultimately reduce the economic strength of the community.[33]

Given these possible outcomes, the Foggin Commission concluded to let local circumstances take their course, with the belief "that the complete re-absorption into Native life of the great majority is not unduly difficult, and that it can be fully achieved in the course of two generations."[34] The commission therefore endorsed the idea of segregation as a compromise strategy with infinite flexibility: the existing system could accommodate this interstitial community temporarily, given its small size.[35] "Halfcastes" could be channeled into "the leadership of the more enlightened section of African opinion," and they should have full rights in local communities and be classified as native, except in cases of those acknowledged and supported by their father.[36] This maneuvering underscored the reluctance to rule on a separate legal status for Coloured people. The racial designation *Coloured* had accrued political currency in Southern Rhodesia by the 1930s due to local organizations as well as state expertise circulating between South Africa and Southern Rhodesia. But it came to be regarded by the commission as a social expression, rather than a legal term imbued with any political entitlement.[37] To repeat its pervasive ambivalence about actively constructing an intermediate community, the Foggin Commission finished its report by justifying intervention in the case of "the half-caste child who is abandoned or grossly neglected by his mother and leads a precarious and furtive existence among Natives," while also recommending further legislation against interracial relationships as the best preventive—despite dissenting opinions that such measures would be ineffective, given earlier legislative debates about the issue in 1921 and 1930.[38] As final recommendations, neither proposal guaranteed solutions. But nor would they create new problems in the purview of the colonial government.

: A SENSE OF PERMANENCE :

Given the first-generation nature of many Coloured and Eurafrican Rhodesians during the 1920s and 1930s, the official attitude against legislating a new racial community into existence appeared reasonable at the time of the Foggin Commission. The 1933 commission could, in effect, ignore the emergent set of politics among these nascent communities. Yet by the Second World War, it had become clear that the population was not diminishing in size. In fact, it was becoming increasingly integrated into the colonial economy. This shift toward permanence needed to be addressed. This turn in the short space of a decade occurred against a backdrop of significant change in Southern Rhodesia's political landscape. The war galvanized a new set of anticolonial politics as well as enhanced economic pressures.[39] Broader in scale and more public in scope, the 1945 commission of inquiry must be understood within this context of state adjustment. Tentative questions of recognition that had animated the Foggin Commission had been replaced by open acceptance, and the new commission focused on economic roles and social welfare that could strengthen the Coloured community and the colony more generally. Signaling its ambition, the commission pursued six lines of investigation, including employment opportunities in industry and agriculture; housing; health services; and education, particularly above the primary level.[40] Headed by Thomas Hugh William Beadle, who later served as chief justice for Southern Rhodesia, the commission was the subject of a publicity campaign via government notices, articles in the local press, and recommendations from various officials. Venues for local testimony were provided in Salisbury, Bulawayo, Umtali, and Gwelo. The commission lasted for nearly four months during the first half of 1945, with its members hearing seventy-nine days of testimony from February to May in Salisbury, ten days of testimony in Bulawayo, two in Umtali, and one in Gwelo. Although 199 witnesses participated, 145 of them were European; only 52 Coloured and Eurafrican Rhodesians and 2 Africans testified. Despite their smaller numbers, the commission's report indicated that Coloured and Eurafrican participants "gave evidence with candour and expressed their grievances freely," such that pronounced disagreements within the community emerged.[41]

In these ways, the Beadle Commission, in contrast to its predecessor, acknowledged the permanent presence of a Coloured and Eurafrican population in Southern Rhodesia. Given this recognition, the tone and content of the later commission's report was far more comprehensive (with over 400 pages of text in two volumes) and accepting of the population, even if it was still uncertain about the group's definition and legal status. Census figures justified both this acknowledgment and legal ambivalence. The 1941 census reported that 3,974 Coloured people lived in Southern Rhodesia, an increase of 1,572 from 1931. This growth was attributed to the birth rate in the colony rather than immigration from South Africa, an indication of stability. But these figures raised questions of who was being counted and therefore the terms of definition. Different classifications in existing legislation generated potential inaccuracies in census taking. The Liquor Act (Chapter 219), Section 2, defined a Coloured person as "any person who is neither white nor an asiatic [sic] nor native."[42] The Old Age Pensions Act (Chapter 287), Section 2, presented a cultural criterion, describing a "Coloured person" as being "any person who is neither white nor (a) a member of any of the aboriginal tribes of Africa, nor (b) a person who has the blood of any such tribes or races and lives among or after the manner thereof."[43] The Firearms Restriction Act No. 16 of 1944, Section 2, used a strict language of racial descent, with a Coloured person defined as "any person other than an Asiatic or native, who has the blood of an Asiatic or native."[44] The commission cited this diverse set of legal definitions and the dilemmas it produced, recalling once more the unresolved debates of the 1930s.[45] A definition of *native* occurred in twenty-four Southern Rhodesian laws alone, using varying criteria of race and culture that reflected the seriousness of the law at hand—owning firearms versus consuming alcohol, for example.[46] For the purpose of census taking, the working definition apparently included "all persons of mixed origin including Hottentot, Cape Malay and Cape Coloured."[47] The commission similarly took the broadest definition possible that permitted "the various classes of persons commonly known as Cape Coloured, Cape Malays, Indo-Africans, Goanese, St. Helenas [sic], Eurasians, persons of the first generation of European and Native unions and Euro-Africans generally."[48] Streamlining this diversity for administrative purposes under the rubric of *Coloured* therefore held sway, with the commission in effect ignoring the complex histories, cultures, and politics of the identity groups in the preceding list.

But this decision to standardize this racial category did not resolve legal matters. More significant legislation that established the pass system— such the Native Registration Act (1936), the Native Pass Consolidation Ordinance Amendment Act (1936), and the Native Passes Act (1937)—had foregrounded a lifestyle measure for determining non-native status, thus avoiding the conferring of status by racial descent alone, which particularly upset local organizations with a Eurafrican membership. The 1938 Education Amendment Act adopted a similar approach.[49] Land tenure also continued to be an issue. The Beadle Commission outlined the worrisome prospect of "different officials administering the same Statute at the same time to regard a man differently," citing as an example a well-known case involving a man named Mondam Adams, "the illegitimate son of a European father and a Native mother." When his father died, he bequeathed his farm to Mondam and his sister, Diana Adams. However, the father's will was deemed invalid. When Mondam subsequently attempted to purchase a portion of the farm on which he was living, officials ruled that he could not, since he "lived after the manner of a native and must, therefore, be regarded as a Native."[50] The land was in an area reserved for whites under the 1930 Land Apportionment Act. When Mondam attempted to buy land in an adjacent native area, the Native Land Board determined that he could not since he had failed to apply for a Native Registration Certificate that would give him legal recognition as a native. Adams consequently could not buy land anywhere.[51] Though this case acknowledged the limitations of specificity, general opinion suggested it was not isolated. The Land Apportionment Act and related legislation from 1930 made no provision for "Coloured" people.[52] The chief native commissioner recommended in his testimony to the Beadle Commission that such situations "cannot be satisfactorily or equitably dealt with until legal recognition is given to the existence of a Coloured community, and land specially set aside for their occupation."[53]

Statutory definition therefore proved to be a persistent problem. The commission naturalized the use of *Coloured* as a standard category for census purposes and to determine the target population for its investigation.[54] But creating a third racial group by law would create further predicaments that were identified during the 1930s. Legal ambiguities could be more useful in the purview of the state, a position confirmed through economic considerations. Native status was not the only identity in question; class status also presented dilemmas of work and place in the colonial economy. Indeed, this dimension posed a paradox—a colonial reluctance to promote non-native standing was balanced by an active concern for improving people's quality of life through employment. But this issue also presented a potential subterfuge by creating a perception of upward mobility without providing for legal recognition as such. As a result, the Beadle Commission explored present and future "avenues of employment" through two general proposals.[55] The first advocated reserving for Coloured workers a number of jobs currently held by whites. The second recommended limitations on job competition between black and Coloured workers. Both proposals complemented the 1934 Industrial Conciliation Act that excluded African workers from certain jobs, wage levels, and labor unions. Unemployment levels had risen during the Depression of the 1930s, with censuses in 1931 and 1936 listing 14 percent of Coloured workers as unemployed. The number of skilled and semiskilled jobs in the Rhodesian Railways, a major employer, had dropped 35 percent between 1926 and 1931.[56] Still, the commission was reluctant to recommend state intervention on behalf of a marginal social group. Initiating opportunities and placing limits could result in "the solving of one problem by the creation of others." Furthermore, Coloured Rhodesians must not be placed in "a water-tight compartment."[57] In general, surveys and testimony from all four towns as well as rural areas pointed to the population's poor viability as a separate workforce. Many were employed in skilled jobs with little distinction in qualifications or performance from white workers. As a rule, however, Coloured workers did not enjoy the same opportunities for advancement as white workers did, indicating a palpable, if not entirely formalized, color bar. Some witnesses testified that "the Coloured man was unreliable, not interested in his job and racially unsuited for these forms of employment."[58] White employers favored white workers as "a natural tendency."[59] The commission sought to uncover "the root of this prejudice," finding that "considerable confusion exists in the minds of many European journey-men as to what the chief reason for the prejudice is."[60] Referring to South Africa, some witnesses held that "Coloured people" were "affected by thriftlessness, irresponsibility, laziness and intemperance."[61]

But economic competition from white and black workers appeared to be the main reason. The Beadle Commission recommended a quota system that would require private industry and the colonial administration to hire a set number of Coloured employees each year. This plan would need an element of "goodwill" to work.[62] The Beadle Commission took account of different industries in its survey to explore this possibility, including auto mechanic, engineering, building, and printing industry positions. Unions were also consulted. The secretary of the Southern Rhodesia section of the South African Typographical Union noted that prejudice in the union had declined, though he urged "natural evolution," not a quota system.[63] Creating new semiskilled positions was perceived as another prospect that would not necessarily create competition with white workers.[64] The furniture, clothing, and tailoring industries welcomed more Coloured workers.[65] Still, some white-owned businesses expressed reluctance to hire them, since "European staff would resent working next to or under a Coloured man in the more highly paid clerical and administrative grades."[66] There were similar obstacles to employment in the civil service since it conflicted with the Public Services Inquiry Commission of 1945, which discouraged Coloured employment in the government "for a long time to come."[67]

Geography, views about upbringing, and medical opinion also informed these economic questions. A prevalent perception existed that Coloured people "mostly prefer living in towns to living in the country," though this insight was not entirely substantiated by statistics. As much as 35–40 percent of the Coloured population lived in rural areas.[68] Yet Coloured men were seen as ill-suited for agricultural work since they lacked "a sufficient sense of responsibility" and fraternized "unduly with the Natives and the Natives soon lose their respect for him and, in fact, resent having a Coloured man placed in a position of authority over them."[69] Witnesses testified that African foremen were better in this capacity. Others claimed that Coloured men excelled in supervisory roles, citing their work as foremen on the Rhodesian Railways. The capacity for such responsibility was due to upbringing: "given the proper background, education and general training many Coloured men of reliable type can undoubtedly be employed as supervisors [over natives]."[70] A health official in Salisbury offered a medical explanation for this variation in ability, stating that many Coloured people "are in a state of high nervous tension, and are constantly conscious of their colour and lack of security in the economic set up in this country." But, he continued, "in spite of this almost pathological state, many of them have shown resourcefulness and moral courage sufficient to overcome their difficulties which is a credit to their race."[71]

At the heart of employment matters, though, was material livelihood, raising the issue of salaries and, by extension, status once again. Better pay could translate into improved well-being, if not separate legal status. According to the report, the question of salary is "generally answered by the statement that an adequate wage is a wage which would enable the Coloured man to maintain a reasonable standard of living, so the question turns largely on answering the query 'What is a reasonable standard of living for a Coloured person?'"[72] The Beadle Commission noted three such standards in the colony, reflecting a colonial racial hierarchy more than the quality of work performed. This structural interpretation produced the tautology that people were paid according to their lifestyle, which in turn determined their pay.[73] The commission members consequently examined the homes of "better paid" Coloured Rhodesians first hand. It was clear that "when the Coloured people can afford it they adopt exactly the same standard of living as the European. They wear similar clothes, eat similar foods, like the same type of houses with similar furnishings and enjoy, where they can afford it, similar luxuries."[74] To further substantiate its findings, the Beadle Commission drew on a study of poverty in Salisbury conducted by Professor Edward Batson of the University of Cape Town, who had done research on Coloured poverty in Cape Town.[75] Using a set of criteria initially established in the Cape Town area, Batson applied a poverty datum line—defined as "an estimate of the income needed by any individual household if it is to attain a defined minimum level of health and decency"—to Salisbury, assessing the "level of health and decency" through measurements of food, clothing, fuel and lighting, hygiene, transportation, and housing costs.[76] The Beadle Commission enumerated the problems posed by this method. It specifically did not account for expenses "for amusements, for sport, for medicine, for education, for saving, for hire purchase, for holidays, for odd bus rides, for newspapers, stationery, tobacco, sweets, hobbies, gifts, pocket money, or comforts or luxuries of any kind." It subsequently could not be defined as "a 'human' standard of living."[77] Batson's assessment revealed "only a purely physical standard of health and decency; a standard which will maintain life."[78]

Despite these caveats, it provided the only readily available means for social scientific measurement. Based on calculations that factored in occupational differences, urban versus rural location, and "Coloured mode of living" versus "Native mode of living," the commission determined that, on average, only 11 percent of Coloured wage earners in urban areas reached "Adequacy or above"—that is, the rank above the intermediate "Effective Minimum Level," which accounted for additional living expenses beyond Batson's poverty datum line, with its absolute bare minimum requirements. Thus, 89 percent of urban Coloured wage earners fell below "Adequacy," with another 47 percent being beneath Batson's poverty line. Among rural wage earners, a slightly higher figure of 16 percent attained adequacy and above, with 44 percent estimated to be below the Batson poverty datum line. In total, the commission considered only 13 percent of Coloured wage earners to be above adequacy across rural and urban areas, leaving a decisive majority of 87 percent below.[79] These statistics clearly portrayed a strong tendency toward poverty. A more focused survey of 250 individual households in Salisbury—containing a total of 697 people—found that 63 percent of the households were below adequacy, although only 13 percent dipped below the Batson poverty datum line. Half hovered within the effective minimum level.[80] A decisive consensus therefore emerged that current salaries in the Coloured community were inadequate. The commission favored establishing a minimum wage to be fixed through an amendment to the Industrial Conciliation Act (1934) and determining salaries on the basis of class and skill, not race.[81] However, the proposal that regulating income could elevate Coloured Rhodesians above poverty generated tense discussions once more about job protection and fair competition. Coloured workers could not numerically compete with African workers. Nor did white workers want to compete with Coloured workers for semiskilled and skilled positions.[82]

Still, poverty compelled attention, a concern further reflected in the matter of housing. "It is no exaggeration to say that in most instances where the lot of the Coloured man is miserable or unhappy the chief contributory cause undoubtedly is the inadequacy and unsuitability of his housing," the Beadle Commission's report stated. "In the conditions under which many Coloured persons in Salisbury and Bulawayo now live it is surprising that there is not more crime and immorality among the Coloured community, as it would seem almost impossible for an adult to retain his self respect or to bring up a family decently when living in the hovels and under the conditions in which many Coloured people now live."[83] Housing in Bulawayo was described as "bad in the extreme," although the conditions in Salisbury were even worse, having "to be seen to be believed."[84] At least seventy families required new housing in Salisbury.[85] There was particular concern about children. "The dirt, lack of washing facilities, inadequate sanitary facilities and general overcrowding are injurious to the health, vitality and character of all individuals living in these conditions," the commission reported. "The evils, therefore, of the living conditions in these types of dwellings cannot be too strongly stressed. They are totally unsuitable for a family with children. Nevertheless to-day 41% of the Coloured children living in Salisbury . . . are being reared in these types of dwellings."[86]

Though conditions varied across Bulawayo, Umtali, Gwelo, and Salisbury, a consensus quickly developed regarding the importance of housing in providing needed "community spirit."[87] Indeed, this issue intersected with ongoing debates about African housing in urban areas, a topic about which the black middle class had been vocal since at least 1915. Two municipal commissions in Salisbury and Bulawayo in 1930 attempted to take stock of the black townships that had grown in these urban areas.[88] As noted earlier, the election of Huggins as prime minister in 1933 led to a more hard-line stance toward urban segregation, with control over housing centralized in the colonial government rather than left in the hands of municipal authorities. The Beadle Commission consequently worked against this backdrop of municipal mismanagement and the renewal of racial anxieties during the Depression.[89] A proposal for a Coloured residential area was first presented in 1932.[90] Although the Rhodesia Teachers' League and the Coloured Community Service League criticized the idea of residential segregation, praise did exist for Coloured housing projects such as Arcadia in Salisbury, and some people advocated that such endeavors be replicated.[91] Vital to such projects would be affordable rent, which generated questions about the quality and location of housing.[92] Some people felt that houses should be available for purchase, since home ownership would generate more care and pride. The feasibility of this plan was not entirely clear, given that up to 65 percent of those needing housing could not afford rent.[93] Still, the commission recommended that suitable housing—defined as detached homes with enough rooms to accommodate families when appropriate—along with community amenities such as sports fields, schools, and community centers be provided and made available at "sub-economic" rates.[94] Other Coloured witnesses testified against such segregated communities, arguing for their right to live anywhere.[95]

As with housing, poverty also raised concerns about public health. Some Coloured witnesses protested against being "accommodated cheek by jowl with the Native patients in the same building," thus displaying an open racism toward black Africans and a claim to non-native entitlement.[96] But primary among health concerns were diet and nutrition. One witness testified that she knew a household that "did not have a sufficient income to maintain an adequate standard of living but who nevertheless spent money they could very ill afford on expensive tinned foods of very low food value. In this respect they differ little from many of the poorer paid European families."[97] This lifestyle choice, reinforced by observations from Batson's study, showed not only the social proximity of Coloured people to poor whites but also the quotidian ways in which aspirations for non-native status could be expressed. Such ambitions clearly faced limitations. Malnutrition among children appeared as the most urgent health care issue, with approximately 15 percent of Coloured children reported to be suffering from malnourishment, compared to 10 percent of white schoolchildren.[98] Plans to provide one hot meal per day in addition to milk, bread, and other food at schools were proposed.[99] The number of Coloured schoolchildren had doubled since the Foggin Commission's report, though conditions had also changed.[100] The 1934 report estimated that there were 903 first-generation children, whereas the 1945 commission received an estimate of 152, marking a decline in interracial relationships.[101] But disagreement reemerged over the laissez-faire policy of the Foggin Commission. "The 'hybrid' child is a misfit in either the European or Native social system," the chief native commissioner testified at the Beadle Commission's hearings, "and I consider that he or she should be brought up as a 'Coloured child' and that generally every effort should be made to give him or her the higher standard of education and living which the Coloured community enjoy."[102] Given the growth and stability of the population, a shift away from passivity appeared more feasible, raising once more matters of accommodation, the collection of children from villages, and "opposition from the Native mothers."[103] The 1945 commission contended that no evidence existed of first-generation children becoming leaders in African communities, a goal expressed in the 1934 report, and that instead their affiliation was chiefly with white communities.[104]

Indeed, the most urgent issue with which the Beadle Commission concluded continued to be the question of "community spirit." In the view of the commission, it was clear that a stable Coloured population existed. But it was unclear if a community as such did. "It seems a characteristic of the Coloured people in this Colony that they lack a community spirit, quarrel readily among themselves, and divide up into groups, organisations and factions which are often definitely antagonistic to each other," the final report noted. "It is thus difficult to find any body or organisation which can speak with authority for the Coloured people of any area, and thus when it is desired to consult the community about matters concerning their own welfare a sad lack of unanimity is found among them."[105] Although debates existed about whether this malaise was a "racial characteristic," the commission recommended environmental improvements through better housing and community centers in the belief that they could enhance community well-being.[106] Moreover, more employment opportunities, adequate housing, and better education could provide avenues for integrating the population into the broader activities of the colony. But racial prejudice remained at the root of many problems. The commission acknowledged a "change of heart" among many white Rhodesians—a shift toward greater acceptance of the presence of Coloured Rhodesians.[107] Yet Coloured Rhodesians needed to work to integrate themselves so that "their place will not only be deservedly won but permanently maintained."[108] With this sentiment, the commission acknowledged Southern Rhodesia's Coloured community as a fixture in the colony but placed its social, economic, and political status in the hands of its members instead of recommending the passage of a uniform legal solution.

: REGIONAL RECOGNITION :

The 1945 Beadle Commission's report surpassed the reports of other regional commissions, before and after, due to its length and coverage. It underscored a transformation of administrative thought, transitioning from an emphasis on children and education during the 1930s to adult employment, housing, health, and general livelihood by the 1940s — a trajectory that mirrored an aging population, as well as a more committed concern for it, given its permanence. This evolution occurred elsewhere. Northern Rhodesia had a series of official inquiries during the same period, including an initial 1941 commission that collected basic information such as census data. The report of that commission was ultimately provisional, due to disagreements over the conduct of the investigation — committee members did not perform firsthand inspections, nor did they gather oral testimony. One commission member, T. S. Page, submitted a separate report outlining in detail issues of education, social status, and economic opportunity. It advocated greater state attention rather than the passivity of the formal report that the government ultimately favored.[109] Page revived the subject after the Second World War, helping form a new commission in 1947 that included Roy Welensky — at the time a representative for Broken Hill on Northern Rhodesia's legislative council and later the second and last prime minister (1956–63), following Godfrey Huggins (1953–56), of the Central African Federation. This committee examined a similar assemblage of topics, most significantly the matter of the franchise, which it initially deferred given the imminence of political change in the region.[110] The Kreft Commission of 1950 consequently set out to resolve these issues and map out a policy prior to the establishment of the Federation.[111]

The Kreft Commission addressed what had become at this point well-established themes for assessing the livelihoods of Coloured people. The 1950 commission's report was shorter than that of the Beadle Commission. Moreover, it was not released publicly. The Kreft Commission began

House in "Straw" Compound, Livingstone.   Occupier uses front verandah as cycle repair shop.

FIGURE 5.3. Coloured housing inspected by the 1950 Kreft Commission, Livingstone, Northern Rhodesia. Used by permission of the National Archives of the United Kingdom (CO 795/170/13).

in April 1950, and over a period of approximately six weeks its members visited all the provinces in the colony except for the Northern Province, where the population was deemed too small to merit a visit. Commission members inspected over fifty houses and four Coloured-owned farms and heard oral testimony from 172 people (see figure 5.3). The commission's report described Northern Rhodesian policy from the first decades of the twentieth century to 1940 as consisting of inaction—in particular, adhering to an African view that "half-caste" children should reside with their mothers, thus echoing the sentiments of the Foggin Commission. A gradual shift took place in 1927, when a missionary conference advocated separate education, which met with state reluctance parallel to that of other regional administrations at the time. Northern Rhodesia did not want to create an "artificial class."[112] However, building on the reports of its predecessors, the Kreft Commission endorsed the recommendations of the 1947 commission—especially that a distinct "Coloured class" should be recognized and that policies acknowledge this fact for future planning purposes.[113] The Kreft Commission therefore positioned its concerns between those of the neighboring territories. The situation in Northern Rhodesia resembled that found in Nyasaland—demographically and politically—more than that of Southern Rhodesia. While the latter colony embraced segregation, Northern Rhodesia tilted toward African concerns through its system of indirect rule, established in 1929 by Gov. James Maxwell. Similar to that of Nyasaland, this policy shaped the political hierarchy, privileging African interests—which affected attitudes toward the colony's Eurafrican community. Yet, despite its greater geographic size, Northern Rhodesia's predicament was parallel in scope to the one in Nyasaland. The total Coloured population of Northern Rhodesia was reported to be 1,240 people in 1950—approximating Nyasaland's population during the 1950s (see table I.1)—and it was distributed primarily across the urban areas of Fort Jameson (252), Lusaka (163), Ndola (161), and Livingstone (124).[114]

But small numbers permitted informal flexibility. Among the key issues debated in Northern Rhodesia, as elsewhere, was legal status. Following the 1948 British Nationality Act, which classified Eurafricans as British Protected Persons, the Kreft Commission recommended that British non-native subject status not be granted automatically by birth—many first-generation Eurafricans had claimed that status through their fathers—but instead require an application for naturalization.[115] The franchise could be achieved in the same manner.[116] This observance of genealogy stirred up existing differences within the population. Similar to the situation in Southern Rhodesia, the commission noted that there was disagreement about identity and the use of the terms *Eurafrican* and *Euro-African* versus *Coloured*. The former terms emphasized paternal affiliations, while the latter was more generalized racially, including Coloured South Africans who had migrated to the colony. As the Beadle Commission had done, the Kreft Commission advocated the universal use of *Coloured*, defining it as "a person not of pure European, pure African, pure Indian or other pure racial descent," yet its definition also excluded "a person who, although not of pure descent, is nevertheless generally accepted as a European, African, Indian or member of some other pure racial group."[117] This softer definition did not generate the same level of debate found farther south, reflecting a greater acceptance of paternity and kin relations. "It was noticeable that all were aware of the identities of their fathers," noted the commission's report. "They not only carried their surnames but also knew their Christian names in full and could state accurately their occupations in the Territory. With one exception they knew or professed to know their present

House occupied by Coloured in Maramba African Compound.
(Livingstone)

FIGURE 5.4. Coloured housing inspected by the 1950 Kreft Commission in Livingstone, Northern Rhodesia. Used by permission of the National Archives of the United Kingdom (CO 795/170/13).

whereabouts."[118] This type of intimate knowledge in principle suggested a familiarity with and potential access to welfare that needed no state intervention.

But this image proved false. Housing highlighted a predicament similar to that in Southern Rhodesia, with many reportedly living in "hovels" (see figures 5.4 to 5.8).[119] The commission was "almost unanimous" in believing that land should be set aside for housing projects and that houses should be available through an affordable mortgage scheme. The commission recognized that the cost of providing housing would be a crucial factor, and that the cost should be shared by the central government and municipal authorities.[120] Connected to housing was the matter of job opportunities and livelihood, also parallel to the situation in Southern Rhodesia. Though some witnesses noted that Eurafricans were "unable to settle down to regular employment," a consensus existed that "a special niche" should be created for these workers to benefit the economy and enable them to become "useful citizens."[121] They could be employed, for example, as teachers, nurses, clerks, farm managers, and mechanics.[122] Coloured workers were

Coloured Person's House (Ndola)

FIGURE 5.5. Coloured home inspected by the 1950 Kreft Commission in Ndola, Northern Rhodesia. Used by permission of the National Archives of the United Kingdom (CO 795/170/13).

Coloured Person's House (Ndola)

FIGURE 5.6. Coloured home inspected by the 1950 Kreft Commission in Ndola, Northern Rhodesia. Used by permission of the National Archives of the United Kingdom (CO 795/170/13).

Coloured Person's House   (Ndola)

FIGURE 5.7. Coloured home inspected by the 1950 Kreft Commission in Ndola, Northern Rhodesia. Used by permission of the National Archives of the United Kingdom (CO 795/170/13).

especially seen as important for establishing secondary industries and as having a certain "mechanical sympathy" that allowed them to handle and operate complex machinery.[123] Wages raised concerns, and the commission echoed the Beadle Commission in proposing that Coloured workers receive three-fifths the pay of white workers when they met comparable qualifications.[124] Coloured teachers, however, would receive four-fifths the pay of whites due to demand.[125] But the subject of employment appeared to involve less pressure and acrimony than in Southern Rhodesia—a reflection of the smaller community in Northern Rhodesia as well as the lower density of white settlement, which mitigated racial tensions.

The issue of employment led to that of education, and the Kreft Commission supported the Beadle Commission's active attention instead of the Foggin Commission's passivity.[126] This position marked a shift in policy. Previously, only children who lived "after the manner of Europeans" had been admitted to the Katapola School (see figures 5.9 and 5.10), the only Coloured school in the colony, since first-generation children in villages grew up "with their African playmates, speak their language and are more

Manda Flats   (Ndola)

FIGURE 5.8. Another Coloured home inspected by the 1950 Kreft Commission in Ndola, Northern Rhodesia. Used by permission of the National Archives of the United Kingdom (CO 795/170/13).

likely to feel happy in these surroundings than elsewhere."[127] In contrast, the Kreft Commission held that "the lot of a Coloured child in an African village was not a happy one" and that the "mother may be proud of bearing the child of a European father, but her action is frowned upon by her fellow-villagers."[128] "Although she is usually forgiven after a while and is accepted into matrimony, the dowry is lower than in normal cases and the stigma on the Coloured child persists," the commission noted.[129] Other Coloured families "found neglected Coloured children and took them into their homes. No pressure was brought to bear on them to restore them to their former surroundings."[130] This anecdotal knowledge echoes discussions in Southern Rhodesia, as well as evidence from Nyasaland discussed earlier. Even alleged physical ailments of multiracial people were reported, examples of a pseudoscientific eugenics discourse of the time. "Being more delicate, they do not stand the climate as well as Africans," one witness testified. "They are often weak-sighted and covered with sores."[131] Still, cultural connections could continue, with the commission's report adding that a number did not speak English since it was not their mother tongue. "Of the forty-four children at the Katapola School who did not speak Eng-

House of Principal, Katapola School.   (Fort Jameson)

FIGURE 5.9. Members of the 1950 Kreft Commission investigating the Katapola School, Fort Jameson, Northern Rhodesia. Used by permission of the National Archives of the United Kingdom (CO 795/170/13).

lish when enrolled, eighteen spoke Ngoni, twelve Nsenga, six Nyanja, six Chewe [*sic*] and two Bemba," the commission described.[132] Many maintained relations with their African families, "wrote regularly to their African mothers," and often sent them money.[133] Thus, while support existed to educate Eurafrican children, these children still resided—even in adulthood—on a social divide in the colonial order.[134]

To summarize, as with the reports of previous commissions in the region, the Kreft Commission's report was preoccupied with social welfare in its various dimensions. The question of definition and status, although present, generated less debate than in the reports of earlier commissions, no doubt reflecting local conditions that contrasted with the distinctive segregation measures in Southern Rhodesia. But this reduced presence also enabled a more pragmatic approach to such issues. Addressing social conditions counted more than pinpointing identity. "Good houses, wholesome food and clean water are the essentials of good health and social stability. As the Coloured people are living to-day, these conditions do not exist," was one concluding remark in the report.[135] Such circumstances had created many people who were "despondent and demoralised" due to "years of struggling against poverty, neglect and grossly inadequate living

Katapola School - Dormitory and Ablution Blocks. (Fort Jameson)

FIGURE 5.10. Another view of the Katapola School inspected by the 1950 Kreft Commission, Fort Jameson, Northern Rhodesia. Used by permission of the National Archives of the United Kingdom (CO 795/170/13).

conditions."[136] Immediate evidence for such sentiments included "the lack of care and attention to their children and their so-called homes," in addition to the "uneconomical and inadequate feeding consequent on purchasing preserved foods, e.g., tinned milk, on credit and frequently at higher prices merely because cash has not been available to buy fresh food."[137] These comments indicate an aspiration for status through mode of life similar to that found in Southern Rhodesia — with the same limits as well. Those families that had care and guidance, as well as good incomes, had better morale.[138] Though the commission did seek to standardize the term *Coloured*, matters of daily life, rather than categorical determination, became the commission's ultimate source of concern.

: COLONIAL GOVERNMENTALITY AND ITS LITERATURE :

Quoting Lord Hailey's *Britain and Her Dependencies* (1943), the report of Southern Rhodesia's Beadle Commission remarked that "the capacity of any community to reach higher standards of living must in the long run depend on the extent of its natural resources and its ability to make the most beneficial use of them."[139] This statement was applied to Southern Rhodesia's Coloured population, but it also characterized the perception of commissions across the region. Commissions presented prima facie a means of addressing social welfare and thus constituting a means of colonial state legitimation. Yet they also comprised a form of anti-politics.[140] They circumvented more meaningful political action through a type of colonial bad faith—creating an appearance of concern, but with few statutory measures that assured progress. Achieving the benefits of non-native status remained elusive for multiracial people. Granting it by law never became an option. Colonial states examined a variety of issues regarding livelihood and community formation. Sharing themes and at times expertise, the three commissions discussed in this chapter demonstrate an evolution of administrative thought that ranged from tentative concern over "half-caste" children to active discussions about housing, employment, and integration into colonial economies. This shift reflected a politics of recognition that stressed ongoing concern for living conditions and their class manifestations while refraining from legal action. In this sense, regional states engaged existing definitions of *native* without any legislative fiat—a strategy that avoided broader complications as discussed previously, but an approach that nevertheless thwarted the aspirations of the communities under examination.

These commissions had an additional effect. They participated in colonial race making by acknowledging these communities and standardizing a certain racial terminology—namely, the use of the term *Coloured* as a practice of state routine. Not only did this impart a false sense of uniformity, but this act of interpellation tacitly diminished the legal claims that multiracial people might have by virtue of racial descent through the enclosure of a distinct racial category, thus mitigating the repercussions of the Reed ruling and evolving British citizenship laws that employed descent as a criterion. The naturalization of this third racial classification therefore marked a taxonomic means for eluding potential legal problems. *Coloured* marked a distinction apart from native, but it did not guarantee non-native privileges as such by law. These commissions did venture beyond race, inspecting the links between race and poverty and demonstrating that such connections were not the sole result of state-imposed hierarchies, but were informed and made by fluctuating social relations of race and class among employers and workers. Class identity not only mattered as much as racial identity, it also informed racial identity. Indeed, officials largely maintained a laissez-faire approach in this economic context by letting market and social forces, rather than state intervention, determine outcomes—yet another technique of avoiding legal decisions.

State ambivalence, building on that discussed in chapters 3 and 4, therefore held sway. But it did not produce political ambivalence among local communities of multiracial people. The gradual standardization of *Coloured* as a normative expression generated new forms of political action. Although people who traced their roots to South Africa embraced this term, its use was not universally accepted. In fact, it often was seen as contrary to the intentions of local communities due to its obfuscation of kinship and genealogy. These commission reports consequently offer further insight into the dimensions of colonial racial state formation and colonial governmentality more generally.[141] If the creation of the customary underscored an ethnic state paradigm, these commissions illuminate how states engaged in racialization. Categories of rule did not simply appear, nor were such identities determined exclusively by local conditions. States sought to control their use and meaning. As the two chapters of this second part of the book demonstrate, colonial states in British Central Africa participated in a wider regional process of bureaucratic modernization that sought taxonomic uniformity. They recognized, attended to, and ultimately sought to limit the claims and responsibilities generated by a politics of racial descent—non-native questions that became intractable. This state strategy would not remain unchallenged.

PART III

:::

COLONIAL KINSHIPS
Regional Histories, Uncustomary Politics, and the Genealogical Imagination

::

Part II marked a turn in the idea of colonial kinships, from a contingent social phenomenon to a legal and political issue that challenged regional states. Part III addresses the way this phenomenon became a schema—a means of interpreting the world. Anglo-African, Euro-African, and Eurafrican people did not see themselves as occupying a fixed place in a colonial racial hierarchy. They constructed a more complex vision—a genealogical imagination—of ancestry, political entitlement, and colonial obligation that joined their interests to those of regional states and the British Empire. Their hyphenated names captured this abridged sensibility, indicating not simply a reconfiguration of Britishness on an imperial periphery, but the invention of a regional Afro-Britishness. As a result, the three chapters in this section of the book focus on descent, culture, and territory, respectively— the three factors involved in determining status as discussed in part II. These interactive criteria formed key sites of struggle for shaping identity. Each of these chapters subsequently presents a variation on situational analysis, an approach that, similar to genealogical histories, allows for the integration of "variations, exceptions and accidents into descriptions of [structural] regularities."[1] As Jaap van Velsen once argued, this method is "particularly suitable for the study of unstable and non-homogeneous societies and communities."[2] The exceptional, yet unstable, imperial identity formations described here that bound African and European aspects together must be comprehended as innovative and strategic, rather than accepting and reinforcing a colonial taxonomy that reduced their social identity and civic status to disparaging terms such as *half-caste* or amorphous racial categories like *Coloured* that implied homogeneity and concealed histories of connection. Indeed, many local activist intellectuals of the time condemned the use of these vague expressions that obscured familial ties. Specificity mattered. Self-fashioned intermediate identities that have fallen into disuse, like Anglo-African, consequently illuminate perspectives and meaning specific to time and place. Reflecting an emergent colonial habitus, these local designations are good to think with. They tell us how history was experienced and understood.[3]

These practices and the schemas they articulate in turn created what I call a politics of the uncustomary—a realm of political engagement that went beyond African authorities and law to challenge once more the structure of colonial state reason centered on native and non-native distinctions.[4] These self-constructed appellations were critical subjectivities. They produced subaltern solidarities with alternative social and political imaginaries. The specific genealogical imagination that emerged through various idioms served as a critical intervention not only against colonial categories, but against a dominant political order—indirect rule. Anglo-African, Euro-African, and Eurafrican communities nurtured a common set of politics based on European racial descent that sought preferential treatment compared to that received by their African counterparts. Indeed, these communities were often transparently racist in their attempts to circumvent African authorities and advance their interests, contributing to a grassroots process of colonial racialization. Adopting and adapting Western racial thought in resourceful ways, these "odd tribes" struggled against both the primacy of a customary elite and the political limits of colonial nativism, at once aspiring for non-native status and challenging state prerogatives that largely restricted official concern to African communities.[5] The politics of the uncustomary are consequently neither a clear account of resistance nor a patent example of consent. The political connections that were cultivated with states and settler communities through ties of kinship and genealogy were persistently tested—at times intimate and convivial, at times fraught with tension. But these connections were not without self-interest. They were sentimental in scope, instrumental in purpose, and reciprocal in meaning.

This uncustomary set of politics also challenges conventional political boundaries of the local by pointing to communities-in-relation across British Central Africa. Moving chronologically from the 1930s to the 1950s, the multi-sited comparative histories in this part of the book are framed by distinctive empirical themes found in Nyasaland, Southern Rhodesia, and Northern Rhodesia, while also tracking connections between colonies.[6] People frequently migrated for reasons of family, education, and employment, generating minor transcolonialisms and regional histories in their wake.[7] As social entanglement and political association became enmeshed over time, "communities of sentiment" emerged that exercised ideas of kinship, loyalty, and racial belonging to establish firm sentiments of allegiance toward the British Empire.[8] These colonial cultures of relatedness insist on a reconsideration of how political histories of colonialism are understood and written as a result. The nation-state-colony should not remain the principal location of historical meaning. Empires were shaped by social and political movement.[9] But equally they took shape through the ways people regarded themselves according to birth, political status, and future disposition.[10] The patrilateral allegiances of Anglo-Africans, Eurafricans, and Euro-Africans attempted to extend the contours of Britishness, underscoring how subaltern communities engaged with empire. These political histories thus challenge the oppositional framing of conventional colonial histories that frequently counterpose state interests against local will. These regional accounts of everyday imperial formation denaturalize such distinctions to reveal hidden political cosmologies that diversify our sense of political imagination under colonial rule.[11]

A politics of the uncustomary is therefore not fixed to the communities in this book, but it is broadly applicable to those who struggled against and envisioned a political future beyond traditional authorities, customary law, and the constraints of the colonial native state. Following the lead of Archie Mafeje, this detribalized concept opens a space for rethinking the parameters of civic and ethical life during the colonial period.[12] We have seen in the previous two parts of this book how colonial nativism marked a set of limits—social, political, and racial—and how these restrictions faced a range of challenges at the time. The chapters of this final section depict a maturation of these efforts through formal political organization. It is important to stress that these emergent collective identifications were not ethnic as such—their shallow histories disqualifying this possibility. Nor are these microhistories about racial passing—the use of intermediate categories forecloses this ambition. Rather, they underscore a desire for political assimilation—a case of going British, in contrast to going native.[13] The popular pressures and political expectations manifested in these relational histories sought what can be called a colonial social contract. Although contractual relationships between states and subject communities proliferated under colonial rule, a social contract in this case was not the result of service or status through education, acculturation, or property. Instead, it was predicated on reasons of birth, kinship, and genealogy.[14] These ontologies of intimacy informed and articulated senses of natural rights and political affiliation. Colonial states, in turn, conveyed responsibility and obligation through legal considerations and regional commissions, as discussed before. But action ultimately rested with these communities. As the following chapters show, Anglo-Africans, Euro-Africans, and Eurafricans repeatedly demanded respect and recognition through conflicts over racial origin, cultural affiliation, and territory—the triumvirate that defined nativeness and non-nativeness. These colonial kinship relations and the desire to move from an uncertain status to one contracted by law tested the liberal tenets of British imperialism.[15] Indeed, these connections ultimately reveal the paradox that racial descent created both opportunities and constraints—an example of what Elizabeth Povinelli has called the restrictive inheritances of genealogical societies.[16]

These subaltern histories therefore raise larger questions regarding colonialism and the mutable forms of reason that circulated and defined it. They enable us to historicize thought as social phenomena with particular uses. More specifically, these histories underscore the limits of Western racial reason. If provincializing European modernity has become a vital recent agenda, one critical technique—beyond rudimentary geographic circumscription—is to trace the inconsistent effects of European rationalism and knowledge.[17] By examining the challenges, practices, and mentalities that influenced and shaped the lifeworlds of these communities, the locally crafted meanings of colonial citizenship in its rhizomatic, incomplete forms can be better grasped and understood.

CHAPTER 6

RACISM AS A WEAPON OF THE WEAK

::

History has taught the world that a child takes after his or her father. All the
nations of the earth originated and have been built up on this simple principle; they
began from one father and one mother and slowly but surely expansion became
conspicuous but they all as a group take after their ancestry or forefathers.
—Anglo-African Association (1934)

While sitting with Dinah Coombes on the front stoop of her house just
outside Zomba, she would recall the 1950s through the prisms of family,
school, and community. Originally from Zomba, the former colonial capital, she grew up there and in Blantyre, where she knew Jessica ("Jess")
and Ann Ascroft. When asked if there was an Anglo-African community as
such, her answer was categorically yes, "we used to mix a lot, and in those
days there wasn't much mixing with others." "We used to have parties,
dances, and all," she said with a tone of nostalgia. "And we were very close
together. We knew each other through going to school. We went to school
and then we used to, say, once a week meet in the evenings, take dancing
lessons together or have a gathering. Most of the time we used to do things
together." She remembered football (American soccer) matches being held,
and the celebration of holidays such as Christmas and the Jacaranda Fair
each austral spring: "Every year in October, we used to hold a dance, the
Jacaranda Fair, and then we'd choose a Jacaranda queen. It used to be very
nice." There were also "rock and roll competitions" and "twisting competitions" to popular music by Elvis Presley, Cliff Richard, and Ricky Nelson at
Ramsey Hall, in Blantyre. "Oh, life used to be fun in those days," she once
finished, before getting up to return a tray of tea to her small kitchen.[1]

Fond memories of the colonial period appear out of place with the politics of writing history after decolonization. They challenge a set of assumptions that emphasize political rights denied, labor demands imposed, and cultural practices censured. As a result, such nostalgia has often been critiqued as an effect of historical and social amnesia—a form of mnemonic ruination substantiating the longevity of imperialism's legacies.[2] The recollections I heard during several afternoons spent with one person who experienced her childhood and adolescence during the late colonial period do not necessarily dispel this view. But such memories diversify perspectives on this era, recovering forgotten cultural aspects and patterns of life that convey the normality of colonial rule for many people. These reminiscences appear unreasonable from our vantage point, unsettling established views of the past, yet it served little purpose to disagree with her. She spoke for herself. It was her version of the past. Indeed, our conversations wandered from that distant time to the uncertainties of the present—a time of HIV/AIDS as well as political change after the Banda presidency. Mrs. Coombes's expressed concerns about higher rates of crime and gender violence generated nostalgia not only for her childhood but also for the Banda era, when gender roles and social mores generally were more conservative. Mrs. Coombes's telling of the past exhibited an interplay of different personal and political temporalities that shaped one another— the postcolonial present shaping the colonial past, the post-Banda period similarly recasting the time of his presidency, her advanced age infusing with warmth and sentiment her remembrances of childhood and adolescence. But a sense of community also anchored her memories, providing a structure of feeling that organized relationships and events that had long since passed.[3]

This chapter addresses the emergence of the Anglo-African community during the period between the world wars. In doing so, it attempts to rethink questions of security and livelihood under colonial rule, thus following the lead of Mrs. Coombes's recollections. It specifically argues for a need to think beyond a dominant political mode of the time—that is, a politics of the customary. Although studies of African nationalism and class formation have pursued the same goal, they have often resorted to the durable role of ethnic identities and affiliations to explain historical continuities, mobilization, and political legitimation.[4] The shallow histories of the regional communities under examination here do not permit an identical approach. Because these communities lacked time-honored political traditions, their experiences push beyond prevalent conventions of the political. The process of defining *community* in turn deserves scrutiny, given the risks of oversimplification and resulting homogeneity that can exclude some from membership and include others who may place their attachments elsewhere. Determining where communities begin and end culturally, geographically, politically, and even historically can pose distinct challenges. But communities remain an essential feature of political life, even if their existence is brief. This chapter consequently courts a definition based on a collective political understanding—a contingent form of communal identification centered on a politics of kinship and European racial descent. In this sense, this emergent political scheme presents prima facie a colonial variation on African corporate lineage groups and acephalous segmentary lineage systems more specifically—so-called stateless societies in which internal structures are weak and authority is diffuse.[5] But these similarities also mask differences. These communities were not without leaders. They viewed colonial states as sovereign authorities, and a shared racial ancestry was a central feature of this perception.[6]

The Anglo-African Association—founded in 1929 in direct response to the Reed ruling as cited in chapter 4—expressed this embryonic communal politics established through an ideology of racial difference. The association echoed the paternalistic tradition of colonial authorities, to paraphrase E. P. Thompson.[7] But it did so by its own initiative, on its own terms.[8] Indeed, its politics was also based on a form of mētis—a local practical knowledge—and can be understood as part of a broader, if variable, transformation in kinship practices since the nineteenth century, as discussed in chapter 1.[9] The political strategy and outlook of the association therefore emerged from two sets of political traditions: African and European alike. It drew upon preexisting cultural repertoires.[10] Though small in size—a 1934 census estimated the Anglo-African population in Nyasaland to consist of 1,202 people, as noted before, and a 1956 census counted 1,199 people—the community attracted the colonial state's attention, and an abundance of documentary material exists for this organization from the interwar period. This situation is not coincidental. This period was a crucial time in the transition to indirect rule—a shift that encouraged the foundation of protonationalist native associations in Nyasaland. But the Anglo-African Association marked a distinct contrast. Its strategic employment of race raised pointed questions about racial privilege at the exact political moment when the Nyasaland administration sought to avoid such a perspective, especially given memories of the 1915 Chilembwe Uprising, which contained distinct components of racial grievance.

Though the organizational rhetoric examined here may not be wholly representative of views cultivated at the time, it provides insight into the dimensions of Anglo-African self-definition and community coherence in Nyasaland's colonial social order during the 1930s. In practice, Anglo-African racial and civic status did not figure into a conventional racial hierarchy, with the structure of indirect rule rendering that hierarchy more a figment of a pseudoscientific racial imagination than an accurate reflection of colonial political life.[11] African communities garnered greater state attention and occupied a position of importance closer to that of the white settler community than did the numerically small Anglo-African population. This marginalization is precisely what motivated the association to invoke ties of agnatic kinship and patrilateral racial belonging. It aggressively critiqued a colonial nativism that privileged African interests, using intrinsic and extrinsic types of racism as a weapon of the weak.[12] Contrary to many popular understandings, racial thought and argument are not the exclusive province of those with power. This minority discourse not only represents a subjugated knowledge and worldview, but this subaltern intellection underscores the versatile uses and rationales of racial difference in out-of-the-way places—a reconfiguration of a derivative ideology that enabled the emergence of conditional forms of community as recalled by Mrs. Coombes and others.

: BLACK ATLANTIC POLITICS IN BRITISH CENTRAL AFRICA :

On a Saturday evening in January 1915, a small dinner party was held at the home of William J. Livingstone, general manager for the A. L. Bruce Estates, one of the larger landholdings in the Shire Highlands of Nyasaland. It was well known among local African communities not only for its size and productivity, but also for the level of coercion and everyday physical abuse meted out to African laborers. John Chilembwe, a young minister who had founded an independent church nearby, was one vocal critic of these essentially unregulated practices. He served a congregation of workers who had numerous grievances about the estate's use of *thangata*, a land-for-labor exchange that amounted to a system of forced labor.[13] This injustice accumulated—compounded by a tax increase in 1912 and food shortages from 1912 to 1914—and gradually converged with Chilembwe's

FIGURE 6.1. The pond where John Chilembwe baptized converts to his church, 2006. Photograph by the author.

theological and political outlooks, which he developed in the United States when he attended the Virginia Theological Seminary in Lynchburg, Virginia, between 1897 and 1900. Exposed to the ideas of Booker T. Washington and radical abolitionists like John Brown, Chilembwe returned to Nyasaland to establish the Providence Industrial Mission, which occupied a place in a broader landscape of independent, African-led missions in British Central Africa during the early twentieth century. By 1914 Chilembwe had converted hundreds to his church (see figure 6.1), a situation viewed with increasing consternation by white landowners and local Yao chiefs, who were predominantly Muslim. These elements combined to spark a rebellion. After Livingstone's dinner party ended, a small group of men under Chilembwe's directive infiltrated the estate to kill Livingstone and another manager, Duncan MacCormick. However, by February 4 the uprising was over, with only one other settler having been killed and Chilembwe himself shot while fleeing to Mozambique. His church was swiftly demolished (see figure 6.2).[14]

Despite its short-lived character, the Chilembwe uprising became one of the most celebrated in Africa's history. Though its motivations were complex in origin, what is clear is that the revolt represented local resistance to labor abuse, racial oppression, and colonial rule more generally. In the words of George Simeon Mwase, Chilembwe was the first and last African to "attack a lion with a maize stalk," and Mwase believed his activ-

FIGURE 6.2. The New Jerusalem Temple, built to replace Chilembwe's church, 2006. Photograph by the author.

ism should be compared with that of such figures as John Brown, Roger Casement, and William Prynne.[15] Soon after it ended, therefore, the Chilembwe revolt became a critical symbol—not only of armed struggle, but also of the political uses of Western education and appropriated Christian ideology as weapons of resistance. It underlined the fact that racial tensions had both quietly and overtly infiltrated Nyasaland's colonial social order through routines of land ownership and labor and such institutional venues as mission stations, despite the small scale of white settlement— what Charles van Onselen has cited as a phenomenon of cultural osmosis to explain the complex origins and local practices of racial difference, in contrast to systemic statutory measures, particularly in rural areas.[16] The 1920s and the 1930s were characterized by two competing developments. On the one hand, the colonial state implemented indirect rule as a means of stabilizing its political control. Indirect rule would ostensibly blunt the aspirations of an emergent Western-educated class, which Chilembwe represented, through reentrenching a customary elite. On the other hand, the ambitions of this new political class did not subside but became more focused through the creation of native associations that provided an organizational framework for popular discussion and petitioning.[17]

The Anglo-African Association formed part of this context of change. With the rise of an educated and politically engaged African elite and the concurrent effort to strengthen customary authorities, the association belonged to a civil society caught between the Western acculturation and "retribalization" that characterized many colonial orders during this period.[18] Though the general emergence of African pressure groups through native associations took hold after the Chilembwe Uprising, the intellectual and institutional origins of these associations preceded the revolt. The North Nyasa Native Association (founded by A. Simon Muhango) started in 1912 in Karonga, while the West Nyasa Native Association was established in 1914 in Bandawe, thus marking the appearance of these organizations on Malawi's political landscape quite early—only twenty years after the commencement of the protectorate.[19] Organizations founded after 1915 include the Mombera Native Association (1920), the Chiradzulu District Native Association (1929), and the Nyasaland (Southern Province) Native Association (1923), which split into the Blantyre Native Association and the Mlanje Native Association. An interassociation committee also formed in Zomba that united the northern associations, which had materialized earlier due to the older presence of missions in that part of the country.[20] This interassociation group, known as the Representative Committee of Northern Province Native Associations, was headed by Levi Z. Mumba, who participated in a number of capacities during this period, including as secretary of the North Nyasa Native Association, founder of the Native Civil Servants' Association, and corresponding secretary of the Lilongwe African Welfare Society. These political roles led in 1944 to Mumba's becoming the first president of the Nyasaland African Congress, the organizational precursor to the Malawi Congress Party.

These native associations therefore formed a vital political element. Yet, in contrast to Chilembwe, their concerns were primarily accommodationist in scope, seeking to revise existing policies rather than overthrow the state as such. They possessed certain tensions, being regional in orientation—and thus modern and forward-looking in their political imagination—but remaining socially and politically attached to the concerns of customary leaders.[21] Given the size of Nyasaland and a close geographic proximity, these connections are perhaps unsurprising. Still, these associations introduced a new format for political engagement and representation—one more broadly construed than any that had existed before, reflecting the associations' selective acceptance of and alignment with the social and political mores introduced by colonialism.[22] As stated in their official documents, the Chiradzulu District Native Association and the Nyasaland (Southern Province) Native Association both sought "to assist the Government in every way, especially by keeping it informed of Native public opinion," while also supporting "the Native by representing him in all political matters, by keeping him informed of and explaining the object of legislations both new and already in force." The Mombera and the West Nyasa Native Associations further advocated "making the people understand the necessity and value of order, and the importance of becoming law-abiding citizens and also of the value and importance of industrious labour—and in short the value of civilization as against ignorance, laziness, disloyalty and anarchy."[23]

Influenced by the emergence of these parallel organizations, the Anglo-African Association shared many of their features. Yusuf Ismael (born in 1908), a man of Indo-African descent and one of the founders of the association, recalled that its original membership consisted primarily of low-level civil servants such as court interpreters, skilled wage earners such as teachers and transport drivers, and generally upwardly mobile men who aspired to better jobs and political recognition. They formed a contingent medial class—to utilize an expression of Philip Zachernuk's—rather than middle class per se, between the European settler presence and the broader peasant milieu.[24] When I asked Mr. Ismael why he had joined the association, he replied that its members were "just my friends, because I had people like Henry Ascroft and James Jamieson as friends. They were advanced men, you know, doing well, doing some business and so on. James Jamieson was a farmer, tobacco grower. And Ascroft was a transporter."[25] Many had received a mission education and belonged to a new intellectual class, like their African counterparts. In similar fashion, the core membership and leadership of the association was predominantly male. The community it represented primarily resided in Zomba and the neighboring commercial towns of Blantyre and Limbe, in southern Nyasaland, though the association was not completely disconnected from the peasant society and economy that surrounded these areas. Regarding the economic condition of the community as a whole, Mr. Ismael told me that although some members—like Jamieson and Thomas Merry, another of the group's founders—had access to land through their white fathers, many faced difficulties: "the biggest group of the people were poor."[26] This impoverished section of the membership shared affinities with Euro-African and Eurafrican communities in Southern and Northern Rhodesia, as discussed in the previous chapter. The concerns and outlooks of the association's members consequently blended with those of a broader regional milieu. Yet the group's organizational papers reveal a distinctive view toward the nature of colonial politics in Nyasaland and how Anglo-Africans interpreted existing structures of power—African and European alike—to claim non-native status. The association, like its African equivalents, wanted to promote a law-abiding colonial citizenry. But the terms through which it expressed its civic loyalty were entirely different.[27]

The Anglo-African Association articulated a contrasting set of politics through a political language that stressed racial connection. Similar to Chilembwe's revolt, it sought to transcend the customary through a form of subaltern racial solidarity. Though its membership was situated primarily in urban areas, the association had a broadly inclusive political outlook, locating the civic status of its members in village politics as well as across the colony—even speculating on their position in the British Empire. As a result, the language of the association captured a complex mix of traditional and modern elements, with ideas of racial endowment grafted onto understandings of agnatic kinship and belonging—a hybridization of elements that resembles Antonio Gramsci's criteria for delineating subaltern political sensibilities. Members of the association can be said to have traced their "origins in pre-existing groups, whose mentality, ideology and aims they conserve for a time," thus reflecting "affiliation to the dominant political formations." But through such attachments, the association equally attempted "to influence the programmes of these formations in order to press claims of their own."[28] The political and moral sensibilities exhibited in the association's intellectual discourse constituted a complex cultural echo that reconfigured ideas of status, responsibility, and entitlement that resonated with British values as well as local African perspectives. The moral economy of loyalty and reciprocal colonial responsibility that emerged borrowed from European and African traditions, with the idiom of kinship not only representing familial bonds but also containing components of local, racial, and imperial belonging that transformed these connections into an engaged political schema and rationale for contractual obligation. This emergent genealogical imagination enabled a type of critical agency—a form of poor theory—that challenged the boundaries of colonial nativism at the grassroots level.[29]

: RACIAL PRIVILEGE AND RESPECTABILITY
IN A TIME OF ETHNIC RULE :

The politics initiated by the Anglo-African Association during the 1930s marked an intersection of the administrative question of native status and issues related to individual self-reflection and self-fashioning among members of the association. Identity was an instrumental means to an end, not the end itself. The association sought jobs, education, and other social and material benefits for its members. Much of the association's political rhetoric consequently emphasized the *Anglo-* prefix in its hyphenated locution to demonstrate loyalty—a sentiment that approximated that of other native associations. However, a stress on agnatic kinship to the British signaled a key difference between the association and these parallel organizations—a genealogical imagination unique and specific to its members' descent background. This sense of family, civilizational attachment, and the subsequent obligation of the state toward the community offered a distinct qualitative valence and modality of critical engagement, with the association's political case resting on an affective racial inheritance rather than more abstract appeals to the liberal values of British colonialism.[30] It presented a version of a neoprimordialist position—which emphasizes the evocative power of imagined racial bonds as having deep emotive meaning in the belief of historical actors—while maintaining a utilitarian purpose and reason for those bonds. As Jonathon Glassman has argued, these two perspectives are not incompatible but can reinforce one another.[31] This intrinsic racism therefore attempted to achieve cohesion and responsibility by asserting a common familial connection that sought a reduction of social marginality.[32] In Kwame Anthony Appiah's words, it is "the assimilation of 'race feeling' to 'family feeling' that makes intrinsic racism seem so much less objectionable than extrinsic [racism]."[33] But it was racism nevertheless. These conjoined sentiments of family and racial difference underpinned the social entitlement, political favor, and racial respectability the association's members demanded.[34]

Though it is difficult to attribute the association's rhetoric to specific members, several key figures can be identified. Of the nineteen men present at its inaugural meeting on July 28, 1929, R. E. Deuss was elected president, S. H. Osman vice president, Thomas B. Merry secretary, and T. D. Duncan as treasurer.[35] Deuss served as president until 1935. He was a first-generation Anglo-African, having an African mother and a father who was either German or Swiss. Purportedly having been educated in the Western Cape of South Africa, Deuss became prosperous through raising stock and dairy cattle, eventually leasing three hundred acres of land from the government in southern Nyasaland, beginning in 1923. He had substantial ties to the white farming community, and he advocated the payment of the non-native poll tax by Anglo-Africans as a bargaining chip to induce the state to grant them other benefits. Another member of the association, who later served as secretary, was George Leyer, the son of a Swedish father and a Bemba (an ethnic group located in Northern Rhodesia) mother. He had worked for the Trans African Continental Telegraphic Company in Kenya, Uganda, and Tanganyika before returning to Nyasaland. Thomas Ravenor, the son of an African mother and an English father who was once involved in the tobacco business in Nyasaland, also achieved a degree of prosperity through a small holding of land and cattle. Overall, the early membership of the association reflected a mildly affluent, first-generation community of mostly local origins, albeit with a diverse range of family backgrounds and personal experience. As indicated by the fathers of these members of the Anglo-African Association, the prefix *Anglo-* did not always denote direct familial ties with Britain. It also signaled cultural affiliation and imperial patriotism.[36]

Among the association's most active members was Henry Ascroft. He was one of the nineteen men who attended the group's initial meeting, and he served as president after the death of Deuss in 1935. Ascroft's term was brief due to his arrest and eighteen-month imprisonment for public intoxication and assaulting a police officer in 1936.[37] But he reemerged as a key figure during the 1940s and 1950s, both as president of the association and through his efforts to build regional connections with parallel communities and their political organizations in Southern and Northern Rhodesia. As early as the 1930s, Ascroft gave speeches at the association's meetings on the meaning of Anglo-African status and the importance of issues like education. His daughters recalled his support for separate education for Anglo-Africans as central to the cohesion and uplift of the community. Ann recollected him telling her how his own father pushed schooling. "He always remembered his father would say to him, 'You must be educated. You must go to school!'" she recounted. "My father was a very intelligent man. He always came first in class at school all along. There was no one who could beat him." Similar to his African counterparts, then, Henry Ascroft attended mission school, in his case the Blantyre Mission of the Church

The Scotch Mission Station Blantyre. School Children.

FIGURE 6.3. Children at the Blantyre Mission, 1886, taken by Consul A. G. H. Hawes. Used by permission of the National Archives of the United Kingdom (CO 1069/108/31).

of Scotland that had been established in 1881 and was headed in Ascroft's student days by the Reverend Doctor Alexander Hetherwick (see figures 6.3 and 6.4). Among the most important missions in Nyasaland due to its early history and ties to David Livingstone and John Chilembwe, who was also a graduate, it offered both liberal arts and technical education. "They could become medical assistants, they could become carpenters, they could become agricultural workers, or they could become teachers," Ann told me in conversation. Henry Ascroft eventually "became a teacher. . . . He loved teaching. He was a very good teacher."[38]

Although Ascroft did not remain a teacher, it left an imprint on his views about the importance of education. Given his own experience working as a domestic servant in Hetherwick's residence to pay his fees, Ascroft acknowledged the material cost of education as well.[39] State intervention was needed. The Anglo-African Association consequently sought such intervention through a dialogue with the state—a strategy including the submission of written petitions, meeting minutes, and transcribed speeches to government departments, as well as having formal appointments with colonial officials. Anglo-African identity and status were constituted inter-actively from the start. Minutes from the inaugural meeting sent to the commissioner of the Southern Province declared that "the most important question above all was that of establishing our status. . . . [W]e humbly ap-peal to the Government that when framing any Ordinances concerning our community, especially with regard to our status, to kindly avoid, as far as possible, the scourge with which we have been initiated, namely, the term, 'HALF-CASTE.'" This term did not offer "any compliment" and "something more appreciative" was needed. The association further desired to estab-lish a "relationship with all sections of the communities of this country" and to raise other issues, including welfare and education for children, taxation, higher wages, and a census of the Anglo-African population.[40] As discussed before, the government initially expressed support for the as-

FIGURE 6.4. The reverend's residence at the Blantyre Mission, where Ascroft worked. 1886, taken by Consul A. G. H. Hawes. Used by permission of the National Archives of the United Kingdom (CO 1069/108/51).

PROVINCE	Under 5 years		5 years to marriageable age		Marriageable age		All ages		TOTAL
	EURO-PEAN ORIGIN	ASIAN ORIGIN	EURO-PEAN ORIGIN	ASIAN ORIGIN	EURO-PEAN ORIGIN	ASIAN ORIGIN	EURO-PEAN ORIGIN	ASIAN ORIGIN	
Southern	103	244	135	233	145	138	383	615	998
Northern	19	56	31	16	62	20	112	92	204
Total	122	300	166	249	207	158	495	707	1,202

TABLE 6.1. The 1934 census of the Anglo-African community conducted by colonial district residents and customary authorities. It is important to observe that the majority lived in the southern province and that the majority were of Asian origin. Among adults, the majority were of European origin. NAM, s1/214/34, Census of Half-Castes in Nyasaland.

sociation, given its loyalty to the British government. But this positive reception gave way to an ongoing ambivalence. Anglo-Africans were not the only ones seeking favor and progress. Native associations expressed similar aspirations. This impasse only spurred the association to strive harder, and its efforts took on a particular urgency after 1933—the year the Native Authority and Native Courts Ordinances were promulgated to institute indirect rule. These two laws were intended to mitigate the political influence of the native associations. But both acts recognized and entrenched African welfare more generally, generating a palpable sense of political marginalization for Anglo-Africans, in the eyes of the association's members. This institutional shift underscored a key distinction between the historical situations in Nyasaland and the Western Cape of South Africa vis-à-vis multiracial people—in Nyasaland, the Anglo-African community did not occupy a stable middle position in a racial hierarchy, but instead became subordinate to black and white interests alike.[41]

Given this context of competition among Anglo-African and African political organizations, the association used as its guiding principle a statement made by Governor Shenton Thomas at a meeting in July 1931, at which he stated that the Anglo-African community should be given opportunities and encouragement.[42] It was generally agreed that this promise had not been kept, particularly after Thomas's departure for the Gold Coast in 1932. Members of the association proposed compiling a list of unemployed Anglo-Africans to be circulated among district commissioners for any vacancies that might exist.[43] Closely connected to this concern was

	Under 5 years	5 years to marriageable age	Marriageable age	Total
Male	234	230	190	654
Female	188	185	175	548

TABLE 6.2. The 1934 census figures in table 6.1 divided by gender. It is important to observe that the majority were children and youth (under marriageable age). NAM, s1/214/34, Census of Half-Castes in Nyasaland.

the issue of education, given the relatively high number of children in the community (see tables 6.1 and 6.2). With education a vital dimension of collective development, Ascroft forcefully argued this matter be raised again in light of Thomas's earlier statement.[44] The issue was addressed in more detail in two meetings in 1933.[45] Prior to the second meeting, Ascroft learned from the Blantyre Mission that education for the Anglo-African community was "a general topic amongst the high Government Officials." With this encouragement, Ascroft made a speech to the association titled "Education for the Anglo-Africans: A Brief Outline on Education as a Result of a Meeting with His Excellency Sir Thomas in 1931."[46] Ascroft's speech is significant for the connections it drew between education, paternal responsibility, and community development. Citing the association's meeting with Thomas in 1931, Ascroft recalled how the association had demanded that it be made "compulsory that every non-native father-parent should deposit a certain sum of money with the Authorities . . . to be used for fees for the child's elementary education." With this funding, the association believed "there would be nothing more to worry about the child because at least there was something with which the child would secure his or her preliminary education; the father of any such child would then be free." Shifting to the present, Ascroft broadened paternal responsibility metaphorically to include the colonial state itself. "It is the Government's charge and not the fathers' alone in every sense," he firmly argued.[47]

This transfiguration of paternal obligation to the colonial state animated much of the association's political discourse. Through these personal and metaphorical kinship relations, Anglo-Africans perceived themselves as different from native Africans. Their intrinsic non-native status by virtue of their racial descent made it "dishonest" for them to be "educated together with natives for an indefinite period."[48] Ascroft continued that when "the

Anglo-african finds out the difference between him and his native class-mates he is scorned, mocked, and abused in such a way that he never forgets." Their sense of inferiority vis-à-vis African and white communities alike would be intensified by "mixed" education—even passed down to subsequent generations if a solution were not devised and implemented. A shared genealogy with European colonists justified such measures. "We are children of non-natives; our thinking, living, [and] social life . . . take after our fathers. We shall always stand by them and be of service to them," Ascroft stressed. "It is for this reason that Government should give us education to shape us into a respectable race and form us into useful citizens of the Government and the British Empire to which unhesitatingly we belong. If we are taught to know ourselves and what we should do there shall be lacking no response on our side because we know what we are and what we owe the Government."[49] The association's members agreed on the importance of education, but skepticism also emerged. One member cited the existence of separate education in South Africa, but "there were some who [still] could not even get a job because of their colour."[50] Ascroft responded that a lack of education would be "the end of our Community."[51] Separate education could circumvent a perceived threat of African acculturation. A Mr. King was "very much grieved to see our people who lived in the villages drinking native beer, dancing with natives with only a blanket or a single cloth tied round their waists or hung over their shoulders . . . [and eating] whatever the primitive native ate."[52] Their condition was "intolerable and would only make one weep . . . if these people had been brought up in a proper elementary school they would be of great service to the Government and would constitute a united Anglo-african Community."[53]

Although copies of these meeting minutes were sent to the government, the official view was that the community's legal status was still under consideration, and the state could not make any formal policy decisions until this question was resolved. However, following the temporary protocol that "no obstacle should be placed in the way of native half-castes being classed among members of a higher civilization where their standard and manner of life justified such classification," the government also held that "no obstacle should be raised to children, legitimate or illegitimate, of European or Indian fathers and native mothers being treated in accordance with the status of their fathers where they have been brought up in a manner suited to that status"—a position reflecting the Colonial Office's stance.[54] Still, the government felt that given this community's small size, there were "comparatively few who would desire to be treated as other than natives" due to the potential for a higher poll tax, but also because the majority lived "in exactly the same manner as natives."[55] Echoing the Foggin Commission's deliberations of the same year, the government felt that these people should not be prevented from "taking their place in the life of a native village."[56] A "distinctive educational programme" would be "premature" and potentially "subversive of general policy" with regard to indirect rule and legal status.[57] Missionary institutions shared these views. "Some people wish to make of the half caste children a middle class, between Europeans and African natives," summarized one mission official. "This is a generous dream, but difficult to realize."[58]

In mid-1934 the government arrived at a clear position. Though the Advisory Committee on Education had heard with "great sympathy the plea of the Anglo-African Association with reference to children of 'mixed' descent being 'hidden in the villages,'" the official consensus was that "there was no difference between the intellectual attainments of the African and the half-caste" and therefore no "educational distinction should be made between them." The committee believed that "full consideration [should] be given to the African point of view" regarding the issue and that any plan of separate education was "undesirable."[59] Levi Mumba, the only African member of the committee, provided this perspective. As mentioned earlier, Mumba was involved in several native organizations as well as having connections with the colonial government. In fact, Judge Haythorne Reed knew Mumba personally, once referring to him as "a really competent Native clerk, typist and interpreter."[60] Mumba's stance consequently offered a meaningful contrast, affirming that Anglo-African status rested at the intersection of not two but three competing points of view—each of which had different rationales for the recognition, or disregard, of this community. Like colonial officials, Mumba considered the question of separate education to be "not only important but difficult and complex" because it entailed racial privilege, separate legal status, and new notions of patrilateral corporate belonging.[61] But Mumba argued that the government should provide free education to Africans and Anglo-Africans alike. He supported the association's efforts in this regard, though he found distinctly problematic the association's patrilineal argument.

Mumba undermined this position by asserting that matrilineal kinship

practices found in many local communities in the Nyasaland region should
take precedence. A gendered politics of kinship thus countered a racial
politics of genealogical descent. Mumba recognized the tensions between
this corporate system and the aspirations of the association's members.
Yet he viewed their claims as not only invented and improvised, but also
as a discriminatory form of cultural and racial subterfuge. The association's
members clearly identified more strongly with their European fathers than
with their African mothers. Mumba conceded that Anglo-Africans were
not responsible for their predicament. But he reasoned that they already
had access to mission schools and believed that if separate facilities were
provided for them, their fathers should bear the burden. Moreover, government concessions would not only result in "wasting public revenue" but
also recognize the "illegal miscegenation of races."[62] Contrasting situations
of legitimacy and illegitimacy in Europe and Africa, Mumba argued that
illegitimate children in Europe had no legal claim on their father. He contended that similarly "among tribes who pay dowry the children belong to
the father and have a claim on him. Among those who do not pay dowry,
they belong to the mother and can [only make a] claim on the [maternal]
uncles." Anglo-Africans, many of whom were "the offspring of unions unauthorised by law, dowry, ankhoswe or other understanding," should fall
under the guardianship of their African relatives, specifically their uncles.
Anglo-African status should therefore be determined by matrilineal practices of enatic descent. As a matter of sentimental emphasis, Mumba added
that African families "never grumbled when nursing or bringing them up,
they care for them with a parental love which is lacking on the part of the
civilized and rich father."[63]

In making these remarks, Mumba detected an animosity toward African values and culture that was inherent in the association's position. He
perceived Anglo-Africans as not only ungrateful, but misguided. He argued
that many "do not wish to see the sight of their mothers, much less that
of their related uncles, for they think that if their identity is known it re-
duces their chance of passing as pure white men or Indians on account of
their light colour and the father's name."[64] He also contended that Anglo-
African claims to status were undermined by their diverse origins. "They
are not an independent race and the term Anglo African does not correctly
describe them all, for it is not only the English who have children from
African women," Mumba stated. "There are German, Italian, Portuguese,

Indian, Greek, Arab and Somali halfcastes as well as Nyasaland African halfcastes (who are the children of African men and halfcaste women)."[65] Mumba asserted that the Anglo-African desire for a separate status "to avoid their growing [up] among Africans in the villages and eating native food" was not only unfounded, but unrealistic.[66] "What force can unite all these diverse offspring into one solid mass when they are removed from the villages?" he asked.[67] Mumba understood that their desire for education was "reasonable and cannot be disputed," but the request for separate education was ultimately unjustified. Anglo-Africans had no basis for claiming such entitlement. Education should be available to all "without distinction."[68]

Mumba's position is significant for its customary rationale. The tensions between Anglo-Africans and Africans not only evince the parsing of political language and contestation over Anglo-African identification. They demonstrate competing conceptualizations of corporate belonging that African authorities had a stake in controlling. Kinship became a site of struggle. Indeed, this debate genuflects toward broader challenges that had been made to customary kinship practices since the nineteenth century. Concern over social boundaries and cultural routine not only affected issues like education. It was rooted in a desire to reinforce existing identities and social relations of power. African leaders, like colonial officials, had incentives for preserving social distinctions when certain political claims and action threatened to undermine their influence.[69] Reflecting these interests, Mumba reinforced a common perspective of illegitimacy, contending that Anglo-Africans were simply the "children of wronged African women" who had borne the responsibility of raising them.[70] "They may be non-natives but have no other home except as natives of Nyasaland," he argued. "It would be a double wrong to the African woman, and no protection to the African race, if their halfcaste children are encouraged to look down on them by being given a higher educational status based on nothing except that they are the accidental children of some foreigner who is ashamed to own them."[71] Customary law, which recognized matrilineal descent, should prevail in determining status. "In the absence of a law to the contrary the halfcaste child is bound to live with his mother and maternal uncles as hitherto and get his education together with other children," he remarked. "The removal of such a child from its African environment of village life" was in his view "impracticable."[72]

: REASONING WITH BLOOD:

CARNAL KNOWLEDGE AS POLITICAL KNOWLEDGE :

The Anglo-African Association responded to Mumba's position by refuting claims of illegitimacy and the primacy of matrilineal practices over their patrilineal birthright. Following the gendered turn in Mumba's argument, the association continued to define and promote a counter-genealogy based on agnatic descent, reinforcing its members' sense of affiliation with their white fathers and the British colonial state. Its criticism of Mumba was frequently racist in tone, perceiving its pleas for separate education as being "criticised and attacked by a native instead of by a person of different status."[73] "The fact that he is the first of the primitive stock to taste the blessings of European education was not considered," argued one member.[74] The association feared that Mumba's opinions would lead to "the doom of the whole halfcaste race," that they would "go down into the jaws of primitive life and its evil influences as if they were born by that inferior race alone without a drop of the blood of the advanced races in their veins."[75] The association further rejected Mumba's argument that African families nurtured Anglo-Africans and that matrilineal relations should take priority. There was not one "who has been educated by his 'African uncle' who has reached any useful standard," one member claimed.[76] They did not see their petitions as a problem for the government, but as a matter of claiming their inheritance. "Who has found it embarrassing to do good to his own child, and why should an outside member or person or servant or slave be jealous and envious of the doings of a father to his child?" one member asked. "Is it embarrassing for a prince to [have a] claim upon his blood father or his father's crown or kingdom? Will the king's servants and slaves have objections to his claims and will their objections be sound within the law?"[77] Invoking the Reed ruling, members continued to justify their claim as non-natives by birth. They "originated from their fathers, the Europeans," and they should be considered similar to their fathers, as "blood-children" of the British government who would "take a hand in the governing of and support the Empire under which they live."[78]

The association's members consequently disputed the claim that they were illegitimate. Although the political language of agnatic kinship clearly conveyed a vertical sense of affiliation with their British fathers and the colonial state, it also presented a horizontal sensibility—a tacit acceptance of the importance of kinship and their ongoing connections with African communities. Kinship provided an indigenous vernacular of legitimation to both African and European communities. The subaltern intellection of the association reflected a form of "rule-governed creativity" structured by competing systems of kinship.[79] It seized on and reworked a gendered epistemology in order to validate Anglo-African claims, despite the enatic views articulated by Mumba. Issues of marriage and abandonment emerged as well, given their ramifications for legitimacy, recalling the oral family histories discussed previously. The association acknowledged the legal predicaments involved in interracial relationships, given their occurrence under "two different and conflicting national or tribal laws."[80] But its members reconfigured this problem by questioning conventional wisdom, arguing that there was no "'illegal miscegenation of races' in us whatsoever," given the regional prevalence of intergroup marriage.[81] Recognizing the matrilocal dimensions (broadly construed) of foreign white settlers having relationships with local African women, the association further professed that European men adapted to and participated in customary marriage practices. As one member stated, slighting African husbands, "nearly all our fathers have paid dowry and performed Chinkhoswe with a few exceptions of course . . . they have not regarded the native women or wives as their slaves capable of being substituted by their sisters."[82] These purported marriages also benefited the wider family. "Our fathers lavished upon those related to their native wives; the village picture of the halfdressed children and women was changed into one of forms decorated with blue calico, grey sheetings, or some cotton blanket," one member remarked. "The father and mother of the native girl received cash to pay their hut tax to the Boma, they also received hoes, and axe-heads by the dozens and their necks were ornamented with beads which they had received from the European son-in-law."[83] European husbands "knew by name and face everyone said to be the relations of his wife and treated them kindly."[84] A European husband would attend to his wife "to see that she led a faithful life now; just the very thing the natives do between themselves in their own life."[85] This obligation extended once more to other members of her family, with husbands helping "brothers and uncles of the wives by giving them decent employments such as field *capitãos* [foremen], cooks, bricklayers, carpenters, sawyers, or any other work which they could do."[86] Families could become prosperous with "a European son or brother-in-law."[87]

These assertions of legality and benefits were intended to buttress Anglo-African claims for legitimacy. But they also marked more affective considerations. This rhetoric extended to the ways Anglo-Africans treated their African mothers, denying that their search for status translated into a complete rejection of their African background. "The fact therefore that we have been nursed by our mothers has been natural but [also] profitable to all the mothers," one member concluded. "We have been left with our mothers either at the death of our fathers or at their departure . . . and she has not lost but gained considerably. In turn for their care which we, the halfcastes, have received, we look after them in a way many times better than they would have been looked after by their own colour or native children. Many native boys do not care for their mothers as we do."[88] The association's members also attacked the view that they sought to pass for white. "There is not one halfcaste who dislikes his mother [so much] that he must pass as a pure white man or as an Indian on account of the colour," one member stated. "The very colour which is neither white nor black is his mark that he is a halfcaste."[89] Fathers received equal respect. Given the strong missionary influence in Nyasaland, a theological sensibility was evident. Biblical ideas of "natural law" and "the law of God" were used as rationalizations for the argument that their identity should follow that of their fathers.[90] One member rhetorically asked, "Why is man endeavouring to reverse the natural and beautiful arrangements . . . [so] that the children must take after their mothers?"[91] The association argued that "we all are 'the children of Adam'" and that "when we want to make reference to our origin . . . we speak of the 'father' and not of the 'mother.'"[92] It was natural to make "a claim upon the 'father.'"[93]

This reasoning with blood signaled a transformation of the carnal knowledge that once had resided in gossip and rumor into a political language intended to achieve non-native entitlement. A hidden transcript of innuendo and purported illegitimacy became a public transcript of open petitions to the state. But members of the Association did not intend to lose their distinctive status by becoming recognized as non-natives. "We are an independent race. We are not black, nor white. We are midway and must remain there—an intermediate race," one member summarized.[94] The term *Anglo-African* was therefore proposed as an accurate representation of who they were and the period in which they lived. The Anglo-African "made his appearance in this country . . . with the settlement of the European."[95] The association further underscored that social diversity was natural, with Great Britain being "a Kingdom of many races or nations."[96] But ultimately the association's claims were intended to produce material benefits beyond status itself. Its members perceived education as a "factory for building individuals into a race and a nation."[97] They claimed their community was bound to persist, remarking we "are increasing year by year; the marriages between halfcastes alone are on the upward tendency."[98] Racial discrimination temporarily aside, they cited as a guiding principle the ethos of Booker T. Washington to mold themselves "into an industrial, useful and respectable people who will in the end be of use to themselves and to the Government."[99] The association's members further requested that their appeals be sent to the Colonial Office in London, since they desired to participate in future policy making.[100]

Yet the Nyasaland administration remained unmoved.[101] Officials did review Southern Rhodesia's Foggin Commission report as outlining a possible model for preferential treatment. But the Nyasaland director of education expressed reservations about "making distinctions, social and economic, between degrees of colour and race" where "these distinctions must be more or less hard and fast." The report gave "the idea of definite strata; below the African and the 'African half-caste'; then the coloured and the 'European' half-caste; then though this is not quite so clear the Indian; and then the European." The appropriateness of legislating such a hierarchy in Nyasaland was deemed unfavorable.[102] Unlike Southern Rhodesia, the Nyasaland government decided to bridge the gap between Africans and Europeans over time, not to harden racial differences permanently by law.

: VERNACULAR INTELLECTUALS, RACIAL THOUGHT,
AND THE POLITICS OF LEGITIMATION :

In depicting struggles over racial descent in Nyasaland during the interwar period, this chapter has underscored the active role intellectuals played in shaping political debate—specifically their ability to reconfigure European racial thought and use local cultural vernaculars to achieve distinct ends.[103] The Anglo-African Association and its members acknowledged the intrinsic racial characteristics of colonial hegemony, even after the establishment of indirect rule. It consequently sought to circumvent customary politics through a political language of loyalty and colonial obligation, using vernacular idioms of kinship and genealogy in its arguments. The association's long conversation with the colonial state must be understood as an engagement with the broader politics of the time, if in an uncustomary fashion. The genealogical imagination the association mobilized was a "regulated improvisation" reworked from local understandings of kinship and racial pedigree that had influenced and shaped an emergent colonial habitus.[104] This imagination attempted to mediate the concerns of the association, the state, and local communities.[105] Members felt these tangible connections made entitlement not only a matter of law, but also an issue of familial heritage and reciprocity—a social contract based on natural rights of descent. But, as Jaap van Velsen has argued, what counts is whether assumed or putative forms of kinship are accepted, and by whom.[106] The association's rhetoric oscillated between consent to governmental policies and condemnation of the government—a type of contradictory consciousness—that echoed patriarchal norms but also criticized those norms when they did not cast favor, given facts of "blood, history backing, [and] prestige."[107] Indeed, although the association sought to evade a customary structure of power institutionalized through indirect rule, the agnatic framework of colonial fathers and Anglo-African children could also work against the latter's intentions, constructing an alternative hierarchy of difference and seniority that was difficult to overcome. A colonial order of paternalism remained.

But Anglo-African claims must be read not only as symptomatic of the broader political conditions and modalities of power transecting Nyasaland's colonial social order. They also reflected, more specifically, emerging self-narratives that countered arguments of illegitimacy. The association redefined its members' uncertain politics of birth by transforming hidden histories of interracial intimacy rendered invisible by colonial domination (due to their potential for scandal) into open knowledge that was critical of colonial policy.[108] The association mobilized a European racial bloodline as a "weapon of the weak" to claim specific entitlements when the state granted favor to African communities, perceiving such actions by the state as violations of a moral reciprocity based on ties of agnatic kinship and genealogy.[109] The assertion by the association's members of a distinctive Anglo-African identity approximates what John Lonsdale has called "moral ethnicity," a concept that stresses how internal understandings of civic virtue map and substantiate patterns of identification.[110] Civic virtue in this instance was determined along racial and patrilateral lines. Asserting agnatic claims of descent sought to establish a form of social dignity and honor to be used against frequent counterclaims of illicit origins.[111]

This intellectual engagement demonstrates that colonial states and settler communities did not have exclusive use of racial ideologies and their modes of reason. Subaltern communities invented little traditions with alternative applications and meanings.[112] The political success of the association was not immediate or complete, with only modest recognition and affluence occurring after World War II. Government officials attempted to gain more accurate figures regarding population numbers, standards of living, and education levels of Anglo-Africans across the protectorate (see tables 6.3 and 6.4). These figures indicated a social group occupying several cultural borderlands, with those of "European" status forming a minority. Nonetheless, a separate school for Anglo-Africans was established in 1946 at Chichiri, near Blantyre.[113] But the 1930s proved to be a defining period, when significant issues such as education and employment and central figures like Ascroft emerged to define the content and contours of the organization and the affective community it represented. Identity and its relation to political and legal status would continue to evolve, and efforts at greater precision, solidarity, and connection would be ongoing (figure 6.5), especially at the regional level as discussed in the next chapter.

When I talked with Yusuf Ismael about these issues in 1999—seventy years after the association's founding and at a time when his health was in dramatic decline after the recent passing of his wife—his memories of the association were primarily related to the friendships he had with people like Ascroft, with whom he attended the Blantyre Mission school. "We were in school together, and when we finished our schooling, we started work and Henry was working as a court interpreter," Mr. Ismael recalled. "We were good friends, of course, good friends from school, but he, himself, made life uncomfortable, not a very happy person, because he was that type of a person who quarreled with people." Prompted by this description, I asked him how Ascroft's politics and community advocacy contributed to his life and death. Mr. Ismael said simply, "He died because the Malawi Congress Party had beaten him so severely. He was so sick in the hospital and then he recovered. After he recovered he couldn't get on. He wasn't very well at all and then suddenly got sick and died."[114] These difficult memories toward the end of Mr. Ismael's life appeared emblematic of the Anglo-African community's persistent struggle for and ultimate failure to achieve the political recognition and elevated status it sought.

But such sorrows did not uniformly define the past. During the same

Northern Province region	Children and youth	Adults	Mode of life	Religion	Literate	Illiterate	Total
Ncheu	61	18	79 Asiatic	79 Muslim	7	72	79
Dedza	19	18	17 European, 11 Asiatic, 9 African	22 Christian, 12 Muslim, 3 Pagan	13	24	37
Lilongwe	36	13	9 European, 31 Asiatic, 9 African	14 Christian, 35 Muslim	15	34	49
Dowa	38	4	9 European, 8 Asiatic, 25 African	11 Christian, 11 Muslim, 20 Pagan	4	38	42
Kota-Kota	11	7	1 Asiatic, 17 African	3 Christian, 15 Muslim	1	17	18
Mzimba	8	0	1 Asiatic, 7 African	3 Christian, 3 Muslim, 2 Pagan	0	8	8
West Nyasa	8	7	9 Asiatic, 6 African	9 Christian, 5 Muslim, 1 Pagan	6	9	15
North Nyasa	13	10	4 European, 3 Asiatic, 16 African	13 Christian, 3 Muslim, 7 Pagan	16	7	23
Northern Province total	194	77	39 European, 143 Asiatic, 89 African	75 Christian, 163 Muslim, 33 Pagan	62	209	271

TABLE 6.3. 1943 "Anglo-Indian-African" census figures for the Northern Province according to age, mode of life, religion, and literacy. "Anglo-Indian-African" referred to the brief name change of the Anglo-African Association to the Anglo-Indo-African Association during the early 1940s. Categories listed (e.g. "Pagan" and "Asiatic") are in the original documentation, though I have changed "Mohammedan" to "Muslim" for the sake of formatting. It is significant to note that the population was predominantly Asiatic (in terms of mode of life), Muslim, and illiterate. It is also important to note the lower total population figure for the northern province as compared to the southern province. NAM, S20-1-1-1, folio 21a.

Southern Province region	Children and youth	Adults	Mode of life	Religion	Literate	Illiterate	Total
South Nyasa	81	51	5 European, 11 Asiatic, 116 African	29 Christian, 86 Muslim, 17 Pagan	25	86	132
Mlanje	95	37	5 European, 43 Asiatic, 84 African	28 Christian, 51 Muslim, X Pagan	58	54	132
Blantyre	428	448	145 European, 98 Asiatic, 203 African	284 Christian, 69 Muslim, 93 Pagan	159	187	876
Zomba	95	55	16 European, 14 Asiatic, 25 African	24 Christian, 16 Muslim, 15 Pagan	29	89	150
Upper Shire	34	9	1 Asiatic, 8 African	5 Christian, 4 Pagan	3	30	43
Cholo	83	31	35 European, 39 Asiatic, 40 African	5 Christian, 30 Pagan	6		114
Port Herald	93	38	20 European, 107 Asiatic, 12 African	35 Christian, 84 Muslim, 20 Pagan	66	73	131
Southern Province total	909	669	226 European, 313 Asiatic, 488 African	410 Christian, 306 Muslim, 179 Pagan	346 (incorrectly listed as 446 in the original)	519	1,578 (incorrectly listed as 1,586 in the original)

TABLE 6.4. 1943 "Anglo-Indian-African" census figures for the Southern Province according to age, mode of life, religion, and.literacy. These figures are incomplete, with the "mode of life" numbers and "literate/illiterate" figures at times not adding up to or exceeding the total population numbers. I have reproduced these numbers as reported in the census, occasional colonial inaccuracies included, except when calculating total population figures (i.e., excluding the numbers for mode of life, religion, and illiteracy/ literacy). It is significant to note that the majority of those counted were children and youth, most maintained an African mode of life, were Christian, and were illiterate. This reporting may likely have been biased to justify colonial inaction on legally ruling Anglo-Africans as uniformly non-native in status. NAM, s20-1-1-1, folio 21a.

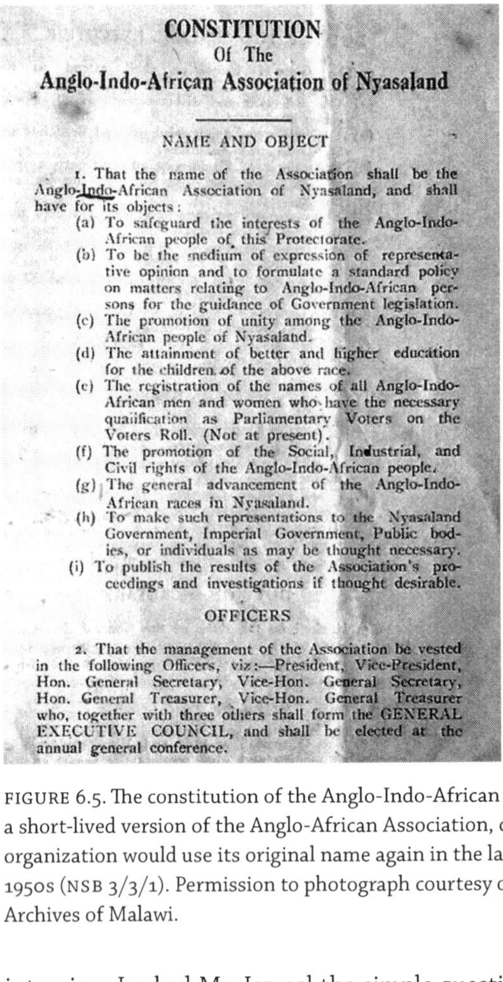

CONSTITUTION
Of The
Anglo-Indo-African Association of Nyasaland

NAME AND OBJECT

1. That the name of the Association shall be the Anglo-Indo-African Association of Nyasaland, and shall have for its objects:
(a) To safeguard the interests of the Anglo-Indo-African people of this Protectorate.
(b) To be the medium of expression of representative opinion and to formulate a standard policy on matters relating to Anglo-Indo-African persons for the guidance of Government legislation.
(c) The promotion of unity among the Anglo-Indo-African people of Nyasaland.
(d) The attainment of better and higher education for the children of the above race.
(e) The registration of the names of all Anglo-Indo-African men and women who have the necessary qualification as Parliamentary Voters on the Voters Roll. (Not at present).
(f) The promotion of the Social, Industrial, and Civil rights of the Anglo-Indo-African people.
(g) The general advancement of the Anglo-Indo-African races in Nyasaland.
(h) To make such representations to the Nyasaland Government, Imperial Government, Public bodies, or individuals as may be thought necessary.
(i) To publish the results of the Association's proceedings and investigations if thought desirable.

OFFICERS

2. That the management of the Association be vested in the following Officers, viz:—President, Vice-President, Hon. General Secretary, Vice-Hon. General Secretary, Hon. General Treasurer, Vice-Hon. General Treasurer who, together with three others shall form the GENERAL EXECUTIVE COUNCIL, and shall be elected at the annual general conference.

FIGURE 6.5. The constitution of the Anglo-Indo-African Association, a short-lived version of the Anglo-African Association, circa 1942. The organization would use its original name again in the late 1940s and 1950s (NSB 3/3/1). Permission to photograph courtesy of the National Archives of Malawi.

interview, I asked Mr. Ismael the simple question as to whether he had a good life or not. "I had a good life. . . . I was one of the fortunate or lucky men who had European friends. People like the district commissioner came to my house and so on," he reflected. "I think I've been one of the lucky men all the time. . . . I've been among friends, European friends, Indian friends, and Africans. . . . I've had a good life. . . . Things have not been difficult for me. . . . Not like other friends who were disappointed in many things."[115] Although I had hoped to see and interview him once more, I was never able to again.

CHAPTER 7

:::

LOYALTY AND DISREGARD

::

It was represented to us that the Coloured communities are under some
disability in that, for certain purposes, they are regarded as forming part of the
native, rather than the non-native, population. The circumstances under which they
are thus placed bear especially hard upon the more enterprising amongst the
Coloured peoples, and apart from any question of closer co-operation or
amalgamation their position is one which calls for sympathetic treatment.
— Bledisloe Commission, *Rhodesia-Nyasaland Royal Commission Report*

"It is an established fact that a newspaper has a powerful tendency for influencing the thoughts of the people, the modern inventions which amplify propaganda have been used in recognition of the very great power
of the Press in our present stage of evolution," declared an editorial in the
Rhodesian Tribune, a Eurafrican periodical published in Southern Rhodesia
during the years immediately after World War II. "The *Rhodesian Tribune* is
divorced from all party disputes, it is just a powerful instrument of imper-
sonal journalism — devoted to the welfare of the community as a whole —
one community. . . . We appeal to every member of the community to support the *Rhodesian Tribune*, our first national community magazine, and let
us go forward and help to create that better social order which is the hope
and aspiration of the common man the world over."[1] These sentiments are
reminiscent of the later views of Benedict Anderson regarding the creation
of national communities through modern print culture.[2] This chapter applies this argument to community formation under colonial rule. It focuses
on how Eurafricans in Southern Rhodesia fought against social and political marginalization by making appeals to the government through the in-

strument of print media. The previous chapter examined racial descent as an issue struggled over given its implications for social identity and political status. This chapter scrutinizes how the politics of heritage and status shaped and were shaped by urban cultural life. Drawing from the influence of Terence Ranger, it is a study of invention.[3] More specifically, it appraises an unofficial culture, to use an expression of Karin Barber's, that emerged in Southern Rhodesia to provide a realm of self-determination for communities of multiracial people that resided in Salisbury and Bulawayo.[4]

The initial purpose of the *Rhodesian Tribune* (1945–50) was to create a new reading public. Published in Salisbury and edited by Ronald A. D. Snapper (born in 1916), a prominent Eurafrican leader, it intervened in a segregated public sphere that was fundamentally defined, if not rendered impermeable, by social boundaries of racial inclusion and exclusion.[5] Colonial urban space more generally was a place of both settlement and un-settlement—struggled over physically, but also discursively and symbolically through the production and dissemination of certain types of social knowledge.[6] Newspapers and magazines were a vital part of this process, providing an effective means of relaying political ideas and proposing strategy, in addition to reporting everyday cultural life.[7] The *Rhodesian Tribune* can be situated in this context. It formed part of an emerging political culture between the dominant and the residual, to paraphrase Raymond Williams.[8]

Published by the Euro-African Patriotic Society (EAPS), a petit bourgeois organization established in 1944, the *Tribune* was a political and cultural periodical that attempted to generate a bounded groupness among Eurafrican and Coloured Rhodesians.[9] It was the first and last publication of its kind in terms of its focus on multiracial people, the depth of its coverage, and the quality of its social and political analysis. Like the Anglo-African Association of Nyasaland, the EAPS was founded as an advocacy group, surfacing in the wake of Southern Rhodesian organizations like the Rhodesia Eurafrican Vigilance Association (established in 1925), the Rhodesia Cape Afrikander Association of Bulawayo (1928), the Cape Afrikander Population of Salisbury (1929), and the Coloured Community Service League (CCSL, 1931).[10] The founding of these organizations should be attributed not only to population growth, but also to the early existence of schools that introduced literacy and addressed the more general needs of Coloured and Eurafrican children. St. Cyril's School (established in 1900) was the first, followed by, among others, the Church of Christ Day

School (1907), the Bethlehem School (1912), the Salisbury Coloured School (1916), the Embakwe Coloured School (1921), and the St. John's Coloured School (1924).[11]

Similar to the Anglo-African Association, these organizations that were founded between the world wars challenged the Rhodesian government to provide various forms of support. Divisions surfaced, however, during the 1930s and early 1940s between Coloured Rhodesians, who located their roots in the Western Cape, and Euro-African or Eurafrican Rhodesians, who were the children of local African-European couples. Indeed, Southern Rhodesia proved to be a regional borderland for the intermingling of these two types of multiracial people. This point is vital to grasp. The microhistorical differences and partisan conflicts that surfaced between these two sections of the population underscore the problem of essentializing multiracial identity under the rubric of *Coloured* in Southern Rhodesia and elsewhere in the region. Issues of terminology and self-naming were actively debated in the pages of the *Tribune*, with vocal resistance against the routine use of the category *Coloured*. The terms *Eurafrican* and *Coloured* were not synonymous in the minds of community members during this period. Yet there were concerted efforts to define and mobilize a sense of unity. The *Tribune* articulated sentiments of affiliation and loyalty to the Rhodesian government and the British Empire through a political language similar to that found in Nyasaland between the world wars—a genealogical imagination that once more demanded material benefits as well as civic recognition through public respect and political entitlement. But, in contrast to Anderson, the political community imagined was also imperial, not simply national, in orientation. Moreover, competing genealogical imaginations surfaced, one citing local ties of patrilineal kinship and another historical origins in the Western Cape. The animated discussion in the *Tribune*'s pages consequently underscores how idioms of kinship and genealogy emerged as regional, not simply local, political tools, indicating once more uncustomary political subcultures that aspired toward a higher status under colonial rule.

: **A WIDER HORIZON** :

World War II had a profound impact on the political landscape of Southern Rhodesia. It revived African political mobilization through new possibilities of conjoining labor activism with African nationalism.[12] There was a concurrent shift in settler politics and Colonial Office policy. The 1930s witnessed the stabilization of segregation and with it the consolidation of the United Party's political power, under the leadership of Godfrey Huggins. The United Party's platform centered on the idea of separate development—the so-called two pyramid scheme—that rationalized segregation yet sought economic growth and, in principle, a sense of parity between white settler and African interests. Competing with this trend was discussion of regional *amalgamation*—a term used at the time—that would integrate the Rhodesias and Nyasaland into a single political entity. Calls for this idea had occurred as early as 1931, in the wake of the 1928 Hilton Young Commission. In 1938 the Bledisloe Commission—named after Lord Bledisloe, a former governor-general of New Zealand—was launched to investigate this political option. The commission found that Northern Rhodesia and Nyasaland shared characteristics of demography and state constitution that made their union plausible, but Southern Rhodesia contrasted both so much that its inclusion would need careful planning. Momentum toward union increased in 1948 with the reelection of Huggins, who had embraced amalgamation, as Southern Rhodesia's prime minister and with the National Party's coming to power in South Africa and implementing its apartheid policy. Developments in South Africa made Huggins seem more liberal in comparison. And they encouraged the Colonial Office to take more seriously the idea of amalgamation—a strategy that could bolster British influence in southern Africa as well as generate a positive image of political liberalism in the face of South Africa's new conservative order. In 1949 the first meeting of many that would lead to the establishment of the Central African Federation in 1953 was held at Victoria Falls.

The *Rhodesian Tribune* and its organizational sponsor, the EAPS, must be situated in this context of political change. Multiracial people presented a challenge to segregation, as discussed in part II. They viewed regional amalgamation as potentially creating opportunities for them. The *Tribune*'s masthead itself marked these intentions, with its three objectives—"opportunities, citizenship, co-operation"—printed just above a rising sun (see figure 7.1). The EAPS took as its motto René Descartes's *cogito ergo sum*—a distinct assertion of self-consciousness—and its optimistic slogan was "the dawn of a new day." It had eight official objectives, the first four being to "formulate a culture, whereby the community could develop racial pride and responsibility"; to preserve "our Racial identity"; to "acquire the correct and acceptable definition of persons of European

FIGURE 7.1. The masthead of the *Rhodesian Tribune*, August 1945.
Permission to photograph courtesy of the National Archives of Zimbabwe.

and African parentage, descent and origin which will honourably aid in the attainment of the fundamental rights of the community"; and to critique the prevalent use of three existing terms, namely "half-caste" (which "places a stigma on the people"), "Coloured" (which "applies generally to nondescripts"), and "Non-European" (a term "which is vague and misleading").[13] The EAPS sought the "abolition" of these "ambiguous terms."[14] The remaining four points addressed community welfare—the importance of charity, financial independence, and community solidarity—and the broad need to "promote a programme of racial development, education and culture as will honourably aid in the raising of the general status of the Euro-African community in a manner befitting their fathers' heritage."[15] This was condensed into a pledge that members of the EAPS took, to be "citizens of Southern Rhodesia [in order] to maintain the heritage handed down to us by our fathers" and to work toward having the term "Eurafrican" become a "National Name" since "it is our heritage."[16]

The inaugural issue of the *Tribune* outlined the situation within the Eurafrican community and the reasons for the publication's creation. It offered both an internal view of the community in Southern Rhodesia and a regional perspective on the rest of British Central Africa. With the intention of "opening the eyes of all citizens of the Rhodesias and Nyasaland," an editorial in the first issue sought to address matters facing the "Eurafrican race," among them the need for "co-operation" and "self-help" in the context of "domestic cleavages and feuds." "It is not merely a question of diversity of opinion in the definition of the community, and of warring out-looks," the editorial noted, but the existence of "a thought vacuum, without ideals, faith, and a sense of belonging" that created "supreme peril" for the community's future—which accounted for the *Tribune*'s Cartesian motto about the importance of active self-realization.[17] The *Tribune* intended to serve as a public platform for the Eurafrican community, to "give voice to its aspirations and feelings" and provide "an intelligent survey of the com-munity's peculiar position in the life of our country, and perhaps in a pan-Rhodesian State including Nyasaland."[18] It thus attempted to be impartial. The use of term *Eurafrican* was not meant to exacerbate tensions between Coloured Rhodesians of South African origin and first-generation Eurafri-can Rhodesians. But this first editorial tacitly suggested that existing ten-sions were a consequence of the former group's reluctance to accept the idea that "the community is a hybrid one, with widely differing elements stemming from various lands."[19] This dissenting group, the editorial noted, "has not yet had sufficient time to sink into Rhodesian soil such roots."[20]

This initial summary of purpose and division animated the issues that followed for much of the publication's life. However, political loyalty to the colonial state united all members of the community. The *Tribune* made explicit its allegiance to the Rhodesian government and the British Em-pire. In the first issue's letter of welcome to Governor William Eric Camp-bell Tait, it stated, "this Society represents the smallest community in this Colony, but our loyalty and devotion to His Majesty the King is and will be found by your Excellency to be no less than that of the rest of the citizens of the Colony."[21] Paternal descent was the key underpinning and rationale for Eurafrican allegiance:

> Euro-Africans possess a natural sense and feeling of pride to be their sub-jects, not by conquest, but by common heritage—strictly speaking the Euro-Africans in the Rhodesias and Nyasaland are 99 per cent Anglo-Africans. This is the secret of their fervent love and affection and loyalty to the throne; it is a virtue inherent from their fathers and forefathers of the British race, who are royalists to the backbone.
>
> Our race that is so uniquely associated by ties of blood and birth to the throne and the British Isles and its people can never be severed from the links which bind us to the King and Great Britain and the Empire.[22]

Such open expressions of loyalty naturally converged with more self-interested community aspirations for a respectability that could transcend

FIGURE 7.2. G. T. Thornicroft addressing an audience, circa 1950. Photograph published in the *Rhodesian Tribune*. Permission to photograph courtesy of the National Archives of Zimbabwe.

racial distinctions.[23] But the *Tribune* and the EAPS actively engaged in a postwar atmosphere of patriotism and devotion to the British Empire — a political gamble, given the parallel emergence of forms of anticolonial activism.[24]

The creation of the *Tribune* did garner visible public backing. The published tributes in its pages included statements from government ministers and the bishop of Southern Rhodesia, as well as avowals of support from prominent members of the Eurafrican community. Among them was Gaston Thomas (G. T.) Thornicroft (figure 7.2), owner of Thornicroft Buildings in Salisbury, from which he operated a general merchant and trucking business, and a founding member of the EAPS. Against the backdrop of the Allied victory in World War II and Eurafrican military service, he noted:

> Though [we are] a minority in the State, we have been able to render service both in the field and otherwise. We have thus contributed in our own small way to the cause for the liberation and freedom of mankind. We are particularly happy that our loyalty and devotion to His Majesty the King and his cause has been second to none in the whole of the British Empire. Our loyalty and services were and are offered willingly and voluntarily, and as such cannot be underrated.[25]

Thornicroft went on to consider what "our position in the makeup of the new world" might be. He viewed the recent Beadle Commission to be an opportunity, "a practical indication of a desire on the part of the State to place the community in its right place as part of the Citizenship of the Colony of Southern Rhodesia. This could and will be achieved if the community is granted full economic status and privileges [such] as those applicable to European citizens."[26] Government interest could therefore lead to full recognition of the "legitimate claims of the community." But "unity of purpose" was needed before "all the privileges of citizenship" could be attained.[27] Thornicroft praised efforts to develop regional connections with Eurafrican communities in Northern Rhodesia and Nyasaland, remarking it was "absolutely essential that we should keep in closer contact with our brothers and sisters in these territories, especially in view of the proposed amalgamation of the three territories at some future date which is inevitable."[28]

These sentiments of local and regional solidarity informed the pages of the *Tribune* in the ensuing years. Indeed, this regionalism can be interpreted as one strategy of negotiating the ongoing tensions between Coloured Rhodesians and Eurafrican Rhodesians.[29] A sense of regional identity tied to first-generation multiracial people served to bolster local demands against the universal application of the South African term *Coloured*. The political emergence of Coloured Rhodesians occurred as early as 1909, when a branch of the African Political Organisation, the most important Coloured political party in the Western Cape at the time, was established by South African party members who had immigrated to Bulawayo.[30] As noted before, there was a flowering of political organizations during the interwar period, with many drawing on a Cape Coloured heritage to the point of excluding those who did not have connections to South Africa. Given this discrimination, other organizations were founded to address first-generation Eurafrican interests, including the short-lived Rhodesia Coloured Society (established in Bulawayo in 1929) and the EAPS after World War II. Professional organizations also appeared, such as the Rhodesia Teachers' League and the CCSL, both established in 1931. Most of the members of these two organizations were teachers, and these new groups shared the outlook of the Coloured Teachers' League of South Africa, even using a version of the latter's motto, "We Must Live for Our Children."[31] For a time, the CCSL was formally affiliated with the African Political Organisation.[32]

But these professional associations also became embroiled in conflict. Class, culture, and geography—in addition to personal ambition—figured into these internal and external divisions, with Coloured Rhodesians viewed as marginally wealthier and retaining South African cultural and geographic ties, in contrast to the Eurafrican population with its local roots.[33] However, the central question of racial identity, which applied to both groups, proved pivotal. Members of the CCSL had expressed concern about definitions since the Foggin Commission released its report in 1934, observing that "the only remedy is to nullify the multifarious definitions and to substitute therefore the following positive definition:- 'That a Coloured person is one of mixed blood originally descended from any two of the following groups: White, Asiatic and African.'"[34] This position stirred vocal debate, however, with Cape Coloured Rhodesians claiming their South African roots, rather than race mixture, as crucial to their identity. In their view, referring openly to histories of interracial liaisons encouraged discriminatory stereotypes of illegitimacy. The CCSL ultimately split in 1943, with Thornicroft, its president since 1933, becoming a founder of the EAPS in the following year.

Despite being more vocal, Cape Coloured Rhodesians comprised only 36 percent of the total multiracial population.[35] Of these, a majority of them were recent immigrants. Their political influence largely derived from their urban middle-class presence and the history they brought with them and promoted. They boasted "of a tradition of close on to 300 years," whereas Eurafricans "have been brought from the kraals."[36] Eurafrican response to this pejorative image was that most of them had "lived with their European fathers, under and according to the manner of Europeans and therefore they can boast of a very much older tradition of western civilization," thus undermining the Cape Coloured attitude that the Eurafrican desire for status amounted to a "kraal fairy-tale."[37] Bitter acrimony continued, though, with the situation once described as "so serious that one might risk a fight if he used a wrong term."[38] Conditions of political nonrecognition and uncertain legal status deepened this persistent division.

But given the multiracial community's small numbers, unity appeared essential. A politics of birth and descent consequently rested at the center of partisan debate in the *Tribune*, with heritage proving to be a decisive factor. A consensus emerged that "the occupation of Africa by the European has created a new Race, generally called 'Half-caste, Coloured and lately Non-European.'" These terms were a source of "self-pity, disillusionment, fear and inferiority complex, and many more negative and vague manifestations." But it was still possible "to formulate a programme for educating the community to think as a group, and to form a common race mind. . . . To formulate a culture, whereby the community could qualify and identify themselves, and command the respect and goodwill of other sections of the community."[39] Terminology was therefore more than an issue of semantics. It also went beyond abstract self-reflection and rhetorical self-making. Such appellations affected legal and civic status and the community's fate in the context of regional change. Common-sense notions of honor and racial respectability additionally emerged.[40] Whether a "common race mind" and "culture" could be attained ultimately depended on reaching a provisional agreement about identities and the histories they told.

: TERMINOLOGY AND ITS COMPETING HISTORIES :

> My point is that this term "Coloured" as its meaning stands in the outside world, applies to persons who are not white. In America it is applied to people of mixed blood, the pure negroes included. In England it is applied to Africans and all non-whites. . . . In South Africa the term "Coloured" is changing to non-European. . . .
> —John Ascroft, "The Term Coloured," *Rhodesian Tribune* (1946)

Use of the term "Coloured" had been forcefully criticized in testimony to the 1945 Beadle Commission. It constituted "a nondescript term under which it was impossible to inculcate any racial pride."[41] Its weakness could be seen in South Africa, "where the Coloureds were divided amongst themselves, where there was no support for any national movement and where they had failed to produce a leader."[42] Indeed, the term guaranteed discrimination on a racial basis.[43] But the responsibility for transforming this situation and its resulting feelings of vulnerability and despair rested with members of the community. Familial descent became a crucial criterion in this regard. J. E. Jones—who was born in 1909 in Southern Rhodesia, educated at Zonnebloem College in Cape Town, served as general secretary of the CCSL, and became chairman of the EAPS—argued for the importance of specificity, explaining that a Eurafrican was "one born or descended from a European on the one side and an african [sic] on the other side," whereas a "Coloured" was characterized as "one who is dark complexioned, having a specious appearance, negro, of some race other than white, not of European descent."[44] In a separate article titled "The Term Coloured," John Ascroft—a bookkeeper who lived in the Arcadia neighborhood of Salisbury, served as the accountant for the *Tribune*, and was Henry

Ascroft's younger brother—argued that its use extended "to any person who is not white, such as the Indians, Japanese and Africans." Echoing his brother's opinions, John Ascroft underscored a sense of patrilateral kinship with the white community. "When the European Pioneers arrived in Africa, there were no white women, and some of them took Native women as their wives, and the Eurafricans were born," he stated. "Some Europeans are still creating more of these children. Those with good fathers are sent to school, and others leave their children to nature's care." But these familial connections had produced limited benefits for the children thus far. "The Eurafricans have no status; they are usually defined to suit the Government," Ascroft noted. "They are non-Africans when it is to their disadvantage, and when it is to their benefit they are told that they are not entitled to that, because they are not Europeans. What are they then? Surely they are Europeans by birth. We all take our race from our fathers. We want our status which affords us 'equal rights' with our fathers."[45]

The Rhodesian terms *Eurafrican* and *Euro-African*—like *Anglo-African* in Nyasaland—therefore proposed a more precise indication of familial, cultural, and political affiliation. They indicated a specific history. But terminology had further implications. It could affect legal status, which in turn could impact social and economic opportunities. Pointing to a broader regional consciousness, the Reed ruling in the case of *Carr v. Karim* was actively cited on at least two occasions in the *Tribune* as a key legal precedent on the importance of origin and its ramifications.[46] Indeed, terminology and its legal consequences was a frequent subject of editorials, articles, and letters to the editor in the *Tribune*. In November 1945 a short article titled "Legal Meaning of Natives and Coloured Persons" discussed the statutory limitations on owning firearms and consuming alcohol based on existing legal definitions of the category *native*.[47] A letter to the *Tribune* in 1946 similarly noted the role of racial descent in defining native and non-native status and its occurrence in a variety of laws. The letter pointed out that persistent state ambiguity created uncertainty for multiracial people.[48] The *Tribune* stressed the difficulties the Beadle Commission had in arriving at a firm definition, criticizing its broad application of the term *Coloured* as a default. "Now if the Commissioners believe that Eurasians, Indo. Africans, Goanese and St. Helenas freely participated in the social and political activities of the Coloured community, they are grossly misinformed," argued one editorial commentary. "These people do not want to be associated with nor do they consider themselves as belonging to the Coloured community. They consider themselves as distinct races."[49] Similarly, the commission embraced "the negative factors, namely, one who has native or Asiatic blood," and thus "their European ancestry is completely ignored." In contrast, using the term *Eurafrican* would enable the "discarding [of] the ambiguous term Coloured."[50] Others, however, "felt that they would be drawing themselves backward" since "the adoption of the term Eurafrican would mean advertising one's [African] origin." These dissenters preferred the word *Coloured* since it did not have "any specific definition."[51]

These debates over definitions renewed sentiments of paternal descent and political association with the Rhodesian government in the postwar period—a time defined by emerging possibilities of self-determination. Feelings that the "world is changing" and Eurafricans "are human beings and not animals which must be given a name" generated urgency and frustration, with people unwilling to accept the government's imposing "one term on the other."[52] The *Tribune* praised the Beadle Commission for "condemning the wicked Foggin Report, which has retarded our progress [by] a generation."[53] But this conflict over terminology and its different histories undermined a sense of bounded groupness. "The terms 'Coloured' and 'Eur-African' are different names for the same community," one article noted. "They are names for the same idea that has animated the minds of the Eurafrican and Coloured leaders of to-day."[54] In December 1945 and January 1946, the Coloured-Eurafrican League of Southern Rhodesia was formed to attempt reconciliation through "a three-fold programme of personal and national development in harmony with the progressive life of the Colony"—an effort that had limited results.[55] The *Tribune* itself became a forum for efforts at compromise. Some proposals were fanciful, shot through with a bleak sense of humor. "Let us face the truth, and that truth is: We are all classified under the general term 'Coloured.' Let us then, for the sake of our children, come together as a united community," urged one article. The writer subsequently recommended "that in place of 'Coloured' we adopt the term 'Heterogenean.'" This neologism referred to "a person of mixed race, originally descended from two or more of the following: White, Asiatic and African," thus achieving resolution through a new expression.[56] Other commentators took a more serious stance. The "battle of definitions" could be resolved only through a proper understanding of history. "The study of the history of one's origin and its place in the world has an intrinsic value of its own equal to that of one's country or more," argued one pseudonymous group of writers called the Magi, "for on the one hand the function of history is to provide training for citizenship. Without racial background, citizenship of any kind is impossible."[57]

Efforts at "putting their house in order" were therefore pursued, to "formulate a definite programme which embodies the maximum of imagination of unity consistent with the maximum of realism."[58] But rapprochement remained elusive. The term *Eurafrican* continued to draw scrutiny for its approximation to an African identity. Arthur S. Rhoades, chairman of the Eurafrican Patriotic Society of Matabeleland, noted: "I have heard many people say that the Eurafrican from the reserve is a menace to the Coloured people, and that they reduce wages and live like Africans, but have they ever tried to study the Eurafrican who has just come into town? He has no friends, and the only one who can help him, [sic] is the African. The first wage of ten pounds is a fortune to him after having been exploited by farmers or miners at four pounds per month."[59] Others viewed the term as simply too limited to unite a community. The "multiplication of groups within a community" is a "sociological eventuality," argued one article, and has questionable benefit. "Simply, the Cape Coloured, Eurafrican and St. Helena groups all face the same oppressive laws throughout Southern and South-Central Africa. . . . It is not a matter of a greater or lesser degree of Europeanised blood, honourable birth or noble parentage that will bring into correct democratic alignment our anomolous [sic] existence; but an unmistakable policy of united effort and indefatigable campaigning for the abolishing of all colour bars in whatever shape or subtle form these exist: a campaign based upon a definitely evolved policy and programme."[60] Regional possibilities suggested that the Eurafrican Association of Northern Rhodesia, the Anglo-African Association of Nyasaland, and the EAPS and the CCSL of Southern Rhodesia could "amalgamate without sacrificing their identities as separate organisations, under the designation of the South-Central African People's Alliance—(SCAPA)."[61] But such proposals of greater solidarity were met with examples of failed coalitions, such as the discord between the African Political Organisation and the Anti-Coloured Affairs Department Movement in South Africa.[62]

This impasse generated additional intellectual impulses and other political directions—at times opposing each other. One trend focused on the importance of the individual, a strategy that mixed the psychology of the day with the political ideal of the liberal subject. "We are fast approaching an era of 'self' consciousness in our evolution," observed an article. "As a community we are faced by many problems. . . . The knowledge of 'self' is the first step required in the attainment of liberty from ignorance and bondage; the pursuit of freedom, therefore, follows naturally as the result of the realisation of one's racial background."[63] Such suggestions — which roughly paralleled the ideas of Frantz Fanon from the same period and presaged later ones by Steve Biko — were balanced with a more community-centered approach. The idea of a "non-European" coalition received some attention, the expression originating from South Africa through the Non-European Unity Movement (NEUM), a Trotskyite organization connected to the Anti-Coloured Affairs Department Movement established in Cape Town in 1943. The author who advocated individual self-empowerment noted "the alarming increase of the term Non-European," describing it as "positively a menace to the posterity of the Eurafrican people in Central Africa." It would be "the beginning of serious trouble for the two-pyramid policy in the Colony," since it would encourage communism, an ideology "admirably suited to the Africans as a basis of incitement to organise strikes and generally to attack the Europeans."[64] Non-Europeanism was consequently viewed as a "disguise" that concealed a revolutionary perspective antithetical to the loyalism of the Eurafrican community.[65] Moreover, similar to the word *Coloured*, the term *non-European* once again negated ties with the white community. Still, some used it to argue that political alternatives should be pursued if "Europeans continue to deny Eurafricans their fathers' rights and force them to unite with the non-Europeans."[66] Indeed, white Rhodesians preferred that people of "mixed" race background "take vague terms, so that their relationship [with whites] should be extinct" rather than embracing "the term 'Eurafrican' [which] maintains that relationship." The state did not want to be "responsible for all the Eurafricans suffering in the Colony, as the result of miscegenation."[67]

These debates expanded into broader questions over race and its uses. Racial difference cut both ways — enabling community solidarity but also reinforcing patterns of exclusion that worked against community interests. The views expressed in the *Tribune* largely reflected the existing policy of segregation that established a hierarchical, yet allegedly evolutionary, racial structure.[68] "The white race had the advantage of being the first race prepared by circumstances for the requirements of civilisation," suggested one article, while "other races such as the Black, if given the opportunity, are found to adapt themselves very readily."[69] This capacity for change encouraged social and political hopes. "Racial and physical differences will disappear in assimilation. . . . Opportunities will be equal," commented the same writer. "Only true superiority will then exist. This will be superiority of the intelligence and initiative of the individual. Such will be found among people of all different racial descents. The idea of racial superiority will then . . . [be] relegated to the place of inglorious myths."[70] This possibility of assimilation affected a range of issues. There was some criticism of "half-caste" children, for example, as a "malignant growth" and "a veritable menace to the body politic of the community."[71] But other opinions considered retrieving such children from villages and educating them.[72] These debates contested specific state measures such as the Education Act of 1938, which barred children living with their African mothers from attending school due to a lifestyle criterion. The first-generation nature of many Eurafrican people, children and adults alike, signaled both the possibility of assimilation as well as the limited vitality of the community more generally, given its historical brevity.[73] Voices materialized against Eurafrican intermarriage with African women and for group endogamy instead, despite parallel declarations that tribute "must be paid to the African mothers for the supreme sacrifices they were called upon to make."[74] The predicament over origins and affiliation therefore surfaced once more, with the perception that "Eurafricans are hemmed [in] between two major races— Europeans on the paternal side and Africans on the maternal side."[75]

This gendered epistemology contributed to additional differences. "The Indo-Africans are those born between Indian fathers and African mothers. We notice that in many instances the Indo-Africans do not suffer the same colour discrimination that the Eurafricans do," commented John Ascroft. "The Indians and the Indo-Africans are of the same colour; most of them live together with their fathers and are legally called Indians. It is advisable that the Indo-Africans should not encourage any racial distinction because they enjoy the rights and privileges of their fathers." This dynamic informed the desire that Eurafricans avoid "mixing politically with the Asiatics and the Africans, or mixing socially with the Africans," since they did not wish to pose "any hostile front against the Europeans, who are our fathers." "It will be beastly if we were to fight and kill our fathers," Ascroft argued. "Our case before the Europeans is that they are responsible for our creation. They must do something for us and not leave us in misery."[76] But others disagreed. A letter to the *Tribune* by "God's Step-Son"—a reference to the "distant relative" attitude toward multiracial people captured in Sarah Gertrude Millin's racist novel *God's Stepchildren* (1924)—argued:

"We complain of colour prejudice and yet display it to the fullest among ourselves! Why should we push aside the Africans and Asiatics who share our grievances and who, through decency, avoid . . . social associations with us—instead we give the men who have ill-treated us and [who are] responsible for our creation the soft-down chairs, heart and soul any time." The writer contended that "unless we try to eliminate that colour distinction inherited from the white men our progress will prove fatal eventually."[77] Another writer similarly urged that Eurafricans and Indo-Africans "have both got African mothers, and I, therefore, see no reason why there should be strife. . . . We are nephews and cousins; we all have African mothers. . . . We cannot be honoured by our fathers—the Europeans—and other races of distinction if we do not build a strong force against this unmoral doctrine of discrimination between cousins and nephews." Emphasizing the framework of family, the writer continued: "No sane people can have respect for a family which is always at loggerheads with one another. . . . We stand a better chance than our African uncles and mothers, and yet we use this opportunity to create hatred from within ourselves."[78] These last remarks capture the genealogical imagination at work—and its limits. Despite their potential uses and putative meaning, affective connections alone could not guarantee community cohesion.

: IMPERIAL FORMATIONS AND CULTURES OF CONSENT :

The issues of racial identity and affiliation addressed by the *Tribune* contributed in turn to its readers' sentiments of political loyalty toward the Rhodesian government and the British Empire. These sentiments shaped a political subculture of allegiance that in turn influenced a broader cultural life that embraced European styles and standards. Such devotion could also lead to disappointment when it was not reciprocated. This tension between popular loyalty and state disregard generated circular feelings of hope and discontent that animated a number of social issues from education to military service. These feelings filtered through editorials and political commentary, as well as reporting of day-to-day events. Media coverage of social events and cultural life led to a sense of community beyond politics. News announcements of seasonal sporting events and weekend dances, birthdays and wedding engagements, and other such celebratory occasions offered the *Tribune*'s reading public a social calendar that helped transcend their differences. On Rhodes's Day in 1945, the *Tribune* reported that the Unity Hall in Salisbury was "packed to capacity" with a "galaxy of dancers," including "soldiers, visiting Soccer [sic] teams from Umtali and Bulawayo, the local dance fans, and visitors from Gwelo, Rusapi and Gatooma."[79] Such festivities had identifiable political backing—"only the Euroafrican Patriotic Society could provide such a barrage of happiness"— but, community politics aside, the *Tribune* took pleasure in describing how "young people swayed dreamily to the strains of the music, while the older ones preferred to talk far into the night, while sitting on the side lines. . . . These were beautiful moments which will someday be joyously recalled as all Eurafricans stroll down memory's highway."[80]

Dances, sporting events, and other social activities certainly created moments of community harmony.[81] But these vivid depictions of cultural life also conveyed senses of racial etiquette, cultural affinity, and political attachment with the Rhodesian and British governments, with Rhodes's Day in particular celebrating the colonial settlement of Southern Rhodesia.[82] But demonstrations of loyalty touched on recent history as well. Military service was a prime example, given the recent denouement of World War II. In an article entitled "The Shadow of Events," Ronald Snapper (see figure 7.3), an editor of the paper, wrote that "the world must turn its attention from winning the war to winning the peace" and that "each citizen of this one world must be made responsible as his brother's keeper." "A crime committed against one race," he wrote, "is a crime committed against all races. . . . Let your post-war planning lay a foundation for an era of fruitful reconstruction."[83] Such thoughts about the postwar period had promoted Eurafrican involvement in the war. The *Tribune* reprinted a presidential address given by G. T. Thornicroft at the eighth annual conference of the CCSL in Bulawayo in July 1939, in which he argued that the government's decision not to call up Coloured men to serve in the armed forces reflected the idea that Coloured people were "not accorded in this Colony the full rights of citizenship." "I want to assure the Government and the European population of this country, that even though we are denied nearly all the privileges and the right of citizenship in this Colony, which is in fact our motherland and permanent home," Thornicroft stated, "we shall be quite ready and willing in the cause of our King to whom we are equally as loyal and devoted, to give service in any way we may be required, up to the last member of our community." He remarked that their birth status demanded such service, that it was "unfair to look upon the Coloured people as mere British subjects" since "the majority of them are British born on their

FIGURE 7.3. Ronald Snapper and his wife, October 1945. Photograph published in the *Rhodesian Tribune*. Permission to photograph courtesy of the National Archives of Zimbabwe.

paternal side and should, therefore, be looked upon and treated as true British citizens."[84] Thornicroft expressed similar sentiments in a speech in July 1941, claiming that "our loyalty and sincerity is second to none" and voicing the regret he felt that Coloured Rhodesians were "not included in the National Conscription Regulations, which require all British male subjects of European descent to be liable for military service."[85]

Such patriotism in the face of discrimination escalated with the return of the Eurafrican men who eventually did serve. The *Tribune* celebrated the members of the Fifty-Fifth General Transport Company of Southern Rhodesia—who had been to Kenya, Ethiopia, Egypt, and Palestine—which

FIGURE 7.4. G. T. Thornicroft (third from the left) with white officers, who supervised the Coloured Mechanical Transport Company, September 1945. Photograph published in the *Rhodesian Tribune*. Permission to photograph courtesy of the National Archives of Zimbabwe.

included the Southern Rhodesia Coloured Mechanical Transport Company, a unit whose soldiers provided service as drivers and mechanics (see figure 7.4).[86] Approximately 230 Eurafrican and Coloured men had served by the end of the war.[87] Celebrations for returning veterans of this unit were also held in Blantyre, Nyasaland, since some Anglo-Africans had served in it. A party hosted by the Anglo-African Association at the Portuguese Nyasa Hotel concluded with Henry Ascroft, then president of the association, declaring, "Long Live Nyasaland and our Imperial Government."[88] But concerns over veteran welfare soon displaced such pride and revelry, initiating a new litmus test for government assistance with employment, housing, and general social welfare. The fact that such help was slow in coming proved discouraging.[89] Moreover, Eurafrican veterans reported experiencing discrimination in the British Empire Service League, a veterans' organization.[90] These developments paralleled occasional assurances by the Rhodesian government. In a Christmas message to the Eurafrican community, Governor Campbell Tait announced: "There is one very important thing for us who are citizens of the great British Commonwealth to remember now that the war is over. It is this: That if we are to enjoy the peace for which we have fought so long, then we must pull together. . . . We must live together in unity. We must all go forward together in this country of ours to make it a united and happy land, able to play its part in the reconstruction of the world."[91]

These expressions of imperial unity were intended to be encouraging. But from a practical standpoint, a number of challenges remained. One article in the *Tribune* asked rhetorically whether Eurafrican war service was being energetically reciprocated through social programs, with an immediate response in the negative—given the government's assistance for the educational needs of the Indian community, but not theirs, and the creation of new segregated housing schemes. "Much is spoken these days of the numerous 'freedoms' for which we were fighting, and freedom from bondage is one of them," the article noted. "It is significant that we have hardly got over the Victory celebrations when our civil right was assailed."[92] The Beadle Commission had placed these social issues in the foreground of early postwar matters. The *Tribune* reprinted portions of the commission's report on several occasions, generating substantial discussion and serious debate. Priorities for the community in the aftermath of the commission focused on employment, wages, education, and a positive definition of Eurafrican status.[93] One of those who viewed the report critically was G. T. Thornicroft, who concluded that it was "in many respects very disappointing," but the Eurafrican community was "grateful" for the attention.[94] The commission's salary recommendations were viewed with particular disdain, with an article in the *Tribune* declaring that the "popular belief that there are three standards of living" is "erroneous." It was seen as unlikely that a Eurafrican would accept the proposed average minimum wages: for a single man, £11 per month; for a couple without children, £17; and for a married couple with children, £25. The commission's recommendations seemed to be "'half doses' of privileges," when "the best solution" would be "equal pay for equal work done."[95]

Still, praise emerged for the commission's work in attracting attention to discrimination and community development. "It now rests with the Government to carry out these recommendations and so bring the Coloured workers within the economic framework of the Colony," an article in the *Tribune* stated.[96] "The Eurafrican community possesses considerable aptitude for skilled work, but that does not mean that they want to be superior to the European skilled worker," noted another article, even though "no avenue of employment should be regarded as a sacred heritage for one section only."[97] Such perspectives highlighted the need for "a sound economic foundation" and made it clear that due to "the stress of discrimination and years of segregation we must foster and develop economic institutions within the community for the community as the first stone in the foundation."[98] Proposals included the formation of a central review board to examine the adequacy of "a man's condition of living" and justifications for a racial hierarchy of wages, since Eurafricans often aspired to a white European lifestyle.[99] The Rhodesian Tribune Foundation and the New Era Investment Corporation were subsequently established with a capital of £15,500, a substantial figure, to provide financial support for the community. "We are faced by four cardinal tasks, turning suffering into achievement, servitude into freedom, egotism into patriotism and dispersion into unity," noted one editorial in the *Tribune*. "In our day of crass economic necessity and strained social demands, self-expression is smothered in uncongenial toil. Natural born artists are made mechanics, natural born business men are made labourers, and many other categories."[100] These aspirations for betterment resulted in a meeting between the CCSL, the EAPS, and government officials over the Beadle Commission's report in May 1947. The government accepted many of the commission's recommendations for increasing education, housing, and job opportunities, reinforcing a sense of political possibility.[101] For the members of these advocacy organizations, these interactions reassured repeated sentiments of affiliation with the Rhodesian government.

: A "NEW BLOODED EMPIRE" :

The most symbolic indications of this political loyalty and alignment occurred in more celebratory moments. When the British royal family visited Salisbury in March 1947 (see figures 7.5 and 7.6), representatives of the CCSL and the EAPS attended the arrival of King George VI, Queen Elizabeth, Princess Elizabeth, and Princess Margaret with Eurafrican veterans of World War II.[102] "Hundreds of Eurafricans had streamed into the City from the bundu," reported the *Tribune*, "to pay homage to a beloved Family."[103] This imperial identification took hold regionally. Ambitions surfaced regarding the creation of intercolonial connections, with the anticipation that the *Tribune* could become the official organ for Eurafrican communi-

FIGURE 7.5. King George VI inspecting Eurafrican veterans in Salisbury, 1947. Photograph published in the *Rhodesian Tribune*. Permission to photograph courtesy of the National Archives of Zimbabwe.

FIGURE 7.6. G. T. Thornicroft greeting Princess Elizabeth in Salisbury, 1947. Photograph published in the *Rhodesian Tribune*. Permission to photograph courtesy of the National Archives of Zimbabwe.

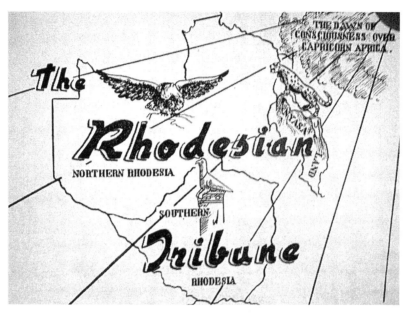

FIGURE 7.7. The new masthead for the *Tribune* in July 1947, with a map including both Rhodesias and Nyasaland and the motto "The Dawn of Consciousness over Capricorn Africa." In September 1947 the motto was revised to "The Dawn of National Consciousness over Capricorn Africa." Capricorn referred to the Tropic of Capricorn. Permission to photograph courtesy of the National Archives of Zimbabwe.

ties across the Rhodesias and Nyasaland (see figure 7.7).[104] Editorials and letters to the editor contributed to this sentiment of regionalism, as did transcolonial news reporting that generated forms of circular discourse — to cite an expression of Carlo Ginzburg's refurbished by Jonathon Glassman — that covered British Central Africa.[105] Henry Ascroft had expressed early support for the *Tribune*. "The Eurafrican community in this country [Nyasaland] is very interested in everything which will promote the welfare of the entire race in this country and the two Rhodesias," he wrote. "There is no reason why the Eurafricans in all the three countries should not come together and . . . ameliorate their lot."[106] Eurafricans should be "prepared for the day when [regional political] amalgamation will be an accomplished fact," he stated, and he recommended that a conference in Salisbury to assemble regional interests should be held. The *Tribune* would have "a good circulation in Nyasaland" and be useful for reporting on "the activities of the communities in the three territories."[107] Jack A. Thornicroft (see figure 7.8) — a businessman involved in tobacco and residential

FIGURE 7.8. Jack A. Thornicroft, October 1945. Photograph published in the *Rhodesian Tribune*. Permission to photograph courtesy of the National Archives of Zimbabwe.

property in Fort Jameson and president of the Eurafrican Association of North-East Rhodesia — expressed similar support: "In the past the terms 'Coloured, half-caste' denoted something low, despisable and uncivilised, but to-day we have evolved a more dignified term, viz: Eurafrican, and with it we hope to give our people a new dignity and a new pride of race."[108] A federation of these organizations was subsequently proposed by another letter writer, since the *Tribune* had "awakened the spirit of every Eurafrican in the Colonies . . . and many of us are surprised at the number of Eurafricans there are in these Colonies. Can we not be better off if we unite? Or should we wait for the Governments of the Rhodesias and Nyasaland to amalgamate first?"[109]

Questions quickly arose about how to attain regional solidarity. One dimension consisted of direct personal connections. The brothers John and Henry Ascroft helped to link Salisbury and Blantyre, their respective homes. G. T. and Jack Thornicroft were also brothers—their father was H. S. Thornicroft, a British district commissioner—with Fort Jameson, Northern Rhodesia, being their place of birth.[110] These transcolonial family ties gave substance and motivation for a regional approach. Indeed, the achievements of local activism encouraged broader ambitions, with the *Tribune* playing a vital role in publicizing them. The *Tribune* reported the appointment of three members of the Anglo-African Association, including Henry Ascroft, to serve on the Eurafrican Education Advisory Committee in Nyasaland in 1945—a clear victory, given the association's repeated petitions during the 1930s.[111] This local accomplishment stirred further aspirations. In an article published later in 1945 on the topic of regional unity, Ascroft wrote: "There is that glittering star now, shining before us, which we must seize if we must secure the future of our children through an organisation—a Federation of Associations—which will be capable of voicing for the people in a constitutional and loyal way." "Nyasaland is a very beautiful country to see and live in," he continued, with characteristic flourish. "I am sure you will like it, for it is a country of British ideals and each section of its community is now busy building up a beautiful future befitting the glory of our Great British Empire."[112] However, an article on the Eurafrican Association of North-East Rhodesia noted that "Many of our kinsfolk in neighbouring Southern Rhodesia are unaware that such an Association as the above exists."[113] Jack Thornicroft, as president of the association and a leader of the community, had succeeded in getting a government-subsidized school, separate hospital facilities from African patients, and exemption from liquor laws for Eurafricans on an individual basis. In spite of its small size, Northern Rhodesia's community was held up by the *Tribune* as a model of success. Furthermore, Thornicroft's organization was interested in joining with others. "We must fight to unite and unite to fight" for the purpose of "the upliftment of our race," despite recognition that "the Eurafrican population is small and widely scattered."[114]

Though the *Tribune* praised the Eurafrican Association of North-East Rhodesia for its achievements, challenges remained. Struggles for residential housing and status continued. One particular worry involved an effort to change "details given in the birth certificates of 'illegitimate children,'" with the "detail to be removed or omitted" being "the fathers' names."[115] An editorial commenting on the debate about this proposed change in the Northern Rhodesia legislative council argued that the proposal was "not in keeping with British principles of justice." Moreover, "Europeans who took unto themselves African women did so according to African Law," and consequently "the question of illegitimacy on the part of the children is not properly founded." Not only did European fathers bear responsibility for their children, but "Eurafricans came in with the Europeans, and . . . they are entitled to their fathers' franchise. The proposed Rhodesias and Nyasaland Eurafrican Federation might well consider sending a delegation to England to lay before His Majesty the King the various hardships and grievances of the community in Southern Africa."[116] The *Tribune* reported a "lengthy and lively discussion" on the question of the franchise, centered on the principle of "no taxation without representation."[117]

Similar to the situation in the Rhodesias, a mix of promise and uncertainty defined the politics of the Anglo-African community during the 1940s, as reported in the *Tribune*. On the one hand, good relations appeared: "It is in Nyasaland where the Europeans are sympathetically disposed towards Eurafricans and this has come about mainly because of the close understanding existing between the two sections. It is there where the salvation of the Eurafrican cause lies."[118] A separate Anglo-African school opened in October 1946 with twenty-seven students, fulfilling the wishes and struggles of the 1930s. Bursaries had also been granted for study in Southern Rhodesia and South Africa.[119] Anglo-Africans did not object to being represented by Europeans on the Nyasaland legislative council, since they viewed its members as "their fathers and to that end they must remain part and parcel of the British people and His Majesty's loyal subjects."[120] On the other hand, perceptions of social and political vulnerability persisted. "My experience in Nyasaland is that many Eurafricans are living with Indians, this is likely to lead them astray, and also likely to end in serious racial disintegration which may prove fatal to the constitution of the Eurafrican race in time," commented one writer in the *Tribune*. "Imagine! Since 1941 only one Eurafrican wedding has been recorded! The cause may be due to the policy of the old Missionaries, who wanted every Eurafrican girl to agree in writing that she will promise to marry an African or someone other than a Eurafrican before she could be admitted to a Mission school. This meant that the old Missionaries had a plan in view of annihilating the Eurafrican race by letting them (or forcing them rather) to be absorbed into African or other communities." These fears of decline through "no social life" led some to relocate to Southern Rhodesia.[121]

These intraregional views were balanced with attitudes about the situation in South Africa. The Cape Coloured community was held in respect, given its size and history. But it was also criticized for its political failures, attributed to its perceived disunity.[122] The *Tribune* reported on the NEUM as noted earlier, with a Rhodesian delegation sent to the second Unity Conference held in Kimberley, South Africa, in December 1945. The conference was "attended by delegates from all parts of the Union as well as from Rhodesia, Nyasaland and the Protectorates."[123] NEUM representatives—including Ali Fataar, a well-known figure in the NEUM—would later travel to Southern Rhodesia to discuss their views.[124] Yet the radical Marxist orientation of the NEUM provoked denunciation. "Non-Europeans, or to be precise, Communists . . . these vocabulary pirates level insults at the King. . . . They abuse the King, and yet they are employed by the King's Government," argued one piece in the *Tribune*.[125] Others found the NEUM's position to be a "pseudo-philosophy of liberation" given the "dual status" it presented—being politically "non-European," but socially "Coloured."[126] These views ultimately compromised its potential as a political model. Noting the paradoxes within the NEUM's approach, one writer observed: "It is not fair for Communists to say that Eurafricans are thinking with their blood when they want to preserve their racial identity. The former contend that the latter should forget their European origin and concentrate on the [*sic*] African origin."[127] But the criticism directed at the NEUM and non-Europeanism more generally formed part of a broader set of pejorative views toward Coloured South Africans, undoubtedly a reflection of shifting local tensions.[128] One article in the *Tribune* on the Cape Coloured community referred to its citizens as "Unhelpables." In contrast, the article commented, "Our Coloured Community [in Southern Rhodesia] is not like that. We want our 5,000 Coloureds to become a self-respecting, respected, healthy [and] useful Community."[129] Indeed, the *Tribune* at times argued that its version of Rhodesian politics could offer a solution to the South African situation. "General Smuts is alleged to have said that Eurafricans are an appendix of the European race," one contribution reminded readers. "The wise statesman perhaps foresees that in a world of changing circumstances, and with the Communistic doctrine upsetting the African and Indian political mentality, the Europeans will find that the creation of a [loyal] Eurafrican race is in the best interests of the realm."[130]

Ambivalence about South Africa motivated unity and a sense of political fate located to British Central Africa, a stance reinforced by the political currents carrying the region toward federation. "The salvation of Central Africa depends on the co-operation between the countries which constitute Capricorn Africa. Whether that co-operation must be in the form of unity in the political or economic set-up is a matter for the States to formulate," argued one article in the *Tribune*. "Now as citizens of one of the member States which falls in this category, we must ask ourselves what part we are going to play in the development of our new Empire. We have said that Cecil Rhodes dreamed of the North and we agree with him, because if the countries between the Equator and the Tropic of Capricorn look South for their regeneration that will be a calamity and the end of a new blooded empire."[131] Embracing this idea of a "new blooded empire," Henry Ascroft claimed in a Christmas message published in the *Tribune* that he and others should seek "justice in its true sense, justice towards the child whose father is a European and mother an African; who is the image of the father but because of his pigment is denied all the kind thought of a father who will have nothing to do with this child as Coloured, Eur-African[, or] Non-European and he must live on the fringe of society's good things." This justice could be achieved only after the end of discriminatory legislation in all three colonies and the birth of a new "uniformity in the treatment of all Eur-Africans."[132]

Political movement toward federation, along with newly proposed measures like a 1947 bill to grant Eurafricans the franchise in Northern Rhodesia, renewed hope.[133] New momentum culminated in two regional meetings. Attention focused in particular on the anticipated effects of the British Commonwealth Nationality Act of 1948, a law that introduced new rules and criteria for citizenship.[134] Optimism grew that this act could affect Eurafrican rights, with legitimacy by descent ultimately granted to them.[135] Indeed, there was some government support for Eurafricans to apply for naturalization as British subjects through the 1948 act.[136] Other regional efforts spurred hope as well. A separate legal development occurred in Nyasaland regarding the Affiliation Ordinance of 1946. Supported by the Nyasaland Council of Women, the ordinance recognized the paternal line of ancestry for Anglo-African children and pushed for the support of such children by their white fathers. The Anglo-African Association by this time had embraced as a legal precedent the Criminal Penal Code of 1928, which defined a European as "any person of European origin or descent," in addition to the 1929 Reed ruling.[137] The association also noted that during World War II, many Anglo-Africans had applied for

"British Subject by Birth" passports and received them, leading to cautious optimism about eventually having legal legitimacy.[138] Yet political changes in the region toward federation added a dose of uncertainty to this positive view of the future.

Held in Salisbury in July 1948, the first conference of the Eurafrican Federation of Central Africa was attended by delegates from the Rhodesias, Nyasaland, and Bechuanaland with the single purpose of coordinating regional efforts to achieve "uniform treatment" socially, politically, and economically.[139] The conference noted constitutional changes taking place, and it sought to take advantage of this political moment. "What about ourselves? Must we be excluded from the constitutions of our motherlands and fatherlands?" asked Ronald Snapper in his opening address. He expressed fear about both apartheid and non-Europeanism in South Africa and argued for Eurafrican status as "British Empire citizens."[140] In a major speech reprinted in the *Tribune*, Henry Ascroft offered a history of the Eurafrican people, reciting a historical genealogy that linked them to Vasco de Gama, David Livingstone, and Cecil Rhodes—thus tying their history to the start of European settlement in southern Africa. "We know that they came into existence only after the white man had set foot on Africa and that they are the offspring of the European. If they are of this origin, why have they been confused for so long on their status?" Ascroft asked. "In Nyasaland we have the national status and rights of our fathers."[141] He cited challenges faced by his "kinsmen" across the region. "From the Cape to Chitambo's village [the site of David Livingstone's death] these European descendants have been confused by the word 'Coloured' which was coined to hide the father's identity. . . . We are descendants of the British. . . . We know the English laws on origin and descent," he argued.[142] Ascroft viewed Eurafricans as "the King's loyal subjects" and argued that "blood is thicker than water" and "the pride of their descent" remained strong within them.[143]

Such sentiments were expressed throughout this first conference, as reported in the *Tribune*. The Reverend Leonard W. S. Price, president of the Eurafrican Patriotic and Benevolent Society of Northern Rhodesia, asked: "Can we at this hour fail in our duty as Patriots? . . . The different territories where we come from may divide us in other respects, but we are united under one great term 'EURAFRICAN.'"[144] He referred to the plight of "our cousins" in South Africa and, in a critique of British policy, contended that the "race that disclaims its offspring just because it is of two nationalities is barbarian. . . . Can the British government reflect without shame upon the fact that it has made a third racial problem — and that this third race is left without sound provision if any at all?"[145] Attaining a high-water mark, Eurafrican leaders including Henry Ascroft met with Arthur Creech Jones, the secretary of state for the colonies (1946–1950), in Blantyre in April 1949, who in turn expressed appreciation for "their special difficulties."[146] Similar meetings occurred in Northern Rhodesia.[147] But loyalty and condemnation both were again on display at a second conference held in Lusaka in October 1949. "We are part and parcel of this country, and in terms of our birth we claim to belong to the family of the British Commonwealth. . . . We therefore claim that we be accorded the full rights of citizenship in terms of the Constitution, not on a differentiation basis but on an equal basis with our European ancestors," declared G. T. Thornicroft. He quoted Cecil Rhodes as saying, "as to the Coloured people, that is to those who carry a good deal of white blood in their bodies, I owe them a deep debt of obligation for the work they have done for me in Rhodesia."[148]

Eurafrican opinion consequently gravitated toward support for federation, provided that they were granted new rights that reflected their desire "to be identified with our fathers (Europeans) racially."[149] "Our birth being exactly the same, our treatment at the hands of the governments concerned with our welfare being identical, our grievances, unhappiness, and distrust of the intentions behind the new laws and the whole of European Society in British Central Africa, all of which promised but a bleak future for us in all the territories of Nyasaland and the two Rhodesias, forced us to unite our strength," summed up one article in 1950.[150] On the eve of federation, different political organizations of regional Eurafrican communities therefore found themselves aligning with the momentum of imperial policy, viewing it as an unparalleled opportunity for unifying their interests and finally achieving non-native legal status across British Central Africa.

: COLONIAL CULTURES OF RELATEDNESS :

By the end of its publication run in 1950, the *Rhodesian Tribune* had managed to cover much of the local and regional political mood during the transition period between World War II and the turn toward federation. It enabled a contingent sense of community through its coverage of issues and events — even if that community faced internal divisions and strife.

The *Tribune* also demonstrated the importance of cultural life in the construction of regional identities. Racial descent alone was not enough. The concerns expressed in its pages reproduced themes that had emerged during the interwar period—issues of identity, legal status, legitimacy, and community strength. But it applied them to a postwar period of renewal and future optimism. Civic feelings of loyalty toward the British Empire reinforced this hopeful outlook. Yet the recurrence of issues from the 1930s equally underscored a sense of political inertia and the difficulty in enacting change. Complaints over terminology persisted throughout the life of the *Tribune*. Although some readers became more willing to accept the Beadle Commission's use of the term *Coloured*, other readers and writers still viewed the term as a "negative way of defining people."[151] There were additional concerns about proposed legal measures. The Native Status Determination Act of 1948 in Southern Rhodesia, for example, caused renewed anxieties, particularly a proposed lifestyle component that could exclude Eurafrican children who had limited choice in such cultural matters, thus circumscribing their status from the start.[152] Issues of status and legitimacy in familial and political forms therefore continued into the 1950s. Indeed, the eventual failure to achieve the franchise in Northern Rhodesia was attributed in part to future federation Prime Minister Roy Welensky's argument that Eurafricans were illegitimate, despite repeated Eurafrican claims to the contrary.[153]

But criticism of current policies and advocacy for change also persisted. G. T. Thornicroft, echoing the sentiments of many of the *Tribune*'s readers, concluded that it was "very unjust to define the racial status of a person against his or her will and merely on the grounds of the circumstances or conditions under which such a person is forced to live."[154] Yet Eurafrican aspirations for social and political recognition were contradicted by their own practices of racial discrimination—a situation reflecting what Carlo Ginzburg has described as the "circular, reciprocal influence" between cultures of the subordinate and those with hegemonic power.[155] An inconsistency existed of fearing racism and denouncing it as unreasonable, while simultaneously engaging in parallel practices of favoritism toward whites and prejudice toward African communities—a paradox generated not only by Eurafrican paternal identification but also by colonial state disregard. Eurafrican leaders, writers, and readers were aware of this tension. "It is then that we must use our positive power of discrimination and be sure that we ourselves are not guilty of the very thing we are resenting in others," commented one writer in an article titled "Discrimination" published in the *Tribune* in 1946. "We must guard our tongues carefully so that our words may always show proper discrimination between what is vital, just and essential and that which is non-essential and often rather trivial in the long run."[156] Reasoning with blood carried distinct ambitions of political recognition, social respectability, and economic security—a social contract with regional colonial states based on perceived natural rights. But the uncustomary nature of this genealogical imagination also reproduced the taint of unreasonable ideologies of racial difference and discrimination that, as acknowledged by Eurafrican writing and protest, continued to oppress them.

CHAPTER 8

URBANIZATION AND SPATIAL BELONGING

::

In July 1960 the *Central African Post* reported a growing problem of "over-spending" on the part of Eurafrican families in Lusaka, Northern Rhodesia. Despite a number of them being behind on rent in the Thorn Park neighborhood (see map 8.1), all had a car and "each family employed an African servant."[1] "One Eurafrican employed a houseboy and a nannie," the article continued, "despite the fact that he was in debt with his rent and overspent on his income."[2] Rent was administered by the city council, which had subsidized and built the neighborhood's housing. Rent varied between £14 and £18 per month, yet most families paid only £6 to £10. Enhancing the problem was a lack of employment opportunities, particularly for women, which placed the burden of income on men. Vasco Thompson, for example, was a thirty-three-year-old mechanic who earned £45 a month. With five children between the ages of ten months and thirteen years, Thompson's monthly expenses—including "entertainment" and a "houseboy and nannie" as well as rent—came to £62. Similarly, H. E. Wightman, a forty-seven-year-old electricity meter reader, had a monthly income of £47, in addition to £8 that his eighteen-year-old daughter, Lilian, brought in by working at a kindergarten. Wightman had five children between the ages of two and eighteen, plus a two-year-old granddaughter. His expenses, including the wages of a servant, came to £65. P. W. Fredman, a thirty-four-year-old warehouseman with an income of £50 per month, had three children between two and a half and eight years old. His expenses came to £61, forcing him to buy on credit on top of owing £20 in back rent. Harry A. Thornicroft, also thirty-four, did slightly better: his income of £48 per month as a lubrication bay superintendent, com-

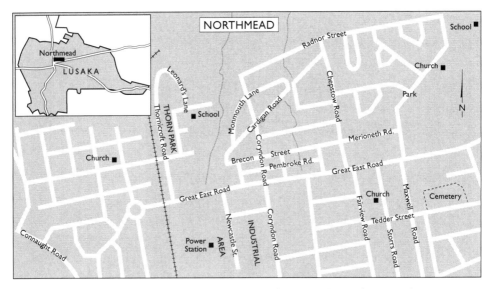

MAP 8.1. Lusaka and the Thorn Park neighborhood. Thorn Park was also referred to as area R.27 by city officials.

bined with his wife's income of £10 to £12 per month through dressmaking, covered almost all of the expenses for his household of six children, ages eighteen months to fourteen years. His monthly deficit was only about £2, but he owed between £12 and £15 in back rent. Both Fredman and Thornicroft were leading members of the local Eurafrican political elite. The descriptions of their circumstances in the *Post* highlighted how the lifestyle of some families in Northern Rhodesia's Eurafrican community exceeded their financial means on a consistent basis, raising fundamental questions about government assistance versus individual responsibility.[3]

This chapter examines the material costs of Eurafrican aspirations during the late colonial period. It tells a story about the municipal politics of poverty, urban development, and civic accountability toward Eurafricans in Northern Rhodesia from the late 1940s to the early 1960s. The preceding two chapters addressed dimensions of racial descent and political culture in establishing identity and status. This chapter turns to the importance of place. Territoriality defined native and non-native categories as much as descent and culture did. Achieving a stable sense of spatial belonging contributed to people's feelings of security, even if beneficial legal measures remained out of reach.[4] It aided Eurafrican aspirations of upward mobility. Indeed, neighborhoods have played an important role in establishing and shaping the histories of multiracial Africans—presenting a type of third space—with District Six in Cape Town and Arcadia in Harare being the prime examples.[5] Like their counterparts elsewhere in the region, Eurafricans in Lusaka faced uncertainty, given their liminal position vis-à-vis policies of urban segregation. Thorn Park, once known as area R.27, provided a measure of hope and stability.

This chapter consequently revisits the role of commissions and the issue of class in defining status, in addition to continuing part III's theme of grassroots activism. Existing scholarship on urbanization in Northern Rhodesia is among the richest in Africa, defining postcolonial Zambia's narrative of modernization.[6] But urban history must be understood as contested rather than teleological, setting a scene of struggle.[7] Concerns about the "urban native" structured labor migration and municipal habitation, often placing African workers within a condition of constant limbo— desired as the main source of labor in towns and cities, but unwelcome as a permanently settled presence. Eurafricans posed a different, if related, challenge given their interstitial racial status. Though many had rural roots, urban connections were equally common among them. Towns were not a place of arrival, nor were villages a place of return. As John Western has written, multiracial people as urban subjects challenged basic assumptions regarding race and place, creating dilemmas of social space and hierarchy.[8] The Eurafrican case in Lusaka reinforces these points. The capital of Northern Rhodesia since 1935, Lusaka became a significant site for urban politics during the late colonial period, a time animated by postwar African nationalism, white political entrenchment, and questions about the costs of colonialism, especially during the period of the Central African Federation (1953–63). Housing proved to be an issue where all three factors intersected, underlining questions of race and displacement that the city government, the central colonial government, and local organizations had to confront to meet the pressing housing needs of the Eurafrican community. This chapter as a result is about the politics of location, but also the location of politics.

: HOUSING AND URBAN POVERTY IN LATE COLONIAL LUSAKA :

The news reports in the *Central African Post* from July 1960 marked the culmination of a particular story that began in the 1940s. Urban housing in Lusaka, as in other parts of Africa, presented an avenue to modern life. Indeed, the paradox of overexpenditure while failing to keep up with rent payments reflected the material costs of Eurafrican aspirations of achieving middle-class status—a situation driven by a desire to approximate themselves with Lusaka's white community rather than the African working class. The expenses described by the *Post*—a newspaper whose readership was predominantly white—included food, entertainment, firewood, water, electricity, child care, cigarettes, car maintenance, and servants' wages, apart from rent. But the larger issue was whether this lifestyle was sustainable—a question that echoed the concerns of the 1945 Beadle Commission in Southern Rhodesia.[9] A month earlier, the *Post* reported that twenty-three Eurafricans in Thorn Park owed £423 in rent collectively, and that a municipal inspection had revealed that "not only are the grounds and surrounds of the houses untidy, but that the houses themselves are in most cases dirty and uncared for."[10] The Eurafrican Society, an organization that represented the interests of the community, was equally aware of the problem, albeit from a different angle.[11] The society had written to the government in April 1959, complaining that the city council was charging too much for rent. The society's members had understood that Eurafricans would not be charged more than one-sixth of their salary. In practice, rent could be as much as one-fourth. Not only did this affect those with housing, but it deterred "many of the lower income group from taking a house."[12]

Yet the issue of rent constituted only one of an intersecting set of concerns. There had long been tensions between the Lusaka municipal government and the Northern Rhodesian central government over costs and responsibility for housing. Thorn Park consisted of thirty houses, including twenty-two recently built for £29,392—the culmination of an extended effort to improve living conditions for Lusaka's Eurafrican community.[13] The incentive for building the new neighborhood reflected years of neglect combined with immediate need. In February 1958 the *Central African Post* reported that "weeks of incessant rain" had taken its toll on "the kimberley brick and pole-and-dagga houses" located at Marrapodi—an authorized African settlement where tenants could pay rent to occupy land— with many Eurafrican homes collapsing (see figure 8.1).[14] By December a number of Eurafrican families had applied to live in Thorn Park, with the central government agreeing to cover 80 percent and the local government 20 percent of the total difference between the cost of rent and one-sixth of the applicant's individual income.[15] This formula had evolved during the mid-1950s, although matching rent estimates with actual costs became an

FIGURE 8.1. Two Eurafrican squatter homes (left and right) in disrepair, 1958. Photograph published in the *Central African Post* (LGH 1/6/23). Permission to photograph courtesy of the National Archives of Zambia.

inexact science. Fearing that they would end up paying more than 20 percent, city officials convinced the central government to raise its maximum level of coverage.[16] The year of 1958 proved to be decisive with all three sides finding common ground. But this one-year snapshot glosses over a complex story of local initiative and bureaucratic maneuvering, underscoring the ways racial status, middle-class aspiration, and financial cost informed and complicated urban planning during the late colonial period.

The parameters of the situation were first established between the end of World War II and the founding of the Central African Federation, in 1953. As in Southern Rhodesia, this period of transition produced opportunity and uncertainty for the Eurafrican community—reflecting renewed state attention to the community's development needs after the war, but also the ambiguous racial politics of the time. During its short life span, the federation attempted to implement a gradualist strategy of new rights and more representation for Africans, but continued power and control for white settlers. These priorities underscored once more the lower-strata marginality of the Eurafrican population vis-à-vis African and British interests. Yet this Federation perspective risks oversimplification at the local level—particularly for one of Northern Rhodesia's most important cities. Initially established as a railway station in 1905, Lusaka was emblematic of colonial urban design, with distinct spaces for white businesses and homes while African migrant workers had only a temporary presence. Pass laws and required identification cards (*situpas*) enforced this order.

However, segregation efforts were far weaker than in South Africa, for example, during the same period. Lusaka's urban development was an ongoing co-creation of white and African interests combined, with squatter compounds and their informal sectors playing a significant role in shaping city life.[17]

The Eurafrican community fit uneasily into this narrative of urban development. During the late 1940s, the Eur-African Association of Lusaka—an organization that preceded the Eurafrican Society of the 1950s—and government officials had focused on a small project of building twelve houses, one of them a boardinghouse.[18] Despite the community's small numbers, Lusaka's representative in the central government legislative council conveyed that Eurafricans had to cope with "very over-crowded conditions."[19] Initial population figures for the community were low—only forty-one Eurafricans lived in the city, according to one estimate—but authorities anticipated the population would increase.[20] Urban census figures were frequently inaccurate, given that their primary concern was employed men.[21] To better assess the circumstances, municipalities across the colony were consulted in 1949 on the status of Eurafrican housing. Lusaka had one of the most challenging situations, though Fort Jameson and Ndola faced similar issues of "degrading" and "inhuman" housing.[22]

By 1950 this concern had become part of a larger effort to address Eurafrican welfare in Northern Rhodesia. The Kreft Commission's *Report of the Committee to Inquire into the Status and Welfare of Coloured Persons in Northern Rhodesia*, released in that year, examined issues such as existing housing and employment based on Eurafrican testimony and government inspections, as discussed in chapter 5 (see figures 8.2, 8.3, and 8.4).[23] "They are not asking for palatial homes, they are not asking for anything to which they are not entitled," commented one government official in the course of these discussions. "I would ask that Government use its influence . . . to do something immediately for the comfort of these unfortunate people."[24] Yet differences quickly emerged. According to one view Eurafrican housing was part of a "much larger problem—that is, the overall question of housing for all sections of the community in this country."[25] The predicament of conspicuous racial preferences consequently arose. "It is really an economic and not a racial question," remarked one official, and the "correct procedure" would be urban zones with housing that offered different rental scales. Such measures "would automatically provide for

House provided for Coloured employees by Nkana Mine (Kitwe)

FIGURE 8.2. Members of the 1950 Kreft Commission inspecting Coloured employee housing, Kitwe, Northern Rhodesia. Used by permission of the National Archives of the United Kingdom (CO 795/170/13).

different economic levels without any racial segregation, which . . . is something to be deprecated on every possible occasion."[26]

The opposition to racial preferences reflected the broader challenges of creating a new multiracial society during this time of transition toward federation. Labor demands of the postwar period had resulted in a shift in attitude toward African migrants, specifically through the 1948 African Urban Housing Ordinance that allowed employers to provide residences for married workers. Four reports and plans in less than a decade—the 1944 Eccles Report, the 1948 Town Planning Scheme, the 1950 Jellicoe Plan, and the 1952 Town Planning Scheme—attempted to accommodate a growing influx of white and African residents, in addition to improving coordination between the governmental and commercial sectors of the city.[27] Still, despite rhetorical claims that racial segregation was being rejected, de facto segregation remained. An early proposal that had Eurafrican interests fall under the existing European Housing Loan Scheme, enabling Eurafricans to apply for home-building loans, met with resistance. Fears of "deterioration" in white areas emerged, with the belief that such a program could lead other racial groups to move in, too. One legislative

FIGURE 8.3. Members of the 1950 Kreft Commission investigating Coloured housing in Ndola, Northern Rhodesia. Used by permission of the National Archives of the United Kingdom (CO 795/170/13).

council member candidly remarked: "We know what happened in Natal and we certainly do not want that here if we can possibly help it."[28] Such racial sincerity spoke in two ways. Though the government should be "thoroughly ashamed of the housing conditions of the Coloured people," it was felt that any special concessions for Eurafricans constituted discrimination against both the African and white communities.[29] Race therefore continued to be a pervasive factor, functioning as a basis for attention and concern, but also offering a rationale for inaction, lest perceptions of unfair treatment be bolstered.

Populist pressure by Eurafricans grew during this period, counterbalancing this inertia. Indeed, local response to the Kreft Commission surfaced in a fashion similar to reactions to the Beadle Commission in Southern Rhodesia. Unlike the mining centers of Ndola and Kitwe, Lusaka maintained a diversity of housing—black municipal townships, employer-provided quarters, and illegal squatter compounds in addition to white neighborhoods—that made housing a distinct political issue as well as

Adshead House - Front view.   Chichele (near Ndola)

FIGURE 8.4. Kreft Commission members viewing another Coloured home near Ndola, Northern Rhodesia, 1950. Used by permission of the National Archives of the United Kingdom (CO 795/170/13).

creating an atmosphere for an urban grassroots politics that contrasted with the labor politics in the Copperbelt.[30] In a letter to the *Central African Post* published in March 1951, C. J. Jones wrote: "We [the] Coloured people of Lusaka are in a great predicament, and our morals are gradually declining due to the lack of homes for families and single people. . . . We hope sincerely that the planned housing scheme will be started as soon as possible."[31] Government discussions continued. The "unhealthy conditions" that Eurafrican people had to endure were "well known or should be" stated one member of the legislative council, with government inaction leaving them to "live under conditions which are a disgrace to Northern Rhodesia."[32] In May officials appeared sympathetic, expressing the belief that the situation was "approaching a crisis" and that "extraordinary measures" would be considered.[33] An August article in the *Northern News*—another newspaper with mostly white readers and the only daily one published between 1953 and 1965—criticized the fact that, despite two commissions in three years, nothing had been done. If this persisted until the next rainy season, "these unfortunate people will not have water, sanitation or housing for another year."[34] By December, the *Central African Post* reported there were "several Coloured people sleeping in their employers' lorries [in Lusaka] because they had nowhere else to go."[35]

Given the predominantly white readership of these newspapers, these depictions should be read as informed by both a political liberalism disapproving of government policy and anxieties about racial degeneracy and public health. Like other media, these newspapers projected certain moral ideals to shape social discourse and political agendas.[36] But solutions beyond government action appeared elusive. The *Report of the Committee to Inquire into the African and Eurafrican Housing Position in Lusaka* (1953) provided further information about and context for the situation, offering an explanation for the continued delay.[37] Lusaka's African population had rapidly increased from 17,000 to approximately 55,000 since 1945. Of these, 24,000 people were adequately housed, with existing plans only accommodating 5,000 more people.[38] A vital need for housing therefore existed to account for an estimated 26,000 people, aside from expectations of 20,000 more over the next five years.[39] These figures contrasted dramatically with the Eurafrican population, estimated by the report to number only 154 persons.[40] This census figure likely reflected only employed Eurafricans, as mentioned before. The majority of the people counted were either government staff or workers in light industry, and only one-fifth—about thirty people—had adequate housing. The report noted that "many families were living as lodgers with other Eurafrican families in houses which were barely sufficient to accommodate the proper tenants."[41] The current location designated for Eurafrican housing had only eight houses, and during the rainy season "the water-table often approached ground level."[42] Sewage disposal was "a major problem."[43] Moreover, current rental rates were seen as "beyond the reach of the majority of the Eurafricans employed in Lusaka."[44] Recommendations included improving sewage, preventing further overcrowding, and exploring an affordable rental or purchase scheme.[45] What became clear was that a sizable subsidy plan was needed—existing Eurafrican incomes alone were not enough to cover living expenses. Any subsidy would have to be shared between local and central governments.

: BUILDING CRITERIA AND HOUSING COSTS :

The 1953 *Report* offered a bird's-eye view of the housing situation in Lusaka. In contrast, local bureaucratic resolutions to the problem largely centered on details. Prior to the report's release, issues of home design, cost, and overall implementation of a plan to begin housing construction had surfaced during the early 1950s. Not only did uncertainty about fiscal accountability between local and central government authorities materialize by the mid-1950s, but indecision affected prosaic material concerns. The initial standards for housing suggested undertones of racial difference, native versus non-native lifestyles, and how such factors took form physically. With Eurafrican housing, "the relaxation of the Building Code should be permitted," remarked one official in April 1950, with regard to "the stability and finish of houses but not to health requirements, relating to light, air and space." "Drainage and sanitation standards as for African houses should be enough," it was decided.[46] Moreover, a "2-bedroom type African house" with fewer square feet was proposed to reduce costs to less than £300 per home rather than upward of £650.[47] By April 1951 construction fees in the bottom range of £200 to £250 had been explored, though the 1950 Kreft Commission's report had recommended expenses between £350 and £500 per home.[48] Further cost-cutting measures included having no electricity and only showers instead of tubs.[49]

Such recommendations, if oriented around pragmatic issues of cost, nevertheless affronted the race and class aspirations of the Eurafrican community. They generated an outcry. In July 1952 leaders of the Eurafrican Patriotic and Benevolent Society complained to government officials that the current houses lacked "a proper kitchen," there were "no ceilings" (with thatch instead) and "no electricity," the houses themselves were "far too small," and in general were "badly built."[50] The government agreed to improve cooking and washing facilities by including stoves, sinks, and "perhaps communal clothes washing points."[51] It also outlined a broader urban vision. First, new houses to be built would be considered "low-income group houses" and "in principle be available for any persons of the low income group irrespective of their race or colour." Second, the government intended to pay for construction, though this initial expenditure would be recovered through rent. Third, Eurafrican employees of the government would receive priority, with the remaining houses to be allocated thereafter. Fourth, a pilot scheme would be implemented first, with twenty houses for Lusaka, twelve for Ndola, and six for Fort Jameson.[52] Accepting higher costs, the government endorsed a three-room house plan costing £1,200 to build, which would include amenities such as water-borne sewage, concrete floors, two beds and mattresses, a dressing table, and basic furniture for the kitchen and living room.[53]

Despite these welcome enhancements, these improvements presented a new challenge. To reimburse the government for the costs, the monthly rent per home would have to be £7.5.0 over a forty-year period. The government would offer an outright grant of £200 per £1,200 house, with the remainder to be paid off through rent under the supervision of local municipal authorities.[54] Tenants were expected to allocate one-sixth of their income for this purpose. But to meet the projected rent, Eurafricans would have to pay more than one-sixth of their average income, which ranged from £24 to £30 a month. As a result, the commissioner for local government felt that it was "of course always tendentious to write of average earnings and the average man but I think it can be accepted that some subsidy will be necessary for Coloured housing. Certainly, in the Union of South Africa most Coloured housing is subsidised."[55] Despite this uncertainty over cost and payment, populist sentiment pushed matters forward. In November Eurafrican leaders wrote the government that "we have no hesitation to inform you that we are nearly drowning and also experiencing very serious road difficulties. . . . Through the dampness we have had several cases of illness. . . . Nearly all the roofs of the houses are leaking and need attention before the heavy rains."[56]

By 1953 a legislative council debate disclosed that the total cost of each house could be lower, at £950, though rent would have to be higher than anticipated—in the range of £9.10—when miscellaneous charges of insurance and maintenance were included.[57] These new figures for new houses did not generate sympathy. The Eurafrican community already expressed "great surprise" at the rent currently charged for "Huts" that were similar to African housing.[58] A firsthand inspection by Lusaka's district commissioner of the current eight houses available in the R.27 area later revealed the disjuncture between rental rates and housing quality.[59] Yet public opinion at this point on the eve of federation, which would be formalized in August, displayed limited compassion. An article in the *Central African Post* in May 1953 expressed a sentiment that captured the broader political mood and implications over the issue:

> We have often pressed the claims of the Coloured people of this country for a fuller recognition of their qualities and for what we consider their rights. They have not been treated with the consideration they deserve. They ought to be British subjects and they should have the vote. Nowadays, in industry they are doing very useful, sometimes excellent, work. They are capable and reliable and their earnings are nearly as high as those of many Europeans. . . . The monthly rental payable is well within

their means. And yet, instead of paying their rents like docile, responsible Europeans, they complain that their houses are no better than many African houses. . . . If well-employed Eurafricans find that they cannot pay the modest economic rent of their houses, let them put the matter before their employers and not ask the ratepayers and the taxpayers to subsidise them. If they wish to be treated as equals, let them behave as equals.[60]

Not only did federation present macroeconomic questions of fiscal viability, but its multiracial political agenda depended on fulfilling its duties for different racial communities simultaneously. Against this backdrop, concerns about and divisions over cost gradually became more pronounced. One legislative council member observed in July 1954:

I have always felt, ever since I first came to this Territory, that the Europeans as a whole owe a deep moral obligation towards the Coloureds of this Territory. . . . It is they as a race that brought them into this world, and it is their duty to look after them. We have heard recently a description of Coloured houses in Lusaka. . . . I cannot emphasise sufficiently my feelings that the Coloured people are a deserted and abandoned race at the present time. Most of them have no recreation, no community hall, no cinemas, no place where they can get together, and the housing generally is absolutely deplorable, and if it is necessary to build uneconomic housing and uneconomic community halls, then in their case, surely, we are only repaying a debt.[61]

Here, a tacit kinship-based sense of responsibility emerged, as discussed in previous chapters. A summary memorandum issued the same month said that because "the special circumstances of the Coloured community create special obligations for the Govt. towards that community," subsidy support should be provided on an annual basis, with the central government covering 60 percent and local authorities 40 percent of the cost.[62]

Despite such positive measures, the Euro-African Patriotic Society, a variation of the earlier organization with connections to the association with the same name in Southern Rhodesia, expressed continued anxiety over housing availability and costs.[63] The society's members believed that "the Government has never admitted responsibility for the provision of houses for Coloured people" and that officials were "distinctly half-hearted about their provision." During a key meeting with officials, the society presented a detailed memorandum stating that the "living condition[s] for

House of Coloured Person - Marrapodi Compound (Lusaka)

FIGURE 8.5. Coloured home in Marrapodi, Lusaka, Northern Rhodesia. Photograph taken during the inspections of the Kreft Commission (1950). Used by permission of the National Archives of the United Kingdom (CO 795/170/13).

the Euro-Africans is shocking. The water supply is obtained from holes dug in the ground and there is no sanitation. Forty of the Euro-Africans live in African's [sic] huts in the Marrapodi Compound, eight sleep in the cars, thirty have no homes whatsoever" (see figures 8.5, 8.6, and 8.7). The memorandum described the existing eight houses as "overcrowded due to lack of accommodation and the willingness of the Euro-African people to help each other." Many had living conditions "infinitely worse than the lower class Africans."[64] The memorandum also reemphasized the problem of high rent and further cited the lack of welfare generally:

Good houses. Wholesome food and clean water are the assencials [sic] of good health and social stability. It is pointed out that a very large number of the Community, consequently on years of struggling against poverty, neglect and grossly inadequate living conditions had become despondent and demoralised. This is seen in the lack of care and attention of our children and our homes due to no Welfare Officers and clinics. We ask

Detached Kitchen of above house   (Lusaka)

FIGURE 8.6. Another view of the same house. Photograph taken during the inspections of the Kreft Commission (1950). Used by permission of the National Archives of the United Kingdom (CO 795/170/13).

the Government to make an outright grant to Local Authorities for the construction of playgrounds, sub economic halls, sport centers and such other projects as may be considered necessary for the Welfare of the Euro-African people.[65]

In response to these demands, officials proposed a new plan allowing Eurafrican individuals to take out twenty-year loans to build their own homes. Loans for as much as 90 percent of the cost of a house would be possible, provided that the borrower could secure the remaining 10 percent. Monthly loan repayments, including interest, would approximate rental rates, though borrowers would own their homes in the end.[66] But

Source of Drinking Water - Marrapodi Compound (Lusaka)
(Note lack of protection.)

FIGURE 8.7. Photograph of a drinking water source in Marrapodi, Lusaka, Northern Rhodesia, taken during the inspections of the Kreft Commission (1950). Used by permission of the National Archives of the United Kingdom (CO 795/170/13).

hesitant views also surfaced, with Tom Sayer, a leader of the Euro-African Patriotic Society, observing that "Euro-Africans would accept the maximum possible Government assistance and would make no effort to better, or even help themselves."[67] Facilities such as a community hall were not approved—even though such services had been provided in African areas—because of the belief that Eurafricans' "underlying trouble was really the lack of sufficient and adequate housing and the consequent hand-to-mouth existence which they were compelled to lead."[68] Such amenities would be established once the housing situation had been stabilized. To justify these proposals, a colonial social welfare officer and Eurafrican leaders inspected several houses in December 1954. Confirming Eurafrican public opinion, existing housing was found to be "poor—there are no ceilings and the walls are very roughly plastered."[69] Many were overcrowded. Twelve children and five adults lived in one three-room house, with each room only ten feet square. Three of the eight houses were occupied by more than one family. A separate inspection found that twenty houses built in a Eurafrican squatter camp were "very poor. . . . Sanitary arrangements are most primitive and the only water supply available is from a crude well."[70] Overcrowding there was not an acute problem, since the houses were mostly occupied by unmarried men and women. But many houses had been built only recently due to "the advent of the rainy season."[71] Some people slept in cars. Other Eurafricans were reported to be living in African compounds. Overall, the need for improved housing appeared obvious. "These people are striving to attain a European standard of living and housing plays a very important role," remarked the welfare officer. "They should be encouraged and helped to uplift themselves."[72]

: POPULAR PRESSURE AND BUREAUCRATIC MOMENTUM :

With these inspections in late 1954 reconfirming the need for action, official inertia was slowly overcome. But disagreements between the central government and municipal officials persisted about the proposed 60–40 plan for sharing the cost. Indeed, an economic downturn that would grip Northern Rhodesia until the late 1950s, postponing the development of African housing, was just taking hold.[73] Lusaka Mayor F. Payne thought that housing "should be a national and not a local government responsibility."[74] He also complained of the difficulty in collecting rent, going so far as to express the wish not to build further housing "even if the Government made available the funds with which it could do so."[75] However, J. R. Brown, the commissioner for local government, argued that Eurafricans "could not be left to stand on their own feet" and that they provided "a useful and low-paid labour force."[76] He observed that working-class housing in Great Britain was subsidized jointly by local municipalities and the national government. Given the Eurafrican community's estimated size, forty more houses would probably be needed. With the central government's views overriding those of the city government, the decision was reached that, despite environmental problems of water drainage, the existing area of R.27 should be developed, since "it was most important to establish the Coloureds in one community as soon as possible." A new plan was to be drawn up by the end of February.[77]

This government action occurred against a backdrop of continued criticism in the local media. In January 1955 articles in the *Northern News* characterized Eurafricans—estimated to total two thousand across the territory—as "forgotten people," with their housing situation being "scandalous" since it was "well known that many are living under the most appalling conditions with a total lack of recreational facilities."[78] This state of affairs in Lusaka was becoming "more acute" daily.[79] Although the community numbered only 300 according to a 1955 estimate, it was expected to double in size soon, with still only eight municipal houses currently available. Yet the report that many residents failed to pay rent in full on current housing did not lead to optimism.[80] An owner-housing scheme, a subeconomic housing scheme, and a plan to sell housing to employers of Eurafrican workers were all mentioned in the media as possible solutions, but financial support from the central government was perceived as the only final means of "rescue."[81] The Euro-African Patriotic Society kept up its pressure on the government, with its chairman, Tom Sayer, arguing that a government loan program needed to take more account of the level of Eurafrican income and their limited ability to pay rent.[82] Moreover, Eurafricans desired that a new location for housing be found—unlike the "bog" where housing currently existed.[83] A letter to the editor of the *Northern News* in February from H. P. Crosby, secretary of the society, put the community's feelings even more bluntly. "Euro-Africans have no social or welfare activities," he wrote. "What they do is just to sit in [a] 10 x 10 roomed house and watch how the meal is being cooked by the mother of a family of 10. We are really God's forgotten children or God's stepchildren on this earth."[84]

By March the city council moved forward with an ambitious proposal to increase the number of houses to 9 per acre to reach a total of 205 houses for the area—191 new houses plus the 14 already built or under construction. Loans would be made for up to 95 percent of the value of the house.[85] By May confidence was being expressed that this more dramatic plan would succeed, though questions remained as to whether there would be enough loan applicants.[86] Through the initiative of P. W. Fredman, the Euro-African Society consequently set up the First Lusaka Euro-African Co-Operative Housing Association in August, which was designed to pool the funds of individual members to secure and pay off government loans.[87] The society expressed its interest in extending the cooperative's membership throughout Northern Rhodesia, noting that it was "the first such [housing] association formed in the history of Euroafricans [sic] in the Territory."[88] Between September and November, the cooperative worked with the government to get loan applications, as well as to address problems such as proper sewage at the squatter compound set up at Marrapodi.[89] In December government officials agreed that working with this association rather than individual applicants would be the most effective approach.[90]

In the meantime, development plans continued to move forward. In 1956 a plan (Plan No. 309/8) was approved for a new Eurafrican residential area in R.27.[91] With the question of Eurafrican housing now fitting into a larger issue of housing for non-Africans as a whole, the *Northern News* reported in October that a census would be taken to account for "all Europeans, Asiatics and Eurafricans without homes."[92] The census would seek information regarding family size, home size desired, and present satisfaction with existing housing. As part of a broader population assessment by the federation, the idea of a census had originated in a debate over African housing beyond Lusaka and in the 1953 report, with 225,000 Africans currently living in urban areas in Northern Rhodesia and 53,000 new houses needed over the next ten years.[93] Housing across the colony was "in a parlous state"—a situation confronting all communities and raising subsequent questions of priority and cost. "The cement that is used in an African house," remarked one official, "is no different from the cement that is used for example, in a European's house or in a Eurafrican's house."[94] With the growing commitment to housing across the federation, some dissenters expressed the fear that "we are heading for the welfare state and the irresponsible attitude of mind which the welfare state has created in Great Britain should be an awful example to us not to encourage it in this Territory."[95]

Continued local pressure managed to dispel these emerging arguments for a time. In March 1956 the *Northern News* repeated the now-familiar refrain that the majority of the Eurafrican community continued to "live in shacks, broken-down hovels of tarpaulin and covered lorries."[96] Despite recent gains, the Eurafrican Society (replacing the previously named Euro-African Society) highlighted Lusaka as doing far less than other municipalities in Northern Rhodesia. The city council had "failed in its duty to the Eurafricans," and current housing in the Thorn Park area remained a health hazard, a "mosquitoes' paradise."[97] "A large proportion of the Eurafricans were becoming despondent and demoralised," the *Northern News* concluded, "and some attempt should be made to lift the community from the morass in which it now lived."[98] In August the central government echoed these sentiments, evincing the tensions and differences of opinion that had surfaced between it and the Lusaka municipal government, with one official acerbically asserting that "the whole history of Coloured housing in Lusaka is one of indifference followed by procrastination followed by muddle." In his opinion, "the problem of the Coloureds is a national problem."[99] E. W. Sergeant, who represented Lusaka and was a member of the 1950 Kreft Commission, called the situation a "white man's burden," that "we are responsible for them . . . coming into this world. . . . We have passed the buck for so long that these people have still not got houses."[100] The Eurafrican Society agreed with this view, stating that "this [failure] is indeed the unkindest cut of all, since a man comes into this world through no fault of his own."[101] The *Central African Post* further acknowledged the ties of racial descent and kinship between Eurafricans and the white community, rhetorically asking: "When is somebody going to do something for these unfortunate people—who, let it never be forgotten, were in many cases fathered by the early civil servants in this country?"[102]

These recurring expressions of connection help explain why officials granted attention and financial backing to such a small community. Eurafricans valued such overtures. The political hopes of the community expanded during the federation period, with the first meeting of the Euro-African Association of Northern Rhodesia, in Ndola in 1956, attracting representatives from across the colony. Support for "a united Euro-African movement in Northern Rhodesia" was expressed as "a long-cherished ambition."[103] Promoting the term *Eurafrican* over *Coloured* in order to "inculcate racial pride," the association noted that its members' welfare could be affected by federation laws currently being considered, such as the Federal Citizenship and Franchise Bill and various constitutional changes concerning Northern Rhodesia's governing status.[104] Even the U.S. Supreme Court decision in *Brown v. Board of Education of Topeka* (1954) was cited as a legal precedent for ending school segregation in Northern Rhodesia.[105] Since a central intention was "to raise the standard of living of the [Eurafrican] people and to open for them a richer and more varied life," housing also became a central issue at the meeting.[106] "A good house is an essential of good health and social stability," it was noted. "The houses being erected fall short of the requirements of the Community. They will provide grossly inadequate living conditions."[107] Governor Arthur Benson of Northern Rhodesia was also quoted as saying Eurafrican housing "has long been regarded by government as being the factor most likely to lead to the stabilisation of Euroafrican Communities in Urban areas."[108]

But municipal authorities bore the local burden of such issues and the accountability that went with it. In August 1956 J. R. Brown, the commissioner for local government, lamented: "On whose shoulders does the responsibility lie? Can we honestly say it lies with the local authority? At the moment there is no legal obligation on the local authority to house 'Coloureds'. Morally, have they any more obligation to 'Coloureds' than to Europeans?"[109] With the Lusaka city council fiscally constrained, Eurafricans unable to pay their rents, and their employers unwilling to offer higher salaries, a final decision awaited the attention of the central government. The *Northern News* continued to criticize the city council for its unresponsiveness. As one observer facetiously explained, "the Europeans have houses, the Africans have houses, so the Eurafricans can sleep where the devil they like."[110] Tensions soon rose again between Lusaka city councilors and central government representatives.[111] The arrival of yet another rainy season added urgency. The *Central African Post* repeated a familiar exhortation that "these people are living in the most primitive conditions under tarpaulins, indifferently constructed tin huts, even old motor-cars." "The Eurafricans are an 'in-between' community. Very much so," noted the article. "There is no fraternisation between them and the Africans. They are left to their own devices."[112] A shorter news piece that reemphasized Eurafricans as "Lusaka's forgotten people" and "the worst-housed people in the Territory" additionally mentioned that a visiting United Nations Relief and Rehabilitation Administration official had judged the situation as "absolutely disgraceful."[113]

Eurafrican protests continued into 1957 in the form of petitions and outcries in the media, despite official efforts to arrive at a new formula for subsidizing housing costs.[114] Referring to the well-known Coloured neighborhood in Cape Town, the *Central African Post* declared in May 1957:

> Lusaka has its own District Six, a squalid shack settlement where disease is rife. . . . In a shack village a mile out of Lusaka on the Kafue Flats Road, about 100 Coloureds live in 10 or 11 mud, dagga, corrugated iron and sacking-draped huts which would make poor pig-sties.
>
> These people have nowhere else to live. Unlike Lusaka's African population they do not have housing areas provided by the Municipality. The Municipality has built only eight small dwellings to house the lucky ones.
>
> In one of these neat, white-walled homes a man and wife live with some of their nine children.

The house has only one bedroom. When the children come back from
boarding school they sleep in the living room or kitchen.

All these small homes are overcrowded.[115]

J. B. Thompson, a member of the Eurafrican community, further commented on the vulnerability of this temporary settlement by depicting it
as "on an industrial site" and observing that the people there were essentially "squatters." The article described the makeshift "village" as having
"no sanitation [so that] the Coloured children are constantly exposed to
disease."[116] In July the Eurafrican Society, under its new president Harry A.
Thornicroft, threatened a street protest, charging that the problem had
been going on for nine years and the time for "dilly-dallying" should end.[117]
"Eurafricans were not getting a square deal in the Federation," the media
reported, "and unless something was done for them they would have to
throw in their [political] lot with either the Indians or the Africans."[118]

But Eurafrican leaders called off the protest after a special meeting between the city council and the Eurafrican Society.[119] In November 1957 officials approved a final plan for four types of homes—two types had three
bedrooms and the other two types had two bedrooms—along with a new
site plan (see figures 8.8 and 8.9).[120] Although cost concerns extended into
1958—with a discrepancy between a housing allocation for £28,000 and the
estimated total cost of the current plan at £29,391—momentum pushed
the scheme forward.[121] In August members of the Eurafrican community
met again with local officials to clarify exactly when and how housing support would be allocated.[122] Twenty-two houses had been approved at a cost
of £1,300 to £1,550 per home, with rents of between £14 and £17.15.6 per
month. These rates were higher than a previous working figure of £12.10.0
and those cited earlier, though further government support was possible.
At this point, ability to pay was not seen as the only criterion for allocat-
ing housing: "the special position and the needs of the Eurafrican community must be borne in mind."[123] Overall, despite a withdrawal of support
for African housing during the same period, 1958 proved to be the turning
point for Eurafrican housing.[124]

Yet the final transition to a new Thorn Park neighborhood for Eurafricans was not without problems. Tensions erupted in 1959, shortly after the
government attempted to close the squatter camp at Marrapodi, particularly over the question of Eurafrican residents who had African wives.[125]
Thornicroft sought to alleviate the situation, saying that he did not want

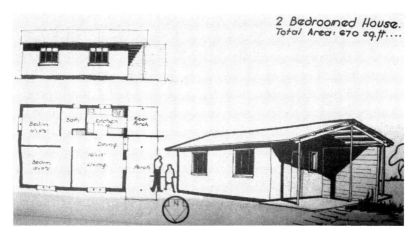

FIGURE 8.8. Detail of two-bedroom house, November 1957 (LUDC 1/22/53). Permission to photograph courtesy of the National Archives of Zambia.

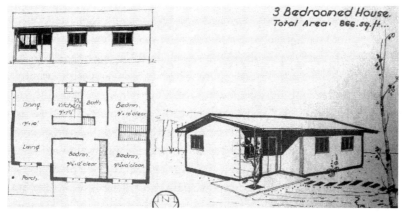

FIGURE 8.9. Detail of three-bedroom house, November 1957 (LUDC 1/22/53). Permission to photograph courtesy of the National Archives of Zambia.

to encourage "friction" between the Eurafrican and African communities. "We were brought up by African mothers," he pointed out, "and there can be no question of us not wanting to live with them at Thorn Park."[126] Still, there were concerns that "the introduction of African wives" to Thorn Park would cause "deterioration not only of the Council's houses built there but also of the whole tone of Thorn Park."[127] Although there were only three Eurafrican men who had African wives, it "was feared that illegal beer brewing would take place on the premises and that the relatives of African wives could cause damage to property and trouble to the neighbours whilst under the influence of such liquor."[128] Others lamented this paradox of racism. Eurafricans were "claiming for recognation [sic] and for rights as citizens of N.R. [Northern Rhodesia]" yet sought to reestablish a "Colour Bar of which we are trying to break."[129] It was "disgraceful" that "a person [could] neglect his mother," given that African mothers lived with some Eurafrican families, while others had African servants and other Eurafrican women had African husbands.[130] Those who opposed allowing African wives to live in Thorn Park were "actually enemies of the two sections of people, and these are the Black from which section their mothers come, and the European from which section their fathers come."[131] To pacify the situation, city officials decided that a welfare officer reviewing applications would determine whether the tenants lived "characteristically as Eurafricans," thus entitling them to live in Thorn Park, or if "their living habits" were "more African in nature."[132]

The intersection of racial descent and lifestyle and their relation to status therefore emerged once more. But this debate about inclusion and exclusion was soon overshadowed by a broader problem of vacancies in the neighborhood. Ten of the thirty houses that had been built were vacant.[133] Despite government aid the Eurafrican Society remained critical, citing that a "fantastic Rental" was being charged.[134] By January 1960 twenty-nine of the thirty houses were occupied. However, all but eleven tenants were behind on rent.[135] In June a grim assessment was submitted—that "little effort is being made by these tenants to meet their rent obligations," that "not only are the grounds and surrounds of the houses untidy but the houses themselves are, in most cases, dirty and uncared for. Windows are broken, door furniture damaged and wash basins broken from the walls."[136] Furthermore, it appeared that "some of the houses are being used for immoral purposes. . . . Wives appear to change hands. . . . unauthorised lodgers are taken into the houses without the permission of the Council being first sought and obtained."[137] Although many of the residents of Thorn Park had skilled occupations—among them mechanics, municipal workers, and small business workers in the laundry and food service industries—keeping up with rent proved to be an ongoing challenge.[138] If the original problem of housing had found a degree of resolution, it had also introduced a new set of challenges and questions regarding the long-term viability of this welfare project and the community it sought to address.

: HOUSING AND ITS MEANINGS :

The extended outlook for the neighborhood ultimately proved limited in the face of federation politics. At the annual conference of the Municipal Association of Northern Rhodesia and Nyasaland in May 1961, the point was made that, despite a policy of racial equality in the federation, Eurafrican subsidies in Lusaka were one of two programs administered on a racially unfair basis. The minister of local government and social welfare called "this so-called subsidy for Eurafrican housing" a "relief payment" that could be "made available to members of other races. . . . I know of no reason why it shouldn't be."[139] However, the plan for rent subsidies to Eurafricans was canceled with the end of the federation and the independence of Zambia in 1964.[140] By this time, it was estimated that only 250 residents inhabited Thorn Park, which was considered on "the low side" from a socioeconomic perspective.[141] Subsidies officially ended on December 31, 1966, with full rents charged thereafter.[142]

This history, then, is ultimately one of failure—a colonial episode of urban displacement, debates over affordability, and the question of civic versus community responsibility. As in previous chapters, the story here describes the "unreasonable" dilemmas that multiracial people posed to colonial policy as urban subjects, but it also shows how colonial political reason permitted, even enabled, intolerable social conditions to exist. It tells once again how community organizations challenged state perspectives on social welfare policies. Eurafricans did not fit into existing plans of urbanization in Lusaka or colonial housing development generally. This chapter consequently highlights the active role Eurafricans played in redefining urban categories of personhood—not only through racial descent and their interstitial identity between European and African settlers, but also through issues of poverty and class aspiration. Their presence and social conditions divided municipal and central government authorities, generating sentiments of duty and obligation as in previous chapters, as well as clear indifference. Eurafricans themselves sought what was a prosaic feature of modern life—affordable housing—yet it was a meaningful ambition, given the enhanced lifestyle and sense of upward mobility that such housing could provide. If status could not be achieved legally, it could still be attained through middle-class attributes of property ownership and a settled lifestyle.

This struggle for housing was ultimately successful, but with distinct costs—both fiscal and political—for the city of Lusaka, the Northern Rhodesian government, and the Eurafrican community. Although the politics of racial descent proved to be a tacit motivating factor for state concern once more, a sense of relatedness alone could not ensure well-being and social gain for Eurafrican families in Lusaka. The narrative that the capital's "forgotten people" belonged to was therefore part of a broader pattern of activism found throughout British Central Africa, as well as a story they wrote themselves.

CONCLUSION

∷∷∷

GENEALOGIES OF COLONIALISM

∷∷

It is remarkable to observe that in the opening chapter of his postapartheid memoir, *The Last Trek* (1998), F. W. de Klerk mentions part of his family's history "of which we did not speak."[1] Tracing his family's origins to the initial wave of French Huguenots who immigrated to the Western Cape in the late seventeenth century, de Klerk describes the role his family played in the storied emergence of the Afrikaner community over the next two and a half centuries, with one ancestor in particular, Hendrik Bibault, being among the first to refer to himself as an "Afrikaander" in 1707.[2] However, it is Bibault's half-sister, Susanna, who places de Klerk's family in a different historical light. Susanna was the illegitimate daughter of Detlef Bibault, Hendrik's father, and Diana of Bengal, a slave from India who arrived in the Cape in 1667. Susanna went on to marry Wilhelm Odenthal in 1711, and her daughter married de Klerk's direct ancestor, Barend de Klerk. It is this genealogical thread—with its suggestion of racially tainted origins—that was kept a secret in the de Klerk family for generations.[3]

This kind of revelation is not unique within the Afrikaner community. But neither is it inconsequential. Indeed, this story can be interpreted as strategic, establishing de Klerk's connections not only to the history of the Afrikaner people, but also to the history of racially oppressed communities in South Africa. This personal retelling gestures toward a new kind of postapartheid legitimacy, interweaving de Klerk's family genealogy to both sides of South Africa's political struggle. This disclosure sharply contrasts with an often-cited public comment by his former wife, Marike de Klerk, who famously referred to Coloured people as a "negative group," as "leftovers . . . after the nations were sorted out" without a common identity due to a lack of racial purity.[4] F. W. de Klerk's delicate embrace of racially mixed origins consequently underscores the transformations—at times subtle, at times dramatic—of identity politics during the postapartheid period.[5] Histories once hidden have been reconfigured into new versions of heritage, laying claim to contemporary forms of nativeness and the political entitlements they have to offer. Though de Klerk's story is anecdotal in nature, the type of entangled politics of genealogy and the mutable social opportunism it evinces has a broad regional history. Reflecting on her anthropological work in central and South Africa, Audrey Richards once remarked that, rather than structurally stable, the societies she had studied were notable for "the lack of permanence of particular lineages or 'segments'; the infinite variety there is in their composition, [and] their liability to change owing to historic factors, [such as] the strength of individual personalities and similar determinants."[6]

This book has been about practices of affiliation and the forms of reason that have rationalized such social and political behavior. By extension, it has examined how reason itself—whether racial, political, or academic, as addressed here—is historically constructed and, as a consequence, subject to change: an observation that demands recurrent reconsideration of the intellectual epistemologies that have determined and shaped the production and structure of knowledge in the past and present, as well as the factors that enable the critical circumvention of such constraints. An underlying question that has persisted throughout this book has been why histories of multiracial Africans have been largely invisible from a historiographical standpoint—why colonial stories of perceived illegitimacy have remained illegitimate as sources of historical knowledge. The answer does not rest with demographic numbers, a common position undermined by the virtues of biography. Rather, these silences point to tacit intellectual continuities between the past and present. The communities examined in this book provide an empirical vantage point that indicates the ways in which the colonial native question still structures and shapes the contours of academic research from behind the curtain of decolonization, with postcolonial nativism—at the complex intersection of racial, territorial, cultural, and national meanings—taking on its mantle. Put simply, because of their uncertain racial background, the lives of multiracial Africans have not fit within the same parameters of concern for colonial or postcolonial states as compared to black African communities. This relative disregard has been repeated by scholars. The preceding histories thus did not end with the arrival of social legitimation or political fulfillment. Instead they received a postcolonial version of the enormous condescension of posterity, to cite E. P. Thompson, both politically and historiographically.[7]

From a political standpoint, the Anglo-African, Euro-African, and Eurafrican activism that emerged during the 1930s and matured through the 1940s shifted by the late 1950s with the ascendance of African nationalism across the region. In Northern Rhodesia the colony-wide Euro-African Association that had been established in 1956 dissolved by 1962, with members like Henry Thornicroft (of the well-known Thornicroft family) and Aaron Milner joining the United National Independence Party under the leadership of Kenneth Kaunda. Both men served as government ministers during the 1960s and 1970s.[8] In Southern Rhodesia a similar generational and political shift transpired, albeit under more difficult circumstances given the prolonged history of white minority rule. The Rhodesia National Association (established in 1952) became the dominant Eurafrican organization during the 1950s, involving G. T. Thornicroft, Ronald Snapper, and John Ascroft once more, along with younger activists such as Gerald Raftopoulos, who embraced a more pluralistic political view reflective of the federation period. Raftopoulos later became a member of parliament representing the United Federal Party in the early 1960s.[9] The Unilateral Declaration of Independence in 1965 under the Rhodesian Front marked a turning point. The 1969 Rhodesian constitution classified "Coloureds" as "Europeans," a goal pursued since the 1920s.[10] However, racism against Coloured Rhodesians persisted.[11] The National Association of Coloured Peoples (founded in 1968) signaled a radical break with a more global outlook, its members being attuned to the U.S. civil rights struggle in addition to regional African nationalisms.[12] The association redefined and promoted the term *Coloured* in positive, self-validating fashion akin to the Black Power and Black Consciousness Movements in the United States and South Africa. Though the community remained politically divided for and against white minority rule until the political independence of Zimbabwe in 1980, its members, like their counterparts to the north, cultivated a flexible citizenship that went both ways, demonstrating the adaptive capacity of a genealogical imagination to rationalize competing sets of familial connections, political sentiment, and racial affinity as changing circumstances dictated.[13]

Nyasaland experienced a transition similar to that of its neighbors, with those supporting the continuation of British rule suffering distinct political consequences as described at the beginning of this book. Shortly after the creation of the federation in 1953, a new organization was founded— the Nyasaland Coloured Community Welfare Association, led by Ismail K. Surtee—that was intended to provide an alternative to the Anglo-African Association.[14] The new association had gained political clout by the end of the 1950s such that it aligned with the Malawi Congress Party (MCP) and Hastings Banda, who considered "all mixed-blooded people" as "Africans," based on matrilineal custom.[15] Echoing the argument of Levi Mumba during the 1930s, Anglo-Africans were, in essence, "his sister's children."[16] By 1961 Surtee had become a member of the MCP, due to his own ambitions and the wider context of African nationalism. He eventually became speaker of the National Assembly of Malawi after independence, a fate sharply contrasting with that of Henry Ascroft. As a coda to this dissimilar outcome, a parliamentary debate took place in April 1969 over "Coloured" status, with N. A. Mwambungu—who represented Karonga in the north— repeating the idea that Coloured people were our "nephews and nieces" and that "we are really their uncles whom they must respect."[17] This social distancing and political diminishment through a terminology of kinship— Coloured people were not, for example, "brothers" or "cousins"—emerged from personal friction with Surtee, as well as from broader tensions within the MCP and its ideas of Malawian nationalism as both were transformed and stabilized during the early postcolonial period. Banda ended the debate on its third day, arguing, to applause, that anyone "who has a drop of African blood in him, or in her, whether it is mixed up with European blood, mixed up with Asian blood, Indian or Arab, so far as I am concerned, he is an African."[18] Banda further noted that "although they have not identified themselves with the other Africans as much as one would like them to," he did have support from "Africans of mixed blood."[19] Surtee himself asserted, "I represent no special community, either in Parliament or outside Parliament."[20]

These debates five years after Malawi's independence underscore the complex transitions that these colonial-era political identities experienced, with new hierarchies of postcolonial credibility ultimately undermining the longevity of their social uses and meaning.[21] These partisan disputes further demonstrate the recurrence of kinship and blood as discursive idioms mobilized for purposes of defining degrees of status and the parameters of political inclusion and exclusion. Yet this occasion proved unique—a postscript to earlier struggles of the colonial period. The term

Coloured is still acknowledged and used today across Malawi, Zimbabwe, and Zambia. But such terminology must be understood as mutable, as a historical creation that can experience different forms of vitality over time. The agnatic ideology cultivated by Anglo-African and Eurafrican communities generated a colonial fathers-and-children structure that not only produced certain constraints of paternalism and dependence, as touched on before, but also ensured the demise of this counter-genealogy given its fixed nature to colonial rule.[22] Such terms as *Anglo-African*, *Eurafrican*, and *Euro-African* imagined establishing a form of perpetual kinship, to borrow an expression from Ian Cunnison, that would secure a lasting privileged status, but this permanence was not to be.[23] Even so, as argued in chapter 1, these colonial histories must be situated as part of a regional fabric of rational social experimentation and cultural change in the *longue durée*. Intergroup conjugal relationships and their histories are an intrinsic part of Africa's past. The roles of kinship and genealogy in defining vernacular notions of autochthony and social belonging form an enduring political pattern found across the continent before, during, and after the period of colonial rule. They offer a principal means for constituting and shaping what Jan Vansina has called the collective imagination of African societies.[24]

This book has examined a colonial adaptation of this longstanding practice. It has traced the social and political construction of a fluid genealogical imagination and its uses through a set of regional histories across British Central Africa. This imagination represented a modern colonial-era invention as well as an evolving set of long-term regional political traditions centered on ideas of natural rights and corporate belonging.[25] It consequently provides an alternative approach to understanding the histories of multiracial people in central and southern Africa with an interpretation anchored in local perspectives that worked against the omniscience of colonial categories. This imagination as a socio-political phenomenon and technique for historical analysis grants critical agency and intellectual insight to historical actors of the time, thus moving beyond the popular treatment of multiracial Africans in either unchanging hierarchical terms (occupying a middle position) or as persistently ambiguous, a variation of the so-called tragic mulatto caught betwixt and between.[26] Both views resemble colonial attitudes of white condescension. This imagination similarly imparts specificity to understandings of creolization, given that this process was not unique to multiracial Africans and, as a method of interpretation, requires historical precision.[27] Most significant of all, this self-crafted genealogical imagination underscores the importance of both local practices and regional histories. The Cape Coloured experience should not remain paradigmatic. Indeed, as addressed in chapter 7, even those embracing Cape origins did so through genealogical connections. This emergent political imagination that took local forms thus comprised a critical strategy against colonial indeterminacy and obfuscation that inhabited state taxonomies. The term *Coloured* became part of a regional process of bureaucratic racial modernization that overwhelmed empirical subtleties. Employing it for analysis in the present without consideration for the layered histories of debate and struggle that occurred risks reproducing a colonial lexicon that had been standardized by the 1950s—one that concealed, rather than revealed, individual historical experience.

But these histories speak beyond these concerns as well. A larger set of issues surface, as I have progressively argued throughout this book. When I began this research, I imagined writing a postcolonial supplement to the formative work of the Rhodes-Livingstone Institute—a study of identity formation and political community that would engage with similar concerns for agency and livelihood amid conditions of social and political change as found in the pathbreaking scholarship of this research center. Although this project draws on the influence of its most well-known affiliates as cited, still adheres to these essential principles, and shares the same geography, it also marks a critical departure from this influential literature. As stated in the introduction, the communities examined here pose fundamental challenges of fragmentary evidence, contingent forms of historical causality, and discontinuous narration. They possess shallow histories that lack longstanding cultural traditions and ongoing practices of social reproduction. Moreover, many, if not all, members of these communities espoused a set of racial politics and moral values supportive of imperial rule that were not only uncustomary in scope, but would sharply contrast with the nation-building interests of the postcolonial period. Above all, multiracial people resided beyond the basic research parameters of the Rhodes-Livingstone Institute: they were not perceived as indigenous, native, and therefore "African" and thus were disqualified as legitimate subject matter for study. In sum, these experiences stand apart from what was and is conventionally understood to be rational, accepted, and justified—in a word, reasonable—from methodological, political, and epistemological standpoints. These antithetical histories confront a colonial and postcolonial reason structured territorially by (what I have critically referred to as) the nation-state-colony, culturally by an ethnic paradigm, and politically by black nationalism.

Yet these antithetical qualities grant value to these difficult histories. They point to a postnationalist research agenda that not only encourages the deterritorialization of historical meaning from the nation-state-colony, but they highlight the oppressive consequences of modern nationalism in Africa, as in other parts of the world. While the achievement of postcolonial independence across the continent should be celebrated, adopting this geopolitical form can have empirical costs. These histories of the excluded demonstrate the demographic complexity that inhabited colonial societies, how native and non-native questions coexisted in mutually constitutive ways, and thus the possibilities of rewriting colonial histories through reconsideration of the nature of the political under colonial rule.[28] Though small population figures offer a reason for minimizing these communities, scholarship should not be governed by demographic data alone. Their experiences underscore the significance of social margins and border histories, which offer perspectives that disrupt our current narratives of the past and the frames of analysis we employ to understand that past.[29] This book has proposed a set of methods for reporting and interpreting such experiences: the genre of histories without groups, the emergence and function of uncustomary political practices, and the uses of region for managing the unwieldiness of empire in more concrete fashion, as well as denaturalizing the nation-state-colony as the location for historical meaning. These histories challenge consensus and, as a result, force a return to fundamental questions about the techniques and politics of doing African history—how, why, for whom, and for what purpose.

But these histories do not simply present new narratives of power and agency under colonial rule. They are a direct effect of them. Colonialism fragmented these histories, and postcolonialism has disregarded them. As described in the introduction, the purpose of the genealogical approach pursued in this book has been anti-teleological in scope, not only to underscore the variability of identity formation, but also to outline the irregular effects of power in different social realms. A genealogical technique can give shape to communities and stories that sit uneasily within conventional accounts of power and duress. Nativism in its colonial and postcolonial forms has been the primary expression of this power. Nativism—not racism—is the central problem raised in this book. To stress race alone oversimplifies the problem at hand. Indeed, while this project deeply sympathizes with work that resists the uncritical reproduction of colonial and racial terminology, it embraces the concurrent argument that recognizing and historicizing colonial and racial difference and their euphemisms is essential to get beyond their influence. Although race and racism are recurring themes that explain patterns of identification and discrimination, a specific ruling language of nativism and non-nativism structured the opportunities and constraints of multiracial people, as it did for other communities under colonial rule.

The term *native* is ubiquitous in colonial documentation, as it was throughout colonial life. Similar to race, it was prosaic and possessed a plasticity that lent itself to wide definition and use, as discussed in part II. But nativism and non-nativism were not about racial distinction and descent alone. They were equally informed by culture and territory. In the purview of colonial administrators, maintaining cultural discretion and territorial segregation were as vital—indeed, typically more vital—to colonial social orders as preventing interracial relationships, even if states never achieved any of these aims. This triumvirate of race, culture, and territory informed and shaped the struggles of multiracial people and the colonized more generally. Engaging with nativism and non-nativism is thus not only historically more accurate. They offer a more focused sense of how colonial difference was structured and rationalized. This terminology provides a critical vantage point for engaging with, rather than being subsumed beneath, what Howard Winant has called a world racial system.[30] Racial thought not only needs to be historicized, but provincialized territorially to better understand its local uses and meanings. The intersectionality of nativism demonstrates that racial politics in British Central Africa was not an uncomplicated derivative of Western thought. It was the result of active local definition and reconfiguration. Multiracial people aspired to non-native status—legally, socially, and politically—but given their self-locutions, they did not desire to pass for white as such. They sought a specific form of colonial livelihood, mobilizing a genealogical imagination to circumvent totalizing colonial categories, generate a contractual reciprocity with regional states, and create a sense of collective well-being and civic virtue based on shared kinship and natural rights by descent.

Another imagination is also at stake: a historical one. The priorities of colonial nativism—that is, the privileging of customary authorities and ethnic communities—ultimately disregarded these alternative communities and their collective concerns. This colonial indifference has since transformed into postcolonial contempt, with the pervasive influence of nativism connecting the two. As addressed in the introduction, nativism has primarily been understood as a postcolonial phenomenon—a response to colonialism that was born in the crucible of decolonization, with intentions to restore and promote precolonial histories and indigenous cultures as a critical means of mitigating the impact of Western colonization and stabilizing postcolonial national identities.[31] Yet postcolonial nativism itself has drawn from colonial sources of knowledge and Western understandings of cultural and national difference. It is a distinct outcome of modern imperialism and the rise of the nation-state. And it has often replicated colonial hierarchies of exclusion. The relative inattention paid in the present to the communities discussed here reflects a colonial nativist reason that has informed postcolonial politics and scholarship, a rationalism that has rendered them unknowable communities.[32] The colonial native question that emerged during the early twentieth century and existed in different variations across Africa has continued to influence our basis of knowledge for defining what counts as African—a deeply racialized epistemology that has foregrounded black political and cultural life exclusively, subjugated alternative assemblages of collective experience and information, and created hidden histories as an aftereffect.[33]

Our understanding of the past—our historical imagination—has been restricted as a result. The "unreasonable" histories depicted here remain outside this intellectual structure—this colonial formation—and thus separate from the political and categorical parameters of African history as conventionally understood. They evince an academic hierarchy of credibility.[34] But in addition to rendering certain social groups and their histories invisible, nativism has organized politics in a rudimentary way by strengthening binary frameworks—domination and resistance, colonizer and colonized, traditional and modern—to the exclusion of intermediate and uncustomary political forms. Important critiques of these mainstream interpretive modes, especially one put forward by Frederick Cooper, demand not only conceptual innovation and a more expansive empiricism.[35] They also require a reconsideration of how the political and the historical have been structured in relation to the economies of knowledge produced by colonialism—a type of epistemic disobedience.[36] Critical histories of colonialism cannot be reduced to choosing sides—writing postcolonial history used to be all too easy from a political standpoint—but can only be achieved once the conditions of power—imperial and local, state and social, and material and discursive—that informed the possibilities and methods of individual and group agency are fully cataloged. Accounting for these conditions in turn necessitates a more expansive definition of the term *African*—beyond the nativist paradigm—that encompasses the social heterogeneity described in this book.

This broader argument about historical practice consequently challenges us to rethink not simply the legacies of colonialism, but its active genealogies in the present. V. Y. Mudimbe, Achille Mbembe, and James Ferguson have shown how Africa—as an idea, place, and historical geography—has been conscripted to contrast Western modernity and its forms of reason.[37] But what is needed, beyond shadowboxing with Hegel, is interrogating the limits of this reason—racial, cultural, and otherwise—at the local level. Indeed, along with being concerned with the unreasonable origins of reason (colonialism's contemporary legacies), scholars should equally consider the reasonable origins of contemporary unreason—how certain ideologies and worldviews that were accepted and cultivated during the early postcolonial period have become irrational, even perverse, in the present.[38] Race as a form of colonial reason has justifiably faced criticism in the postcolonial period, and its use as a statutory method for organizing political order by law, census, and similar state means has suitably declined. But nativism has become a prevalent mode of postcolonial reason, playing out in different ways dependent on time and place. It has revitalized African histories and cultures in positive fashion on the one hand. It has also generated practices of political exclusion and violence on the other hand—from genocide in Rwanda and xenophobic bloodshed in South Africa to ethnic massacres and tense land struggles in Zimbabwe.[39] Some of these cases have involved racial difference. Politically constructed notions of autochthony have been crucial to all of them.[40] Nativism remains a legitimate political ideology in the postcolony, a fact increasingly lamented by scholars.[41] Mbembe has spoken to this broad issue, decrying the fact that race has become the core of a "restricted civic relatedness" found across sub-Saharan Africa, with "everything that is not black . . . out of place, and thus [unable to] claim any sort of Africanity."[42] Francis Nyamnjoh has posed a similar reflexive critique specific to anthropology, calling for an "epistemological conviviality" that breaks from racialized perspectives rooted in colonial nativism that would have the subject of ethnographic study always be black.[43] These recent positions extend a critical tradition situated in southern Africa as cited in the introduction, building upon earlier observations by such scholars as Max Gluckman. This book seeks to do the same. It shares the same geography that Gluckman's later work inhabited, though it addresses a set of empirical questions beyond the research imagination of the Rhodes-Livingstone Institute that he once headed.

To be clear, making these points is not to suggest that postcolonial scholarship to this point has inherited a colonial epistemology without critical revision. Moreover, the case put forward here is not ultimately about sources. Using colonial archives in some form, whether through primary or secondary means, is an ineluctable aspect of practicing African history. Neither do these remarks encourage a return to an older argument regarding social pluralism that underestimated the sources and function of power.[44] What is principally argued for is a renewal of interpretation that allows for a more capacious historical sensibility to address the diverse multitudes that have shaped Africa's past. In the same way that European and North American historiographies were once empirically and intellectually diminished by the absence of serious scholarship on racial, religious, and other cultural minorities, so too does Africa's historiography remain under-researched and incomplete until such communities are accounted for. Indeed, in the same way that the innovative contributions by historians of women and gender in Africa have now become mainstream, so too must work on the range of racial minority groups found across the continent find universal acceptance. As noted in the introduction, recent scholarship has indicated that a turn in this direction is under way, with new, more textured understandings of African life emerging. In contrast to many histories of colonial racism, this book has summoned realms of connection, rather than conflict. It has worked against discrete forms of colonial and contemporary analytic categorization with the purpose of diversifying identities, worldviews, and historical experiences. And though this study shares affinities with the new imperial history, it does so with the intention of unsettling working assumptions about the boundaries, meanings, and possibilities of African history—and British imperial history.[45]

Nativism as a problem can, of course, appear too monolithic, generating epistemic anxieties and an unhelpful intellectual claustrophobia.[46] Variations between colonies and imperial territories must be pointed to and engaged with as addressed in this book. But it is also remarkably cohesive as a structure of knowledge, a quality that can be attributed to its racial character and the intellectual reach of European colonial rule itself. Work remains. In the same manner that former colonial boundaries have left a lingering political geography on the continent, so too have colonial questions of knowledge and definition left an intellectual imprint that has often pre-determined our research imagination, a situation making critical engagement with persistent genealogies of colonialism still an essential task. Indeed, the line between colonialism and postcolonialism has often been too starkly drawn, adhering to the signposts of political timelines rather than being alert to the continuities of tacit knowledge across space and time. Attention must be paid to what forms of knowledge have transcended these political temporalities, how so, and why. Anthropology has been criticized periodically as being complicit with colonialism.[47] History must similarly be understood and interrogated as an instrument of postcolonialism. If African history as an emancipatory practice is to persevere, it must resist easy claims of intellectual transcendentalism and consistently revisit the colonial origins of contemporary issues—even in the face of political optimism—given the recurrence of these legacies and the ongoing need to define what emancipation itself means.[48]

Colonialism was not merely a struggle for territory or resources. It was a struggle over knowledge—a confrontation, debate, and at times open fight over worldviews and the senses of social status and place that emanated from them. Decolonization subsequently reflected not only a political occasion, but also an intellectual moment and opening—the initial possibilities of which still remain unfulfilled.

: COLONIAL HAUNTOLOGIES :

Genealogies of colonialism persist not only in the realm of knowledge. They also endure at the personal level. In my conversations with various informants, the differences between the past and present would inevitably come up, as touched upon earlier. The people I spoke to came from different generations, with some having experienced the meanings of community—people like Ann and Jessica Ascroft, Dinah Coombes, and Yusuf Ismael—whereas others had a fainter sense of what had occurred during the colonial period, either because they were too young to appreciate such matters of collective interest or because they were members of a separate generation entirely, with this history a figment of memory that had been handed down, its contemporary uses unclear.

The Banda regime had a decisive impact on identification and social memory, even after the parliamentary debate of 1969. During his presidency increased state centralization resulted in practices of censorship and political imprisonment. The regime additionally imposed a form of Chewa nationalism—Banda's version of nativism—that suppressed other identities. Nationalism in its most strident form often occurs after independence, not before as so frequently assumed. The reemergence of regional and ethnic identities following the death of Banda has consequently been significant.[49] But not all groups experienced this revival. Some had a different fate. Postcolonial nativism, apart from nationalism, undermined the permanence of the Anglo-African community.[50] This decline of community—the ways in which people collectively engaged in forms of connection through shared understandings of affiliation, loyalty, and friendship—challenges conventional ethnic teleologies that depict the creation of identities, but express less concern for their historical ends—their precarity, failure, and even disappearance.[51] Kwame Anthony Appiah has noted that, beyond arguments for agency and social construction, identities must be understood as having the capacity to be rational or irrational, and that certain identities can be self-undermining if group members do not adjust in rational ways to changing conditions.[52] The moribund status of Anglo-African, Eurafrican, and similar colonial-era identities underscores their innate temporality and their dependence on active community effort—the consistent intellectual rationalization of difference and the simultaneous articulation of connection through strategic practices of self-naming and group constitution.[53] These social identities counted on the agency of individuals who embraced them, not a reductive condition of race mixture. In contrast, the relative persistence of the term *Coloured* without formal political recognition, statutory measures, or regular community activism signals its standing as a racial stereotype and the endurance of colonial language in popular discourse.

"I think it is from before. You know, the colonial period," said one person, when I asked her about Coloured identity and the politics of race in Malawi. "There were places where they would say 'this is for white people only,' you see? 'No blacks allowed to stay here,' you see? This is 'only for the blacks,' this is 'only for the Indians.'" When I pushed her to see if any issues of race remained, she suggested they were still present, if in a subsumed form. "That has been going on for many years now," she told me, sounding apprehensive. "It's going to take quite a long time. We have just come out from the dark, so it is very difficult just to change overnight. The doctrine of Dr. Banda is still living in people's minds."[54] Some felt less trepidation talking about matters of difference and discrimination. "I think it's no secret that there has always been a policy, unofficial policy, in government to sideline us," remarked Robert Jamieson, a descendant of James Jamieson and once the publisher of a national newspaper in Malawi, the *Chronicle*. "Not to allow us to get into positions of prominence. And it was more difficult for the Anglo-African than for the Eurasian African because the Eurasian African, or the Asian African, actually took a stand very early on in the late 1950s to work with the indigenous people and to fight for independence from Britain. The Anglo-African wanted to a large extent to maintain the status quo, not that they didn't want independence for Malawi, but they felt an affinity toward both sides rather than just one side." "I think the problem is that the term 'Coloured' has been shifting considerably. There was a time when we were trying to get recognition as a people, as a separate entity, and during the thirty years of dictatorship our status was much reduced," he continued. "We certainly were not recognized for what we were and in the last five or six years of multiparty democracy, that position from thirty years of dictatorship has not changed much, has not altered. I think there are questions being asked amongst ourselves as to whether or not we should pursue the situation, and try and gain recognition for being who we are, rather than just being assimilated into local populations."[55]

These conversations offer some validation that revisiting these histories still bears usefulness in the present. They have value for the descendants of those who experienced them. But these histories also demonstrate how certain regimes of truth and the forms of reason they promote can subside, even fall into permanent decline—a cause for optimism, not nostalgia. Unlike other works that have critically mobilized culture and class against race, this book places its convictions in empiricism and the passage of time—the ability of political struggle and historical change to inaugurate social transformation, to revise values, and to invalidate forms of colonial and postcolonial reason in their wake. The end of Banda's presidency has created new opportunities to reassess Malawi's history, to explore themes and subjects that were previously prohibited from study.[56] The end of apartheid in South Africa has similarly afforded an occasion to reconsider the politics of scholarship on race throughout the continent. We can now examine racial communities in a way that we previously could not, due to anxieties of political misinterpretation. To historicize white settler communities once posed the risk of tacitly valorizing and legitimating a politics of racist minority rule—a view that has become too limited and unwarranted.[57] Departing from such critical unease is essential to mounting an effective antiracism that moves past race as an incontrovertible condition. The aura of universality that has granted race its importance must be balanced with an examination of how it historically intersected with local definitions and uses. Racial thought must be provincialized to understand how difference was employed and inhabited, how race became encoded in colonial euphemisms and concealed through forms of common sense. To debate whether race as a concept originated elsewhere, beyond the continent, raises significant questions of intellectual history. But such attention can also miss a fundamental empirical point: people had to manage the social and political conditions they encountered without choice, epistemological or otherwise.

Subaltern histories of the kind addressed in this book can contribute to this new agenda. They serve to outline a broader critical project in southern Africa after apartheid. Matters of race, culture, and territoriality undoubtedly continue to affect the region. Genealogies of colonial thought also endure. Though categories of native and non-native are technically moribund, the legacies they structured persist. They can be witnessed in terms of where people live, how people perceive one another, and how people identify. Yet the impermanence of such features must also be recognized. At a different, more local, level, it makes perfect sense in retrospect that colonial kinship relations and the political schema they generated should decline with the end of colonialism. However, the genealogical imagination that emerged did not entirely vanish. It was altered once more, receding to the realm of family memory from where it started, a point repeated in the stories I heard. It remains a critical practice, albeit a private one against forgetting. Returning to Kwame Anthony Appiah, in his separate philosophical meditation *In My Father's House*, he stages a comprehensive critique of race, nativism, and Africa as orientations for identity, concluding with a personal rumination on the lasting meanings of kinship and family—a reflection and way of embracing his own multiracial identity.[58] This perspective speaks to the ends of history in this book.

But the lives I encountered can still stand for something larger—beyond colonial gossip and rumor, beyond postcolonial social death, and beyond family recollection. These historically ephemeral communities once unconcealed instruct us to see the past differently. They demonstrate the existence of unusual lives of texture and sophistication that can exceed our intellectual grasp. Indeed, they serve as reminders of the outsized reality of Africa's past, which we, as students, must always assume surpasses our current understanding. Situated between private lives and public histories, these experiences ultimately provide a vital juncture of social, political, and historical opportunity to diversify the meanings of being African in the past and present — and for the future.

NOTES

::

INTRODUCTION. COLONIALISM, NATIVISM, AND THE GENEALOGICAL IMAGINATION

1. Quoted in Short, *Banda*, 2.

2. Kaunda and Morris, *A Humanist in Africa*, 61, 62. Kaunda's comment references British Prime Minister Harold Macmillan's "wind of change" speech to the South African parliament in 1960, when he criticized South Africa's policy of apartheid at a time of decolonization in Africa.

3. On the federation and the politics of this period, see Hyam, "The Geopolitical Origins of the Central African Federation"; Murphy, "'Government by Blackmail'"; Rotberg, *The Rise of Nationalism in Central Africa*.

4. As explained in this book's note on terminology, I use the term *multiracial* at the outset as a translation term that converses with contemporary work in critical race theory. For discussion and debate over this expanding issue, see, for example, DaCosta, *Making Multiracials*; Elam, *The Souls of Mixed Folk*; Ifekwuniqwe, *'Mixed Race' Studies*, parts 2 and 3; Joseph, *Transcending Blackness*; Root, *The Multiracial Experience*; Sexton, *Amalgamation Schemes*.

5. Interview with Ann and Jessica Ascroft, November 9, 1999, Blantyre, Malawi.

6. On Surtee, see Baker, *Revolt of the Ministers*, 38.

7. On the Banda regime and after, see Phiri and Ross, *Democratization in Malawi*; Englund, *A Democracy of Chameleons*.

8. Interview with Dinah Coombes, November 11, 1999, Zomba, Malawi. On the ambiguities of decolonization and the often personal effects of Malawi's political transition, see Baker, *Revolt of the Ministers*; McCracken, "The Ambiguities of Nationalism" and *A History of Malawi*, chapters 15 and 16; Power, "Remembering Du."

9. On genealogy and political imagination more generally, see Anderson, *Imagined Communities*; Appadurai, *Modernity at Large*; Crais, *The Politics of Evil*; Shryock, *Nationalism and the Genealogical Imagination*; Vergès, *Monsters and Revolutionaries*. On the politics of writing critically about race and racism, see, for example, Fields and Fields, *Racecraft*; Painter, *The History of White People*; Roediger, *The Wages of Whiteness*.

10. For recent discussion of this terminology, see, for example, Brennan, *Taifa*, chapter 1; Mamdani, *Define and Rule*, chapters 1 and 2; Pierre, *The Predicament of Blackness*, chapters 1 and 2.

11. For a critique of histories of race and their search for origins, see Stoler, "Racial Histories and Their Regimes of Truth."

12. Stoler, *Carnal Knowledge and Imperial Power*, 160.

13. My thoughts here have been stimulated by Brennan, *Taifa*; Evans, *Bureaucracy and Race*; Glassman, *War of Words*.

14. Cohen and Odhiambo, *Siaya*, 6. See also Gordon, "Vagrancy, Law and 'Shadow Knowledge.'" On racial marking and racial thought, see, for example, Glassman, *War of Words*; Holt, "Marking"; Jackson, *Real Black*; Stoler, "Racial Histories and Their Regimes of Truth"; Wacquant, "For an Analytic of Racial Domination." On identity and the cognitive turn more generally, see Brubaker, *Ethnicity without Groups*, especially chapter 3.

15. On the tension between using race as a category for historical analysis and the problem of perpetuating race, see, for example, Fields, "Ideology and Race in American History"; Holt, *The Problem of Race in the Twenty-First Century*; Roediger, *Colored White*.

16. Here, I paraphrase Fields, "Of Rogues and Geldings," 1400, and Smedley and Smedley, "Race as Biology Is Fiction, Racism as a Social Problem Is Real."

17. Engagement with race and racism took political form early on. For activist critiques, see Biko, *I Write What I Like*; Fanon, *Black Skin, White Masks* and *The Wretched of the Earth*. For more recent critical engagements not yet cited on this large issue, see Appiah, *In My Father's House*, chapter 2; Desai, *Subject to Colonialism*, chapter 1; Fyfe, "Race, Empire, and the Historians." For treatments in southern Africa, see particularly Dubow, *Scientific Racism in Modern South Africa*; Summers, *From Civilization to Segregation*. On the challenges of defining race and racism given the former's plasticity, see, for example, Banton, *Racial Theories*; Goldberg, "The Semantics of Race"; Hall, "Race, Articulation, and Societies Structured in Dominance"; Miles and Brown, *Racism*, introduction.

18. The literature on this issue is equally vast. See, for example, Comaroff and Comaroff, *Ethnicity, Inc.*; Comaroff, "Of Totemism and Ethnicity"; Dubow, "Ethnic Euphemisms and Racial Echoes"; Iliffe, *A Modern History of Tanganyika*, chapter 10; Lonsdale, "The Moral Economy of Mau Mau"; Lonsdale, "When Did the Gusii or Any Other Group Become a 'Tribe'?"; Mamdani, *Citizen and Subject*, chapters 3 and 4; Spear, "Neo-Traditionalism and the Limits of Invention in British Colonial Africa"; Spear and Waller, *Being Maasai*; Vail, *The Creation of Tribalism in Southern Africa*; Young, *The Politics of Cultural Pluralism*.

19. Exemplary works by Boas and Herskovits include Boas, *The Mind of Primitive Man* and Herskovits, *The Myth of the Negro Past*. See also Baker, *From Savage to Negro*; Williams, *Rethinking Race*. Scholars have debated these earlier positions, further critiquing and supporting the idea of culture against race. See Hartigan, "Culture against Race"; Michaels, "Race into Culture" and "The No-Drop Rule"; Visweswaran, *Un/common Cultures*, chapters 2 and 3.

20. For work citing the importance of the precolonial past, see, for example, Schoenbrun, "Conjuring the Modern in Africa" and Vansina, *Paths in the Rainforests*. For recent work addressing the issue of race prior to European control, see Glassman, *War of Words*, chapter 2; Hall, *A History of Race in Muslim West Africa*, chapters 1 and 2.

21. A tradition of Marxist thought played a role in marginalizing the issue of race for a time. On the relative absence of race, see Posel, Hyslop, and Nieftagodien, "Editorial." For scholarship that marked this turn in the South African historiography,

see Dubow, *Racial Segregation and the Origins of Apartheid in South Africa, 1919–36*; Marks and Trapido, *The Politics of Race, Class, and Nationalism in Twentieth-Century South Africa*. Comparative work with the United States also influenced this shift, as did the Black Consciousness Movement of the 1970s. See Cell, *The Highest Stage of White Supremacy*; Fredrickson, *White Supremacy*.

22. Examples of this continuing turn include Brennan, *Taifa*; Glassman, *War of Words*; Hall, *A History of Race*.

23. Though Nyasaland was referred to as British Central Africa prior to its protectorate status, I use the term as shorthand to designate the three colonies of Nyasaland, Northern Rhodesia, and Southern Rhodesia—a common practice during the middle decades of the twentieth century.

24. This study takes into account what Howard Winant has called a "world racial system" centered in the West (*The World Is a Ghetto*, 20, 21, 35). Other relevant literature includes Clarke and Thomas, *Globalization and Race*; Fredrickson, *Racism*; Lake and Reynolds, *Drawing the Global Colour Line*. On peripheries and out-of-the-way places, see Appadurai, "Theory in Anthropology"; Comaroff, *Body of Power, Spirit of Resistance*; Cooper et al., *Confronting Historical Paradigms*; Gupta and Ferguson, "Beyond 'Culture'"; Piot, *Remotely Global*; Tsing, *In the Realm of the Diamond Queen*; Wilmsen, *Land Filled with Flies*.

25. On British Central Africa as a defined region of study, see the work of the Rhodes-Livingstone Institute, such as Colson and Gluckman, *Seven Tribes of British Central Africa*; Gluckman, "Anthropology in Central Africa" and "Tribalism in Modern British Central Africa"; Schumaker, *Africanizing Anthropology*. For engagements with the uses of region generally, see, for example, Cohen and Odhiambo, *Siaya*, 4; Feierman, *The Shambaa Kingdom*, 6, 7; Martin, "Region Formation under Crisis Conditions." For a study that asserts the significance of histories of "the trivial and the ephemeral" in the making of regional histories, see White, "The Traffic in Heads," 326.

26. On the connections between race and nation, see, for example, Anderson, *Imagined Communities*, chapter 8; Balibar and Wallerstein, *Race, Nation, Class*; Marx, *Making Race and Nation*; Glassman, *War of Words*; Brennan, *Taifa*. On race and empire, see McClintock, *Imperial Leather*; Stoler, *Carnal Knowledge and Imperial Power*; Levine, *Prostitution, Race, and Politics*.

27. On the rule of difference, see Chatterjee, *The Nation and Its Fragments*, chapter 2; Scott, "Colonial Governmentality," 194–98; Steinmetz, *The Devil's Handwriting*, 27–41.

28. For arguments that have stressed examining other forms of agency and political imagination as addressed in this book, see Cooper, "Conflict and Connection"; Ortner, "Resistance and the Problem of Ethnographic Refusal." On political language and the politics of language, see, for example, Comaroff and Comaroff, *Of Revelation and Revolution*, chapters 1 and 2; Cooper, *Decolonization and African Society*, 4, 5; Feierman, *Peasant Intellectuals*, 3; Landau, *The Realm of the Word*; Mann, *Native Sons*, 5; Stedman Jones, *Languages of Class*.

29. Mamdani, *Define and Rule*, chapters 1 and 2.

30. Mudimbe, *The Invention of Africa*, x. For extensions of the parameters of Mudimbe's argument, see Amselle, *Mestizo Logics*; Desai, *Subject to Colonialism*.

31. "Africanism" is Mudimbe's term for this order of knowledge, an analogue to

Edward Said's *Orientalism*. See Mudimbe, *The Invention of Africa*, introduction and chapter 1; Said, *Orientalism*.

32. Mbembe, "African Modes of Self-Writing," 256. Mbembe's point generated considerable debate. See Diagne, "Keeping Africanity Open"; Guyer, "Contemplating Uncertainty"; Jewsiwickie, "The Subject in Africa"; Quayson, "Obverse Denominations." For a response, see Mbembe, "On the Power of the False." On the development of the native question and the native problem, see Ashforth, *The Politics of Official Discourse in Twentieth-Century South Africa*; Dubow, *Racial Segregation*. On their repercussions for knowledge, see, for example, Tilley, *Africa as a Living Laboratory*, chapters 5 and 6.

33. Mudimbe has outlined the deep legacies of Africanism, including critical (though limited in his view) challenges made by African intellectuals. See Mudimbe, *The Invention of Africa*, chapters 3 and 4. In a separate vein, not only has a great deal of scholarship been committed to underscoring African agency under colonial rule, but much work has focused on how defining ethnic groups and practices was a negotiated process. In addition to customary authorities and state officials, folk ethnographers, local historians, and trained anthropologists contributed in various ways to this expansive structure of colonial knowledge. For critical discussion, see Berry, *No Condition Is Permanent*; Chanock, *Law, Custom and Social Order*; Hamilton, *Terrific Majesty*; Moore, *Social Facts and Fabrications*; Peterson, *Creative Writing*. On the role of local historians in particular, see Peterson and Macola, *Recasting the Past*. On the connections between ethnography and colonialism, see Asad, *Anthropology and the Colonial Encounter*; Stocking, *Colonial Situations*.

34. Recent scholarship that arguably belongs to this critical tradition, which has attempted to unravel intellectual continuities, includes Vaughan, "Reported Speech and Other Kinds of Testimony"; Landau, *Popular Politics in the History of South Africa, 1400–1948*.

35. For this fascinating political and intellectual history, see Cocks, "Max Gluckman and the Critique of Segregation in South African Anthropology, 1921–1940"; Macmillan, "Return to the Malungwana Drift."

36. Macmillan, *The Cape Colour Question*. For a parallel study from the same period, see Marais, *The Cape Coloured People*. See also the work by a former student of Marais and Schapera, Patterson's *Colour and Culture in South Africa*.

37. These earlier connections have been less explored in recent literature, which has focused on the twentieth century. Recent influential work includes Erasmus, *Coloured by History, Shaped by Place*; Adhikari, *Not White Enough, Not Black Enough*. For a comparative view that returns to and recenters interracial relationships, see the family histories in Milner-Thornton, *The Long Shadow of the British Empire*.

38. Cocks, "Max Gluckman and the Critique of Segregation in South African Anthropology, 1921–1940," 754; Macmillan, "Return to the Malungwana Drift," 48. In addition to *The Cape Colour Question*, Macmillan wrote a second important work that positioned this argument entitled *Bantu, Boer, and Briton* (1929). For a discussion of his influence on South Africa's liberal and Marxist historiography, see Macmillan and Marks, *Africa and the Empire*. For a noted example of Macmillan's influence, see Legassick, *The Politics of a South African Frontier*. Macmillan's work also generated later debates over pluralism and the importance of class analysis. See Magubane, "Plural-

ism and Conflict Situation in Africa"; Van den Berghe, "Pluralism and Conflict Situations in Africa: A Reply to B. Magubane."

39. Cocks, "Max Gluckman and the Critique of Segregation in South African Anthropology, 1921–1940," 754. On Gluckman's intervention itself, see Gluckman, "Analysis of a Social Situation in Modern Zululand" and "Analysis of a Social Situation in Modern Zululand (continued)." For a French parallel, see Balandier, "The Colonial Situation."

40. Mafeje, "The Ideology of 'Tribalism,'" 261. Mafeje further remarked that "if tribalism is thought of as peculiarly African, then the ideology [of tribalism] itself is particularly European in origin" (253). Though he and Gluckman shared a Marxist orientation, it should be noted that Mafeje critiqued Gluckman in the same article for not fulfilling his critical ambition. For further discussion, see Gluckman, "Anthropologists and Apartheid." For a critical engagement with Schapera, see Dubow, *Scientific Racism*, 53, 54. Landau, *Popular Politics*, 223–27, 232–38, 240. For related work and work that has responded to Mafeje's critical intervention, see Amselle, *Mestizo Logics*, chapter 1; Ekeh, "Social Anthropology and Two Contrasting Uses of Tribalism in Africa"; Ojiaku, "European Tribalism and African Nationalism"; Ranger, "The Invention of Tradition Revisited"; Southall, "The Illusion of Tribe."

41. Apter, "Africa, Empire, and Anthropology"; Mafeje, "Anthropology and Independent Africans."

42. While a great deal of intellectual energy has been committed to interrogating essentialist, instrumentalist, and social constructionist interpretations of ethnicity, less attention has extended beyond the ethnic paradigm to interrogate other racial subjectivities in the same fashion. For an overview, see Glassman, *War of Words*, chapter 1.

43. On writing for the nation, see Lonsdale, "States and Social Processes in Africa," 143. On "unofficial" histories and culture, see Barber, "Popular Arts in Africa," 11–13. Luise White, among others, has already made a point of critiquing nationalist histories, remarking that "Early nationalist historiography did not problematise its goals." Moreover, it must be stressed that postcolonial nativism has also created hierarchies of exclusion among ethnic groups, with indigeneity itself often being a political construction. Derek Peterson has recently written that "the era of African independence was marked by increasing intolerance of minorities, by the solidification of unequal gender roles, and by the multiplication of nativisms." Though they could overlap as suggested in this book, postcolonial nativism and black nationalism must not always be equated. For critical discussion of these issues, see Hodgson, *Being Maasai, Becoming Indigenous*; Peterson, *Ethnic Patriotism and the East African Revival*, 281; Ranger, "Nationalist Historiography, Patriotic History and the History of the Nation"; White, "The Traffic in Heads," 326. On postcolonial nativism more generally, see, for example, Appiah, *In My Father's House*, chapter 3; Mamdani, *When Victims Become Killers*, chapter 1; Ndlovu-Gatsheni, "Tracking the Historical Roots of Post-Apartheid Citizenship Problems"; Ngũgĩ, *Decolonising the Mind*.

44. On hierarchies of credibility, see Stoler, "'In Cold Blood.'" On a related formulation of invisible histories, see Feierman, "Colonizers, Scholars, and the Creation of Invisible Histories." For a recent study of autochthony, see Geschiere, *The Perils of Belonging*.

45. Said, *Culture and Imperialism*, xxiv, 42, 228.

46. See Brennan, *Taifa*; Glassman, *War of Words*; Hall, *A History of Race*. This recent work has followed the lead of many historians of women and gender, who have sought to complicate male-centered narratives of anti-colonial struggle. See, for example, Geiger, *TANU Women*; Lyons, "Guerrilla Girls and Women in the Zimbabwean National Liberation Struggle"; Schmidt, "'Emancipate Your Husbands!'" On political alternatives in Africa after the Second World War, see Cooper, "Possibility and Constraint." For related discussion on challenging the nation-state as overdeterming historical narratives, see Burton, *After the Imperial Turn*, introduction, and *Empire in Question*, chapters 2 and 5.

47. See, for example, Akyeampong, "Race, Identity and Citizenship in Black Africa"; Arsan, "Failing to Stem the Tide"; Brennan, *Taifa*; Dotson and Dotson, *The Indian Minority of Zambia, Rhodesia, and Malawi*; Freund, *Insiders and Outsiders*; Glassman, *Feasts and Riot*; Hall, *A History of Race*; Hansen, *Melancholia of Freedom*; Hughes, *Whiteness in Zimbabwe*; Kennedy, *Islands of White*; Mangat, *A History of the Asians in East Africa*. On imperialism and cultural management, see Burbank and Cooper, *Empires in World History*; Cannadine, *Ornamentalism*.

48. White, *The Middle Ground*, chapters 5 and 8. For other studies in a similar vein, see Ballantyne and Burton, *Bodies in Contact*; Ghosh, *Sex and the Family in Colonial India*; Hodes, *Sex, Love, Race*; Ray, "Interracial Sex and the Making of Empire"; Stoler, *Haunted by Empire*.

49. Brooks, *Eurafricans in Western Africa*; Jones, *The Métis of Senegal*; Mark, *"Portuguese" Style and Luso-African Identity*; Rodney, *A History of the Upper Guinea Coast, 1545–1800*, 221, 222; White, *Children of the French Empire*.

50. Glassman, *War of Words*, chapter 2.

51. For Mozambique, see Isaacman, *Mozambique*; Penvenne, "'We Are All Portuguese!'" and "João dos Santos Albasini (1876–1922)."

52. Historians of nineteenth-century South Africa have located the term's origins in the 1820s and 1830s, the period when slavery was abolished in the Western Cape, when a free person of color was considered "Coloured." But the category "Coloured" had a British imperial presence across the slaveholding Atlantic world. See Adhikari, "The Sons of Ham"; Bickford-Smith, *Ethnic Pride and Racial Prejudice in Victorian Cape Town*; Jordan, "American Chiaroscuro."

53. Landau, *Popular Politics*, chapters 2 and 5. For other studies of the Griqua, see Legassick, "The Northern Frontier to c.1840"; Ross, *Adam Kok's Griquas*; Waldman, *The Griqua Conundrum*. For a historiographical overview, see Cavanagh, *The Griqua Past and the Limits of South African History*.

54. Landau, *Popular Politics*, 4, 11.

55. Giliomee, "The Beginnings of Afrikaner Ethnic Consciousness, 1850–1915," 23. See also Giliomee, "The Non-Racial Franchise and Afrikaner and Coloured Identities."

56. On postcolonial nationalism and elite historiographies, see, for example, Guha, "On Some Aspects of the Historiography of Colonial India"; Prakash, "Writing Post-Orientalist Histories of the Third World." On subject races, see Mamdani, "Beyond Settler and Native as Political Identities."

57. I place "transgressive" in quotes to signal my criticism of this discriminatory

colonial attitude toward interracial relationships. For a study of such attitudes, see Young, *Colonial Desire*, chapters 1 and 6.

58. I borrow this expression from Wolf, *Europe and the People without History*.

59. The authoritative statement on this agenda is Cooper, "Conflict and Connection." See also Abu-Lughod, "The Romance of Resistance"; Hunt, *A Colonial Lexicon*, introduction; Johnson, "On Agency"; Ortner, "Resistance and the Problem of Ethnographic Refusal."

60. For pathbreaking work on the role of intellectuals in identity formation, which this book builds upon, see Vail, "Introduction: Ethnicity in Southern African History."

61. Posel, "Race as Common Sense," 89, 90.

62. Macmillan, *Cape Colour Question*, 266, note 1.

63. Muzondidya, *Walking a Tightrope*, 26–28.

64. There is also evidence that the term *Anglo-African* was used earlier in southern Africa to refer loosely to whites either born or settled in Africa, similar to the term *Anglo-Indian* in India. This usage may reflect the aftermath of the South African War (also known as the Anglo-Boer War) and the search for a new terminology to include settlers of both British and Afrikaner descent. See Wills and Barrett, *The Anglo-African Who's Who and Biographical Sketch-Book*.

65. For a study of Coloured identity as a state instrument, see Goldin, *Making Race*.

66. Curiously, the only census I could find that uses "Eurafrican" as a standard category is from outside the region, in Swaziland. See Swaziland, *Swaziland Census, 1962*.

67. For other studies in the region, see Dotson and Dotson, "Indians and Coloureds in Rhodesia and Nyasaland"; Mandaza, *Race, Colour, and Class in Southern Africa*; Milner-Thornton, *The Long Shadow of the British Empire*; Wheeldon, "The Operation of Voluntary Associations and Personal Networks in the Political Processes of an Inter-Ethnic Community." For a southern Africa approach, see Adhikari, *Burdened by Race*.

68. The literature for South Africa is primarily centered in the Western Cape, especially Cape Town. For an overview, see Lee, "Voices from the Margins." Some exceptions include Carstens, *The Social Structure of a Cape Coloured Reserve*; Dickie-Clark, *The Marginal Situation*; Sales, *Mission Stations and the Coloured Communities of the Eastern Cape, 1800–1852*. For studies that have extended beyond history and sociology to the fields of literature and ethnomusicology, see Farred, *Midfielder's Moment*; February, *Mind Your Colour*; Jorritsma, *Sonic Spaces of the Karoo*.

69. I sympathize with an argument made by Edward Cavanagh regarding the erasure of Griqua history and the homogenizing effect of much South African Coloured history (*The Griqua Past*, 5, 38). James Brennan strikes a similar cautionary note (*Taifa*, 3).

70. On Anglo-Indians, see Caplan, *Children of Colonialism*.

71. My thinking here has been inspired by Frederick Cooper's useful distinction between analytic terms and historical terms. As he writes, we tend to "lose sight of the quest of people in the past to develop connections or ways of thinking that mattered to them but not to us." See Cooper, *Colonialism in Question*, 18. On a separate

note, South African histories have tended toward political and intellectual histories as a means of addressing social formation—an approach pursued in part III of this book. See Adhikari, *Not White Enough, Not Black Enough*; Lewis, *Between the Wire and the Wall*; van der Ross, *The Rise and Decline of Apartheid*.

72. On structures of feeling, see Williams, *Marxism and Literature*, 128–35.

73. This position draws from social constructionist arguments. See Adhikari, *Not White Enough, Not Black Enough*, 13; Brubaker and Cooper, "Beyond 'Identity'"; Vail, *The Creation of Tribalism in Southern Africa*, introduction. Examples of conflict histories include Crais, *White Supremacy and Black Resistance in Pre-Industrial South Africa*; Evans, *Cultures of Violence*; Glassman, *War of Words*. The politics of descent have also been vital to recent histories of race, see Brennan, *Taifa*, chapters 1, 2, and 4; Glassman, *War of Words*, chapters 2, 3, and 4; Hall, *A History of Race*, chapter 1.

74. These specific forms are discussed in van Velsen, *The Politics of Kinship*, 185, 186.

75. This argument builds on a turn in kinship studies away from structuralism and biological determinism to local history and social construction in the making of kin relations. See Carsten, *After Kinship*; Collier and Yanagisako, *Gender and Kinship*; Franklin and McKinnon, *Relative Values*; McKinnon, "Domestic Exceptions"; Schneider, *A Critique of the Study of Kinship*; Strathern, *After Nature*. On "cultures of relatedness," see Carsten, *Cultures of Relatedness*.

76. Darnton, *The Great Cat Massacre and Other Episodes in French Cultural History*; Ginzburg, *The Cheese and the Worms*; Stoler, *Carnal Knowledge and Imperial Power*; van Onselen, *New Babylon, New Ninevah*; Vaughan, *Curing Their Ills*; White, *Speaking with Vampires*.

77. Eze, *On Reason*, chapter 1.

78. Gramsci, *Selections from the Prison Notebooks of Antonio Gramsci*, 52, 54, 55. On applying subaltern studies to Malawi, see Kalinga, "Resistance, Politics of Protest, and Mass Nationalism in Colonial Malawi, 1950–1960."

79. Foucault, *Language, Counter-Memory, Practice*, 139.

80. Foucault, "Nietzsche, Genealogy, History," 2:374. See also Asad, *Genealogies of Religion*, 16.

81. It should be noted that the genealogical history pursued in this book works forward, not backward, to avoid a retrospective analysis that can produce anachronisms. See Cooper, *Colonialism in Question*, 18, 19.

82. Foucault, *"Society Must Be Defended,"* 7, 9.

83. I place "transgression" in quotes to critique the idea of racial purity that underpins the use of this word. The relative historical shallowness of these identities and the communities they represent is also one reason why I resist calling them "ethnic" groups.

84. My thoughts on historicizing reason and unreason have been influenced by Chakrabarty, *Provincializing Europe*, 238, 239; Derrida, *Writing and Difference*, chapter 2; Foucault, *Madness and Civilization*; Foucault and Gérard Raulet, "Structuralism and Post-Structuralism."

85. Mbembe, "African Modes of Self-Writing," 241.

I. HISTORIES WITHOUT GROUPS

1. On the importance of enduring traditions, see Ajayi, "The Continuity of African Institutions under Colonialism."

2. On colonialism, knowledge, and categories, see Cohn, *Colonialism and Its Forms of Knowledge*; Dirks, *Castes of Mind*; Mamdani, *Define and Rule*; Mitchell, *Colonising Egypt*; Said, *Orientalism*. On uncovering this complexity, see Landau, *Popular Politics in the History of South Africa, 1400–1948*, chapter 2; Vaughan, "Reported Speech and Other Kinds of Testimony." On ephemeral histories, see White, "The Traffic in Heads."

3. My thoughts here are influenced by Guha, "The Prose of Counter-Insurgency."

4. On colonial fabrication, see, for example, Afigbo, *The Warrant Chiefs*; Hamilton, *Terrific Majesty*.

5. Wolf, *Europe and the People without History*.

6. Williams, *Marxism and Literature*, 126. My thinking here is influenced by Brubaker, *Ethnicity without Groups*, chapter 3; Brubaker and Cooper, "Beyond 'Identity'"; Landau, *Popular Politics*, chapter 2.

7. On the citation of peoplehood in this paragraph, see Smith, *Stories of Peoplehood*. On sources and the archival turn, see, for example, Barber, *Africa's Hidden Histories*; Burton, *Archive Stories*; Cohen, *The Combing of History*; Hamilton et al., *Refiguring the Archive*; Stoler, *Along the Archival Grain*.

8. On Freud and slips of history, see Sarkar, "The Kalki-Avatar of Bikrampur."

9. Chakrabarty, *Habitations of Modernity*, 34, 35.

1. IDIOMS OF PLACE AND HISTORY

1. On folk sociologies and local theory, see, for example, Geertz, *Local Knowledge*, chapters 3 and 4.

2. It should be noted that Wolf's historical concerns were the rise of a world capitalist system and how peoples outside the West (those "without history") shaped this global process (*Europe and the People without History*, chapter 1).

3. For a critique of Ann Laura Stoler's work on this point, see Loos, "Transnational Histories of Sexualities in Asia," 1314. For sexuality and the precolonial period in Africa, see, for example, Epprecht, *Hungochani*, chapter 1, and "Sexuality, History, Africa," 1268.

4. Livingstone and Livingstone, *Narrative of an Expedition*, 50; Johnston, *British Central Africa*, 390.

5. Livingstone and Livingstone, *Narrative of an Expedition to the Zambesi and Its Tributaries*, 24, 37, 43, 193, 201, 217, 397, 402, 423.

6. Hailey, *Native Administration in the British African Territories*, 25. For a parallel study from the same period, see Baker and White, "The Distribution of Native Population over South-East Central Africa."

7. My thoughts here critique understandings of creolization or hybridity that locate such processes to the arrival of Western colonialism, the work of Jean Comaroff and John L. Comaroff being an example. See Elbourne, "Word Made Flesh," 443–53; Landau, "Hegemony and History in Jean and John L. Comaroff's *Of Revelation and Revolution*," 511, 512.

8. For discussion and debate over the Mfecane, see Hamilton, *The* Mfecane *Aftermath*.

9. On the *jumbe*, see Morris, "The Ivory Trade and Chiefdoms in Pre-Colonial Malawi." On the Chikunda, see Isaacman and Isaacman, *Slavery and Beyond*. On this period in Malawi generally, see McCracken, *A History of Malawi*, 26–37.

10. An argument for the diminution of matrilineal practices over time can be found in Phiri, "Some Changes in the Matrilineal Family System among the Chewa of Malawi since the Nineteenth Century," 272–74. For an argument that these practices persisted, see Peters, "Against the Odds"; Vaughan, *The Story of an African Famine*, 124–44. On continuity and change in kinship practices more generally, see Mandala, "Capitalism, Kinship and Gender in the Lower Tchiri (Shire) Valley of Malawi, 1860–1960"; Mitchell, *The Yao Village*; Northrup, "The Migrations of Yao and Kololo into Southern Malawi"; Read, *The Ngoni of Nyasaland*; van Velsen, *The Politics of Kinship*. On Malawi's precolonial history, see Alpers, *Ivory and Slaves in East Central Africa*; Mandala, *Work and Control in a Peasant Economy*; McCracken, "The Nineteenth Century in Malawi"; Power, *Political Culture and Nationalism in Malawi*, 10–12. It should be noted that regional upheaval and migration have continued as a historical pattern, most recently with the Mozambican civil war (1977–92). See Englund, *From War to Peace on the Mozambique-Malawi Borderland*.

11. Quoted in Vail and White, "Tribalism in the Political History of Malawi," 153.

12. Abdullah, *Chiikala Cha Wa Yao (The Story of the Yao)*; Mwase, *Strike a Blow and Die*; Vaughan, "Mr. Mdala Writes to the Governor."

13. Tew, *Peoples of the Lake Nyasa Region*, ix.

14. Chanock, *Law, Custom and Social Order*, 31–34.

15. Mitchell, foreword, vi, vii. See also Young, "Tribal Intermixture in Northern Nyasaland."

16. Amselle, *Mestizo Logics*, x, 10.

17. On marriage, see, for example, Colson, *Marriage and the Family among the Plateau Tonga of Northern Rhodesia*; Mitchell, *The Yao Village*, chapter 7; Read, *The Ngoni of Nyasaland*, chapter 3; van Velsen, *The Politics of Kinship*, chapter 4. On knowledge and wealth, see Guyer and Belinga, "Wealth in People as Wealth in Knowledge." On territory, see Schoffeleers, *River of Blood*.

18. Vaughan, "Reported Speech and Other Kinds of Testimony," 59. For similar critiques, see Landau, *Popular Politics in the History of South Africa, 1400–1948*, chapter 2; McKinnon, "Domestic Exceptions."

19. The notion of racial frontiers is from Stoler, *Carnal Knowledge and Imperial Power*, chapter 4.

20. National Archives of Malawi (hereafter NAM), Zomba, s1/705^i/30, Folio 44a, 4, 5. See also NAM, s1/705^i/30, Folio 46, Copy 9.

21. On disease and degeneration, see Levine, *Prostitution, Race, and Politics*; Vaughan, *Curing Their Ills*, chapter 6. On empire and sexual opportunity, see Hyam, *Empire and Sexuality*.

22. A distinction must be drawn between miscegenation and "black peril" (for which there were laws in Southern Rhodesia), discussed further in the next chapter. See Ibbo Mandaza, *Race, Colour, and Class in Southern Africa*, 157.

23. Kennedy, *Islands of White*, 147.

24. McCracken, *A History of Malawi*, 80–82, 92.

25. McCracken, *A History of Malawi*, 138, 139.

26. Mwase, *Strike a Blow and Die*, 95.

27. On the size of the Anglo-African community see NAM, s1/705¹/30, Folio 27, January 4, 1934. On population figures for Nyasaland more generally, see Rotberg, "The African Population of Malawi"; Superintendent of the Census, *Census of the Nyasaland Protectorate, 1921*.

28. As discussed in chapter 2, black peril scares typically generated scandal. In addition, homosexuality could produce public displays of outrage and purported disgrace. See Epprecht, *Hungochani*; Rich, "Torture, Homosexuality, and Masculinities in French Central Africa"; Schmidt, "Colonial Intimacy."

29. Hyam, *Empire and Sexuality*, 158.

30. NAM, s2/62/19, Minutes Section, No. 18.

31. White, *Speaking with Vampires*, 75.

32. NAM, s2/62/19, Enclosure "B" in Circular of 11th January 1909, Folio 1. See also Mandaza, *Race, Colour, and Class*, chapter 3. For differences between British colonies and Portuguese and French ones, see Bender, *Angola under the Portuguese*, chapters 1 and 2; White, *Children of the French Empire*.

33. NAM, J 4/3/1, Judgments of 1901, High Court of the British Central Africa Protectorate, *Storey vs. Registrar of Marriages*.

34. For this issue in Southern Rhodesia, see McCulloch, *Black Peril, White Virtue*, 73; Schmidt, *Peasants, Traders, and Wives*, 174–78. As McCulloch notes, one definition of "white peril" in Southern Rhodesia concerned "degenerate" white women consorting with black men, essentially the same white woman–black man formula as with black peril. For comparison with West Africa, see also Ray, "Decrying White Peril."

35. For an overview of tightening control in different realms in Southern Rhodesia, see Jeater, *Marriage, Perversion, and Power* and *Law, Language, and Science*; Summers, *From Civilization to Segregation*.

36. National Archives of Zimbabwe (hereafter NAZ), Harare, Letter from the native commissioner, Chilimanzi, to the superintendent of natives, Victoria, A 3/18/35, June 16, 1921.

37. NAZ, A 3/18/35, Letter from the native commissioner, Plumtree, to the superintendent of natives, Bulawayo, June 16, 1921.

38. NAZ, A 3/18/35, Letter from the native commissioner, Rusapi, to the superintendent of natives, Umtali, June 10, 1921.

39. NAZ, A 3/18/35, Letter from the native commissioner, Umtali, to the chief native commissioner, Salisbury, June 23, 1921.

40. Gluckman, "Gossip and Scandal"; White, *Speaking with Vampires*, 59–66.

41. White, *Speaking with Vampires*, 62, 63. On respectability and why it mattered, see Stoler, "Making Empire Respectable."

42. NAZ, A 3/18/35, Letter from the native commissioner, Mazoe, to the superintendent of natives, Salisbury, June 20, 1921.

43. NAZ, A 3/18/35, Letter from the native commissioner, Inyati, to the superintendent of natives, Bulawayo, June 14, 1921.

44. White, *Speaking with Vampires*, 62, 84.

45. NAM, s2/31/20, Letter from magistrate, Ncheu, to the attorney general, Zomba, Folio 1, September 25, 1920.

46. NAM, s2/31/20, Letter from magistrate, Ncheu, to the attorney general, Zomba, Folio 1, September 25, 1920. On the history of marriage law and the particular significance of the 1923 Native Marriage (Christian Rites) Ordinance, see Power, "Marrying on the Margins."

47. Power, *Political Culture and Nationalism in Malawi*, 30.

48. NAM, s2/31/20, Letter from attorney general, Zomba, to the magistrate, Ncheu, Folio 1, October 12, 1920.

49. NAM, s2/31/20, Letter from the resident, Ncheu, to the chief secretary, Zomba, Folio 1, October 16, 1920.

50. NAM, s2/31/20, Minute Comments 2, October 21, 1920.

51. NAZ, A 3/18/35, Letter from the native commissioner, M'Toko, to the superintendent of natives, Salisbury, June 24, 1921.

52. NAZ, A 3/18/35, Letter from the native commissioner, M'Toko, to the superintendent of natives, Salisbury, June 24, 1921.

53. Emphasis in the original. NAZ, A 3/18/35, Letter from the native commissioner, Marandellas, to the superintendent of natives, Salisbury, June 13, 1921.

54. NAZ, A 3/18/35, Letter from the native commissioner, Chilimanzi, to the superintendent of natives, Victoria, June 16, 1921.

55. NAZ, A 3/18/35, Letter from the native commissioner, Chilimanzi, to the superintendent of natives, Victoria, June 16, 1921.

56. Quoted in Crowder, *The Flogging of Phinehas McIntosh*, 42.

57. NAM, s2/31/20, Minute Comments 2, October 21, 1920.

58. NAM, s2/31/20, Letter from the resident, Fort Johnston, to the chief secretary, Zomba, Folio 8, January 1, 1921.

59. NAM, s2/31/20, Letter from the resident, Mlanje, to the chief secretary, Zomba, Folio 18, December 20, 1920.

60. NAM, s2/31/20, Letter from the resident, Mzimba, to the chief secretary, Zomba, Folio 13, December 31, 1921.

61. NAM, s2/31/20, Letter from the acting resident, Karonga, to the chief secretary, Zomba, Folio 23, January 27, 1921, 1.

62. NAM, s2/31/20, Letter from the resident, Chinteche, to the chief secretary, Zomba, Folio 22, January 14, 1921.

63. NAM, s2/31/20, Letter from the resident, Dedza, to the chief secretary, Zomba, Folio 7, December 22, 1920.

64. NAM, s2/31/20, Letter from the acting resident, Kota Kota, to the chief secretary, Zomba, Folio 11, January 2, 1920.

65. NAM, s2/31/20, Letter from the assistant resident, Liwonde, to the chief secretary, Zomba, Folio 19, December 21, 1920, 1.

66. NAM, s2/31/20, Letter from the resident, Blantyre, to the chief secretary, Zomba, Folio 12, January 10, 1921, 2.

67. NAM, s2/31/20, Letter from the resident, Fort Johnston, to the chief secretary, Zomba, Folio 8, January 1, 1921.

68. NAM, s2/31/20, Letter from the resident, Mzimba, to the chief secretary, Zomba, Folio 13, December 31, 1921.

69. The first quote is from NAM, s2/31/20, Letter from the assistant resident, Chiradzulu, to the chief secretary, Zomba, Folio 16, December 21, 1920, and the second quote is from NAM, s2/31/20, Letter from the acting resident, Karonga, to the chief secretary, Zomba, Folio 23, January 27, 1921, 1.

70. NAM, s2/31/20, Letter from the resident, Mlanje, to the chief secretary, Zomba, Folio 18, December 20, 1920.

71. White, *Speaking with Vampires*, 81.

72. White, *Speaking with Vampires*, 76, 77.

73. For an auto-ethnographic study that similarly touches on personal family histories in Northern Rhodesia, see Milner-Thornton, *The Long Shadow of the British Empire*.

74. This point is discussed at greater length in the book's conclusion.

75. Interview with Ann and Jessica Ascroft, November 9, 1999, Blantyre, Malawi.

76. White, "'Tribes' and the Aftermath of the Chilembwe Rising," 516.

77. On land tenure, see Kandawire, "Thangata in Precolonial and Colonial Systems of Land Tenure in Southern Malawi"; McCracken, "'Marginal Men'" and *A History of Malawi*, 168–71; Ng'ong'ola, "The State, Settlers, and Indigenes in the Evolution of Land Law and Policy in Colonial Malawi," 32; Power, "'Eating the Property,'" 101, note 5.

78. Interview with Ann and Jessica Ascroft, November 9, 1999, Blantyre, Malawi.

79. Interview with Eunice Mussa, October 4, 1999, Zomba, Malawi.

80. Interview with Yusuf Ismael, October 17, 1999, Blantyre, Malawi.

81. For a further discussion of Indian communities, see Dotson and Dotson, *The Indian Minority of Zambia, Rhodesia, and Malawi*, 281.

82. Turner, *Schism and Continuity in an African Society*, 82.

83. Appadurai, "The Past as a Scarce Resource."

84. I borrow "elective affinities" from Jackson, *The Palm at the End of the Mind*, xiii, 4, 104.

85. Interview with Robert Jamieson, November 15, 1999, Lilongwe, Malawi.

86. Interview with Robert Jamieson, November 15, 1999, Lilongwe, Malawi.

87. van Velsen, *The Politics of Kinship*, 47, 268.

88. Stoler, *Carnal Knowledge and Imperial Power*, 215.

89. On remains, see Stoler, "Imperial Debris."

90. Megan Vaughan raises a similar set of issues regarding kinship and defining household in "Which Family?"

91. My thoughts here draw on the tensions between individual and collective history as discussed by Michel-Rolph Trouillot in *Silencing the Past*, 15, 16.

92. White, "Telling More," 16.

93. Interview with Dinah Coombes, November 8, 1999, Zomba, Malawi. On genealogical time, see Jackson, *The Palm at the End of the Mind*, xiii.

94. See Kopytoff, "The Internal African Frontier."

95. I borrow the term *hauntology* from Jacques Derrida, who invented it as an elaboration on ontology to capture the ends of being. See Derrida, *Specters of Marx*, 10, 63, 202.

2. ADAIMA'S STORY

1. On silences surrounding sex, the existing South African literature has rarely addressed this topic in serious historical fashion, focusing on political and intellectual history instead. See, for example, Adhikari, *Not White Enough, Not Black Enough*; Lewis, *Between the Wire and the Wall*. On dissident sexualities, see Epprecht, *Hungochani*, 11, 12.

2. Wolfe, "Land, Labor, and Difference," 904. For comparative discussions on this topic, see Hodes, *White Women, Black Men*; Ghosh, "National Narratives and the Politics of Miscegenation."

3. On "ethically constitutive" stories, which have the capacity to establish a sense of "normative worth," see Smith, *Stories of Peoplehood*, 59.

4. On the evolution of oral history as methodology, see Cohen, Miescher, and White, "Introduction: Voices, Words, and African History."

5. See Guha, "Chandra's Death." Other key references include Spivak, "The Rani of Sirmur" and "Can the Subaltern Speak?"

6. This expression is from Hawkins, *Writing and Colonialism in Northern Ghana*.

7. On mining in the Rhodesias, see, for example, Parpart, *Labor and Capital on the African Copperbelt*; van Onselen, *Chibaro*. On agricultural production in Nyasaland, see, for example, McCracken, *A History of Malawi*, chapter 3; White, *Magomero*, 168–71.

8. McCulloch, *Black Peril, White Virtue*, chapter 1. For earlier studies, see Kennedy, *Islands of White*, chapter 7; Pape, "Black and White." For a broader discussion of social "scares," see Rose, "Cultural Analysis and Moral Discourses."

9. On Natal, see Etherington, "Natal's Black Rape Scare of the 1870s." On Johannesburg, see van Onselen, *New Babylon, New Ninevah*, 237–39, 247, 257–74. See also Keegan, "Gender, Degeneration and Sexual Danger"; Anderson, "Sexual Threat and Settler Society."

10. In fact, the original 1903 legislation grew out of preexisting legislation, the Criminal Law Amendment Ordinance of 1900, which was intended to protect young women from sexual exploitation by brothel owners and similar means of prostitution. See McCulloch, *Black Peril, White Virtue*, 4, 5, 57. For other important studies on women and morality generally during this period, see Jeater, *Marriage, Perversion, and Power*; Schmidt, *Peasants, Traders, and Wives*. For comparison in British Africa, see Thomas, *Politics of the Womb*, chapters 1–4.

11. On this distinction, see Kennedy, *Islands of White*, 174–79. For studies of this issue from other parts of Africa, see, for example, Jean-Baptiste, "'A Black Girl Should Not be With a White Man'"; Ray, "Decrying White Peril"; Rich, "'Une Babylone Noire.'"

12. Hunt, "Noise over Camouflaged Polygamy," 471.

13. For this issue in Southern Rhodesia, see McCulloch, *Black Peril, White Virtue*, 73; Pape, "Black and White"; Schmidt, *Peasants, Traders, and Wives*, 174–78.

14. Ibbo Mandaza, *Race, Colour, and Class in Southern Africa*, 160–72.

15. Plaatje, "The Mote and the Beam," 87. The South African writer Sarah Gertrude Millin engaged in similar commentary, though in a more racist vein by addressing white anxieties over racial "contamination" and "degeneration" in books like *God's*

Stepchildren. For a commentary on this issue, see Coetzee, *White Writing*, chapter 6. See also Cornwell, "George Webb Hardy's *The Black Peril*."

16. On morality, see Jeater, *Marriage, Perversion, and Power*. For the broader political context, see Summers, *From Civilization to Segregation*.

17. Note: this transcription is complete, with the exception of a few sentences where the writing was illegible, as I have indicated with ellipses. Words that are in italics are emphasized in the original. National Archives of Malawi (hereafter NAM), Zomba, Native Secretariat (hereafter NS) 1/35/3, Folio 7, 1–4.

18. Stoler, *Along the Archival Grain*, 106.

19. Burton, "Introduction: Archive Fever, Archive Stories," 14.

20. Conceptualizing archives has been a topic of much attention, to a great extent building on Michel Foucault's work. See Foucault, *The Archaeology of Knowledge*; Hamilton et al., *Refiguring the Archive*; Steedman, *Dust*.

21. On the size of the Anglo-African community, see NAM, S1/705ⁱ/30, Folio 27, January 4, 1934.

22. The full title of the report is *Report of the Committee appointed by the Government of Southern Rhodesia to Enquire into Questions Concerning the Education of Coloured and Half-Caste Children in the Colony*. See NAM, S26/2/4/5, Folio 14.

23. On public and private transcripts, see Scott, *Domination and the Arts of Resistance*, chapter 1.

24. The Yao were involved in the East African slave trade as discussed in the previous chapter, thus explaining the use of a Swahili name. My thanks to Sam Mchombo for explaining the potential colloquial use of this name as well. The concurrent use of both meanings is also possible.

25. My thanks to Joey Power for alerting me to the relevance of this name.

26. On the persistence of slaves and slave-wives among the Yao, see, for example, Vaughan, *The Story of an African Famine*, 126.

27. On mobility, see Chirwa, "Child and Youth Labour on the Nyasaland Plantations, 1890–1953," 672–76; Power, "'Eating the Property.'"

28. On anonymity and agency, see Newell, *The Power to Name*, introduction.

29. On settler life in Nyasaland, see McCracken, "Planters, Peasants and the Colonial State" and "Economics and Ethnicity."

30. On secrets as a form of history, see White, "Telling More."

31. NAM, Judgments of 1901, High Court of British Central Africa, *Storey vs. Registrar of Marriages*, J 4/3/1.

32. Emphasis in the original. NAM, NS 1/35/3, Folio 7, 3.

33. NAM, NS 1/35/3, Folio 7, 3.

34. NAM, NS 1/35/3, Folio 7, 3.

35. NAM, NS 1/35/3, Folio 7, 3.

36. On historicizing domestic violence in Africa, see Burrill, Roberts, and Thornberry, "Introduction: Domestic Violence and the Law in Africa."

37. NAM, NS 1/35/3, Folio 7, 1.

38. NAM, NS 1/35/3, Folio 7, 1.

39. NAM, NS 1/35/3, Folio 7, 2.

40. On the instability of domestic spaces, see Clancy-Smith and Gouda, *Domesticating the Empire*; Stoler, *Race and the Education of Desire*, chapter 5.

41. On hysteria and race (with the exposure to "civilization" as a cause for the former), see Briggs, "The Race of Hysteria."

42. NAM, NS 1/35/3, Folio 7, 1, 2, 3.

43. Emphasis in the original. NAM, NS 1/35/3, Folio 7, 1, 2.

44. Scott, *Weapons of the Weak*, 29, 30.

45. NAM, NS 1/35/3, Folio 7, 1.

46. NAM, NS 1/35/3, Folio 7, 1, 2.

47. NAM, NS 1/35/3, Folio 7, 1, 2.

48. NAM, NS 1/35/3, Folio 7, 1, 2.

49. Emphasis added. NAM, NS 1/35/3, Folio 7, 2.

50. NAM, NS 1/35/3, Folio 7, 2.

51. On the issue of female desire under colonialism, see, for example, Gengenbach, "'What My Heart Wanted.'" On material motivations and sex, see White, *The Comforts of Home*, chapters 1 and 5. On thinking through the multiple dimensions of resistance, see Abu-Lughod, "The Romance of Resistance"; Ortner, "Resistance and the Problem of Ethnographic Refusal."

52. White, "Telling More," 22.

53. Marks, *"Not Either an Experimental Doll"*; Wright, *Strategies of Slaves and Women*. On restoring women's history in southern Africa, see Bozzoli, "Marxism, Feminism and South African Studies"; Bradford, "Women, Gender and Colonialism" and "Peasants, Historians, and Gender"; Marks, "Changing History, Changing Histories."

54. Though it is possible that the writer is lying about the extent of Adaima's behavior, I am reluctant to think his story is a complete fabrication. If she were not destructive, or did not take James away, why would he have gone public to a state official? On secrets and lies, again see White, "Telling More," 15–22. On possibilities of archival fictions, see Davis, *Fiction in the Archives*.

55. Scott, "The Evidence of Experience," 777.

3. COMING OF AGE

1. Ariès, *Centuries of Childhood*, 15.

2. For a study of absent fathers in Northern Rhodesia, see Milner-Thornton, "Absent White Fathers."

3. Hunt, "Letter-Writing, Nursing Men and Bicycles in the Belgian Congo," 192.

4. On negotiating this difficult, if not impossible, challenge, see Miescher, *Making Men in Ghana*; Smith, *Baba of Karo*; van Onselen, *The Seed Is Mine*. For a broader project that has productively interrogated this issue, see Weinbaum et al., *The Modern Girl around the World*.

5. At times, children could introduce political change. See Cohen, *Womunafu's Bunafu*, chapter 1. For a classic study of childhood in Nyasaland, see Read, *Children of Their Fathers*. For a more recent study of child and youth agency, see Grier, *Invisible Hands*.

6. Thompson, "The Crime of Anonymity," 304. See also Barber, *Africa's Hidden Histories*.

7. This view contrasts with Read's study of childhood that examines "ideal" patterns and uniformity. See Read, *Children of Their Fathers*, 30.

8. Translated with the assistance of Sam Mchombo. The surnames "Swan" and "Swann" are both used in the letter, with the latter likely being the correct version. National Archives of Malawi (hereafter NAM), Zomba, Letter from Alfred Swann of Kota Kota to Mr. Ambrostra of Fort Johnston, Native Secretariat (hereafter NS) 1/35/3, October 26, 1917.

9. The word *Father* suggests a religious official, though it could denote seniority more generally.

10. NAM, Letter from the acting superintendent of native affairs, Zomba, to A. J. Swann, NS 1/35/3, Folio 6, March 16, 1918.

11. NAM, Letter from the acting superintendent of native affairs, Zomba, to A. J. Swann, NS 1/35/3, Folio 6, March 16, 1918.

12. NAM, Letter from the acting superintendent of native affairs, Zomba, to A. J. Swann, NS 1/35/3, Folio 6, March 16, 1918.

13. NAM, NS 1/35/3, Letter from Henry Munby to Mr. Costley White, Folio 6b, March 26, 1919; NAM, NS 1/35/3, Letter from the acting superintendent of native affairs, Zomba, to H. Munby, Kota Kota, Folio 6c, April 21, 1919; NAM, NS 1/35/3, Letter from St. Augustine's Mission, Southern Rhodesia, to Mr. Costley White, Zomba, Folio 6e, September 10, 1919.

14. NAM, NS 1/35/3, Letter from St. Augustine's Mission, Southern Rhodesia, to Mr. Costley White, Zomba, Folio 6e, September 10, 1919.

15. The literature on moral economy is extensive, though most of it focuses on local communities, not states. See Thompson, "The Moral Economy of the English Crowd in the Eighteenth Century"; Scott, *The Moral Economy of the Peasant*. On states, see Munro, *The Moral Economy of the State*, chapter 1.

16. NAM, NS 1/35/3, Letter from the acting superintendent of native affairs, Zomba, to the reverend father superior of the Nguludi Mission, Folio 2, January 1, 1917.

17. Linden with Linden, *Catholics, Peasants, and Chewa Resistance in Nyasaland*, 67. See also 70, 82n.

18. NAM, NS 1/35/3, Letter from the acting superintendent of native affairs, Zomba, to the reverend father superior of the Nguludi Mission, Folio 2, January 1, 1917.

19. NAM, NS 1/35/3, Letter from M. Cadaret, Folio 2a, January 5, 1917.

20. NAM, NS 1/35/3, Letter from the acting superintendent of native affairs, Zomba, to the reverend father superior of the Roman Catholic Mission, Beira, Folio 2b, March 1917.

21. NAM, NS 1/35/3, Letter from the acting superintendent of native affairs, Zomba, to the reverend father superior of the Roman Catholic Mission, Beira, Folio 2b, March 1917.

22. NAM, NS 1/35/3, Letter from the acting superintendent of native affairs, Zomba, to the reverend father superior of the Roman Catholic Mission, Beira, Folio 2c, September 3, 1917.

23. NAM, NS 1/35/3, Letter from the acting superintendent of native affairs, Zomba, to the reverend father superior of the Roman Catholic Mission, Beira, Folio 2c, September 3, 1917.

24. NAM, NS 1/35/3, Letter from the acting superintendent of native affairs, Zomba, to the reverend father superior of the Roman Catholic Mission, Nguludi, Folio 2d, October 31, 1917.

25. NAM, NS 1/35/3, Letter from the acting superintendent of native affairs, Zomba, to the reverend father superior of the Roman Catholic Mission, Beira, Folio 2c, September 3, 1917.

26. NAM, NS 1/35/3, Letter from the acting superintendent of native affairs, Zomba, to the reverend father superior of the Roman Catholic Mission, Beira, Folio 2e, March 16, 1918; NAM, NS 1/35/3, Letter from the reverend father superior of the Roman Catholic Mission, Beira, to the acting superintendent of native affairs, Zomba, Folio 6a, April 10, 1918; NAM, NS 1/35/3, Letter from the chief secretary, Zomba, to the reverend father superior of the Roman Catholic Mission, Beira, Folio 6f, October 29, 1919; NAM, NS 1/35/3, Letter from the reverend father superior of the Roman Catholic Mission, Beira, Folio 6g, December 13, 1919; NAM, NS 1/35/3, Letter from the reverend father superior of the Roman Catholic Mission, Beira, Folio 6h, January 28, 1920.

27. NAM, NS 1/35/3, Letter from the acting superintendent of native affairs, Zomba, to the resident, Fort Johnston, Folio 3, March 5, 1917.

28. NAM, NS 1/35/3, Letter from the acting superintendent of native affairs, Zomba, to H. Woodard, Folio 3a, March 7, 1917.

29. NAM, NS 1/35/3, Letter from the acting superintendent of native affairs, Zomba, to H. Woodard, Folio 3a, March 7, 1917.

30. NAM, NS 1/35/3, Letter from H. Woodard, March 21, 1918; NAM, NS 1/35/3, Letter from the reverend father superior of the Roman Catholic Mission, Beira, to the chief secretary, Zomba, Folio 8, September 2, 1920; NAM, NS 1/35/3, Letter from acting first assistant secretary, Zomba, to the medical officer, Zomba, Folio 8a, September 18, 1920.

31. NAM, NS 1/35/3, Letter from A. S. Chalmers, Overtoun Institution, to A. J. Mallet Veale, Zomba, Folio 1f, November 12, 1917.

32. On Livingstonia and its educational facilities, see McCracken, *Politics and Christianity in Malawi, 1875–1940*, chapter 6.

33. NAM, NS 1/35/3, Letter from A. S. Chalmers, Overtoun Institution, to A. J. Mallet Veale, Zomba, Folio 1f, November 12, 1917; NAM, NS 1/35/3, Letter from the superintendent of native affairs, Zomba, to J. Chalmers, Livingstonia, Folio 1h, November 13, 1917.

34. NAM, NS 1/35/3, Letter from the superintendent of native affairs, Zomba, to J. Chalmers, Livingstonia, Folio 1h, November 13, 1917; NAM, NS 1/35/3, Letter from the acting superintendent of native affairs, Zomba, to A. S. Chalmers, Overtoun Institute, Folio 1l, December 17, 1917.

35. NAM, NS 1/35/3, Letter from the assistant attorney general, Zomba, to E. Costley-White, Blantyre, Folio 1m, December 21, 1917, 1, 2.

36. NAM, NS 1/35/3, Letter to Mr. Anderson, Folio 1q, January 10, 1918.

37. NAM, NS 1/35/3, Letter from the superintendent of native affairs, Zomba, to Mr. Anderson, Folio 1s, January 19, 1918.

38. NAM, NS 1/35/3, Letter from the acting superintendent of native affairs, Zomba, to H. Woodard, Folio 3a, March 7, 1917.

39. White, *Children of the French Empire*, chapter 2.

40. The relatively informal nature of African-European relationships may also have disrupted birth-spacing practices, thus making the children of these relation-

ships more expendable than those conceived under normal conditions. See Vaughan and Moore, *Cutting Down Trees*, 201.

41. NAM, s1/705ᶦ/30, Folio 37.

42. Mandala, *Work and Control in a Peasant Economy*, 32–36.

43. Fetter, "Colonial Microenvironments and the Mortality of Educated Young Men in Northern Malawi, 1897–1927."

44. Read, *Children of Their Fathers*, 25–28. See also Read, "The Ngoni and Western Education."

45. Page, *The Chiwaya War*, 135, 136, 142.

46. Vaughan, *The Story of an African Famine*, 36, 117.

47. Ibbo Mandaza discusses how many well-known people had half-caste children. See Mandaza, *Race, Colour, and Class in Southern Africa*, 130, 131.

48. Bennett, introduction, vii, xlv, xlvi.

49. The English translation is based on an 1889 Portuguese original, with "1888–1891" added to the English title.

50. Langworthy, "Introduction," 10.

51. Langworthy, "Introduction," 4. See also NAM, NS 1/35/3, Letter from the custodian of enemy property, Blantyre, to the acting superintendent of native affairs, Zomba, Folio 4a, July 20, 1917; Wiese became involved with the Anglo-African Association during the 1930s. See NAM, s1/309/33, Folios 2, 3, and 4, July 30, 1933.

52. Page, *The Chiwaya War*, 146. Though the precise origins and meaning of the word *majoni* are unknown, it is likely a neologism with the suffix *-joni* referring to Johannesburg. Men from Nyasaland frequently migrated to South Africa to work in the mining industry, and this word could have been invented as a result. My thanks to Sam Mchombo for his views on this word.

53. The case of the Deuss family can be found in NAM, NS 1/35/3, Letter from the acting superintendent of native affairs, Zomba, to the custodian of enemy property, Blantyre, Folio 4, July 17, 1917; NAM, NS 1/35/3, Letter from the custodian of enemy property, Blantyre, to the acting superintendent of native affairs, Zomba, Folio 4a, July 20, 1917.

54. On this period, see McCracken, *A History of Malawi*, chapter 8.

55. Chirwa, "Child and Youth Labour on the Nyasaland Plantations, 1890–1953," 672–76.

56. NAM, NS 1/35/3, Letter from the superintendent of police, Mlanje District, to the chief commissioner of police, Zomba, July 22, 1931.

57. NAM, NS 1/35/3, Letter from the district commissioner, Mlanje, to the provincial commissioner, southern province, Blantyre, Folio 11, August 13, 1931.

58. NAM, NS 1/35/3, Letter from the district commissioner, Mlanje, to the provincial commissioner, southern province, Blantyre, Folio 11, August 13, 1931.

59. NAM, NS 1/35/3, Letter from the district commissioner, Mlanje, to the provincial commissioner, southern province, Blantyre, Folio 11, August 13, 1931.

60. NAM, NS 1/35/3, Letter from the district commissioner, Fort Johnston, to the provincial commissioner, southern province, Blantyre, Folio 12, May 6, 1932.

61. NAM, NS 1/35/3, Letter from the district commissioner, Fort Johnston, to the provincial commissioner, southern province, Blantyre, Folio 12, May 6, 1932.

62. NAM, NS 1/35/3, Letter from the district commissioner, Fort Johnston, to the provincial commissioner, southern province, Blantyre, Folio 12, May 6, 1932.

63. NAM, NS 1/35/3, Letter from the provincial commissioner, southern province, Blantyre, to the secretary for native affairs, Zomba, Folio 13/12, May 9, 1932.

64. Translated with the assistance of Sam Mchombo. NAM, NS 1/35/3, Letter from Anderson J. Bishop to the Universities' Mission to Central Africa, Fort Johnston, Folios 16 and 17, August 29, 1934.

65. Translated with the assistance of Sam Mchombo. NAM, NS 1/35/3, Letter from Anderson J. Bishop to the Universities' Mission to Central Africa, Fort Johnston, Folios 16 and 17, August 29, 1934.

66. Translated with the assistance of Sam Mchombo. NAM, NS 1/35/3, Letter from Anderson J. Bishop to the Universities' Mission to Central Africa, Fort Johnston, Folios 16 and 17, August 29, 1934.

67. Translated with the assistance of Sam Mchombo. NAM, NS 1/35/3, Letter from Anderson J. Bishop to the Universities' Mission to Central Africa, Fort Johnston, Folios 16 and 17, August 29, 1934.

68. NAM, NS 1/35/3, Letter from the senior provincial commissioner to the office of superintendent, Zomba, Folio 18, September 17, 1934.

69. NAM, NS 1/35/3, Letter from Anderson J. Bishop to the Universities' Mission to Central Africa, Fort Johnston, Folios 36/18 and 35, July 2, 1935.

70. NAM, NS 1/35/3, Letter from Anderson J. Bishop to the Universities' Mission to Central Africa, Fort Johnston, Folios 36/18 and 35, July 2, 1935; NAM, NS 1/35/3, Translated paraphrase of a letter from Anderson J. Bishop, Folio 38a, July 2, 1935; NAM, NS 1/35/3, Letter from Anderson J. Bishop to the Universities' Mission to Central Africa, Fort Johnston, Folio 37, July 12, 1935; NAM, NS 1/35/3, Letter to P. D. Bishop, Folio 38, January 14, 1936.

71. NAM, NS 1/35/3, Letter from Anderson J. Bishop to the Universities' Mission to Central Africa, Fort Johnston, Folio 40/39, September 8, 1936; NAM, NS 1/35/3, Letter from acting provincial commissioner to Anderson J. Bishop, Folio 41/40, September 14, 1936.

72. NAM, NS 1/35/3, Letter from Christopher H. Findler to the Blantyre Mission, Folio 19, February 9, 1935, 1.

73. NAM, NS 1/35/3, Letter from the senior provincial commissioner, Blantyre, to the district commissioner, Liwonde, Folio 30, February 11, 1935; NAM, NS 1/35/3, Letter from the district commissioner, Liwonde, Folio 30, February 15, 1935.

74. NAM, NS 1/35/3, Letter from Clement K. Msamu to the senior provincial commissioner, Blantyre, Folio 23, February 28, 1935. The term *bwana* is equivalent to *sir,* expressing respect or acknowledging the addressee's seniority.

75. There was some confusion about the father's surname, and officials identified two men who might have been the father. NAM, NS 1/35/3, Letter from the district commissioner, Fort Manning, to the senior provincial commissioner, Blantyre, Folio 25, March 13, 1935; NAM, NS 1/35/3, Letter from the district commissioner, Fort Manning, to the senior provincial commissioner, Blantyre, Folio 28, March 13, 1935; NAM, NS 1/35/3, Letter from the district commissioner, Cholo, to the senior provincial commissioner, Blantyre, Folio 27, April 16, 1935.

76. NAM, NS 1/35/3, Letter from the senior provincial commissioner, Blantyre,

to Christopher H. Findler, Folio 32/19, May 2, 1935; NAM, NS 1/35/3, Letter from Christopher H. Findler to the senior provincial commissioner, Blantyre, Folio 34/32, May 18, 1935; NAM, NS 1/35/3, Letter to the provincial commissioner, southern province, Blantyre, Folio 39/19, September 4, 1936; NAM, NS 1/35/3, Letter from the district commissioner, Liwonde, Folio 42, September 19, 1936.

77. "The Census," *Nyasaland Times*, January 12, 1922, 3.

78. NAM, s1/129/32, Folio 2, March 16, 1932.

79. NAM, s1/129/32, Folio 3, March 31, 1932; NAM, s1/129/32, Folio 4, April 2, 1932.

80. NAM, s1/129/32, Folio 6, April 30, 1932.

81. NAM, s1/129/32, Folio 6, April 30, 1932.

82. NAM, s1/129/32, Folio 7; Folio 8.

83. NAM, s1/129/32, Folio 11, August 1, 1932; NAM, s1/129/32, Folio 12, October 11, 1932.

84. NAM, s1/129/32, Folio 15.

85. NAM, s1/129/32, Folio 16, March 28, 1933.

86. NAM, s1/129/32, Folio 17, August 2, 1933; NAM, s1/129/32, Folios 18 and 19.

87. NAM, s1/129/32, Folio 20, March 6, 1933.

88. NAM, s1/129/32, Folio 21, April 16, 1933.

89. NAM, s1/129/32, Folio 22.

90. NAM, s1/129/32, Folio 23, October 16, 1933.

91. NAM, s1/129/32, Folio 24, November 4, 1933.

92. NAM, s1/129/32, Folio 24, November 4, 1933.

93. NAM, s1/129/32, Folio 25, November 25, 1933.

94. NAM, s1/129/32, Folio 26, December 5, 1933.

95. Emphasis in the original. NAM, NS 1/35/3, Letter from the district commissioner, Fort Johnston, to the provincial commissioner, southern province, Blantyre, Folio 10, July 23, 1931.

96. NAM, NS 1/35/3, Letter from the district commissioner, Fort Johnston, to the provincial commissioner, southern province, Blantyre, Folio 10, July 23, 1931. This fact may explain his involvement a year later in the case of Mussa Omar Mahomed.

97. NAM, NS 1/35/3, Letter from M. G. Dharap to the assistant district commissioner, Fort Johnston, Folio 2, February 9, 1931.

98. NAM, NS 1/35/3, Letter from Kassam Ismail to M. G. Dharap, Folio 3a, June 12, 1931. There are two versions of the name in the documents: Allimahomed Abba and Ali Mahomed Aba. I have used the former for consistency.

99. NAM, NS 1/35/3, Letter from M. G. Dharap to the district commissioner, Fort Johnston, Folio 3, July 8, 1931.

100. NAM, NS 1/35/3, Letter from M. G. Dharap to the district commissioner, Fort Johnston, Folio 3, July 8, 1931.

101. NAM, NS 1/35/3, Letter from the district commissioner, Fort Johnston, to the provincial commissioner, southern province, Blantyre, Folio 10, July 23, 1931.

102. NAM, NS 1/35/3, Letter from the provincial commissioner to the chief secretary, Zomba, July 28, 1931.

103. NAM, NS 1/35/3, Letter from the chief secretary, Zomba, to the provincial commissioner, southern province, Blantyre, Folio 10b, August 8, 1931. Some confusion over "dowry" and "bride price" (or bridewealth) emerges in this correspondence.

Dowry is wealth transferred to the husband's family from the wife's family. Bride price (or bridewealth) is compensation paid by the husband's family to the bride's family. Jileka seeks a bride price, not a dowry, perhaps a mistaken report by colonial officials.

104. NAM, NS 1/35/3, Letter from the district commissioner, Fort Johnston, to the provincial commissioner, southern province, Blantyre, Folio 10c, September 1, 1931; NAM, NS 1/35/3, Letter from the provincial commissioner to the chief secretary, Zomba, Folio 10d, September 17, 1931.

105. NAM, NS 1/35/3, Letter from the chief secretary, Zomba, to the provincial commissioner, southern province, Blantyre, Folio 10e, September 23, 1931; NAM, NS 1/35/3, Letter from the provincial commissioner to M. G. Dharap, Folio 10f, September 24, 1931.

106. NAM, S1/705^I/30, Folio 23, September 13, 1933.

107. NAM, S1/705^I/30, Folio 24, 1, 2.

108. Although not intentional, the repeated usage of *children* imparts a sense of infantilization, which was a key aspect of colonial paternalism. White, *Children of the French Empire*; Caplan, *Children of Colonialism*; Saada, *Empire's Children*.

109. Stoler, *Carnal Knowledge and Imperial Power*, 114.

II. NON-NATIVE QUESTIONS

1. On the issues of nativism and non-nativism, see Mamdani, *When Victims Become Killers*, chapter 1, and *Define and Rule*, chapters 1 and 2. On bureaucratic reason, see Crais, *The Politics of Evil*, 110, 111. On legibility, see Scott, *Seeing Like a State*, 2. On "impossible" legal subjects, see Ngai, *Impossible Subjects*.

2. Assimilation was also debated in the French case with a policy of association replacing its initial promise. See Saada, *Empire's Children*, chapter 4; White, *Children of the French Empire*.

3. On the limits of British imperial liberalism, see Mehta, *Liberalism and Empire*; Pitts, *A Turn to Empire*.

4. For broader discussion of challenges to colonial categories of rule, see Stoler and Cooper, "Between Metropole and Colony."

4. THE NATIVE UNDEFINED

1. National Archives of Malawi (hereafter NAM), Zomba, High Court of Nyasaland, J5/2/73:46, Folio 1.

2. NAM, High Court of Nyasaland, J5/2/73:46, Folio 1.

3. For overviews, see Mehta, *Liberalism and Empire*, chapters 1 and 2; Pitts, *A Turn to Empire*, parts 1 and 2.

4. NAM, High Court of Nyasaland, J5/2/73:46. See also NAM, S1/705^I/30, April 19, 1929, Folio 3.

5. NAM, High Court of Nyasaland, J5/2/73:46.

6. NAM, High Court of Nyasaland, J5/2/73:46.

7. NAM, High Court of Nyasaland, J5/2/73:46.

8. For an overview, see Cooper, *Decolonization and African Society*, 59 and chapter 3 generally.

9. This case study also challenges the idea that the hypodescent rule (that is, anyone descended from a black person is black) has been unique to the United States, where it is colloquially known as the one-drop rule. For discussions, see Daniel, "Multiracial Identity in Global Perspective"; Hollinger, "Amalgamation and Hypodescent."

10. Chatterjee, *The Nation and Its Fragments*, 18. For engagement with this topic beyond South Africa, see, for example, Glassman, *War of Words*, chapter 2; Penvenne, *African Workers and Colonial Racism*, chapters 1 and 5.

11. Mamdani, *Citizen and Subject*, 90. For Mamdani's discussion of subject races versus subject ethnicities, see also his "Beyond Settler and Native as Political Identities."

12. This view forms the broad argument of Mamdani, *Citizen and Subject*, part 1. On the apartheid state, see also Posel, *The Making of Apartheid, 1948–1961*. For the interwar origins of apartheid thinking, see Dubow, "Afrikaner Nationalism, Apartheid and the Conceptualization of 'Race.'"

13. Goldberg, *The Racial State*, 104.

14. For an early observation of this issue, see Robinson, "The Administration of African Customary Law," 159.

15. For a historical comparison, see Pedersen, "'Special Customs'"; Stoler, *Carnal Knowledge and Imperial Power*, 98–100. For a further discussion of their meanings, see Brubaker, *Citizenship and Nationhood in France and Germany*, especially chapters 5 and 6.

16. Such cases are particularly common in the American context. See Clifford, *The Predicament of Culture*, chapter 12; Gross, *What Blood Won't Tell*; Pascoe, *What Comes Naturally*.

17. NAM, Native Secretariat (hereafter NS) 1/3/2, Folio 1, 1.

18. NAM, NS 1/3/2, Folio 1, 1.

19. NAM, s1/705^i/30, Folio 1, March 31, 1930. See also NAM, s1/705^i/30, Minutes Section, No. 5, April 24, 1930; NAM, s1/705^i/30, Folio 1a, July 28, 1929, 3; NAM, NS 1/3/2, 1–8.

20. NAM, s1/705^i/30, Minutes Section, No. 5, April 24, 1930.

21. For an overview, see Muzondidya, *Walking a Tightrope*, chapter 1.

22. NAM, s1/705^i/30, Minutes Section, No. 5, April 24, 1930.

23. Elias, *British Colonial Law*, 9.

24. Elias, *British Colonial Law*, especially chapters 1 and 3–5.

25. NAM, s1/420/33, Folio 1. For the general file on this issue, see NAM, s1/420/33, "The Definition of the Expression 'Native.'"

26. NAM, s1/705^i/30, Minutes Section, No. 6, April 30, 1930.

27. This measure attempted to account for children born overseas, while the first-generation clause limited its application to avoid multiple generational claims. Successive revisions in 1918 and 1922 further extended the descent principle. Karatani, *Defining British Citizenship*, 85–87.

28. NAM, s1/705^i/30, Minutes Section, No. 7, May 16, 1930.

29. This uncertainty was not unique. The category of "European British subject" had circulated as a means of instituting white privilege, though who was included within this category had also been debated. Jordanna Bailkin has written that European British subjects, as defined by the European Vagrancy Act of 1874, were "persons of European extraction," thus utilizing a *jus sanguinis* rationale ("The Boot and the Spleen," 472). Yet the principle of *jus soli* was also present, since birth in certain territories—including Australia, New Zealand, and the Cape and Natal Colonies—was a qualification for this status. Moreover, according to the 1874 law, being homeless disqualified one from this status. "Behavior that damaged white prestige, such as homelessness or vagrancy," writes Bailkin, "was thus criminalized and rendered non-British" ("The Boot and the Spleen," 473).

30. Adding another layer of consideration was the fact that Nyasaland (like Northern Rhodesia) was a protectorate, which meant that those born in the territory were technically British Protected Persons, not subjects per se. This difference did not affect the descent clause nor did this status, like subject status, decisively impact native and non-native status. For example, there were native and non-native subjects alike in the British Empire.

31. NAM, s1/705ⁱ/30, Minutes Section, No. 7, May 16, 1930.

32. NAM, s1/705ⁱ/30, Minutes Section, No. 7, May 16, 1930. See also NAM, s1/705ⁱ/30, Folio 4, July 14, 1930; NAM, s1/705ⁱ/30, Folio 5, July 14, 1930; NAM, s1/705ⁱ/30, Folio 6, July 16, 1930; NAM, s1/705ⁱ/30, Folio 7, August 6, 1930; NAM, s1/705ⁱ/30, Folio 8, August 4, 1930.

33. NAM, s1/705ⁱ/30, Letter from Governor Shenton Thomas of Nyasaland to Lord Passfield, Secretary of State for the Colonies, Folio 10, November 6, 1930, 1, 2.

34. NAM, s1/705ⁱ/30, Folio 10, November 6, 1930, 1, 2.

35. National Archives of the United Kingdom (hereafter NAUK), London, Colonial Office (hereafter CO) 822/36/16, Folio 39.

36. NAUK, CO 822/36/16, Folio 40.

37. NAUK, CO 822/36/16, Folio 42.

38. For a discussion of the uncertainties involved in determining racial categories in South Africa, see Posel, "Race as Common Sense," 89–98.

39. NAUK, CO 822/36/16, Folio 43.

40. NAUK, CO 822/36/16, Folio 43. See also NAUK, CO 822/36/16, Folio 44.

41. NAUK, CO 822/36/16, Folio 44.

42. NAUK, CO 822/36/16, Folios 2–10.

43. NAUK, CO 822/36/16, Folio 1b, 55.

44. NAUK, CO 822/36/16, Folio 1b, 56.

45. NAUK, CO 822/36/16, Folio 1b, 57.

46. For the New Zealand case, see NAUK, CO 822/36/16, Folio 1a, 76, 77.

47. NAUK, CO 822/36/16, Folio 1b, 57, 58. West African colonies were considered as well, though persons of mixed descent were not an issue there. See NAUK, CO 822/36/16, Folio 1b, 59.

48. NAUK, CO 822/36/16, Folio 1b, 11.

49. NAM, s1/705ⁱ/30, Folio 11, April 22, 1931.

50. Karatani, *Defining British Citizenship*, chapter 3.

51. NAM, s1/705^i/30, Folio 12a, April 20, 1931. See also NAM, s1/705^i/30, Folio 11a, April 20, 1931.

52. NAM, s1/705^i/30, Folio 12a, April 20, 1931. See also NAM, s1/705^i/30, Folio 11a, April 20, 1931.

53. NAM, s1/705^i/30, Folio 12a, April 20, 1931.

54. NAM, s1/705^i/30, Folio 12a, April 20, 1931. See also NAM, s1/705^i/30, Folio 11a, April 20, 1931.

55. NAM, s1/705^i/30, Folio 12a, April 20, 1931. See also NAM, s1/705^i/30, Folio 11a, April 20, 1931.

56. NAM, s1/705^i/30, Folio 12, May 21, 1931.

57. NAM, s1/705^i/30, Folio 15, August 1, 1931, 1.

58. NAM, s1/705^i/30, Folio 16, August 18, 1931, 1–3.

59. NAM, s1/705^i/30, Folio 17d, August 27, 1931. See also NAM, s1/705^i/30, Folio 17h, July 8, 1931. Uganda also agreed with this position. See NAM, s1/705^i/30, Folio 21, Annexure IIIa, March 10, 1933, 45. With regard to separate education and how it might create a separate class, see NAM, s1/705^i/30, Folio 17g.

60. NAM, s1/705^i/30, Folio 17c, September 10, 1931. See also NAUK, CO 822/36/16, Folio 26, September 10, 1931.

61. NAM, s1/705^i/30, Folio 17c, September 10, 1931. See also NAUK, CO 822/36/16, Folio 26, September 10, 1931.

62. NAM, s1/705^i/30, Folio 17b, July 9, 1931. See also NAUK, CO 822/36/16, Folio 25, July 9, 1931.

63. NAM, s1/705^i/30, Folio 17b, July 9, 1931. See also NAUK, CO 822/36/16, Folio 25, July 9, 1931.

64. NAM, s1/705^i/30, Folio 17b, July 9, 1931. See also NAUK, CO 822/36/16, Folio 25, July 9, 1931.

65. NAM, s1/705^i/30, Folio 17, January 12, 1932, 1.

66. NAM, s1/705^i/30, Folio 21.

67. NAM, s1/705^i/30, Folio 21. See also NAM, s1/705^i/30, Folios 29 and 30. On Tanganyika's mandate status, see Brennan, *Taifa*, 23.

68. NAM, s1/705^i/30, Folio 21.

69. NAM, s1/705^i/30, Folio 21, Annexure VIII, 53, 54.

70. NAM, s1/705^i/30, Folio 21, Annexure VIII, 53, 54.

71. NAM, s1/705^i/30, Folio 21, Annexure VIII, 53, 54.

72. NAM, s1/705^i/30, Folio 21, Annexure VIII, 53, 54.

73. NAM, s1/420/33, "A Bill to Amend and Define in More Precise Terms the Definition of the Expression 'Native,'" Clause 2, Folio 2. Also included in NAM, s1/420/33, Folio 1, December 8, 1933.

74. NAM, s1/420/33, "A Bill to Amend and Define in More Precise Terms the Definition of the Expression 'Native,'" Clause 2, Folio 2. Also included in NAM, s1/420/33, Folio 1, December 8, 1933.

75. For recent work on the categories of native and non-native in urban Tanzania, see Brennan, *Taifa*, 22–34.

76. NAM, s1/420/33, Folio 2, Clause 3; NAM, s1/420/33, Folio 3, Clause 5; NAM, s1/420/33, Folio 5.

77. NAM, s1/420/33, Folio 2, Clause 3; NAM, s1/420/33, Folio 3, Clause 5; NAM, s1/420/33, Folio 5.

78. For a comparison with South Africa, which followed similar lines, see Posel, "Race as Common Sense," 90–95.

79. NAM, s1/420/33, Folio 1, December 8, 1933.

80. NAM, s1/420/33, Folio 9, March 1, 1934.

81. NAM, s1/420/33, Folio 17, April 30, 1934.

82. NAM, s1/420/33, Folios 19–25.

83. NAM, s1/420/33, Folio 28, December 2, 1935.

84. NAM, s1/420/33, Folio 26, December 3, 1935.

85. NAM, s1/420/33, Folio 31, October 21, 1937; NAM, s1/420/33, Folio 32, October 25, 1937.

86. NAM, s1/420/33, Folio 34, January 12, 1938.

87. NAM, s1/420/33, Folio 35, January 17, 1938; NAM, s1/420/33, Folios 38–41; NAM, s1/420/33, Folio 42, February 9, 1938; NAM, s1/420/33, Folio 43, February 9, 1938.

88. NAM, s1/420/33, Folio 44.

89. Domínguez, *White by Definition*, chapter 3.

90. This notion of a colonial native state resembles the "native state apparatus" described by Mahmood Mamdani. In his use, it refers (prosaically) to a pre-existing indigenous state system or one created by colonial officials, which in both cases is appropriated for colonial ruling purposes. It offers a point of departure for addressing problems of ethnic conflict. The native state model proposed here draws primarily from Goldberg. Rather than being a basis for addressing ethnicity, this conceptual paradigm draws attention to how (paraphrasing Goldberg) populations were determined, defined, and structured on the basis of native and non-native categories. Attention is focused on the dimensions, meaning, and use of these terms; it is not a platform for engaging ethnicity. See Mamdani, *Citizen and Subject*, 62, 79.

91. This term has been popularized by Giorgio Agamben. For a discussion of it, see Agamben, *Homo Sacer*, 183–84. For an exploration of its implications for postcolonial Africa, see Mbembe, "Necropolitics."

5. COMMISSIONS AND CIRCUMVENTION

1. On commissions and state legitimation in South Africa, see Ashforth, *The Politics of Official Discourse in Twentieth-Century South Africa*. On the Wilcocks Commission, see Lewis, *Between the Wire and the Wall*, 158–70. On the Carnegie commission, see Bell, "American Philanthropy, the Carnegie Corporation and Poverty in South Africa."

2. Southern Rhodesia Land Commission, *Report of the Land Commission*. For a further discussion, see Alexander, *The Unsettled Land*, 20; Palmer, *Land and Racial Domination in Rhodesia*, chapter 7.

3. Crais, *The Politics of Evil*, chapters 2 and 3; Wilder, "Colonial Ethnology and Political Rationality in French West Africa."

4. On interpellation, see Althusser, "Ideology and Ideological State Apparatuses (Notes towards an Investigation)."

5. Clarke and Newman, *The Managerial State*, chapters 4 and 5.

6. On naturalizing categories, see Domínguez, *White by Definition*, chapter 2.

7. For a parallel process in South Africa, see Posel, "Race as Common Sense."

8. Stoler, *Along the Archival Grain*, 143.

9. "A Message from Mr. G. Thomas Thornicroft," *Rhodesian Tribune*, vol. 1, no. 1, August 1945.

10. Concerns over education had been reported earlier to the Tate Commission (1929), if in a less comprehensive manner. Mandaza, *Race, Colour, and Class in Southern Africa*, 72.

11. Muzondidya, *Walking a Tightrope*, 53–63, and "Race, Ethnicity and the Politics of Positioning," 164–66.

12. The Foggin Commission's report is included in administrative files in Malawi, indicating its regional circulation as well. See National Archives of Malawi (hereafter NAM), Zomba, s26/2/4/5, Folio 14.

13. NAM, s26/2/4/5, Folio 14.

14. These figures are quoted in McCulloch, *Black Peril, White Virtue*, 243 fn38.

15. Alexander, *The Unsettled Land*, 21; Palmer, *Land and Racial Domination*, 135.

16. Palmer, *Land and Racial Domination*, 168.

17. NAM, s26/2/4/5, Folio 14, 4.

18. NAM, s26/2/4/5, Folio 14, 4. On the emergence of Coloured education prior to the commission, see Mandaza, *Race, Colour, and Class in Southern Africa*, 28–39.

19. NAM, s26/2/4/5, Folio 14, 5, 6.

20. NAM, s26/2/4/5, Folio 14, 6, 7.

21. NAM, s26/2/4/5, Folio 14, 7.

22. NAM, s26/2/4/5, Folio 14, 8, 9, 10.

23. NAM, s26/2/4/5, Folio 14, 13, 14, 15.

24. NAM, s26/2/4/5, Folio 14, 15.

25. NAM, s26/2/4/5, Folio 14, 15.

26. NAM, s26/2/4/5, Folio 14, 15, 16.

27. NAM, s26/2/4/5, Folio 14, 15.

28. NAM, s26/2/4/5, Folio 14, 17, 18.

29. NAM, s26/2/4/5, Folio 14, 17, 18.

30. NAM, s26/2/4/5, Folio 14, 18.

31. NAM, s26/2/4/5, Folio 14, 18.

32. NAM, s26/2/4/5, Folio 14, 21.

33. NAM, s26/2/4/5, Folio 14, 21, 22.

34. NAM, s26/2/4/5, Folio 14, 22.

35. Summers, *From Civilization to Segregation*, 269.

36. NAM, s26/2/4/5, Folio 14, 23.

37. NAM, s26/2/4/5, Folio 14, 25, 26.

38. NAM, s26/2/4/5, Folio 14, 26, 27; Mandaza, *Race, Colour, and Class in Southern Africa*, 155, 160–72.

39. The railway strike of October 1945 reflected sharp grievances among the African proletariat about substandard living conditions, low wages, and rising inflation. The general strike of 1948 signaled a more ambitious attempt to align elite African and working-class interests across the colony. Although it failed, this activism repre-

sented a new political and economic environment. On this period, see Scarnecchia, *The Urban Roots of Democracy and Political Violence in Zimbabwe*, chapters 1 and 2.

40. Southern Rhodesia (hereafer SR), *Report of the Commission of Inquiry Regarding the Social Welfare of the Coloured Community of Southern Rhodesia*, 2.

41. SR, *Report of the Commission of Inquiry*, 4.

42. SR, *Report of the Commission of Inquiry*, 9.

43. SR, *Report of the Commission of Inquiry*, 9.

44. SR, *Report of the Commission of Inquiry*, 9.

45. SR, *Report of the Commission of Inquiry*, 9.

46. SR, *Report of the Commission of Inquiry*, 11.

47. SR, *Report of the Commission of Inquiry*, 9.

48. SR, *Report of the Commission of Inquiry*, 11.

49. Mandaza, *Race, Colour, and Class in Southern Africa*, 255.

50. SR, *Report of the Commission of Inquiry*, 12.

51. SR, *Report of the Commission of Inquiry*, 12, 13.

52. Mandaza, *Race, Colour, and Class in Southern Africa*, 250.

53. SR, *Report of the Commission of Inquiry*, 13.

54. Ferguson, *The Anti-Politics Machine*, part III.

55. SR, *Report of the Commission of Inquiry*, 18.

56. Muzondidya, *Walking a Tightrope*, 49–50.

57. SR, *Report of the Commission of Inquiry*, 19.

58. SR, *Report of the Commission of Inquiry*, 21.

59. SR, *Report of the Commission of Inquiry*, 22.

60. The first quote is from SR, *Report of the Commission of Inquiry*, 22, and the second quote is from SR, *Report of the Commission of Inquiry*, 23.

61. SR, *Report of the Commission of Inquiry*, 23.

62. SR, *Report of the Commission of Inquiry*, 26.

63. Quoted in SR, *Report of the Commission of Inquiry*, 30.

64. SR, *Report of the Commission of Inquiry*, 33–34.

65. SR, *Report of the Commission of Inquiry*, 43, 49, 51.

66. SR, *Report of the Commission of Inquiry*, 55.

67. SR, *Report of the Commission of Inquiry*, 75.

68. SR, *Report of the Commission of Inquiry*, 66.

69. SR, *Report of the Commission of Inquiry*, 61.

70. SR, *Report of the Commission of Inquiry*, 62.

71. Quoted in SR, *Report of the Commission of Inquiry*, 24.

72. SR, *Report of the Commission of Inquiry*, 98.

73. SR, *Report of the Commission of Inquiry*, 99.

74. SR, *Report of the Commission of Inquiry*, 99.

75. Lewis, *Between the Wire and the Wall*, 170. On the work of Batson more generally, see Davie, *Poverty Knowledge in South Africa*.

76. Quoted in SR, *Report of the Commission of Inquiry*, 101, 102.

77. SR, *Report of the Commission of Inquiry*, 102.

78. SR, *Report of the Commission of Inquiry*, 104.

79. SR, *Report of the Commission of Inquiry*, 111, 112. Though Batson's study was based in Salisbury, its figures were viewed in this instance as applicable for the whole colony (e.g., 106).

80. SR, *Report of the Commission of Inquiry*, 114.

81. SR, *Report of the Commission of Inquiry*, 115, 129, 131.

82. SR, *Report of the Commission of Inquiry*, 117.

83. SR, *Report of the Commission of Inquiry*, 134.

84. SR, *Report of the Commission of Inquiry*, 135.

85. SR, *Report of the Commission of Inquiry*, 138.

86. SR, *Report of the Commission of Inquiry*, 139.

87. SR, *Report of the Commission of Inquiry*, 144, 146, 147, 148.

88. The Native Urban Locations Ordinance (1906) had enabled some degree of management in Salisbury, but the situation in Bulawayo was more laissez-faire, with a housing program not in place until the 1920s.

89. West, *The Rise of an African Middle Class*, 100–103, 108–10.

90. Mandaza, *Race, Colour, and Class in Southern Africa*, 99–103.

91. SR, *Report of the Commission of Inquiry*, 140–42; Muzondidya, *Walking a Tightrope*, 84.

92. SR, *Report of the Commission of Inquiry*, 149.

93. SR, *Report of the Commission of Inquiry*, 156, 161.

94. SR, *Report of the Commission of Inquiry*, 169. The commission also proposed the formation of a permanent housing commission, together with statutory powers for the central government to compel local authorities to address housing needs when necessary (169–72).

95. SR, *Report of the Commission of Inquiry*, 154.

96. SR, *Report of the Commission of Inquiry*, 176. See also 172–74.

97. SR, *Report of the Commission of Inquiry*, 184.

98. SR, *Report of the Commission of Inquiry*, 189–93.

99. SR, *Report of the Commission of Inquiry*, 186, 187.

100. SR, *Report of the Commission of Inquiry*, 219.

101. SR, *Report of the Commission of Inquiry*, 205.

102. Quoted in SR, *Report of the Commission of Inquiry*, 209.

103. SR, *Report of the Commission of Inquiry*, 209–11.

104. SR, *Report of the Commission of Inquiry*, 213.

105. SR, *Report of the Commission of Inquiry*, 227, 228.

106. SR, *Report of the Commission of Inquiry*, 228.

107. SR, *Report of the Commission of Inquiry*, 31.

108. SR, *Report of the Commission of Inquiry*, 31.

109. Mandaza, *Race, Colour, and Class in Southern Africa*, 418–23.

110. Mandaza, *Race, Colour, and Class in Southern Africa*, 427–33.

111. Mandaza, *Race, Colour, and Class in Southern Africa*, 422.

112. The report was published, if not released publicly. A copy of the report is in the file: National Archives of the United Kingdom (hereafter NAUK), London, Colonial Office (hereafter CO) 795/170/13, Northern Rhodesia (hereafter NR), *Report of the Committee to Inquire into the Status and Welfare of Coloured Persons in Northern Rhodesia*, 4.

113. NAUK, CO 795/170/13, NR, *Report of the Committee to Inquire*, 5.

114. NAUK, CO 795/170/13, NR, *Report of the Committee to Inquire*, 6, 7. Numbers were difficult to confirm conclusively, especially since the proportion of children was

deemed to be quite large. Readers should additionally note the differences in this reported figure for 1950 and the lower figure for 1951 in table I.1, signaling the potential for inconsistency in colonial census taking.

115. This classification was due to the protectorate status of Northern Rhodesia. See Milner-Thornton, *The Long Shadow of the British Empire*, 144, 216. For a broader discussion, see Hansen, "The Politics of Citizenship in 1940s Britain."

116. NAUK, CO 795/170/13, NR, *Report of the Committee to Inquire*, 7.

117. NAUK, CO 795/170/13, NR, *Report of the Committee to Inquire*, 8, 9.

118. NAUK, CO 795/170/13, NR, *Report of the Committee to Inquire*, 10.

119. NAUK, CO 795/170/13, NR, *Report of the Committee to Inquire*, 11.

120. NAUK, CO 795/170/13, NR, *Report of the Committee to Inquire*, 12, 13.

121. NAUK, CO 795/170/13, NR, *Report of the Committee to Inquire*, 15.

122. NAUK, CO 795/170/13, NR, *Report of the Committee to Inquire*, 15, 16, 17.

123. NAUK, CO 795/170/13, NR, *Report of the Committee to Inquire*, 16.

124. NAUK, CO 795/170/13, NR, *Report of the Committee to Inquire*, 24.

125. NAUK, CO 795/170/13, NR, *Report of the Committee to Inquire*, 25.

126. NAUK, CO 795/170/13, NR, *Report of the Committee to Inquire*, 20.

127. NAUK, CO 795/170/13, NR, *Report of the Committee to Inquire*, 19. The government invested in Katapola after the commission issued its report. See (no author), "Development in Northern Rhodesia (Tables)," 155 (which uses the spelling "Katopola").

128. NAUK, CO 795/170/13, NR, *Report of the Committee to Inquire*, 19.

129. NAUK, CO 795/170/13, NR, *Report of the Committee to Inquire*, 19.

130. NAUK, CO 795/170/13, NR, *Report of the Committee to Inquire*, 19.

131. Quoted in NAUK, CO 795/170/13, NR, *Report of the Committee to Inquire*, 19.

132. NAUK, CO 795/170/13, NR, *Report of the Committee to Inquire*, 21.

133. NAUK, CO 795/170/13, NR, *Report of the Committee to Inquire*, 19.

134. NAUK, CO 795/170/13, NR, *Report of the Committee to Inquire*, 19.

135. NAUK, CO 795/170/13, NR, *Report of the Committee to Inquire*, 31.

136. NAUK, CO 795/170/13, NR, *Report of the Committee to Inquire*, 31.

137. NAUK, CO 795/170/13, NR, *Report of the Committee to Inquire*, 31.

138. NAUK, CO 795/170/13, NR, *Report of the Committee to Inquire*, 31.

139. SR, *Report of the Commission of Inquiry*, 96.

140. Ferguson, *The Anti-Politics Machine*, chapter 9.

141. Scott, "Colonial Governmentality," 204–5.

III. COLONIAL KINSHIPS

1. Van Velsen, *The Politics of Kinship*, xxviii.

2. Van Velsen, *The Politics of Kinship*, xxviii.

3. Lévi-Strauss, *Totemism*, 89. A difference must subsequently be drawn between indigenous and analytic categories. See Cooper, *Colonialism in Question*, 18. On the importance of intellectuals in the construction of identities, see Vail, "Introduction: Ethnicity in Southern African History."

4. Juliette Milner-Thornton has mentioned that Coloured people in Northern Rhodesia are stereotyped as "chiefless" (*The Long Shadow of the British Empire*, 13).

5. Hartigan, *Odd Tribes*. For a separate critique of customary politics, see Spear, "Neo-Traditionalism and the Limits of Invention in British Colonial Africa."

6. On comparative work, see Stoler, "Tense and Tender Ties." On multi-sited research, see Feierman, *The Shambaa Kingdom*, 6, 7; Fields, *Revival and Rebellion in Colonial Central Africa*; Marcus and Fischer, *Anthropology as Cultural Critique*, 90–95; Marcus, *Ethnography through Thick and Thin*, 52–53; Simone, *For the City Yet to Come*; Steinmetz, *The Devil's Handwriting*; Thornton, "The Rhetoric of Ethnographic Holism"; White, *Speaking with Vampires*. Specific to this study, see Dotson and Dotson, *The Indian Minority of Zambia, Rhodesia, and Malawi*; Mandaza, *Race, Colour, and Class in Southern Africa*.

7. My expression *minor transcolonialisms* is inspired by Lionnet and Shih, eds., *Minor Transnationalism*. For discussions on region, see Malkki, "National Geographic"; Rafael, "Regionalism, Area Studies, and the Accidents of Agency"; Shohat, "Area Studies, Gender Studies, and the Cartographies of Knowledge."

8. Weber, *From Max Weber*, 176.

9. On imperial circulation, see Cooper and Stoler, *Tensions of Empire*; Dirks, *Colonialism and Culture*; Said, *Culture and Imperialism*.

10. According to Ho, "the British became an imperial people—that is to say, they became *a people* as they became *an empire*" (emphasis in the original, "Empire through Diasporic Eyes," 214). My thoughts here are also informed by Burton, "Who Needs the Nation?"

11. My thoughts here are influenced by Joseph and Nugent, *Everyday Forms of State Formation*.

12. Mafeje, "The Ideology of 'Tribalism.'"

13. On comparative patterns of assimilation, see Spitzer, *Lives in Between*.

14. My thoughts here are influenced by Mill, *The Racial Contract*, chapter 1.

15. Cohn, "From Indian Status to British Contract."

16. Povinelli, *The Empire of Love*, 4.

17. Chakrabarty, *Provincializing Europe*, 43. For a related argument, see Appiah, *In My Father's House*, 72.

6. RACISM AS A WEAPON OF THE WEAK

Epigraph from National Archives of Malawi (hereafter NAM), Zomba, author unknown, s1/705[1]/30, Folio 44a, 5.

1. Interview with Dinah Coombes, November 8, 1999, Zomba, Malawi.

2. Rosaldo, "Imperialist Nostalgia"; Stoler, "Imperial Debris."

3. Interviews with Coombes, November 8 and 11, 1999, Zomba, Malawi. On nostalgia as a feature of paradox and rational reflection both, see Dlamini, *Native Nostalgia*.

4. For a classic study, see Allman, *The Quills of the Porcupine*. For a recent history that examines challenges to this framework, see Peterson, *Ethnic Patriotism and the East African Revival*.

5. This argument is made in Wheeldon, "The Operation of Voluntary Associations and Personal Networks in the Political Processes of an Inter-ethnic Community," 131. For a classic study of "statelessness," see Evans-Pritchard, *The Neur*.

6. On community, see Chatterjee, "Agrarian Relations and Communalism in Ben-

gal, 1926–1935" and "More on Modes of Power and the Peasantry"; Piot, *Remotely Global*, 131–34.

7. Thompson, "The Moral Economy of the English Crowd in the Eighteenth Century," 79.

8. Here I disagree with Ibbo Mandaza's argument regarding a "Coloured ideology" that was strictly derived from white supremacy (*Race, Colour, and Class in Southern Africa*, 464).

9. Mētis is not to be confused with métis (as some editors have done). See Scott, *Seeing Like a State*, 313.

10. This kind of resourcefulness and creativity is similar to that found in studies of religious converts. See, for example, Peel, *Religious Encounter and the Making of the Yoruba*, 216.

11. On hierarchies as sociohistorical constructions, see Appadurai, "Putting Hierarchy in Its Place"; Dickie-Clark, *The Marginal Situation*, chapter 2.

12. On these forms, see Appiah, *In My Father's House*, 13, 14, 17.

13. On this practice and its relation to Chilembwe, see White, *Magomero*, chapters 2 and 3.

14. The first and still authoritative study of Chilembwe's revolt is Shepperson and Price, *Independent African*. On independent church movements more generally, see Fields, *Revival and Rebellion in Colonial Central Africa*.

15. Mwase, *Strike a Blow and Die*, 78–80.

16. Van Onselen, "Race and Class in the South African Countryside," 101, 107.

17. On this period, see Power, *Political Culture and Nationalism in Malawi*, chapters 1 and 2.

18. On the concept of "retribalization," see Cohen, *Custom and Politics in Urban Africa*, 1–6.

19. Van Velsen, "Some Early Pressure Groups in Malawi," 377.

20. For an authoritative study of mission history in the north, see McCracken, *Politics and Christianity in Malawi, 1875–1940*.

21. For files concerning native associations, see NAM, Native Secretariat (hereafter NS) 1/3/1, 1/3/3 through 1/3/8, 1/3/10, 1/3/12; NAM, S1/3263/23.

22. Chanock, "Ambiguities in the Malawian Political Tradition," 327, 329. For a broader discussion of this issue, see Ekeh, "Colonialism and the Two Publics in Africa."

23. Quoted in van Velsen, "Some Early Pressure Groups in Malawi," 380. For a further discussion on native associations, see Chanock, "The New Men Revisited"; Power, *Political Culture*, chapter 3; McCracken, *A History of Malawi, 1859–1966*, chapter 9; Tangri, "Inter-War 'Native Associations' and the Formation of the Nyasaland African Congress"; White, "'Tribes' and the Aftermath of the Chilembwe Rising." For studies of the relationships between missions and local communities, see McCracken, *Politics and Christianity*; Linden with Linden, *Catholics, Peasants, and Chewa Resistance in Nyasaland*.

24. Zachernuk, *Colonial Subjects*, 14. See also McCracken, "'Marginal Men.'"

25. Interview with Yusuf Ismael, October 17, 1999, Blantyre, Malawi.

26. Interview with Yusuf Ismael, December 16, 1999, Blantyre, Malawi.

27. Interviews with Ann and Jessica Ascroft, November 9, 1999, Blantyre, Malawi;

Eunice Mussa, October 4, 1999, Zomba, Malawi; Robert Jamieson, November 15, 1999, Lilongwe, Malawi. On membership and occupation, see also the petition in NAM, s20/1/2/1, Folios 23 through 26, September 16, 1938 and Power, "Race, Class, Ethnicity, and Anglo-Indian Trade Rivalry in Colonial Malawi."

28. Gramsci, *Selections from the Prison Notebooks*, 52, 54, 55.

29. On critical agency, see Apter, *Beyond Words*. My thoughts here also draw from Larson, "'Capacities and Modes of Thinking.'" On poor theory, see "Poor Theory: Notes toward a Manifesto," unpublished document, available online at https://www.humanities.uci.edu/critical/poortheory.pdf (accessed May 1, 2014).

30. On the significance of modality, see Guha, *Elementary Aspects of Peasant Insurgency in Colonial India*, chapter 4.

31. Glassman, *War of Words*, 14, 15.

32. On the reduction of marginality as discussed in studies of slavery, see Kopytoff and Miers, "Introduction."

33. Appiah, *In My Father's House*, 17.

34. Paul Gilroy has similarly discussed race, kinship, and family. See Gilroy, "It's a Family Affair."

35. NAM, NS 1/3/2, Folio 1, 1. See also NAM, s1/705ᶦ/30, Folio 1, March 31, 1930, and Folio 1a, July 28, 1929, 1.

36. The prefix "Euro-" or "Eur-" in Northern and Southern Rhodesia also captured this broader sensibility. On the association's membership, see Mandaza, *Race, Colour, and Class in Southern Africa*, 154, 482–86.

37. NAM, POL 2/15/1, Rex vs. Ascroft, October 1936 to April 1937.

38. Interviews with Ann and Jessica Ascroft, November 9, 1999. For a general history of the Blantyre Mission and its historical importance, see Ross, *Blantyre Mission and the Making of Modern Malawi*.

39. Interviews with Ann and Jessica Ascroft, November 9, 1999.

40. NAM, s1/705ᶦ/30, Folio 1, March 31, 1930. See also NAM, s1/705ᶦ/30, Folio 1a, July 28, 1929, 3; NAM, s1/705ᶦ/30, Minutes Section, no. 5, April 24, 1930; NAM, NS 1/3/2, 1–8.

41. This middle position perspective is a central part of Mohamed Adhikari's argument in *Not White Enough, Not Black Enough*, which focuses primarily on the Western Cape. For an earlier account of this position that stresses its flexibility and adaptation drawn from the context of Durban, see Dickie-Clark, *The Marginal Situation*, chapter 2.

42. NAM, s1/309/33, Folios 2 through 4, July 30, 1933.

43. NAM, s1/309/33, August 15, 1933; NAM, s1/309/33, Folio 6, August 25, 1933; NAM, s1/309/33, Folios 2 through 4, July 30, 1933.

44. NAM, s1/309/33, Folios 2 through 4, July 30, 1933; NAM, s1/309/33, Folios 22 through 27, 27a, October 1, 1933.

45. Minutes of these meeting were forwarded to the chief secretary, Zomba, on October 16, 1933, in the hope that they would reach Governor Hubert Young. NAM, s1/309/33, Folio 8; NAM, s1/309/33, Folios 9 through 11, September 17, 1933; NAM, s1/309/33, Folios 12 through 21, October 1, 1933.

46. NAM, s1/309/33, Folios 12 through 21, October 1, 1933; NAM, s1/309/33, Folios 22 through 27, 27a, October 1, 1933.

47. NAM, s1/309/33, Folios 22 through 27, 27a, October 1, 1933.

48. NAM, s1/309/33, Folios 22 through 27, 27a, October 1, 1933.

49. NAM, s1/309/33, Folios 22 through 27, 27a, October 1, 1933.

50. NAM, s1/309/33, Folios 12 through 21, October 1, 1933.

51. NAM, s1/309/33, Folios 12 through 21, October 1, 1933.

52. NAM, s1/309/33, Folios 12 through 21, October 1, 1933.

53. NAM, s1/309/33, Folios 12 through 21, October 1, 1933.

54. NAM, s1/705^i/30, Folio 24, September 22, 1933, 1, 2.

55. NAM, s1/705^i/30, Folio 24, September 22, 1933, 1, 2.

56. NAM, s1/705^i/30, Folio 24, September 22, 1933, 1, 2.

57. NAM, s1/705^i/30, May 30, 1933.

58. NAM, s1/705^i/30, Folio 26, November 27, 1933.

59. For these two quotes and those in the preceding sentence, see NAM, s1/705^i/30, Folio 33, May 29 and 30, 1934; NAM, s1/705^i/30, Folio 34, July 13, 1934; NAM, s1/705^i/30, Folio 36, July 25, 1934. See also NAM, s1/705^i/30, Folio 46, copy 4.

60. Quoted in van Velsen, "Some Early Pressure Groups," 378.

61. For Mumba's testimony, see NAM, s1/705^i/30, Folio 31, May 29 and 30, 1934. See also NAM, s1/705^i/30, Folio 33a; NAM, s1/705^i/30, Folio 46, copy 7.

62. NAM, s1/705^i/30, Folio 31, May 29 and 30, 1934.

63. NAM, s1/705^i/30, Folio 31, May 29 and 30, 1934.

64. NAM, s1/705^i/30, Folio 31, May 29 and 30, 1934, 1, 2. See also NAM, s1/705^i/30, Folio 33a; NAM s1/705^i/30, Folio 46, Copy 7.

65. NAM, s1/705^i/30, Folio 31, May 29 and 30, 1934, 1, 2. See also NAM, s1/705^i/30, Folio 33a; NAM, s1/705^i/30, Folio 46, Copy 7.

66. NAM, s1/705^i/30, Folio 31, May 29 and 30, 1934, 1, 2. See also NAM, s1/705^i/30, Folio 33a; NAM, s1/705^i/30, Folio 46, Copy 7.

67. NAM, s1/705^i/30, Folio 31, May 29 and 30, 1934, 1, 2. See also NAM, s1/705^i/30, Folio 33a; NAM, s1/705^i/30, Folio 46, Copy 7.

68. NAM, s1/705^i/30, Folio 31, May 29 and 30, 1934, 1, 2. See also NAM, s1/705^i/30, Folio 33a; NAM, s1/705^i/30, Folio 46, Copy 7.

69. For a comparable discussion, see Brennan, *Taifa*, 128–36.

70. NAM, s1/705^i/30, Folio 31, May 29 and 30, 1934, 1, 2. See also NAM, s1/705^i/30, Folio 33a; NAM, s1/705^i/30, Folio 46, Copy 7.

71. NAM, s1/705^i/30, Folio 31, May 29 and 30, 1934, 1, 2. See also NAM, s1/705^i/30, Folio 33a; NAM, s1/705^i/30, Folio 46, Copy 7.

72. NAM s1/705^i/30, Folio 31, May 29 and 30, 1934, 1, 2. See also NAM, s1/705^i/30, Folio 33a; NAM, s1/705^i/30, Folio 46, Copy 7.

73. NAM, s1/705^i/30, Folio 44, September 15, 1934.

74. NAM, s1/705^i/30, Folio 44a, 1–16. See also NAM, s1/705^i/30, Folio 46, Copy 9.

75. NAM, s1/705^i/30, Folio 44a, 1–16. See also NAM, s1/705^i/30, Folio 46, Copy 9; NAM, s1/705^i/30, Folio 37.

76. NAM, s1/705^i/30, Folio 44a, 1–16. See also NAM, s1/705^i/30, Folio 46, Copy 9.

77. NAM, s1/705^i/30, Folio 44a, 1–16. See also NAM, s1/705^i/30, Folio 46, Copy 9.

78. NAM, s26/2/4/5, Folio 2, April 5, 1935; NAM, s26/2/4/5, Folio 3, April 5, 1935.

79. Giddens, *Central Problems in Social Theory*, 17, 18.

80. NAM, S1/705^i/30, Folio 44a, 4.

81. NAM, S1/705^i/30, Folio 44a, 4.

82. NAM, S1/705^i/30, Folio 44a, 7. There is confusion in the quote regarding the term *dowry*, which is typically wealth paid by the bride's family to the groom and his family. In contrast a bride price is wealth paid to the bride and her family by the prospective husband.

83. NAM, S1/705^i/30, Folio 44a, 8.

84. NAM, S1/705^i/30, Folio 44a, 8.

85. NAM, S1/705^i/30, Folio 44a, 8.

86. NAM, S1/705^i/30, Folio 44a, 8.

87. NAM, S1/705^i/30, Folio 44a, 8.

88. NAM, S1/705^i/30, Folio 44a, 9.

89. NAM, S1/705^i/30, Folio 44a, 10.

90. NAM, S1/705^i/30, Folio 44a, 5.

91. NAM, S1/705^i/30, Folio 44a, 5.

92. NAM, S1/705^i/30, Folio 44a, 5.

93. NAM, S1/705^i/30, Folio 44a, 5.

94. NAM, S1/705^i/30, Folio 44a, 5.

95. NAM, S1/705^i/30, Folio 44a, 11.

96. NAM, S1/705^i/30, Folio 44a, 11.

97. NAM, S1/705^i/30, Folio 44a, 11.

98. NAM, S1/705^i/30, Folio 44a, 12.

99. NAM, S1/705^i/30, Folio 44a, 12.

100. NAM, S1/705^i/30, Folio 44, September 15, 1934.

101. NAM, S1/705^i/30, Folio 45, October 5, 1934. See also NAM, S1/705^i/30, Folio 46, Copy 10; NAM, S1/705^i/30, 1a, 1–4; NAM, S1/309/33, Folios 22–27, 27a, October 1, 1933.

102. NAM, S26/2/4/5, Folio 16, September 18, 1935. For conditions in Southern Rhodesia, see Mandaza, *Race, Colour, and Class in Southern Africa*, chapter 5.

103. On the vital role of intellectuals, see Vail, "Introduction: Ethnicity in Southern African History" and the rest of the contributions to *The Creation of Tribalism in Southern Africa*.

104. Bourdieu, *Outline of a Theory of Practice*, 78.

105. On mediation, see Feierman, *Peasant Intellectuals*, 4–5.

106. Van Velsen, *Politics of Kinship*, 186.

107. NAM, S1/705^i/30, Folio 44a, 6. On contradictory consciousness, see Glassman, *Feasts and Riot*, 18–19.

108. Scott, *Domination and the Arts of Resistance*, 27.

109. I use this expression with some revision, since James Scott stresses actions more than ideas (*Weapons of the Weak*, 29).

110. Lonsdale, "Moral Ethnicity and Political Tribalism," 131. See also Lonsdale, "The Moral Economy of Mau Mau"; White, "Civic Virtue, Young Men, and the Family."

111. On racial honor, see Iliffe, *Honour in African History*, 306–27.

112. On little traditions, see Redfield, *The Little Community*, 42, 43, 48, 49. See also Ranger, "The Invention of Tradition Revisited"; Zachernuk, *Colonial Subjects*, 6.

113. On this later period, see Mandaza, *Race, Colour, and Class in Southern Africa*, 491–93.

114. Interview with Yusuf Ismael, December 16, 1999.

115. Interview with Yusuf Ismael, December 16, 1999.

7. LOYALTY AND DISREGARD

1. Editorial, "Thought of the Month," *Rhodesian Tribune*, vol. 1, no. 2, September 1945, 3, 4.

2. Anderson, *Imagined Communities*.

3. Ranger, "The Invention of Tradition."

4. On unofficial culture, see Barber, "Popular Arts in Africa," 9–12, 34–40.

5. Muzondidya, *Walking a Tightrope*, 86. For Snapper's biography, see no author, "Personalia," *Rhodesian Tribune*, vol. 1, no. 3, October 1945, 10.

6. On urban politics in Zimbabwe, see Barnes, *We Women Worked So Hard*; Raftopoulos and Yoshikuni, *Sites of Struggle*; Ranger, *Bulawayo Burning*; Scarnecchia, *The Urban Roots of Democracy and Political Violence in Zimbabwe*; Yoshikuni, *African Urban Experiences in Colonial Zimbabwe*.

7. See, for example, Glassman, "Sorting Out the Tribes" and *War of Words*, chapter 5; Brennan, "Politics and Business in the Indian Newspapers of Colonial Tanganyika"; Limb, *The People's Paper*.

8. Williams, *Marxism and Literature*, 121–27.

9. On bounded groupness, see Cooper, *Colonialism in Question*, 71, 75–77.

10. The Coloured Community Service League was not the first organization to use the term *Coloured* in its name and it was not the first to have Cape Coloured members. The term *Coloured* was often scrutinized. For example, the Rhodesia Cape Afrikander Association, despite having a membership with ties to the Cape, fined members for using the term *Coloured*. There were fears that its use would result in discrimination against them. See Mandaza, *Race, Colour, and Class in Southern Africa*, 84, 99.

11. The student body of these schools was not always uniformly Coloured or Eurafrican. See Mandaza, *Race, Colour, and Class in Southern Africa*, 18–19, 29, 31, 35; Muzondidya, *Walking a Tightrope*, 25, 112–13.

12. Scarnecchia, *The Urban Roots of Democracy and Political Violence in Zimbabwe*, chapters 1–3; West, *The Rise of an African Middle Class*, chapter 6.

13. Euro-African Patriotic Society, "Aims and Objects," *Rhodesian Tribune*, vol. 1, no. 1, August 1945, 1.

14. Euro-African Patriotic Society, "Aims and Objects," *Rhodesian Tribune*, vol. 1, no. 1, August 1945, 1.

15. Euro-African Patriotic Society, "Aims and Objects," *Rhodesian Tribune*, vol. 1, no. 1, August 1945, 1.

16. Euro-African Patriotic Society, "Member's Creed," *Rhodesian Tribune*, vol. 1, no. 3, October 1945, 1.

17. Editorial, "A Priority Message to Readers," *Rhodesian Tribune*, vol. 1, no. 1, August 1945, 3.

18. Editorial, "A Priority Message to Readers," *Rhodesian Tribune*, vol. 1, no. 1, August 1945, 3.

19. Editorial, "A Priority Message to Readers," *Rhodesian Tribune*, vol. 1, no. 1, August 1945, 4.

20. Editorial, "A Priority Message to Readers," *Rhodesian Tribune*, vol. 1, no. 1, August 1945, 4.

21. Euro-African Patriotic Society, "Message of Welcome to the Governor," *Rhodesian Tribune*, vol. 1, no. 1, August 1945, 5.

22. Euro-African Patriotic Society, "Message of Welcome to the Governor," *Rhodesian Tribune*, vol. 1, no. 1, August 1945, 5.

23. For studies of respectability, see Iliffe, *Honour in African History*, 246–61; Ross, *Status and Respectability in the Cape Colony, 1750–1870*; Zachernuk, *Colonial Subjects*, chapters 3 and 4. For related work in Zimbabwe, see Burke, *Lifeboy Men, Lux Women*; Shutt, "'The Natives Are Getting out of Hand'" and "'I Told Him I Was Lennox Njokweni.'"

24. Black Rhodesians also pursued ideas of broader citizenship. See West, *The Rise of an African Middle Class*, chapter 7; Scarnecchia, *The Urban Roots of Democracy and Political Violence in Zimbabwe*, chapter 1; Ranger, *Are We Not Also Men?*

25. G. Thomas Thornicroft, "A Message from Mr. G. Thomas Thornicroft," *Rhodesian Tribune*, vol. 1, no. 1, August 1945, 8.

26. G. Thomas Thornicroft, "A Message from Mr. G. Thomas Thornicroft," *Rhodesian Tribune*, vol. 1, no. 1, August 1945, 8.

27. G. Thomas Thornicroft, "A Message from Mr. G. Thomas Thornicroft," *Rhodesian Tribune*, vol. 1, no. 1, August 1945, 8.

28. G. Thomas Thornicroft, "A Message from Mr. G. Thomas Thornicroft," *Rhodesian Tribune*, vol. 1, no. 1, August 1945, 8.

29. No author, "Euro-African–Coloured Reconciliation," *Rhodesian Tribune*, vol. 1, no. 1, August 1945, 9, 10.

30. Muzondidya, *Walking a Tightrope*, 39.

31. No author, "Conflict of Interests," *Rhodesian Tribune*, vol. 1, no. 10, May 1946, 5. For a study of this South African organization, see Adhikari, *"Let Us Live for Our Children."*

32. Mandala, "The Sound and the Fury," *Rhodesian Tribune*, vol. 1, no. 9, April 1946, 8.

33. Muzondidya, *Walking a Tightrope*, 87–90.

34. Mandala, "The Sound and the Fury," *Rhodesian Tribune*, vol. 1, no. 9, April 1946, 7.

35. This figure is from Muzondidya, *Walking a Tightrope*, 65.

36. Mandala, "The Sound and the Fury," *Rhodesian Tribune*, vol. 1, no. 9, April 1946, 7.

37. Mandala, "The Sound and the Fury," *Rhodesian Tribune*, vol. 1, no. 9, April 1946, 9.

38. The Patriot, "Digest of Current Affairs," *Rhodesian Tribune*, vol. 1, no. 7, February 1946, 5.

39. Euro-African Patriotic Society, "Preamble," *Rhodesian Tribune*, vol. 1, no. 1, August 1945, 11.

40. Iliffe, *Honour in African History*, 306–27.

41. This article is listed as a reprint from the *Rhodesia Herald*, February 16, 1945. No author, "Euro-African Society Protests against Use of Term Coloured," *Rhodesian Tribune*, vol. 1, no. 1, August 1945, 12.

42. No author, "Euro-African Society Protests against Use of Term Coloured," *Rhodesian Tribune*, vol. 1, no. 1, August 1945, 12.

43. No author, "Euro-African Society Protests against Use of Term Coloured," *Rhodesian Tribune*, vol. 1, no. 1, August 1945, 12.

44. J. E. Jones, letter to the editor, *Rhodesian Tribune*, vol. 1, no. 3, October 1945, 15. On his biography, see no author, "Personalia," *Rhodesian Tribune*, vol. 1, no. 3, October 1945, 11.

45. John Ascroft, "The Term Coloured," *Rhodesian Tribune*, vol. 1, no. 8, March 1946, 15. For biographical information on Ascroft, see no author, "Personalia," *Rhodesian Tribune*, vol. 1, no. 2, September 1945, 8.

46. See, for example, no author, "Race or Origin," *Rhodesian Tribune*, vol. 1, no. 4, November 1945, 11; no author, "Race or Origin," *Rhodesian Tribune*, vol. 1, no. 11, June 1946, 4. Though not in these instances, Reed was sometimes referred to as "Haythorne-Reed."

47. Reprinted from the Department of Internal Affairs, Southern Rhodesia, August 30, 1935. No author, "Legal Meaning of Natives and Coloured Persons," *Rhodesian Tribune*, vol. 1, no. 4, November 1945, 14.

48. D. M. Desai, letter to the editor, "The Term Coloured," *Rhodesian Tribune*, vol. 1, no. 9, April 1946, 16, 17.

49. Editorial, "'As You Were'—Only Offer," *Rhodesian Tribune*, vol. 1, no. 11, June 1946, 3.

50. Editorial, "'As You Were'—Only Offer," *Rhodesian Tribune*, vol. 1, no. 11, June 1946, 3.

51. Editorial, "'As You Were'—Only Offer," *Rhodesian Tribune*, vol. 1, no. 11, June 1946, 3. On the Beadle Commission, see also no author, "The Social Welfare Commission: Definition of a Coloured Person," *Rhodesian Tribune*, vol. 1, no. 11, June 1946, 11–13.

52. No author, "Race or Origin," *Rhodesian Tribune*, vol. 1, no. 11, June 1946, 4.

53. No author, "Race or Origin," *Rhodesian Tribune*, vol. 1, no. 11, June 1946, 4.

54. The Magi, "What Are the Prospects of Eurafrican Coloured Union," *Rhodesian Tribune*, vol. 1, no. 4, November 1945, 3.

55. The Coloured-Eurafrican League of Southern Rhodesia, "The Coloured-Eurafrican League of Southern Rhodesia: Incorporating the Euro-African Patriotic and Benevolent Society," *Rhodesian Tribune*, vol. 1, no. 9, April 1946, 19.

56. No author, "Coloureds Propose New Term," *Rhodesian Tribune*, vol. 1, no. 4, November 1945, 18.

57. The Magi, "Inside Stuff and Debunking the Myth: Asking Your Indulgence for the Use of the Personal Pronoun," *Rhodesian Tribune*, vol. 1, no. 5, December 1945, 10.

58. The Magi, "Inside Stuff and Debunking the Myth: Asking Your Indulgence for the Use of the Personal Pronoun," *Rhodesian Tribune*, vol. 1, no. 5, December 1945, 10.

59. Arthur S. Rhoades, "New Year Message from Mr. Arthur S. Rhoades (Chairman, Eurafrican Patriotic Society, Matabeleland)," *Rhodesian Tribune*, vol. 1, no. 6, January 1946, 5.

60. F. C. Grainger-Rousseau, "Boos and Bouquets: Case for Unity," *Rhodesian Tribune*, vol. 1, no. 5, December 1945, 11.

61. F. C. Grainger-Rousseau, "Boos and Bouquets: Case for Unity," *Rhodesian Tribune*, vol. 1, no. 5, December 1945, 11.

62. The Magi, "Inside Stuff and Debunking the Myth: Asking Your Indulgence for the Use of the Personal Pronoun," *Rhodesian Tribune*, vol. 1, no. 5, December 1945, 10.

63. The Patriot, "A Cogito Ego [*sic*] Sum," *Rhodesian Tribune*, vol. 1, no. 7, February 1946, 5.

64. The Patriot, "A Cogito Ego [*sic*] Sum," *Rhodesian Tribune*, vol. 1, no. 7, February 1946, 5. See also no author, "Complex Ideas," *Rhodesian Tribune*, vol. 2, no. 4, November 1946, 11, 12.

65. No author, "Should There Be a Third Problem?" *Rhodesian Tribune*, vol. 3, no. 8/9, March–April 1948, 5.

66. The Patriot, "A Cogito Ego [*sic*] Sum," *Rhodesian Tribune*, vol. 1, no. 7, February 1946, 5.

67. The Patriot, "A Cogito Ego [*sic*] Sum," *Rhodesian Tribune*, vol. 1, no. 7, February 1946, 6.

68. No author, "Why Racial Discrimination Exists," *Rhodesian Tribune*, vol. 1, no. 7, February 1946, 7–9.

69. No author, "Why Racial Discrimination Exists," *Rhodesian Tribune*, vol. 1, no. 7, February 1946, 9.

70. No author, "Why Racial Discrimination Exists," *Rhodesian Tribune*, vol. 1, no. 7, February 1946, 9.

71. J. Gunther Stuhardt, "Ninth Annual Conference Rhodesia Teachers' League: Presidential Address," *Rhodesian Tribune*, vol. 1, no. 12, July 1946, 11.

72. No author, "Education of First Generation Coloured Children," *Rhodesian Tribune*, vol. 2, no. 8, March 1947, 11–13; no author, "Illegitimate Children: Responsibility of Father," *Rhodesian Tribune*, vol. 2, no. 9, April 1947, 9.

73. Editorial, "First Generation," *Rhodesian Tribune*, vol. 2, no. 10, May 1947, 3, 4.

74. Editorial, "Should Miscegenation Be Stopped?," *Rhodesian Tribune*, vol. 3, no. 1/2, September 1947, 5, 6; F. R. Old, "Northern Rhodesia News: A Simple Advice to Eurafrican People Regarding Marriage," *Rhodesian Tribune*, vol. 3, no. 6, January 1948, 9, 10.

75. No author, "Should There Be a Third Problem?," *Rhodesian Tribune*, vol. 3, no. 8/9, March–April 1948, 5.

76. John Ascroft, "The Term Coloured," *Rhodesian Tribune*, vol. 1, no. 8, March 1946, 15.

77. God's Step-Son, letter to the editor, *Rhodesian Tribune*, vol. 1, no. 12, July 1946, 16.

78. Freshman Gladstone Brown, letter to the editor, "The Eurafricans and Success in Southern Rhodesia," *Rhodesian Tribune*, vol. 2, no. 5, December 1946, 17.

79. No author, "News from the Unity Hall, Salisbury," *Rhodesian Tribune*, vol. 1, no. 2, September 1945, 19. For a study of similar celebrations, see Shutt and King, "Imperial Rhodesians."

80. No author, "News from the Unity Hall, Salisbury," *Rhodesian Tribune*, vol. 1, no. 2, September 1945, 19.

81. Editorial, "First Anniversary," *Rhodesian Tribune*, vol. 1, no. 12, July 1946, 3.

82. On these kinds of interactions, see Shutt, "'I Told Him I Was Lennox Njokweni.'"

83. R. A. D. Snapper, "The Shadow of Events," *Rhodesian Tribune*, vol. 1, no. 2, September 1945, 13.

84. No author, "Reminiscence from the Past," *Rhodesian Tribune*, vol. 1, no. 2, September 1945, 12. Though Coloured people were not conscripted, they had begun to volunteer by December 1939. See Muzondidya, *Walking a Tightrope*, 103–4.

85. No author, "Reminiscence from the Past," *Rhodesian Tribune*, vol. 1, no. 2, September 1945, 12.

86. No author, "55 G. T. Company," *Rhodesian Tribune*, vol. 1, no. 3, October 1945, 12; no author, "Flags and Bands Greet Repatriates," *Rhodesian Tribune*, vol. 1, no. 3, October 1945, 12; no author, "Final Parade before Discharge of 55th General Transport Coy. Personnel," *Rhodesian Tribune*, vol. 1, no. 4, November 1945, 8, 9.

87. Muzondidya, *Walking a Tightrope*, 103–4. On military service and patriotism, see also Nasson, *Abraham Esau's War*, chapter 3.

88. Quoted in no author, "Blantyre's Victory Parade," *Rhodesian Tribune*, vol. 1, no. 11, June 1946, 17.

89. See the editorials "Current Opinion" and "What Does the Future Hold?," *Rhodesian Tribune*, vol. 1, no. 4, November 1945, 5.

90. No author, "British Empire Service League," *Rhodesian Tribune*, vol. 1, no. 11, June 1946, 5.

91. Governor Campbell Tait, "Message to Eurafricans," *Rhodesian Tribune*, vol. 1, no. 5, December 1945, 5.

92. Editorial, "Thought of the Month," *Rhodesian Tribune*, vol. 1, no. 2, September 1945, 4.

93. No author, "Building Costs Commission Recommendations to Reduce Building Costs in the Colony," *Rhodesian Tribune*, vol. 1, no. 6, January 1946, 11; no author, "Report of the Commission of Inquiry," *Rhodesian Tribune*, vol. 1, no. 12, July 1946, 12–15; no author, "Report of the Commission of Inquiry," *Rhodesian Tribune*, vol. 2, no. 1, August 1946, 11–15; Editorial, "About Priorities," *Rhodesian Tribune*, vol. 2, no. 2, September 1946, 3.

94. G. Thomas Thornicroft, letter to the editor, *Rhodesian Tribune*, vol. 1, no. 12, July 1946, 7.

95. Editorial, "What Is an Adequate Wage?" *Rhodesian Tribune*, vol. 2, no. 1, August 1946, 3.

96. Editorial, "What Is an Adequate Wage?" *Rhodesian Tribune*, vol. 2, no. 1, August 1946, 3.

97. Editorial, "Is It an Economic or Social Problem?" *Rhodesian Tribune*, vol. 2, no. 3, October 1946, 3.

98. Editorial, "The Economic Plan," *Rhodesian Tribune*, vol. 1, no. 10, May 1946, 3.

99. No author, "The Social Welfare Commission: Definition of a Coloured Person," *Rhodesian Tribune*, vol. 1, no. 11, June 1946, 13.

100. Editorial, "First Anniversary," *Rhodesian Tribune*, vol. 1, no. 12, July 1946, 4.

101. Editorial, "Change in Standard of Education Unlikely," *Rhodesian Tribune*, vol. 2, no. 11, June 1947, 3; Editorial, "Minister Meets Leaders," *Rhodesian Tribune*, vol. 2, no. 11, June 1947, 3, 4.

102. Editorial, "God Save the King," *Rhodesian Tribune*, vol. 2, no. 8, March 1947, 3; Editorial, "God Save the King," *Rhodesian Tribune*, vol. 2, no. 9, April 1947, 3.

103. Editorial, "God Save the King," *Rhodesian Tribune*, vol. 2, no. 9, April 1947, 3.

104. J. E. Jones, "Chairman's Report," *Rhodesian Tribune*, vol. 1, no. 1, August 1945, 13, 14.

105. Glassman, "Sorting Out the Tribes," 400.

106. Henry Ascroft, letter to the editor, *Rhodesian Tribune*, vol. 1, no. 2, September 1945, 5.

107. Henry Ascroft, letter to the editor, *Rhodesian Tribune*, vol. 1, no. 2, September 1945, 5.

108. Jack A. Thornicroft, letter to the editor, *Rhodesian Tribune*, vol. 1, no. 3, October 1945, 14. The organization that Thornicroft headed was also referred to as the Eurafrican Association of the Eastern Province. See Mandaza, *Race, Colour, and Class*, 589. As for his business activities, they can be gleaned from advertisements in the *Rhodesian Tribune*.

109. Harry Cox, letter to the editor, *Rhodesian Tribune*, vol. 1, no. 3, October 1945, 14.

110. Mandaza, *Race, Colour, and Class in Southern Africa*, 401.

111. No author, "News from Nyasaland," *Rhodesian Tribune*, vol. 1, no. 2, September 1945, 7.

112. Henry Ascroft, Response to F. C. Grainger-Rousseau, "Boos and Bouquets: Case for Unity," *Rhodesian Tribune*, vol. 1, no. 5, December 1945, 12.

113. G. A. Mehl, "The True North: The Eurafrican Association of N.-E. Rhodesia," *Rhodesian Tribune*, vol. 1, no. 6, January 1946, 10.

114. The first quote is by Jack Thornicroft and the second by the article's author. See G. A. Mehl, "The True North: The Eurafrican Association of N.-E. Rhodesia," *Rhodesian Tribune*, vol. 1, no. 6, January 1946, 10. For the third quote, see editorial, "About Northern Rhodesia," *Rhodesian Tribune*, vol. 1, no. 12, July 1946, 5.

115. James L. Gardner, "The Eurafrican Association, N. E. Rhodesia," *Rhodesian Tribune*, vol. 1, no. 4, November 1945, 17.

116. Editorial, "N. Rhodesia Legislative Council," *Rhodesian Tribune*, vol. 1, no. 3, October 1945, 6.

117. Editorial, "The National Organisation," *Rhodesian Tribune*, vol. 1, no. 7, February 1946, 3.

118. No author, "Fair Comparison," *Rhodesian Tribune*, vol. 2, no. 4, November 1946, 13.

119. No author, "Nyasaland Topics—The Eurafrican School," *Rhodesian Tribune*, vol. 2, no. 4, November 1946, 7.

120. No author, "Convention of Associations," *Rhodesian Tribune*, vol. 3, no. 1/2, September 1947, 7.

121. No author, "Plea for Social Life in Nyasaland," *Rhodesian Tribune*, vol. 2, no. 2, September 1946, 13.

122. No author, "Why Unity?," *Rhodesian Tribune*, vol. 2, no. 1, August 1946, 11.

123. No author, "Condemnation of Racial Hatred," *Rhodesian Tribune*, vol. 1, no. 6, January 1946, 13.

124. No author, "Mr. Fataar Addresses Literary and Debating Club," *Rhodesian Tribune*, vol. 2, no. 12, July 1947, 7.

125. Bulldog Breed, "Non-Europeanism in Retrospect," *Rhodesian Tribune*, vol. 2, no. 12, July 1947, 9.

126. No author, "Pseudo-Philosophy of Liberation," *Rhodesian Tribune*, vol. 3, no. 1/2, September 1947, 11.

127. No author, "Pseudo-Philosophy of Liberation," *Rhodesian Tribune*, vol. 3, no. 1/2, September 1947, 13. For a further discussion of the NEUM, see Adhikari, "Fiercely Non-Racial?"

128. Editorial, "To Be or Not To Be," *Rhodesian Tribune*, vol. 3, no. 4, November 1947, 5, 6.

129. Tilda, "Coloured Community," *Rhodesian Tribune*, vol. 2, no. 3, October 1946, 11.

130. No author, "Our Second Birthday Greetings of Amity," *Rhodesian Tribune*, vol. 2, no. 12, July 1947, 4.

131. Editorial, "Capricorn Africa," *Rhodesian Tribune*, vol. 2, no. 5, December 1946, 3.

132. Henry Ascroft, "Applying the Spirit of Christmas to the People," *Rhodesian Tribune*, vol. 2, no. 6, January 1947, 3.

133. No author, "Coloured Vote in North," *Rhodesian Tribune*, vol. 2, no. 7, February 1947, 7.

134. Editorial, "The New Look," *Rhodesian Tribune*, vol. 4, no. 14, January–February 1949, 3.

135. Editorial, "The British . . . the Nationalists . . . and Eurafricans," *Rhodesian Tribune*, vol. 5, no. 1, October 1949, 3.

136. No author, "The Reply from the Law Officers between the Eurafrican Association and the Governor: 16th September, 1949," *Rhodesian Tribune*, vol. 5, no. 3, November–December 1949, 11.

137. No author, "Meeting with the Colonial Secretary, National Status, Anglo-African Association," *Rhodesian Tribune*, vol. 5, no. 4, March 1950, 4.

138. No author, "Meeting with the Colonial Secretary, National Status, Anglo-African Association," *Rhodesian Tribune*, vol. 5, no. 4, March 1950, 4.

139. R. A. D. Snapper, "Official Welcome Address," *Rhodesian Tribune*, vol. 4, no. 13, September–October 1948, 3.

140. R. A. D. Snapper, "Official Welcome Address," *Rhodesian Tribune*, vol. 4, no. 13, September–October 1948, 4.

141. Henry Ascroft, "Address delivered to the First Conference of the Eurafrican Federation of Central Africa Conference [*sic*] held at Salisbury, Southern Rhodesia, on the 10th July, 1948, by Henry Ascroft, President of the Anglo-African Association of Nyasaland," *Rhodesian Tribune*, vol. 4, no. 13, September–October 1948, 5.

142. Henry Ascroft, "Address delivered to the First Conference of the Eurafrican Federation of Central Africa Conference [*sic*] held at Salisbury, Southern Rhodesia, on the 10th July, 1948, by Henry Ascroft, President of the Anglo-African Association of Nyasaland," *Rhodesian Tribune*, vol. 4, no. 13, September–October 1948, 6.

143. Henry Ascroft, "Address delivered to the First Conference of the Eurafrican Federation of Central Africa Conference [*sic*] held at Salisbury, Southern Rhodesia, on the 10th July, 1948, by Henry Ascroft, President of the Anglo-African Association of Nyasaland," *Rhodesian Tribune*, vol. 4, no. 13, September–October 1948, 7.

144. Leonard W. S. Price, "Presidential Address by Rev. Leonard W. S. Price," *Rhodesian Tribune*, vol. 4, no. 13, September–October 1948, 9.

145. Leonard W. S. Price, "Presidential Address by Rev. Leonard W. S. Price," *Rhodesian Tribune*, vol. 4, no. 13, September–October 1948, 9.

146. No author, "Meeting with Secretary of State for the Colonies," *Rhodesian Tribune*, vol. 5, no. 1, October 1949, 4. See also Henry Ascroft, "Address of Welcome and Memorandum Delivered," *Rhodesian Tribune*, vol. 5, no. 1, October 1949, 5–7; no author, "Meeting with the Colonial Secretary, National Status, Anglo-African Association," *Rhodesian Tribune*, vol. 5, no. 4, March 1950, 3–5, 8–12.

147. No author, "Mr. Cheech [*sic*] Jones Welcomed at Fort Jameson," *Rhodesian Tribune*, vol. 5, no. 1, October 1949, 12; Leonard W. S. Price, "Presidential Address, Federation of Central Africa, Held on 24th to 26th October, 1949," *Rhodesian Tribune*, vol. 5, no. 3, November/December 1949, 5, 6.

148. G. Thomas Thornicroft, "Address by G. Thomas Thornicroft, of Salisbury," *Rhodesian Tribune*, vol. 5, no. 3, November–December 1949, 8.

149. No author, "Meeting with the Colonial Secretary, National Status, Anglo-African Association," *Rhodesian Tribune*, vol. 5, no. 4, March 1950, 12.

150. No author, "Meeting with the Colonial Secretary, National Status, Anglo-African Association," *Rhodesian Tribune*, vol. 5, no. 4, March 1950, 4.

151. Editorial, "Review of the Year," *Rhodesian Tribune*, vol. 3, no. 6, January 1948, 3.

152. Editorial, "The New Bills," *Rhodesian Tribune*, vol. 3, no. 11/12, July–August 1948, 3.

153. Editorial, "The Franchise in the North," *Rhodesian Tribune*, vol. 3, no. 10/11, May–June 1948, 3.

154. G. Thomas Thornicroft, "Definition of a Native," *Rhodesian Tribune*, vol. 3, no. 11/12, July–August 1948, 3.

155. Ginzburg, *The Cheese and the Worms*, xvii.

156. Editorial, "Discrimination," *Rhodesian Tribune*, vol. 1, no. 9, April 1946, 3.

8. URBANIZATION AND SPATIAL BELONGING

1. National Archives of Zambia (hereafter NAZAM), Lusaka, Local Government and Housing (hereafter LGH) 1/6/23, Lusaka Eurafrican Housing, C.A.P. Reporter, "Rent in Arrears and Overspending Too—It's Uphill for Lusaka's Eurafricans," *Central African Post*, July 8, 1960.

2. NAZAM, LGH 1/6/23, Lusaka Eurafrican Housing, C.A.P. Reporter, "Rent in Arrears and Overspending Too—It's Uphill for Lusaka's Eurafricans," *Central African Post*, July 8, 1960.

3. NAZAM, LGH 1/6/23, Lusaka Eurafrican Housing, C.A.P. Reporter, "Rent in Arrears and Overspending Too—It's Uphill for Lusaka's Eurafricans," *Central African Post*, July 8, 1960. See also NAZAM, LGH 1/6/23, Lusaka Eurafrican Housing, no author, "Eurafricans in Lusaka Overspend on Income," *Central African Post*, July 9, 1960.

4. For a recent study, see Hughes, *Whiteness in Zimbabwe*, chapters 1 and 6.

5. On "third space," see Bhabha, *The Location of Culture*, 56, 311, 312. On District Six, see Jeppie and Soudien, *The Struggle for District Six*. On Arcadia, see Seirlis, "Islands and Autochthons."

6. On urbanization, see Epstein, *Politics in an Urban African Community*; Mitchell, *Cities, Society, and Social Perception*; Powdermaker, *Copper Town*. On modernization, see Ferguson, *Expectations of Modernity*. For a recent debate, see Ferguson, "Mobile Workers, Modernist Narratives," parts 1 and 2, and "Modernist Narratives, Conven-

tional Wisdoms, and Colonial Liberalism"; Macmillan, "The Historiography of Transition on the Zambian Copperbelt—Another View."

7. Mabogunje, "Urban Planning and the Post-Colonial State in Africa," 121. For classic studies of urban space and political struggle, see Harvey, *Social Justice and the City*; Lefebvre, *The Production of Space*. For recent work in Africa, see Simone, *For the City Yet to Come*, especially chapter 1.

8. Western, *Outcast Cape Town*, 8.

9. NAZAM, LGH 1/6/23, Lusaka Eurafrican Housing, C.A.P. Reporter, "Rent in Arrears and Overspending Too—It's Uphill for Lusaka's Eurafricans," *Central African Post*, July 8, 1960; NAZAM, LGH 1/6/23, Lusaka Eurafrican Housing, no author, "Eurafricans in Lusaka Overspend on Income," *Central African Post*, July 9, 1960. On the *Central African Post*, see Kallmann, "Projected Moralities, Engaged Anxieties," 103, footnote 116.

10. NAZAM, LGH 1/6/23, Lusaka Eurafrican Housing, C.A.P. Reporter, "Eurafricans Owe £423 in Rents," *Central African Post*, June 29, 1960.

11. This society was previously called the Euro-African Society. It was based in Lusaka and led by H. P. Crosby, H. A. Thornicroft, P. W. Fredman, K. F. Blockley, and C. C. Henderson. Mandaza, *Race, Colour, and Class in Southern Africa*, 494.

12. NAZAM, LGH 1/6/23, Lusaka Eurafrican Housing, letter from P. W. Fredman to secretariat, lands and local government, Lusaka, April 25, 1959.

13. NAZAM, LGH 1/6/23, Lusaka Eurafrican Housing, letter from the town clerk to the commissioner for local government, March 13, 1958; NAZAM, LGH 1/6/23, Lusaka Eurafrican Housing, extract from agenda of municipal council of Lusaka, January 30, 1958. It is noted that this figure differs from footnote 121.

14. On Marrapodi, see Collins, "Lusaka," 108.

15. NAZAM, LGH 1/6/23, Lusaka Eurafrican Housing, letter from the director of welfare and probation services to the town clerk, December 3, 1958.

16. NAZAM, LGH 1/6/23, Lusaka Eurafrican Housing, report of the works committee, Eurafrican housing scheme, rentals for housing units, January 1958.

17. Hansen, *Distant Companions*, 22–28, 33. On Lusaka's development, see also Hawkesworth, *Local Government in Zambia*; Western, "Undoing the Colonial City?"; Williams, *Lusaka and Its Environs*. On segregation in Northern Rhodesia, see, for example, Ambler, "Alcohol, Racial Segregation and Popular Politics in Northern Rhodesia"; Berger, *Labour, Race and Colonial Rule*; Powdermaker, *Copper Town*.

18. NAZAM, Lusaka Urban District Council (hereafter LUDC) 1/22/5, Eurafrican Housing, letter from the Eur-African Association, Lusaka, to the native affairs department, March 17, 1948.

19. NAZAM, LGH 1/16/50, Local Government—Lusaka, Eurafrican Housing, letter from member for health and local government to commissioner for local government, July 18, 1949. See also NAZAM, LGH 1/16/50, Local Government—Lusaka, Eurafrican Housing, letter from the director of development to member for health and local government, July 7, 1949.

20. NAZAM, LGH 1/16/50, Local Government—Lusaka, Eurafrican Housing, letter from the commissioner for local government to the member for health and local government, September 16, 1949.

21. Hansen, *Keeping House in Lusaka*, 33.

22. NAZAM, LGH 1/16/49, Housing for Eurafricans, summary of local authorities from the commissioner for local government and African housing to the member for health and local government, April 22, 1950, 2. See also NAZAM, LGH 1/16/49, Housing for Eurafricans, letter from the commissioner for local government to local authorities at Livingstone, Ndola, Lusaka, Broken Hill, Fort Jameson, Mufulira, Chingola, Kitwe, and Luanshya, October 26, 1949.

23. As cited in chapter 5, a copy of the report is in the file: National Archives of the United Kingdom, London, Colonial Office 795/170/13, Northern Rhodesia, *Report of the Committee to Inquire into the Status and Welfare of Coloured Persons in Northern Rhodesia.*

24. NAZAM, LGH 1/16/49, Housing for Eurafricans, legislative council minutes, Hansard No. 67, January 11, 1950, column 201.

25. NAZAM, LGH 1/16/49, Housing for Eurafricans, legislative council minutes, Hansard No. 70, November 22, 1950, columns 228, 229.

26. NAZAM, LGH 1/16/49, Housing for Eurafricans, legislative council minutes, Hansard No. 70, November 22, 1950, column 229.

27. Collins, "Lusaka," 104–14.

28. NAZAM, LGH 1/16/50, Local Government-Lusaka, Eurafrican Housing, legislative council minutes, Hansard No. 65, September 14, 1949, column 149.

29. NAZAM, LGH 1/16/49, Housing for Eurafricans, legislative council minutes, Hansard No. 70, November 22, 1950, columns 207–9.

30. Hansen, *Keeping House in Lusaka*, 31.

31. The letter itself is dated February 27, 1951. See NAZAM, LGH 1/16/50, Local Government—Lusaka, Eurafrican Housing, C. J. Jones, letter to the editor, "No Houses for Coloureds," *Central African Post*, March 8, 1951.

32. NAZAM, LGH 1/16/50, Local Government—Lusaka, Eurafrican Housing, letter from a member of the legislative council chamber to the secretariat, April 23, 1951.

33. NAZAM, LUDC 1/22/5, Eurafrican Housing, letter from the commissioner for local government to Lusaka management board, May 8, 1951.

34. NAZAM, LGH 1/16/49, Housing for Eurafricans, Staff Reporter, "Coloureds' Call for Better Housing," *Northern News*, August 3, 1951. On the *Northern News*, see Kallmann, "Projected Moralities, Engaged Anxieties."

35. NAZAM, LGH 1/16/49, Housing for Eurafricans, C.A.P. Reporter, "Housing Plight of Coloured People," *Central African Post*, December 13, 1951.

36. Kallmann, "Projected Moralities, Engaged Anxieties."

37. Though this report was published, I draw upon the copy included in the following archival file: NAZAM, LGH 1/16/49, Housing for Eurafricans, *Report of the Committee to Inquire into the African and Eurafrican Housing Position in Lusaka*, 1953.

38. NAZAM, LGH 1/16/49, Housing for Eurafricans, *Report of the Committee to Inquire into the African and Eurafrican Housing Position in Lusaka*, 1953, 2. The African suburbs then consisted of Old Chilenje and Kanyama, built during World War II, and New Chilenje and Matero, started in 1950 and 1951, respectively. Hansen, *Keeping House in Lusaka*, 28.

39. NAZAM, LGH 1/16/49, Housing for Eurafricans, *Report of the Committee to Inquire into the African and Eurafrican Housing Position in Lusaka*, 1953, 2.

40. NAZAM, LGH 1/16/49, Housing for Eurafricans, *Report of the Committee to Inquire into the African and Eurafrican Housing Position in Lusaka*, 1953, 8.

41. NAZAM, LGH 1/16/49, Housing for Eurafricans, *Report of the Committee to Inquire into the African and Eurafrican Housing Position in Lusaka*, 1953, 9.

42. NAZAM, LGH 1/16/49, Housing for Eurafricans, *Report of the Committee to Inquire into the African and Eurafrican Housing Position in Lusaka*, 1953, 9.

43. NAZAM, LGH 1/16/49, Housing for Eurafricans, *Report of the Committee to Inquire into the African and Eurafrican Housing Position in Lusaka*, 1953, 9.

44. NAZAM, LGH 1/16/49, Housing for Eurafricans, *Report of the Committee to Inquire into the African and Eurafrican Housing Position in Lusaka*, 1953, 9.

45. NAZAM, LGH 1/16/49, Housing for Eurafricans, *Report of the Committee to Inquire into the African and Eurafrican Housing Position in Lusaka*, 1953, 6.

46. NAZAM, LGH 1/16/49, Housing for Eurafricans, letter from the commissioner for local government and African housing to the member for health and local government, April 22, 1950.

47. NAZAM, LUDC 1/22/5, Eurafrican Housing, letter from the commissioner for local government to the Lusaka Management Board, December 21, 1950.

48. NAZAM, LUDC 1/22/5, Eurafrican Housing, letter from the works committee to the commissioner for local government, April 6, 1951.

49. NAZAM, LUDC 1/22/5, Eurafrican Housing, works committee memo on low income group housing, August 8, 1951.

50. NAZAM, LUDC 1/22/5, Eurafrican Housing, "Memorandum of a Meeting between the Acting Secretary of the Lusaka Management Board and Representatives of the Eurafrican Patriotic and Benevolent Society held in the Board Room at Boleyn's Buildings on 28th July, 1952, at 3.0 P.M.," 1, 2. See also NAZAM, LUDC 1/22/5, Eurafrican Housing, letter from the Eurafrican Patriotic and Benevolent Society to the secretary/solicitor, May 15, 1952.

51. NAZAM, LUDC 1/22/5, Eurafrican Housing, letter from the commissioner for local government to the Lusaka Management Board, November 3, 1952.

52. NAZAM, LGH 1/16/49, Housing for Eurafricans, "Notes of Meeting Held in the Development Secretary's Office on the 18th August, 1952, to Discuss Housing Standards for Coloured Persons," 1.

53. NAZAM, LGH 1/16/49, Housing for Eurafricans, "Notes of Meeting Held in the Development Secretary's Office on the 18th August, 1952, to Discuss Housing Standards for Coloured Persons," 1–2.

54. NAZAM, LGH 1/16/49, Housing for Eurafricans, "Notes of a Meeting Held in the Development Secretary's Office on 5th September, 1952, to Discuss Housing Standards for Coloured Persons."

55. NAZAM, LGH 1/16/49, Housing for Eurafricans, letter from the commissioner for local government to the member for health and local government, Lusaka, October 8, 1952. This correspondence gives the figure of £7.10.0 for rent.

56. NAZAM, LUDC 1/22/5, Eurafrican Housing, letter from the Eurafrican Association to the Lusaka Management Board, November 15, 1952.

57. NAZAM, LGH 1/16/49, Housing for Eurafricans, legislative council minutes, April 24, 1953, columns 258–59. This item refers to an actual rent of £9.2.6 charged by the Lusaka Municipal Board.

58. NAZAM, LUDC 1/22/41, Housing-Coloured Housing Policy, letter from Eur-African Group to the town clerk, March 29, 1953.

59. NAZAM, LUDC 1/22/41, Housing-Coloured Housing Policy, letter from the district commissioner (urban) to the town clerk, May 6, 1953; NAZAM, LUDC 1/22/41, Housing-Coloured Housing Policy, extract from the minutes of the finance committee meeting, October 22, 1953.

60. NAZAM, LGH 1/16/49, Housing for Eurafricans, no author, "Coloureds' Housing," *Central African Post*, May 1, 1953.

61. NAZAM, LGH 1/16/49, Housing for Eurafricans, legislative council minutes, July 1, 1954, column 65.

62. NAZAM, LGH 1/16/49, Housing for Eurafricans, untitled memo, July 14, 1954, 2.

63. NAZAM, LUDC 1/22/41, Housing-Coloured Housing Policy, letter from the Euro-African Patriotic Society to the town clerk, Lusaka, October 12, 1954; NAZAM, LGH 1/16/50, Local Government—Lusaka, Eurafrican Housing, "Resolution of the Euro-African Patriotic Society," October 24, 1954; NAZAM, LGH 1/16/50, Local Government—Lusaka, Eurafrican Housing, letter from the secretary of the Euro-African Patriotic Society to the member for health, land, and local government, October 24, 1954; NAZAM, LUDC 1/22/41, Housing-Coloured Housing Policy, letter from the Euro-African Patriotic Society to the town clerk, Lusaka, November 1, 1954; NAZAM, LUDC 1/22/41, Housing-Coloured Housing Policy, letter from the Euro-African Patriotic Society to the town clerk, Lusaka, November 10, 1954.

64. NAZAM, LGH 1/16/50, Local Government—Lusaka, Eurafrican Housing, memorandum to the government on houses, welfare, and living conditions of Euro-African people in Lusaka and Broken Hill, November 24, 1954, 1.

65. NAZAM, LGH 1/16/50, Local Government—Lusaka, Eurafrican Housing, memorandum to the government on houses, welfare, and living conditions of Euro-African people in Lusaka and Broken Hill, November 24, 1954, 2.

66. NAZAM, LGH 1/16/50, Local Government—Lusaka, Eurafrican Housing, record of a meeting with a delegation from the Euro-African Patriotic Society, November 25, 1954, 1.

67. NAZAM, LGH 1/16/50, Local Government—Lusaka, Eurafrican Housing, record of a meeting with a delegation from the Euro-African Patriotic Society, November 25, 1954, 2.

68. NAZAM, LGH 1/16/50, Local Government—Lusaka, Eurafrican Housing, record of a meeting with a delegation from the Euro-African Patriotic Society, November 25, 1954, 2. See also Hansen, *Keeping House in Lusaka*, 28.

69. NAZAM, LGH 1/16/50, Local Government—Lusaka, Eurafrican Housing, brief by the social welfare officer on Eurafrican housing, December 12, 1954, 1.

70. NAZAM, LGH 1/16/50, Local Government—Lusaka, Eurafrican Housing, brief by the social welfare officer on Eurafrican housing, December 12, 1954, 1.

71. NAZAM, LGH 1/16/50, Local Government—Lusaka, Eurafrican Housing, brief by the social welfare officer on Eurafrican housing, December 12, 1954, 1.

72. NAZAM, LGH 1/16/50, Local Government—Lusaka, Eurafrican Housing, brief by the social welfare officer on Eurafrican housing, December 12, 1954, 2.

73. Hansen, *Keeping House in Lusaka*, 28.

74. NAZAM, LUDC 1/22/41, Housing-Coloured Housing Policy, "Record of a Meet-

ing Held with Representatives of the Lusaka Municipal Council in the Office of the Member for Health, Lands and Local Government at 10 A.M. on the 24th January, 1955, to Discuss the Problem of Housing of Euro-African People in Lusaka," 1.

75. NAZAM, LUDC 1/22/41, Housing-Coloured Housing Policy, "Record of a Meeting Held with Representatives of the Lusaka Municipal Council in the Office of the Member for Health, Lands and Local Government at 10 A.M. on the 24th January, 1955, to Discuss the Problem of Housing of Euro-African People in Lusaka," 2.

76. NAZAM, LUDC 1/22/41, Housing-Coloured Housing Policy, "Record of a Meeting Held with Representatives of the Lusaka Municipal Council in the Office of the Member for Health, Lands and Local Government at 10 A.M. on the 24th January, 1955, to Discuss the Problem of Housing of Euro-African People in Lusaka," 2.

77. NAZAM, LUDC 1/22/41, Housing-Coloured Housing Policy, "Record of a Meeting Held with Representatives of the Lusaka Municipal Council in the Office of the Member for Health, Lands and Local Government at 10 A.M. on the 24th January, 1955, to Discuss the Problem of Housing of Euro-African People in Lusaka," 1–4. For a copy of the eventual loan regulations, see NAZAM, LUDC 1/22/41, Housing-Coloured Housing Policy, Municipality of Lusaka, "Owner Housing Loan Scheme Regulations," 1–6.

78. NAZAM, LGH 1/16/50, Local Government—Lusaka, Eurafrican Housing, Our Correspondent, "Coloureds in N.R. are Becoming 'Forgotten People'—Gaunt," *Northern News*, January 13, 1955. See also NAZAM, LGH 1/16/50, Local Government—Lusaka, Eurafrican Housing, Our Correspondent, "Roberts Holding Meeting to Discuss Coloured Housing," *Northern News*, January 15, 1955.

79. NAZAM, LGH 1/16/50, Local Government—Lusaka, Eurafrican Housing, Our Correspondent, "Lusaka's Coloured Housing Problem Is Acute," *Northern News*, January 20, 1955.

80. NAZAM, LGH 1/16/50, Local Government—Lusaka, Eurafrican Housing, Our Correspondent, "Lusaka's Coloured Housing Problem Is Acute," *Northern News*, January 20, 1955.

81. NAZAM, LGH 1/16/50, Local Government—Lusaka, Eurafrican Housing, Our Correspondent, "Lusaka's Coloured Housing Problem Is Acute," *Northern News*, January 20, 1955.

82. NAZAM, LGH 1/16/50, Local Government—Lusaka, Eurafrican Housing, C.A.P. Reporter, "Euro-Africans Not Satisfied with Housing Proposals," *Central African Post*, January 28, 1955.

83. NAZAM, LGH 1/16/50, Local Government—Lusaka, Eurafrican Housing, C.A.P. Reporter, "Biggest Single Step," *Central African Post*, January 31, 1955.

84. NAZAM, LGH 1/16/50, Local Government—Lusaka, Eurafrican Housing, H. P. Crosby, letter to the editor, *Northern News*, February 22, 1955.

85. NAZAM, LGH 1/16/50, Local Government—Lusaka, Eurafrican Housing, council meeting agenda, Lusaka, February 24, 1955; NAZAM, LUDC 1/22/41, Housing-Coloured Housing Policy, report of the works committee, February 21, 1955; NAZAM, LGH 1/16/50, Local Government—Lusaka, Eurafrican Housing, letter on Eurafrican housing in Lusaka from the town clerk, March 9, 1955.

86. NAZAM, LGH 1/16/50, Local Government—Lusaka, Eurafrican Housing, supplementary report of the town clerk to works committee," May 1955; NAZAM,

LGH 1/16/50, Local Government—Lusaka, Eurafrican Housing, C.A.P. Reporter, "Euro-African Housing Probe by Lusaka Municipality," *Central African Post*, May 25, 1955.

87. As indicated in this sentence, an organizational name change appears once more in 1955, with the resignation of Sayer. See NAZAM, LGH 1/16/79, Welfare for Coloured Persons, C.A.P. Reporter, "Euro-African Head Resigns," *Central African Post*, May 11, 1955.

88. NAZAM, LGH 1/16/50, Local Government—Lusaka, Eurafrican Housing, C.A.P. Reporter, "Euro-Africans Building Co-Operative," *Central African Post*, August 17, 1955. See also NAZAM, LGH 1/16/50, Local Government—Lusaka, Eurafrican Housing, Our Correspondent, "Housing Co-Op," *Northern News*, August 18, 1955. On the functioning of the cooperative, see NAZAM, LUDC 1/22/53, Housing-Coloured Housing Policy, "By Laws of the First Lusaka Euro-African Co-Operative Housing Association Limited," 1–18.

89. For documents from this period, see NAZAM, LUDC 1/22/53, Housing-Coloured Housing Policy.

90. NAZAM, LGH 1/16/50, Local Government—Lusaka, Eurafrican Housing, letter to the commissioner for local government from the director of co-operatives and African marketing, December 10, 1955.

91. NAZAM, LUDC 1/1/27, Eurafrican Areas Establishment, Thorn Park, 1955–1965, approval of detail plans, town planning board, November 10, 1955; NAZAM, LUDC 1/1/27, Eurafrican Areas Establishment, Thorn Park, 1955–1965, report of the town planning committee, January 27, 1956; NAZAM, LUDC 1/1/27, Eurafrican Areas Establishment, Thorn Park, 1955–1965, extract from report of the town planning committee to the municipal council Lusaka at the meeting held on March 29, 1956; NAZAM, LUDC 1/1/27, Eurafrican Areas Establishment, Thorn Park, 1955–1965, letter from the town clerk to the town engineer, August 13, 1956.

92. NAZAM, LGH 1/14/17, Census of Non-European Housing, no author, "A Census to Tackle Housing," *Northern News*, October 22, 1956.

93. NAZAM, LGH 1/14/17, Census of Non-European Housing, letter from the commissioner for local government to the secretary, Municipal Association of Northern Rhodesia, April 20, 1956; NAZAM, LGH 1/14/17, Census of Non-European Housing, letter from the commissioner for local government to the Office of the Regional Director of Census, March 29, 1956; NAZAM, LGH 1/14/17, Census of Non-European Housing, statutory African housing board, legislative council minutes, March 16, 1956, 384.

94. NAZAM, LGH 1/14/17, Census of Non-European Housing, motions—statutory African housing board, legislative council minutes, March 20, 1956, 416.

95. NAZAM, LGH 1/14/17, Census of Non-European Housing, motions—statutory African housing board, legislative council minutes, March 20, 1956, 424.

96. NAZAM, LGH 1/16/50, Local Government—Lusaka, Eurafrican Housing, no author, "No Homes Still for Coloureds in Hovels," *Northern News*, March 29, 1956.

97. NAZAM, LGH 1/16/50, Local Government—Lusaka, Eurafrican Housing, no author, "No Homes Still for Coloureds in Hovels," *Northern News*, March 29, 1956.

98. NAZAM, LGH 1/16/50, Local Government—Lusaka, Eurafrican Housing, no author, "No Homes Still for Coloureds in Hovels," *Northern News*, March 29, 1956.

99. NAZAM, LGH 1/16/50, Local Government—Lusaka, Eurafrican Housing, legislative council minutes, Hansard No. 885, August 1, 1956, column 1210.

100. NAZAM, LGH 1/16/50, Local Government—Lusaka, Eurafrican Housing, legislative council minutes, Hansard No. 885, August 1, 1956, column 1214.

101. Quoted in NAZAM, LGH 1/16/50, Local Government—Lusaka, Eurafrican Housing, no author, "Lusaka Considers Plan for Housing Eurafricans," *Northern News*, August 23, 1956.

102. NAZAM, LGH 1/16/50, Local Government—Lusaka, Eurafrican Housing, untitled and unsigned clipping from the *Central African Post*, August 29, 1956.

103. NAZAM, LGH 1/18/23, Euro-African Association of Northern Rhodesia, minutes of the proceedings of the inaugural meeting, July 7–9, 1956, 2.

104. NAZAM, LGH 1/18/23, Euro-African Association of Northern Rhodesia, minutes of the proceedings of the inaugural meeting, July 7–9, 1956, 6.

105. NAZAM, LGH 1/18/23, Euro-African Association of Northern Rhodesia, minutes of the proceedings of the inaugural meeting, July 7–9, 1956, 12–13.

106. NAZAM, LGH 1/18/23, Euro-African Association of Northern Rhodesia, minutes of the proceedings of the inaugural meeting, July 7–9, 1956, 16.

107. NAZAM, LGH 1/18/23, Euro-African Association of Northern Rhodesia, minutes of the proceedings of the inaugural meeting, July 7–9, 1956, 17.

108. NAZAM, LGH 1/18/23, Euro-African Association of Northern Rhodesia, minutes of the proceedings of the inaugural meeting, July 7–9, 1956, 17.

109. NAZAM, LGH 1/6/23, Lusaka Eurafrican Housing, letter from the commissioner for local government to the assistant secretary, August 14, 1956.

110. NAZAM, LGH 1/6/23, Lusaka Eurafrican Housing, no author, "Lusaka Council to Be Met over Coloureds' Housing," *Northern News*, August 3, 1956.

111. NAZAM, LGH 1/16/50, Local Government—Lusaka, Eurafrican Housing, C.A.P. Reporter, "Lusaka Councillor Indignant with Sergeant and Gaunt," *Central African Post*, August 31, 1956; NAZAM, LGH 1/16/50, Local Government—Lusaka, Eurafrican Housing, "Record of Meeting Held at the Secretariat at 2.15 P.M. on Thursday, 30th August, 1956, to Consider How the Alienation of Plots at Thorn Park for Coloured Housing Could Be Expedited."

112. NAZAM, LGH 1/16/50, Local Government—Lusaka, Eurafrican Housing, no author, "Lusaka Lags Behind," *Central African Post*, October 31, 1956.

113. NAZAM, LGH1/16/50, Local Government—Lusaka, Eurafrican Housing, C.A.P. Reporter, "The Capital's Forgotten People," *Central African Post*, October 31, 1956.

114. NAZAM, LGH 1/16/50, Local Government—Lusaka, Eurafrican Housing, C.A.P. Reporter, "Eurafricans—Subsidy Plan Soon?," *Central African Post*, November 9, 1956.

115. NAZAM, LGH 1/16/50, Local Government—Lusaka, Eurafrican Housing, no author, "Coloureds Form a 'District 6' for Lusaka," *Central African Post*, May 15, 1957.

116. NAZAM, LGH 1/16/50, Local Government—Lusaka, Eurafrican Housing, no author, "Coloureds Form a 'District 6' for Lusaka," *Central African Post*, May 15, 1957. See also NAZAM, LGH 1/16/50, Local Government—Lusaka, Eurafrican Housing, Staff Reporter, "Lusaka's Coloureds Live in a Squalid Shack Settlement," *Northern News*, May 16, 1957.

117. NAZAM, LGH 1/16/50, Local Government—Lusaka, Eurafrican Housing, no author, "Lusaka Coloureds to Stage Protest March over Poor Housing," *Central African Post*, July 19, 1957.

118. NAZAM, LGH 1/16/50, Local Government—Lusaka, Eurafrican Housing, no author, "Lusaka Coloureds to Stage Protest March over Poor Housing," *Central African Post*, July 19, 1957. See also NAZAM, LGH 1/16/50, Local Government—Lusaka, Eurafrican Housing, no author, "Lusaka Coloureds to Stage Protest March on Housing," *Northern News*, July 20, 1957.

119. NAZAM, LGH 1/16/50, Local Government—Lusaka, Eurafrican Housing, no author, "Sergeant Warns Coloureds," *Central African Post*, July 22, 1957; NAZAM, LGH 1/16/50, Local Government—Lusaka, Eurafrican Housing, no author, "Sergeant Deplores Plan for Protest March," *Northern News*, July 23, 1957; NAZAM, LGH 1/16/50, Local Government—Lusaka, Eurafrican Housing, no author, "New Homes Plan for Coloureds," *Central African Post*, July 24, 1957; NAZAM, LGH 1/16/50, Local Government—Lusaka, Eurafrican Housing, no author, "Coloured March Off," *Central African Post*, July 29, 1957; NAZAM, LUDC 1/22/53, Housing-Coloured Housing Policy, letter from the Eurafrican Society to the town clerk, July 29, 1957.

120. NAZAM, LUDC 1/22/53, Housing-Coloured Housing Policy, supplementary report of the works committee, municipal council of Lusaka, November 1957.

121. NAZAM, LUDC 1/22/53, Housing-Coloured Housing Policy, Report of the Town Engineer to the Works Committee, January 16, 1958; NAZAM, LUDC 1/22/53, Housing-Coloured Housing Policy, report of the works committee to the council, January 30, 1958; NAZAM, LUDC 1/22/53, Housing-Coloured Housing Policy, letter from the town engineer to the town clerk, March 27, 1958.

122. NAZAM, LGH 1/6/23, Lusaka Eurafrican Housing, "Record of a Meeting Held with Representatives of the Eurafrican Community, Lusaka, in the Office of the Assistant Secretary, 'G' Division, at 8.00 A.M. on Saturday, 16th of August, 1958."

123. NAZAM, LGH 1/6/23, Lusaka Eurafrican Housing, letter from the acting commissioner for local government to the member for local lands and government, Lusaka, regarding "Subsidy Scheme—Eurafrican Housing," August 14, 1958, 2.

124. NAZAM, LGH 1/6/23, Lusaka Eurafrican Housing, letter from the acting commissioner for local government to the member for local lands and government, Lusaka, regarding "Subsidy Scheme—Eurafrican Housing," August 14, 1958.

125. NAZAM, LUDC 1/22/73, Housing-Coloured Housing Policy, report of the town clerk to the works committee, October 12, 1959.

126. Quoted in NAZAM, LUDC 1/22/73, Housing-Coloured Housing Policy, no author, "Coloureds with African Wives May Live at Thorn Park," *African Eagle*, February 3, 1959.

127. NAZAM, LUDC 1/22/73, Housing-Coloured Housing Policy, report of town clerk to works committee, June 8, 1959, 1.

128. NAZAM, LUDC 1/22/73, Housing-Coloured Housing Policy, report of town clerk to works committee, June 8, 1959, 1.

129. NAZAM, LUDC 1/22/73, Housing-Coloured Housing Policy, letter from G. L. Horne to the town clerk, June 9, 1959.

130. NAZAM, LUDC 1/22/73, Housing-Coloured Housing Policy, letter from G. L. Horne to the town clerk, June 9, 1959.

131. NAZAM, LUDC 1/22/73, Housing-Coloured Housing Policy, letter from G. L. Horne to the town clerk, June 9, 1959.

132. NAZAM, LUDC 1/22/73, Housing-Coloured Housing Policy, report of the town clerk to the works committee, October 12, 1959.

133. NAZAM, LUDC 1/22/73, Housing-Coloured Housing Policy, letter from the town clerk to E. W. Sergeant, May 1, 1959.

134. NAZAM, LUDC 1/22/73, Housing-Coloured Housing Policy, letter from Eurafrican Society to the minister of local government and social welfare, December 16, 1959.

135. NAZAM, LUDC 1/22/73, Housing-Coloured Housing Policy, report of the works committee to the council, January 28, 1960.

136. NAZAM, LUDC 1/22/73, Housing-Coloured Housing Policy, report of the town clerk to the works committee, June 9, 1960, 1.

137. NAZAM, LUDC 1/22/73, Housing-Coloured Housing Policy, report of the town clerk to the works committee, June 9, 1960, 2.

138. NAZAM, LUDC 1/22/86, Housing-Eurafrican Housing Policy, letter from the social welfare officer to the city treasurer, September 6, 1962; NAZAM, LUDC 1/22/86, Housing-Eurafrican Housing Policy, letter from the social welfare officer to the city treasurer, October 22, 1962.

139. NAZAM, LUDC 1/22/73, Housing-Coloured Housing Policy, proceedings of the annual conference of the municipal association of Northern Rhodesia and Nyasaland, May 10–12, 1961, 52.

140. NAZAM, LGH 2/5/15, Broken Hill Eurafrican Housing, letter from the director of social welfare to the assistant secretary, July 28, 1964.

141. NAZAM, LUDC 1/1/27, Eurafrican Areas Establishment, Thorn Park, 1955–1965, letter from the city engineer to the town clerk, May 7, 1964.

142. NAZAM, LUDC 1/22/86, Housing-Eurafrican Housing Policy, memorandum from the city treasurer to the town clerk, November 17, 1966. For discussion of the period after independence, see Milner-Thornton, *The Long Shadow of the British Empire*, chapter 1. On the effects of spatial segregation, see Milner-Thornton, "Absent White Fathers," 201–2.

CONCLUSION. GENEALOGIES OF COLONIALISM

1. de Klerk, *The Last Trek*, 4.

2. The surname "Bibault" is also sometimes spelled "Biebouw."

3. de Klerk, *The Last Trek*, 3–4.

4. Quoted in Adhikari, *Not White Enough, Not Black Enough*, 13.

5. For discussion of such fabrications and "genealogical fictions," see Bystrom, "The DNA of the Democratic South Africa."

6. Quoted in McKinnon, "Domestic Exceptions," 35. For the original article, which was a critical review of the work of E. E. Evans-Pritchard on the Nuer, see Richards, "A Problem of Anthropological Approach," 49–51.

7. Thompson, *The Making of the English Working Class*, 12.

8. Mandaza, *Race, Colour, and Class in Southern Africa*, 817. For Milner, see also Milner-Thornton, *The Long Shadow of the British Empire*, 7, 12, 106, 148, 154, 196, 239.

9. Muzondidya, *Walking a Tightrope*, 156–65.

10. Mandaza, *Race, Colour, and Class in Southern Africa*, 688; Muzondidya, *Walking a Tightrope*, 208.

11. Muzondidya, *Walking a Tightrope*, 201–14.

12. Muzondidya, *Walking a Tightrope*, 218–30.

13. I draw the notion of "flexible citizenship" from Ong, *Flexible Citizenship*.

14. For a brief discussion of the Nyasaland Coloured Community Welfare Association, see National Archives of the United Kingdom, London, Colonial Office 1015/1170.

15. Paraphrased by Ismail Surtee in Mandaza, *Race, Colour, and Class in Southern Africa*, 601.

16. Paraphrased by Ismail Surtee in Mandaza, *Race, Colour, and Class in Southern Africa*, 602.

17. Quoted in Mandaza, *Race, Colour, and Class in Southern Africa*, 622.

18. Quoted in Mandaza, *Race, Colour, and Class in Southern Africa*, 632.

19. Quoted in Mandaza, *Race, Colour, and Class in Southern Africa*, 633.

20. Quoted in Mandaza, *Race, Colour, and Class in Southern Africa*, 632. For more of the content of these debates, see Malawi Parliament, *Malawi Government Hansard: Official Verbatim Report of the Debates of the Sixth Session, Third Meeting of Parliament*, 289–377.

21. Stoler, "'In Cold Blood.'"

22. For a study of agnatic ideology, its resilience, and transformation, see Comaroff, *Body of Power*.

23. Cunnison, *The Luapula Peoples of Northern Rhodesia*, 105.

24. Vansina, *How Societies Are Born*, 101, 172.

25. My thoughts on the modern emerging from ongoing traditions draw from Feierman, "Colonizers, Scholars, and the Creation of Invisible Histories"; Schoenbrun, "Conjuring the Modern in Africa." For similar studies of the political manipulation of descent, see Brennan, "Realizing Civilization through Patrilineal Descent"; Eltringham, "'Invaders Who Have Stolen the Country'"; Kaplan, "Genealogies and Gene-Ideologies"; Zachernuk, "Of Origins and Colonial Order."

26. On the stereotype of Coloured ambiguity in South African literature, see February, *Mind Your Colour*.

27. On creolization, hybridity, and entanglement as common conditions, see, for example, Bhabha, *The Location of Culture*; Hannerz, "The World in Creolization"; Nuttall, *Entanglement*; Young, *Colonial Desire*.

28. I draw the phrase "histories of the excluded" from Giblin, *A History of the Excluded*.

29. On conceptualizing border histories, which Latin American studies has taken further than African studies, see Anzaldúa, *Borderlands/La Frontera*; Mignolo, *Local Histories/Global Designs*.

30. Winant, *The World Is a Ghetto*, 20, 21, 35

31. On postcolonial nativism, see, variously, Appiah, *In My Father's House*, chapter 3; Mamdani, *When Victims Become Killers*, chapter 1; Ndlovu-Gatsheni, "Tracking the Historical Roots of Post-Apartheid Citizenship Problems"; Ngũgĩ, *Decolonising the Mind*.

32. Here I draw on Raymond Williams's concept of the "knowable community" (*The Country and the City*, 165–81).

33. Indeed, given its imperial origins, this issue extends beyond African studies. Arjun Appadurai has lamented the role of "natives" in anthropology, how the word designates people and groups outside the West by definition. Natives are ultimately "creatures of the anthropological imagination" in his estimation—ostensibly a source of authentic knowledge, but only as a result of cultures and histories being incarcerated in certain places ("Putting Hierarchy in Its Place," 39).

34. Pels, "The Anthropology of Colonialism," 168.

35. Cooper, "Conflict and Connection."

36. I draw the expression "economies of knowledge" from Cohen and Odhiambo, *The Risks of Knowledge*, 20. On epistemic disobedience, see Mignolo, *Local Histories/Global Designs*, xxi.

37. Ferguson, *Global Shadows*; Mbembe, *On the Postcolony*; Mudimbe, *The Invention of Africa*. See also Thomas, "Modernity's Failings, Political Claims, and Intermediate Concepts."

38. The phrasing "the unreasonable origins of reason" draws from a discussion of Hegel by Alexandre Kojève as described in Descombes, *Modern French Philosophy*, 14. See also Chakrabarty, "Radical Histories and Question of Enlightenment Rationalism."

39. Mamdani, *When Victims Become Killers*, chapter 1. Ndlovu-Gatsheni, "Tracking the Historical Roots of Post-Apartheid Citizenship Problems" and "Nativism and the Debate on African Public Sphere in Postcolonial Africa."

40. Understandings of indigeneity are also constructed. For discussion, see Hodgson, "Becoming Indigenous in Africa."

41. Mamdani, *When Victims Become Killers*, chapter 1; Ranger, "Nationalist Historiography, Patriotic History and the History of the Nation."

42. Mbembe, "African Modes of Self-Writing," 256. Ato Quayson has extended this critique by arguing there are no blacks in Africa—race remains a Western construction ("Obverse Denominations," 586). See also Mbembe, "Ways of Seeing."

43. Nyamnjoh, "From Quibbles to Substance," 133. See also Nyamnjoh, "Blinded by Sight."

44. See, for example, Magubane, "Pluralism and Conflict Situation in Africa"; van den Berghe, "Pluralism and Conflict Situations in Africa."

45. For discussion of the new imperial history, see Burton, *Empire in Question*, chapter 2.

46. The expression "epistemic anxieties" is from Stoler, *Along the Archival Grain*, 19.

47. Asad, *Anthropology and the Colonial Encounter*. For further discussion, see Clifford, *The Predicament of Culture*, chapter 1.

48. Lalu, *The Deaths of Hintsa*, 192, 193, 228, 229.

49. On the transition, see Englund, "Between God and Kamuzu"; Newell, "'A Moment of Truth'?"; Posner, "Malawi's New Dawn." On the politics of ethnicity during and after Banda, see Chirwa, "Democracy, Ethnicity, and Regionalism"; Kamwendo, "Ethnic Revival and Language Association in the New Malawi"; Kaspin, "The Politics of Ethnicity in Malawi's Democratic Transition"; Vail and White, "Tribalism in the Political History of Malawi."

50. See chapter 2 for a discussion of how my informants identified themselves as Malawian.

51. I perceive this fact as one shortcoming of Vail's *The Creation of Tribalism in Southern Africa*.

52. Appiah, *The Ethics of Identity*, 181–84.

53. My thoughts here draw on Watts, "Space for Everything (A Commentary)," 124; Hall, "Who Needs 'Identity'?," 16–17.

54. Interview with Eunice Mussa, October 4, 1999, Zomba, Malawi.

55. Interview with Robert Jamieson, November 15, 1999, Lilongwe, Malawi.

56. On the possibility of new work, see Kalinga, "Resistance, Politics of Protest, and Mass Nationalism in Colonial Malawi, 1950–1960"; Mapanje, "The Orality of Dictatorship."

57. For critical engagements with whiteness elsewhere, see Jacobson, *Whiteness of a Different Color*; Roediger, *The Wages of Whiteness*.

58. Appiah, *In My Father's House*, 181–92.

BIBLIOGRAPHY

: :

PRIMARY SOURCES

Archives Consulted

National Archives of Malawi (NAM), Zomba
National Archives of the United Kingdom (NAUK), London
National Archives of Zambia (NAZAM), Lusaka
National Archives of Zimbabwe (NAZ), Harare

Interviews

A note on interviews: I met and conversed with a number of people in my research. The list below indicates only formal conversations I had. I stayed with Graham and Annia Stewart in Harare twice, for example, and we had numerous discussions during those periods. I have cited in the text interviews that I have quoted from directly or that were particularly pertinent to the point being made.

Ann and Jessica Ascroft, November 9, 1999, Blantyre, Malawi
Sam Bhima, December 12, 1999, Blantyre, Malawi
Effie Buelle, December 16, 1999, Blantyre, Malawi
Dinah Coombes, November 8, 1999, Zomba, and November 11, 1999, Zomba, Malawi
Yusuf Ismael, October 17 and December 16, 1999, Blantyre, Malawi
Robert Jamieson, October 17, 1999, Blantyre, Malawi, and November 15, 1999, Lilongwe, Malawi
Robert Jamieson and family, October 16, 1999, Blantyre, Malawi
Doris Joubert, December 16, 1999, Blantyre, Malawi
Florence Mudaliar, December 12, 1999, Blantyre, Malawi
Thambi Mudaliar, December 12, 1999, Blantyre, Malawi
Eunice Mussa, October 4, 1999, Zomba, Malawi
Brian Raftopoulos, July 14, 2004, Harare, Zimbabwe
Ishmael Sabadiya, December 15, 1999, Blantyre, Malawi
Graham and Annia Stewart, July 2004, and March and April 2006, Harare, Zimbabwe
David White, December 17, 1999, Blantyre, Malawi

Newspapers and Periodicals Consulted

African Eagle (Northern Rhodesia)
Central African Post (Northern Rhodesia)
Northern News (Northern Rhodesia)
Nyasaland Times (Nyasaland)
Rhodesian Tribune (Southern Rhodesia)

Government Publications

Beadle, Thomas Hugh William. *Report of the Commission of Inquiry Regarding the Social Welfare of the Coloured Community of Southern Rhodesia*. Salisbury, Southern Rhodesia: Government Printer, 1946.

Bledisloe Commission. *Rhodesia-Nyasaland Royal Commission Report*. London: His Majesty's Stationery Office, 1939.

Hailey, William Malcolm. *Native Administration in the British African Territories. Part II. Central Africa: Zanzibar, Nyasaland, Northern Rhodesia*. London: His Majesty's Stationery Office, 1950.

Malawi Parliament. *Malawi Government Hansard: Official Verbatim Report of the Debates of the Sixth Session, Third Meeting of Parliament*. Zomba: Government of Malawi, 1969.

Northern Rhodesia. *Report of the Committee to Inquire into the Status and Welfare of Coloured Persons in Northern Rhodesia*. Lusaka, Northern Rhodesia: Government Printer, 1950.

Rhodesia and Nyasaland. *Federation of Rhodesia and Nyasaland: Census of Population, 1956*. Salisbury, Rhodesia: Central Statistical Office, 1960.

Southern Rhodesia. *1961 Census of the European, Asian and Coloured Population*. Salisbury, Rhodesia: Central Statistical Office, 1961.

Southern Rhodesia. *Report of the Committee appointed by the Government of Southern Rhodesia to Enquire into Questions Concerning the Education of Coloured and Half-Caste Children in the Colony*. Salisbury, Southern Rhodesia: Government Printer, 1934.

Southern Rhodesia Land Commission. *Report of the Land Commission, 1925*. Salisbury, Southern Rhodesia: Government Printer, 1925.

Superintendent of the Census. *Census of the Nyasaland Protectorate Census, 1921*. Zomba, Nyasaland: Government Printer, 1921.

Swaziland. *Swaziland Census, 1962: European and Eurafrican*. Mbabane, Swaziland: The Secretariat, 1962.

SELECTED SECONDARY SOURCES

Abdullah, Y. B. *Chiikala Cha Wa Yao (The Story of the Yao)*. Edited and translated by Meredith Sanderson. Zomba, Malawi: Government Press, 1919.

Abu-Lughod, Lila. "The Romance of Resistance: Tracing Transformations of Power through Bedouin Women." *American Ethnologist* 17, no. 1 (1990): 41–55.

Adhikari, Mohamed, ed. *Burdened by Race: Coloured Identities in Southern Africa*. Cape Town: UCT Press, 2009.

Adhikari, Mohamed. "Fiercely Non-Racial? Discourses and Politics of Race in the Non-European Unity Movement, 1943–70." *Journal of Southern African Studies* 31, no. 2 (2005): 403–18.

Adhikari, Mohamed. *"Let Us Live for Our Children": The Teachers' League of South Africa, 1913–1940*. Cape Town: UCT Press, 1993.

Adhikari, Mohamed. *Not White Enough, Not Black Enough: Racial Identity in the South African Coloured Community*. Athens: Ohio University Press, 2005.

Adhikari, Mohamed. "The Sons of Ham: Slavery and the Making of Coloured Identity." *South African Historical Journal* 27, no. 1 (1992): 95–112.

Afigbo, A. E. *The Warrant Chiefs: Indirect Rule in South Eastern Nigeria, 1891–1929*. 2nd ed. London: Longman, 1980.

Agamben, Giorgio. *Homo Sacer: Sovereign Power and Bare Life*. Translated by Daniel Heller-Roazen. Stanford, CA: Stanford University Press, 1998.

Ajayi, J. F. Ade. "The Continuity of African Institutions under Colonialism." In *Emerging Themes of African History*, edited by T. O. Ranger, 189–200. Dar es Salaam: East African Publishing House, 1968.

Akyeampong, Emmanuel. "Race, Identity and Citizenship in Black Africa: The Case of the Lebanese in Ghana." *Africa* 76, no. 3 (2006): 297–323.

Alexander, Jocelyn. *The Unsettled Land: State-Making and the Politics of Land in Zimbabwe, 1893–2003*. Athens: Ohio University Press, 2006.

Allman, Jean Marie. *The Quills of the Porcupine: Asante Nationalism in an Emergent Ghana*. Madison: University of Wisconsin Press, 1993.

Alpers, Edward A. *Ivory and Slaves in East Central Africa*. Berkeley: University of California Press, 1975.

Althusser, Louis. "Ideology and Ideological State Apparatuses (Notes towards an Investigation)." In Louis Althusser, *Lenin and Philosophy and Other Essays*, 127–86. Translated by Ben Brewster. New York: Monthly Review, 1971.

Ambler, Charles. "Alcohol, Racial Segregation and Popular Politics in Northern Rhodesia." *Journal of African History* 31, no. 2 (1990): 295–313.

Amselle, Jean-Loup. *Mestizo Logics: Anthropology of Identity in Africa and Elsewhere*. Translated by Claudia Royal. Stanford, CA: Stanford University Press, 1998.

Anderson, Benedict. *Imagined Communities: Reflections on the Origin and Spread of Nationalism*. Rev. ed. London: Verso, 2006.

Anderson, David M. "Sexual Threat and Settler Society: 'Black Perils' in Kenya, c. 1907–30." *Journal of Imperial and Commonwealth History* 38, no. 1 (2010): 47–74.

Anzaldúa, Gloria. *Borderlands/La Frontera: The New Mestiza*. San Francisco: Spinsters/Aunt Lute, 1987.

Appadurai, Arjun. *Modernity at Large: Cultural Dimensions of Globalization*. Minneapolis: University of Minnesota Press, 1996.

Appadurai, Arjun. "The Past as a Scarce Resource." *Man* 16, no. 2 (1981): 201–19.

Appadurai, Arjun. "Putting Hierarchy in Its Place." *Cultural Anthropology* 3, no. 1 (1988): 36–49.

Appadurai, Arjun. "Theory in Anthropology: Center and Periphery." *Comparative Studies in Society and History* 28, no. 1 (1986): 356–61.

Appiah, Kwame Anthony. *The Ethics of Identity*. Princeton, NJ: Princeton University Press, 2005.

Appiah, Kwame Anthony. *In My Father's House: Africa in the Philosophy of Culture*. Oxford: Oxford University Press, 1992.

Apter, Andrew. "Africa, Empire, and Anthropology: A Philological Exploration of Anthropology's Heart of Darkness." *Annual Review of Anthropology* 28 (1999): 577–98.

Apter, Andrew. *Beyond Words: Discourse and Critical Agency in Africa*. Chicago: University of Chicago Press, 2007.

Ariès, Philippe. *Centuries of Childhood: A Social History of Family Life*. Translated by Robert Baldick. New York: Knopf, 1962.

Arsan, Andrew. "Failing to Stem the Tide: Lebanese Migration to French West Africa and the Competing Prerogatives of the Imperial State." *Comparative Studies in Society and History* 53, no. 3 (2011): 450–78.

Asad, Talal, ed. *Anthropology and the Colonial Encounter*. London: Ithaca, 1973.

Asad, Talal. *Genealogies of Religion: Discipline and Reasons of Power in Christianity and Islam*. Baltimore, MD: Johns Hopkins University Press, 1993.

Ashforth, Adam. *The Politics of Official Discourse in Twentieth-Century South Africa*. Oxford: Clarendon Press of Oxford University Press, 1990.

Bailkin, Jordanna. "The Boot and the Spleen: When Was Murder Possible in British India?" *Comparative Studies in Society and History* 48, no. 2 (2006): 462–93.

Baker, Colin. *Revolt of the Ministers: The Malawi Cabinet Crisis, 1964–1965*. New York: St. Martin's, 2001.

Baker, Lee D. *From Savage to Negro: Anthropology and the Construction of Race, 1896–1954*. Berkeley: University of California Press, 1998.

Baker, S. J. K., and R. T. White. "The Distribution of Native Population over South-East Central Africa." *Geographical Journal* 108, nos. 4–6 (1946): 198–210.

Balandier, Georges. "The Colonial Situation: A Theoretical Approach." In *Africa: Social Problems of Change and Conflict*, edited by Pierre L. van den Berghe, 34–61. San Francisco: Chandler, 1965.

Balibar, Étienne, and Immanuel Wallerstein. *Race, Nation, Class: Ambiguous Identities*. London: Verso, 1992.

Ballantyne, Tony, and Antoinette Burton, eds. *Bodies in Contact: Rethinking Colonial Encounters in World History*. Durham, NC: Duke University Press, 2005.

Banton, Michael. *Racial Theories*. 2nd ed. Cambridge: Cambridge University Press, 1998.

Barber, Karin, ed. *Africa's Hidden Histories: Everyday Literacy and Making the Self*. Bloomington: Indiana University Press, 2006.

Barber, Karin. "Popular Arts in Africa." *African Studies Review* 30, no. 3 (1987): 1–78.

Barnes, Teresa A. *We Women Worked So Hard: Gender, Urbanization, and Social Reproduction in Colonial Harare, Zimbabwe, 1930–1956*. Portsmouth, NH: Heinemann, 1999.

Bell, Morag. "American Philanthropy, the Carnegie Corporation and Poverty in South Africa." *Journal of Southern African Studies* 26, no. 3 (2000): 481–504.

Bender, Gerald J. *Angola under the Portuguese: The Myth and the Reality*. Berkeley: University of California Press, 1978.

Berger, Elena L. *Labour, Race and Colonial Rule: The Copperbelt from 1924 to Independence.* Oxford: Clarendon Press of Oxford University Press, 1974.

Berry, Sara S. *No Condition Is Permanent: The Social Dynamics of Agrarian Change in Sub-Saharan Africa.* Madison: University of Wisconsin Press, 1993.

Bhabha, Homi K. *The Location of Culture.* New York: Routledge, 1994.

Bickford-Smith, Vivian. *Ethnic Pride and Racial Prejudice in Victorian Cape Town: Group Identity and Social Practice, 1875–1902.* Cambridge: Cambridge University Press, 1995.

Biko, Steve. *I Write What I Like: Selected Writings.* Edited by Aelred Stubbs. Chicago: University of Chicago Press, 2002.

Boas, Franz. *The Mind of Primitive Man.* New York: Macmillan, 1911.

Bourdieu, Pierre. *Outline of a Theory of Practice.* Translated by Richard Nice. Cambridge: Cambridge University Press, 1977.

Bozzoli, Belinda. "Marxism, Feminism and South African Studies." *Journal of Southern African Studies* 9, no. 2 (1983): 139–71.

Bradford, Helen. "Peasants, Historians, and Gender: A South African Case Study Revisited, 1850–1886." *History and Theory* 39, no. 4 (2000): 86–110.

Bradford, Helen. "Women, Gender and Colonialism: Rethinking the History of the British Cape Colony and Its Frontier Zones, c. 1806–70." *Journal of African History* 37, no. 3 (1996): 351–70.

Brennan, James R. "Politics and Business in the Indian Newspapers of Colonial Tanganyika." *Africa* 81, no. 1 (2011): 42–67.

Brennan, James R. "Realizing Civilization through Patrilineal Descent: The Intellectual Making of an African Racial Nationalism in Tanzania, 1920–1950." *Social Identities* 12, no. 4 (2006): 405–23.

Brennan, James R. *Taifa: Making Nation and Race in Urban Tanzania.* Athens: Ohio University Press, 2012.

Briggs, Laura. "The Race of Hysteria: 'Overcivilization' and the 'Savage' Woman in Late Nineteenth-Century Obstetrics and Gynecology." *American Quarterly* 52, no. 2 (2000): 246–73.

Brooks, George E. *Eurafricans in Western Africa: Commerce, Social Status, Gender, and Religious Observance from the Sixteenth to the Eighteenth Century.* Athens: Ohio University Press, 2003.

Brubaker, Rogers. *Citizenship and Nationhood in France and Germany.* Cambridge, MA: Harvard University Press, 1998.

Brubaker, Rogers. *Ethnicity without Groups.* Cambridge, MA: Harvard University Press, 2004.

Brubaker, Rogers, and Frederick Cooper. "Beyond 'Identity.'" *Theory and Society* 29 (2000): 1–47.

Burbank, Jane, and Frederick Cooper. *Empires in World History: Power and the Politics of Difference.* Princeton, NJ: Princeton University Press, 2010.

Burke, Timothy. *Lifeboy Men, Lux Women: Commodification, Consumption, and Cleanliness in Modern Zimbabwe.* Durham, NC: Duke University Press, 1996.

Burrill, Emily S., Richard L. Roberts, and Elizabeth Thornberry. "Introduction: Domestic Violence and the Law in Africa." In *Domestic Violence and the Law in*

Colonial and Postcolonial Africa, edited by Emily S. Burrill, Richard L. Roberts, and Elizabeth Thornberry, 1–29. Athens: Ohio University Press, 2010.

Burton, Antoinette, ed. *After the Imperial Turn: Thinking with and through the Nation.* Durham, NC: Duke University Press, 2003.

Burton, Antoinette, ed. *Archive Stories: Facts, Fictions, and the Writing of History.* Durham, NC: Duke University Press, 2005.

Burton, Antoinette. *Empire in Question: Reading, Writing, and Teaching British Imperialism.* Durham, NC: Duke University Press, 2011.

Burton, Antoinette. "Introduction: Archive Fever, Archive Stories." In *Archive Stories: Facts, Fictions, and the Writing of History*, edited by Antoinette Burton, 1–24. Durham, NC: Duke University Press, 2005.

Burton, Antoinette. "Who Needs the Nation? Interrogating 'British History.'" *Journal of Historical Sociology* 10, no. 3 (1997): 227–48.

Bystrom, Kerry. "The DNA of the Democratic South Africa: Ancestral Maps, Family Trees, Genealogical Fictions." *Journal of Southern African Studies* 35, no. 1 (2009): 223–35.

Cannadine, David. *Ornamentalism: How the British Saw Their Empire.* New York: Oxford University Press, 2002.

Caplan, Lionel. *Children of Colonialism: Anglo-Indians in a Postcolonial World.* Oxford: Berg, 2001.

Carsten, Janet. *After Kinship.* Cambridge: Cambridge University Press, 2004.

Carsten, Janet, ed. *Cultures of Relatedness: New Approaches to the Study of Kinship.* Cambridge: Cambridge University Press, 2000.

Carstens, Peter. *The Social Structure of a Cape Coloured Reserve: A Study of Racial Integration and Segregation in South Africa.* Cape Town: Oxford University Press, 1966.

Cavanagh, Edward. *The Griqua Past and the Limits of South African History, 1902–1994.* Bern, Switzerland: Peter Lang, 2011.

Cell, John. *The Highest Stage of White Supremacy: The Origins of Segregation in South Africa and the American South.* Cambridge: Cambridge University Press, 1982.

Chakrabarty, Dipesh. *Habitations of Modernity: Essays in the Wake of Subaltern Studies.* Chicago: University of Chicago Press, 2002.

Chakrabarty, Dipesh. *Provincializing Europe: Postcolonial Thought and Historical Difference.* Princeton, NJ: Princeton University Press, 2000.

Chakrabarty, Dipesh. "Radical Histories and Question of Enlightenment Rationalism: Some Recent Critiques of *Subaltern Studies*." *Economic and Political Weekly* 30, no. 14 (1995): 751–59.

Chanock, Martin. "Ambiguities in the Malawian Political Tradition." *African Affairs* 74, no. 296 (1975): 326–46.

Chanock, Martin. *Law, Custom and Social Order: The Colonial Experience in Malawi and Zambia.* Cambridge: Cambridge University Press, 1985.

Chanock, Martin. "The New Men Revisited: An Essay on the Development of Political Consciousness in Colonial Malawi." In *From Nyasaland to Malawi: Studies in Colonial History*, edited by Roderick J. Macdonald, 234–53. Nairobi: East African Publishing House, 1975.

Chatterjee, Partha. "Agrarian Relations and Communalism in Bengal, 1926–1935."

In *Subaltern Studies: Writings on South Asian History and Society*, edited by Ranajit Guha, 1:9–38. New Delhi: Oxford University Press, 1982.

Chatterjee, Partha. "More on Modes of Power and the Peasantry." In *Subaltern Studies: Writings on South Asian History and Society*, edited by Ranajit Guha, 2:311–49. New Delhi: Oxford University Press, 1983.

Chatterjee, Partha. *The Nation and Its Fragments: Colonial and Postcolonial Histories.* Princeton, NJ: Princeton University Press, 1993.

Chirwa, Wiseman Chijere. "Child and Youth Labour on the Nyasaland Plantations, 1890–1953." *Journal of Southern African Studies* 19, no. 4 (1993): 662–80.

Chirwa, Wiseman Chijere. "Democracy, Ethnicity, and Regionalism: The Malawian Experience, 1992–1996." In *Democratization in Malawi: A Stocktaking*, edited by Kings M. Phiri and Kenneth R. Ross, 52–69. Zomba, Malawi: Kachere, 1998.

Clancy-Smith, Julia, and Frances Gouda, eds. *Domesticating the Empire: Race, Gender, and Family Life in French and Dutch Colonialism.* Charlottesville: University of Virginia Press, 1998.

Clarke, John H., and Janet E. Newman. *The Managerial State: Power, Politics, and Ideology in the Remaking of Social Welfare.* London: Sage, 1997.

Clarke, Kamari Maxine, and Deborah A. Thomas, eds. *Globalization and Race: Transformations in the Cultural Production of Blackness.* Durham, NC: Duke University Press, 2006.

Clifford, James. *The Predicament of Culture: Twentieth-Century Ethnography, Literature, and Art.* Cambridge, MA: Harvard University Press, 1988.

Cocks, Paul. "Max Gluckman and the Critique of Segregation in South African Anthropology, 1921–1940." *Journal of Southern African Studies* 27, no. 4 (2001): 739–56.

Coetzee, J. M. *White Writing: On the Culture of Letters in South Africa.* New Haven, CT: Yale University Press, 1988.

Cohen, Abner. *Custom and Politics in Urban Africa.* London: Routledge and Kegan Paul, 1969.

Cohen, David William. *The Combing of History.* Chicago: University of Chicago Press, 1994.

Cohen, David William. *Womunafu's Bunafu: A Study of Authority in a Nineteenth-Century African Community.* Princeton, NJ: Princeton University Press, 1977.

Cohen, David William, and E. S. Atieno Odhiambo. *The Risks of Knowledge: Investigations into the Death of the Honorable Minister John Robert Ouko in Kenya, 1990.* Athens: Ohio University Press, 2004.

Cohen, David William, and E. S. Atieno Odhiambo. *Siaya: The Historical Anthropology of an African Landscape.* London: James Currey, 1989.

Cohen, David William, Stephan F. Miescher, and Luise White. "Introduction: Voices, Words, and African History." In *African Words, African Voices: Critical Practices in Oral History*, edited by Luise White, Stephan F. Miescher, and David William Cohen, 1–27. Bloomington: Indiana University Press, 2001.

Cohn, Bernard S. *Colonialism and Its Forms of Knowledge.* Princeton, NJ: Princeton University Press, 1996.

Cohn, Bernard S. "From Indian Status to British Contract." *Journal of Economic History* 21, no. 4 (1961): 613–28.

Collier, Jane F., and Sylvia Y. Yanagisako, eds. *Gender and Kinship: Essays toward a Unified Analysis.* Stanford, CA: Stanford University Press, 1987.

Collins, John. "Lusaka: The Historical Development of a Planned Capital, 1931–1970." In *Lusaka and Its Environs: A Geographical Study of a Planned Capital City in Tropical Africa*, edited by G. J. Williams, 95–137. Lusaka: Zambia Geographical Association, 1986.

Colson, Elizabeth. *Marriage and the Family among the Plateau Tonga of Northern Rhodesia.* Manchester, UK: Manchester University Press, 1958.

Colson, Elizabeth, and Max Gluckman, eds. *Seven Tribes of British Central Africa.* Manchester, UK: Manchester University Press, 1951.

Comaroff, Jean. *Body of Power, Spirit of Resistance: The Culture and History of a South African People.* Chicago: University of Chicago Press, 1985.

Comaroff, Jean, and John L. Comaroff. *Ethnicity, Inc.* Chicago: University of Chicago Press, 2009.

Comaroff, Jean, and John L. Comaroff. *Of Revelation and Revolution. Volume Two: The Dialectics of Modernity on a South African Frontier.* Chicago: University of Chicago Press, 1997.

Comaroff, John L. "Of Totemism and Ethnicity: Consciousness, Practice and the Signs of Inequality." *Ethnos* 52, nos. 3–4 (1987): 301–23.

Cooper, Frederick. *Colonialism in Question: Theory, Knowledge, History.* Berkeley: University of California Press, 2005.

Cooper, Frederick. "Conflict and Connection: Rethinking Colonial African History." *American Historical Review* 99, no. 5 (1994): 1516–45.

Cooper, Frederick. *Decolonization and African Society: The Labor Question in French and British Africa.* New York: Cambridge University Press, 1996.

Cooper, Frederick. "Possibility and Constraint: African Independence in Historical Perspective." *Journal of African History* 49, no. 2 (2008): 167–96.

Cooper, Frederick, et al. *Confronting Historical Paradigms: Peasants, Labor, and the Capitalist World System in Africa and Latin America.* Madison: University of Wisconsin Press, 1993.

Cooper, Frederick, and Ann Laura Stoler, eds. *Tensions of Empire: Colonial Cultures in a Bourgeois World.* Berkeley: University of California Press, 1997.

Cornwell, Gareth. "George Webb Hardy's *The Black Peril* and the Social Meaning of 'Black Peril' in Early Twentieth-Century South Africa." *Journal of Southern African Studies* 22, no. 3 (1996): 441–53.

Crais, Clifton C. *The Politics of Evil: Magic, State Power, and the Political Imagination in South Africa.* New York: Cambridge University Press, 2002.

Crais, Clifton C. *White Supremacy and Black Resistance in Pre-Industrial South Africa: The Making of the Colonial Order in the Eastern Cape, 1770–1865.* Cambridge: Cambridge University Press, 1992.

Crowder, Michael. *The Flogging of Phinehas McIntosh: A Tale of Colonial Folly and Injustice, Bechuanaland, 1933.* New Haven, CT: Yale University Press, 1988.

Cunnison, Ian G. *The Luapula Peoples of Northern Rhodesia: Custom and History in Tribal Politics.* Manchester, UK: Manchester University Press, 1959.

DaCosta, Kimberly McClain. *Making Multiracials: State, Family, and Market in the Redrawing of the Color Line.* Stanford, CA: Stanford University Press, 2007.

Daniel, G. Reginald. "Multiracial Identity in Global Perspective: The United States, Brazil, and South Africa." In *New Faces in a Changing America: Multiracial Identity in the 21st Century*, edited by Loretta I. Winters and Herman L. DeBose, 247–86. Thousand Oaks, CA: Sage, 2003.

Darnton, Robert. *The Great Cat Massacre and Other Episodes in French Cultural History*. New York: Basic, 1984.

Davie, Grace. *Poverty Knowledge in South Africa: A Social History of Human Science, 1855–2005*. Cambridge: Cambridge University Press, forthcoming.

Davis, Natalie Zemon. *Fiction in the Archives: Pardon Tales and Their Tellers in Sixteenth-Century France*. Stanford, CA: Stanford University Press, 1990.

De Klerk, F. W. *The Last Trek—A New Beginning: The Autobiography*. New York: St. Martin's, 1999.

Derrida, Jacques. 1994. *Specters of Marx: The State of the Debt, the Work of Mourning, and the New International*. New York: Routledge, 2006.

Derrida, Jacques. 1967. *Writing and Difference*. Chicago: University of Chicago Press, 1980.

Desai, Gaurav. *Subject to Colonialism: African Self-Fashioning and the Colonial Library*. Durham, NC: Duke University Press, 2001.

Descombes, Vincent. *Modern French Philosophy*. Cambridge: Cambridge University Press, 1980.

"Development in Northern Rhodesia (Tables)." *African Affairs* 50, no. 199 (1951): 154–59.

Diagne, Souleymane Bachir. "Keeping Africanity Open." *Public Culture* 14, no. 3 (2002): 621–23.

Dickie-Clark, H. F. *The Marginal Situation: A Sociological Study of a Coloured Group*. London: Routledge and Kegan Paul, 1966.

Dirks, Nicholas B. *Castes of Mind: Colonialism and the Making of Modern India*. Princeton, NJ: Princeton University Press, 2001.

Dirks, Nicholas B., ed. *Colonialism and Culture*. Ann Arbor: University of Michigan Press, 1992.

Dlamini, Jacob. *Native Nostalgia*. Auckland Park, South Africa: Jacana, 2009.

Domínguez, Virginia R. *White by Definition: Social Classification in Creole Louisiana*. New Brunswick, NJ: Rutgers University Press, 1986.

Dotson, Floyd, and Lillian O. Dotson. *The Indian Minority of Zambia, Rhodesia, and Malawi*. New Haven, CT: Yale University Press, 1968.

Dotson, Floyd, and Lillian O. Dotson. "Indians and Coloureds in Rhodesia and Nyasaland." *Race & Class* 5, no. 1 (1963): 61–75.

Dubow, Saul. "Afrikaner Nationalism, Apartheid and the Conceptualization of 'Race.'" *Journal of African History* 33, no. 2 (1992): 209–37.

Dubow, Saul. "Ethnic Euphemisms and Racial Echoes." *Journal of Southern African Studies* 20, no. 3 (1994): 355–70.

Dubow, Saul. *Racial Segregation and the Origins of Apartheid in South Africa, 1919–36*. New York: St. Martin's, 1989.

Dubow, Saul. *Scientific Racism in Modern South Africa*. New York: Cambridge University Press, 1995.

Ekeh, Peter. "Colonialism and the Two Publics in Africa: A Theoretical Statement." *Comparative Studies in Society and History* 17, no. 1 (1975): 91–112.

Ekeh, Peter. "Social Anthropology and Two Contrasting Uses of Tribalism in Africa." *Comparative Studies in Society and History* 32, no. 4 (1990): 660–700.

Elam, Michele. *The Souls of Mixed Folk: Race, Politics, and Aesthetics in the New Millennium*. Stanford, CA: Stanford University Press, 2011.

Elbourne, Elizabeth. "Word Made Flesh: Christianity, Modernity, and Cultural Colonialism in the Work of Jean and John Comaroff." *American Historical Review* 108, no. 2 (2003): 435–59.

Elias, T. Olawale. *British Colonial Law: A Comparative Study of the Interaction between English and Local Laws in British Dependencies*. London: Stevens and Sons, 1962.

Eltringham, Nigel. "'Invaders Who Have Stolen the Country': The Hamitic Hypothesis, Race and the Rwandan Genocide." *Social Identities* 12, no. 4 (2006): 425–46.

Englund, Harri. "Between God and Kamuzu: The Transition to Multiparty Politics in Central Malawi." In *Postcolonial Identities in Africa*, edited by Richard Werbner and Terence Ranger, 107–35. London: Zed, 1996.

Englund, Harri, ed. *A Democracy of Chameleons: Politics and Culture in the New Malawi*. Stockholm: Elanders Gotab, 2002.

Englund, Harri. *From War to Peace on the Mozambique-Malawi Borderland*. Edinburgh: Edinburgh University Press, 2001.

Epprecht, Marc. *Hungochani: The History of a Dissident Sexuality in Southern Africa*. Montreal: McGill-Queen's University Press, 2004.

Epprecht, Marc. "Sexuality, History, Africa." *American Historical Review* 114, no. 5 (2009): 1258–72.

Epstein, A. L. *Politics in an Urban African Community*. Manchester, UK: Manchester University Press, 1958.

Erasmus, Zimitri, ed. *Coloured by History, Shaped by Place: New Perspectives on Coloured Identities in Cape Town*. Cape Town: Kwela, 2002.

Etherington, Norman. "Natal's Black Rape Scare of the 1870s." *Journal of Southern African Studies* 15, no. 1 (1988): 36–53.

Evans, Ivan. *Bureaucracy and Race: Native Administration in South Africa*. Berkeley: University of California Press, 1997.

Evans, Ivan. *Cultures of Violence: Racial Violence and the Origins of Segregation in South Africa and the American South*. Manchester, UK: Manchester University Press, 2011.

Evans-Pritchard, E. E. *The Nuer: A Description of the Modes of Livelihood and Political Institutions of a Nilotic People*. 1940. Oxford: Oxford University Press, 1969.

Eze, Emmanuel Chukwudi. *On Reason: Rationality in a World of Cultural Conflict and Racism*. Durham, NC: Duke University Press, 2008.

Fanon, Frantz. *Black Skin, White Masks*. 1952. Translated by Richard Philcox. New York: Grove, 2008.

Fanon, Frantz. *The Wretched of the Earth*. 1961. Translated by Richard Philcox. New York: Grove, 2005.

Farred, Grant. *Midfielder's Moment: Coloured Literature and Culture in Contemporary South Africa*. Boulder, CO: Westview, 1999.

February, Vernie A. *Mind Your Colour: The "Coloured" Stereotype in South African Literature*. London: Kegan Paul International, 1981.

Feierman, Steven. "Colonizers, Scholars, and the Creation of Invisible Histories." In *Beyond the Cultural Turn: New Directions in the Study of Society and Culture*, edited by Victoria E. Bonnell and Lynn Hunt, 182–216. Berkeley: University of California Press, 1999.

Feierman, Steven. *Peasant Intellectuals: Anthropology and History in Tanzania*. Madison: University of Wisconsin Press, 1990.

Feierman, Steven. *The Shambaa Kingdom: A History*. Madison: University of Wisconsin Press, 1974.

Ferguson, James. *The Anti-Politics Machine: Development, Depoliticization, and Bureaucratic Power in Lesotho*. Minneapolis: University of Minnesota Press, 1994.

Ferguson, James. *Expectations of Modernity: Myths and Meanings of Urban Life on the Zambian Copperbelt*. Berkeley: University of California Press, 1999.

Ferguson, James. *Global Shadows: Africa in the Neoliberal World Order*. Durham, NC: Duke University Press, 2006.

Ferguson, James. "Mobile Workers, Modernist Narratives: A Critique of the Historiography of Transition on the Zambian Copperbelt [Part One]." *Journal of Southern African Studies* 16, no. 3 (1990): 385–412.

Ferguson, James. "Mobile Workers, Modernist Narratives: A Critique of the Historiography of Transition on the Zambian Copperbelt [Part Two]." *Journal of Southern African Studies* 16, no. 4 (1990): 603–21.

Ferguson, James. "Modernist Narratives, Conventional Wisdoms, and Colonial Liberalism: Reply to a Straw Man." *Journal of Southern African Studies* 20, no. 4 (1994): 633–40.

Fetter, Bruce. "Colonial Microenvironments and the Mortality of Educated Young Men in Northern Malawi, 1897–1927." *Canadian Journal of African Studies* 23, no. 3 (1989): 399–415.

Fields, Barbara J. "Ideology and Race in American History." In *Region, Race, and Reconstruction: Essays in Honor of C. Vann Woodward*, edited by J. Morgan Kousser and James M. McPherson, 143–77. New York: Oxford University Press, 1982.

Fields, Barbara J. "Of Rogues and Geldings." *American Historical Review* 108, no. 5 (2003): 1397–405.

Fields, Barbara J., and Karen E. Fields. *Racecraft: The Soul of Inequality in American Life*. London: Verso, 2012.

Fields, Karen E. *Revival and Rebellion in Colonial Central Africa*. Princeton, NJ: Princeton University Press, 1985.

Foucault, Michel. *The Archaeology of Knowledge*. Translated by A. M. Sheridan Smith. New York: Pantheon, 1972.

Foucault, Michel. *Language, Counter-Memory, Practice: Selected Essays and Interviews*. Translated by Donald F. Bouchard and Sherry Simon. Ithaca, NY: Cornell University Press, 1980.

Foucault, Michel. *Madness and Civilization: A History of Insanity in the Age of Reason*. Translated by Richard Howard. 1965. New York: Vintage, 1988.

Foucault, Michel. "Nietzsche, Genealogy, History." In Michel Foucault, *Aesthetics, Method, and Epistemology: Essential Works of Foucault, 1954–1984*, translated by

Robert Hurley and others, edited by James D. Faubion, 2:369–91. New York: New Press, 1998.

Foucault, Michel. *"Society Must Be Defended": Lectures at the Collège de France, 1975–1976*. Translated by David Macey. New York: Picador, 2003.

Foucault, Michel, and Gérard Raulet. "Structuralism and Post-Structuralism." In Michel Foucault, *Aesthetics, Method, and Epistemology: Essential Works of Foucault, 1954–1984*, translated by Robert Hurley and others, edited by James D. Faubion, 2:433–58. New York: New Press, 1998.

Franklin, Sarah, and Susan McKinnon, eds. *Relative Values: Reconfiguring Kinship Studies*. Durham, NC: Duke University Press, 2002.

Fredrickson, George M. *Racism: A Short History*. Princeton, NJ: Princeton University Press, 2002.

Fredrickson, George M. *White Supremacy: A Comparative Study in American and South African History*. New York: Oxford University Press, 1981.

Freund, Bill. *Insiders and Outsiders: The Indian Working Class of Durban, 1910–1990*. Portsmouth, NH: Heinemann, 1995.

Fyfe, Christopher. "Race, Empire, and the Historians." *Race and Class* 33, no. 4 (1992): 15–30.

Geertz, Clifford. *Local Knowledge: Further Essays in Interpretive Anthropology*. New York: Basic, 1983.

Geiger, Susan. *TANU Women: Gender and Culture in the Making of Tanganyikan Nationalism, 1955–1965*. Portsmouth, NH: Heinemann, 1997.

Gengenbach, Heidi. "'What My Heart Wanted': Gendered Stories of Early Colonial Encounters in Southern Mozambique." In *Women in African Colonial Histories*, edited by Jean Allman, Susan Geiger, and Nakanyike Musisi, 19–47. Bloomington: Indiana University Press, 2002.

Geschiere, Peter. *The Perils of Belonging: Autochthony, Citizenship, and Exclusion in Africa and Europe*. Chicago: University of Chicago Press, 2009.

Ghosh, Durba. "National Narratives and the Politics of Miscegenation: Britain and India." In *Archive Stories: Facts, Fictions, and the Writing of History*, edited by Antoinette Burton, 27–44. Durham, NC: Duke University Press, 2005.

Ghosh, Durba. *Sex and the Family in Colonial India: The Making of Empire*. Cambridge: Cambridge University Press, 2008.

Giblin, James L. *A History of the Excluded: Making Family a Refuge from State in Twentieth-Century Tanzania*. Athens: Ohio University Press, 2006.

Giddens, Anthony. *Central Problems in Social Theory: Action, Structure, and Contradiction in Social Analysis*. Berkeley: University of California Press, 1979.

Giliomee, Hermann. "The Beginnings of Afrikaner Ethnic Consciousness, 1850–1915." In *The Creation of Tribalism in Southern Africa*, edited by Leroy Vail, 21–54. Berkeley: University of California Press, 1989.

Giliomee, Hermann. "The Non-Racial Franchise and Afrikaner and Coloured Identities." *African Affairs* 94, no. 375 (1995): 199–225.

Gilroy, Paul. "It's a Family Affair: Black Culture and the Trope of Kinship." In Paul Gilroy, *Small Acts: Thoughts on the Politics of Black Cultures*, 192–207. London: Serpent's Tail, 1993.

Ginzburg, Carlo. *The Cheese and the Worms: The Cosmos of a Sixteenth-Century Miller*.

Translated by John Tedeschi and Anne C. Tedeschi. Baltimore, MD: Johns Hopkins University Press, 1980.

Glassman, Jonathon. *Feasts and Riot: Revelry, Rebellion, and Popular Consciousness on the Swahili Coast, 1856–1888*. Portsmouth, NH: Heinemann, 1995.

Glassman, Jonathon. "Sorting Out the Tribes: The Creation of Racial Identities in Colonial Zanzibar's Newspaper Wars." *Journal of African History* 41, no. 3 (2000): 395–429.

Glassman, Jonathon. *War of Words, War of Stones: Racial Thought and Violence in Colonial Zanzibar*. Bloomington: Indiana University Press, 2011.

Gluckman, Max. "Analysis of a Social Situation in Modern Zululand." *Bantu Studies* 14, no. 1 (1940): 1–30.

Gluckman, Max. "Analysis of a Social Situation in Modern Zululand (Continued)." *Bantu Studies* 14, no. 1 (1940): 147–74.

Gluckman, Max. "Anthropologists and Apartheid: The Work of South African Anthropologists." In *Studies in African Social Anthropology*, edited by M. Fortes and S. Patterson. London: Academic, 1975.

Gluckman, Max. "Anthropology in Central Africa." *Journal of the Royal Society of Arts* 103, no. 4957 (1955): 645–65.

Gluckman, Max. "Gossip and Scandal." *Current Anthropology* 4, no. 3 (1963): 307–16.

Gluckman, Max. "Tribalism in Modern British Central Africa." *Cahiers d'Études Africaines* 1, no. 1 (1960): 55–70.

Goldberg, David Theo. *The Racial State*. London: Wiley-Blackwell, 2001.

Goldberg, David Theo. "The Semantics of Race." *Ethnic and Racial Studies* 15, no. 4 (1992): 543–69.

Goldin, Ian. *Making Race: The Politics and Economics of Coloured Identity in South Africa*. New York: Longman, 1988.

Gordon, Robert J. "Vagrancy, Law and 'Shadow Knowledge': Internal Pacification 1915–1939." In *Namibia under South African Rule: Mobility and Containment, 1915–1946*, edited by Patricia Hayes, Jeremy Silvester, Marion Wallace, and Wolfram Hartmann, 51–77. Athens: Ohio University Press, 1998.

Gramsci, Antonio. *Selections from the Prison Notebooks of Antonio Gramsci*. Edited and translated by Quintin Hoare and Geoffrey Nowell Smith. New York: International, 1971.

Grier, Beverly Carolease. *Invisible Hands: Child Labor and the State in Colonial Zimbabwe*. Portsmouth, NH: Heinemann, 2005.

Gross, Ariela J. *What Blood Won't Tell: A History of Race on Trial in America*. Cambridge, MA: Harvard University Press, 2010.

Guha, Ranajit. "Chandra's Death." In *Subaltern Studies: Writings on South Asian History and Society*, edited by Ranajit Guha, 5:135–65. Delhi: Oxford University Press, 1987.

Guha, Ranajit. *Elementary Aspects of Peasant Insurgency in Colonial India*. Duke paperback edition. Durham, NC: Duke University Press, 1999.

Guha, Ranajit. "On Some Aspects of the Historiography of Colonial India." In *Selected Subaltern Studies*, edited by Ranajit Guha and Gayatri Chakravorty Spivak, 37–44. Oxford: Oxford University Press, 1988.

Guha, Ranajit. "The Prose of Counter-Insurgency." In *Subaltern Studies: Writings on*

South Asian History and Society, edited by Ranajit Guha, 2:1–42. Oxford: Oxford University Press, 1983.

Gupta, Akhil, and James Ferguson. "Beyond 'Culture': Space, Identity, and the Politics of Difference." *Cultural Anthropology* 7, no. 1 (1992): 6–23.

Guyer, Jane I. "Contemplating Uncertainty." *Public Culture* 14, no. 3 (2002): 599–602.

Guyer, Jane I., and Samuel M. Eno Belinga. "Wealth in People as Wealth in Knowledge: Accumulation and Composition in Equatorial Africa." *Journal of African History* 36, no. 1 (1995): 91–120.

Hall, Bruce S. *A History of Race in Muslim West Africa, 1600–1960.* Cambridge: Cambridge University Press, 2011.

Hall, Stuart. "Race, Articulation, and Societies Structured in Dominance." In *Race Critical Theories: Text and Context*, edited by Philomena Essed and David Theo Goldberg, 38–68. Malden, MA: Blackwell, 2002.

Hall, Stuart. "Who Needs 'Identity'?" In *Identity: A Reader*, edited by P. du Gay, J. Evans, and P. Redman, 15–30. London: Sage, 2000.

Hamilton, Carolyn, ed. *The* Mfecane *Aftermath: Reconstructive Debates in Southern African History.* Johannesburg: Wits University Press, 1995.

Hamilton, Carolyn. *Terrific Majesty: The Powers of Shaka Zulu and the Limits of Historical Invention.* Cambridge, MA: Harvard University Press, 1998.

Hamilton, Carolyn, et al., eds. *Refiguring the Archive.* Cape Town: David Philip, 2002.

Hannerz, Ulf. "The World in Creolization." *Africa* 57, no. 4 (1987): 546–59.

Hansen, Karen Tranberg. *Distant Companions: Servants and Employers in Zambia, 1900–1985.* Ithaca, NY: Cornell University Press, 1989.

Hansen, Karen Tranberg. *Keeping House in Lusaka.* New York: Columbia University Press, 1996.

Hansen, Randall. "The Politics of Citizenship in 1940s Britain: The British Nationality Act." *Twentieth Century British History* 10, no. 1 (1999): 67–95.

Hansen, Thomas Blom. *Melancholia of Freedom: Social Life in an Indian Township in South Africa.* Princeton, NJ: Princeton University Press, 2012.

Hartigan, John, Jr. "Culture against Race: Reworking the Basis for Racial Analysis." *South Atlantic Quarterly* 104, no. 3 (2005): 543–60.

Hartigan, John, Jr. *Odd Tribes: Toward a Cultural Analysis of White People.* Durham, NC: Duke University Press, 2005.

Harvey, David. *Social Justice and the City.* 1973. Athens: University of Georgia Press, 2009.

Hawkesworth, Nigel R., ed., *Local Government in Zambia: Papers Published on the Occasion of the Diamond Jubilee Celebrations of the City Council of Lusaka, 1913–1973.* Lusaka: Lusaka City Council, 1974.

Hawkins, Sean. *Writing and Colonialism in Northern Ghana: The Encounter between the Lodagaa and the "World on Paper."* Toronto: University of Toronto Press, 2002.

Herskovits, Melville J. *The Myth of the Negro Past.* 1941. Boston: Beacon Press, 1990.

Ho, Engseng. "Empire through Diasporic Eyes: A View from the Other Boat." *Comparative Studies in Society and History* 46, no. 2 (2004): 210–46.

Hodes, Martha, ed. *Sex, Love, Race: Crossing Boundaries in North American History.* New York: New York University Press, 1999.

Hodes, Martha. *White Women, Black Men: Illicit Sex in the Nineteenth-Century South.* New Haven, CT: Yale University Press, 1999.

Hodgson, Dorothy L. "Becoming Indigenous in Africa." *African Studies Review* 52, no. 3 (2009): 1–32.

Hodgson, Dorothy L. *Being Maasai, Becoming Indigenous: Postcolonial Politics in a Neoliberal World.* Bloomington: Indiana University Press, 2011.

Hollinger, David A. "Amalgamation and Hypodescent: The Question of Ethnoracial Mixture in the History of the United States." *American Historical Review* 108, no. 5 (2003): 1363–90.

Holt, Thomas C. "Marking: Race, Race-Making, and the Writing of History." *American Historical Review* 100, no. 1 (1995): 1–20.

Holt, Thomas C. *The Problem of Race in the Twenty-First Century.* Cambridge, MA: Harvard University Press, 2000.

Hughes, David McDermott. *Whiteness in Zimbabwe: Race, Landscape, and the Problem of Belonging.* London: Palgrave Macmillan, 2010.

Hunt, Nancy Rose. *A Colonial Lexicon: Of Birth Ritual, Medicalization, and Mobility in the Congo.* Durham, NC: Duke University Press, 1999.

Hunt, Nancy Rose. "Letter-Writing, Nursing Men and Bicycles in the Belgian Congo: Notes towards the Social Identity of a Colonial Category." In *Paths toward the Past: African Historical Essays in Honor of Jan Vansina,* edited by Robert W. Harms, Joseph C. Miller, David S. Newbury, and Michele D. Wagner, 187–210. Atlanta: African Studies Association, 1994.

Hunt, Nancy Rose. "Noise over Camouflaged Polygamy, Colonial Morality Taxation, and a Woman-Naming Crisis in Belgian Africa." *Journal of African History* 32, no. 3 (1991): 471–94.

Hyam, Ronald. *Empire and Sexuality: The British Experience.* Cambridge: Cambridge University Press, 1990.

Hyam, Ronald. "The Geopolitical Origins of the Central African Federation: Britain, Rhodesia and South Africa, 1948–1953." *Historical Journal* 30, no. 1 (1987): 145–72.

Ifekwuniqwe, Jayne O. *"Mixed Race" Studies: A Reader.* New York: Routledge, 2004.

Iliffe, John. *Honour in African History.* Cambridge: Cambridge University Press, 2005.

Iliffe, John. *A Modern History of Tanganyika.* Cambridge: Cambridge University Press, 1979.

Isaacman, Allen F. *Mozambique: The Africanization of a European Institution, the Zambesi Prazos, 1750–1902.* Madison: University of Wisconsin Press, 1972.

Isaacman, Allen F., and Barbara Isaacman. *Slavery and Beyond: The Making of Men and Chikunda Ethnic Identities in the Unstable World of South-Central Africa, 1750–1920.* Portsmouth, NH: Heinemann, 2004.

Jackson, John L., Jr. *Real Black: Adventures in Racial Sincerity.* Chicago: University of Chicago Press, 2005.

Jackson, Michael. *The Palm at the End of the Mind: Relatedness, Religiosity, and the Real.* Durham, NC: Duke University Press, 2009.

Jacobson, Matthew Frye. *Whiteness of a Different Color: European Immigrants and the Alchemy of Race.* Cambridge, MA: Harvard University Press, 1999.

Jean-Baptiste, Rachel. "'A Black Girl Should Not be With a White Man': Sex, Race, and African Women's Social and Legal Status in Colonial Gabon, c. 1900–1946." *Journal of Women's History* 22, no. 2 (2010): 56–82.

Jeater, Diana. *Law, Language, and Science: The Invention of the "Native Mind" in Southern Rhodesia, 1890–1930*. Portsmouth, NH: Heinemann, 2006.

Jeater, Diana. *Marriage, Perversion, and Power: The Construction of Moral Discourse in Southern Rhodesia, 1894–1930*. Oxford: Clarendon Press of Oxford University Press, 1993.

Jeppie, Shamil, and Crain Soudien, eds. *The Struggle for District Six: Past and Present*. Cape Town: Buchu Books, 1990.

Jewsiwickie, Bogumil. "The Subject in Africa: In Foucault's Footsteps." *Public Culture* 14, no. 3 (2002): 593–98.

Johnson, Walter. "On Agency." *Journal of Social History* 37, no. 1 (2003): 113–24.

Johnston, Sir Harry H. *British Central Africa: An Attempt to Give Some Account of a Portion of the Territories under British Influence North of the Zambezi*. 1897. New York: Negro Universities Press, 1969.

Jones, Hilary. *The Métis of Senegal: Urban Life and Politics in French West Africa*. Bloomington: Indiana University Press, 2013.

Jordan, Winthrop D. "American Chiaroscuro: The Status and Definition of Mulattoes in the British Colonies." *William and Mary Quarterly*, 3rd ser., 19, no. 2 (1962): 183–200.

Jorritsma, Marie. *Sonic Spaces of the Karoo: The Sacred Music of a South African Coloured Community*. Philadelphia: Temple University Press, 2011.

Joseph, Gilbert, and Daniel Nugent, eds. *Everyday Forms of State Formation: Revolution and the Negotiation of Rule in Modern Mexico*. Durham, NC: Duke University Press, 1994.

Joseph, Ralina L. *Transcending Blackness: From the New Millenium Mulatta to the Exceptional Multiracial*. Durham, NC: Duke University Press, 2012.

Kalinga, Owen J. M. "Resistance, Politics of Protest, and Mass Nationalism in Colonial Malawi, 1950–1960: A Reconsideration." *Cahiers d'Études Africaines* 36, no. 143 (1996): 443–54.

Kallmann, Deborah. "Projected Moralities, Engaged Anxieties: Northern Rhodesia's Reading Publics, 1953–1964." *International Journal of African Historical Studies* 32, no. 1 (1999): 71–117.

Kamwendo, Gregory H. "Ethnic Revival and Language Association in the New Malawi: The Case of Chitumbuka." In *A Democracy of Chameleons: Politics and Culture in the New Malawi*, edited by Harri Englund, 140–50. Stockholm: Elanders Gotab, 2002.

Kandawire, J. A. K. "Thangata in Precolonial and Colonial Systems of Land Tenure in Southern Malawi with Special Reference to Chingale." *Africa* 47, no. 2 (1977): 185–91.

Kaplan, Steven. "Genealogies and Gene-Ideologies: The Legitimacy of the Beta Israel (Falasha)." *Social Identities* 12, no. 4 (2006): 447–55.

Karatani, Rieko. *Defining British Citizenship: Empire, Commonwealth and Modern Britain*. London: Frank Cass, 2003.

Kaspin, Deborah. "The Politics of Ethnicity in Malawi's Democratic Transition." *Journal of Modern African Studies* 33, no. 4 (1995): 595–620.

Kaunda, Kenneth D., and Colin M. Morris. *A Humanist in Africa: Letters to Colin M. Morris from Kenneth D. Kaunda, President of Zambia*. New York: Abingdon, 1966.

Keegan, Timothy. "Gender, Degeneration and Sexual Danger: Imagining Race and Class in South Africa, ca. 1912." *Journal of Southern African Studies* 27, no. 3 (2001): 459–77.

Kennedy, Dane. *Islands of White: Settler Society and Culture in Kenya and Southern Rhodesia, 1890–1939*. Durham, NC: Duke University Press, 1987.

Kopytoff, Igor. "The Internal African Frontier: The Making of African Political Culture." In *The African Frontier: The Reproduction of Traditional African Societies*, edited by Igor Kopytoff, 3–84. Bloomington: Indiana University Press, 1987.

Kopytoff, Igor, and Suzanne Miers. "Introduction: African 'Slavery' as an Institution of Marginality." In *Slavery in Africa: Historical and Anthropological Perspectives*, edited by Suzanne Miers and Igor Kopytoff, 3–84. Madison: University of Wisconsin Press, 1977.

Lake, Marilyn, and Henry Reynolds. *Drawing the Global Colour Line: White Men's Countries and the International Challenge of Racial Equality*. Cambridge: Cambridge University Press, 2008.

Lalu, Premesh. *The Deaths of Hintsa: Post-Apartheid South Africa and the Shape of Recurring Pasts*. Cape Town: HSRC Press, 2009.

Landau, Paul S. "Hegemony and History in Jean and John L. Comaroff's *Of Revelation and Revolution*." *Africa* 70, no. 3 (2000): 501–19.

Landau, Paul S. *Popular Politics in the History of South Africa, 1400–1948*. New York: Cambridge University Press, 2010.

Landau, Paul S. *The Realm of the Word: Language, Gender, and Christianity in a Southern African Kingdom*. Portsmouth, NH: Heinemann, 1995.

Langworthy, Harry W. "Introduction: Carl Wiese and Zambezia." In Carl Wiese, *Expedition in East-Central Africa, 1888–1891, A Report*, edited by Harry W. Langworthy, 3–46. Translated by Donald Ramos. Norman: University of Oklahoma Press, 1983.

Larson, Pier M. "'Capacities and Modes of Thinking': Intellectual Engagements and Subaltern Hegemony in the Early History of Malagasy Christianity." *American Historical Review* 102, no. 4 (1997): 969–1002.

Lee, Christopher J. "Voices from the Margins: The 'Coloured' Factor in Southern African History." *South African Historical Journal* 56, no. 1 (2006): 201–19.

Lefebvre, Henri. *The Production of Space*. Translated by Donald Nicholson-Smith. London: Blackwell, 1991.

Legassick, Martin. "The Northern Frontier to c.1840: The Rise and Decline of the Griqua People." In *The Shaping of South African Society, 1652–1840*, edited by Richard Elphick and Hermann Giliomee, 358–420. Middletown, CT: Wesleyan University Press, 1988.

Legassick, Martin. *The Politics of a South African Frontier: The Griqua, the Sotho-Tswana, and the Missionaries, 1780–1840*. Basel, Switzerland: Basler Afrika Bibliographien, 2010.

Levine, Philippa. *Prostitution, Race, and Politics: Policing Venereal Disease in the British Empire*. New York: Routledge, 2003.

Lévi-Strauss, Claude. *Totemism*. Translated by Rodney Needham. Boston: Beacon, 1963.

Lewis, Gavin. *Between the Wire and the Wall: A History of South African Coloured Politics*. New York: St. Martin's, 1987.

Limb, Peter, ed. *The People's Paper: A Centenary History and Anthology of Abantu-Batho*. Johannesburg: Wits University Press, 2012.

Linden, Ian, with Jane Linden. *Catholics, Peasants, and Chewa Resistance in Nyasaland, 1889–1939*. Berkeley: University of California Press, 1974.

Lionnet, Françoise, and Shu-mei Shih, eds. *Minor Transnationalism*. Durham, NC: Duke University Press, 2005.

Livingstone, David, and Charles Livingstone. *Narrative of an Expedition to the Zambesi and Its Tributaries; and of the Discovery of the Lakes Shirwa and Nyassa, 1858–1864*. London: John Murray, 1865.

Lonsdale, John. "The Moral Economy of Mau Mau: Wealth, Poverty and Civic Virtue in Kikuyu Political Thought." In *Unhappy Valley: Conflict in Kenya and Africa*, edited by Bruce Berman and John Lonsdale, 2:315–467. London: James Currey, 1992.

Lonsdale, John. "Moral Ethnicity and Political Tribalism." In *Inventions and Boundaries: Historical and Anthropological Approaches to the Study of Ethnicity and Nationalism*, edited by P. Kaarsholm and J. Hultin, 131–50. Roskilde, the Netherlands: Institute for Development Studies, Roskilde University, 1994.

Lonsdale, John. "States and Social Processes in Colonial Africa: A Historiographical Survey." *African Studies Review* 24, nos. 2–3 (1981): 139–225.

Lonsdale, John. "When Did the Gusii or Any Other Group Become a 'Tribe'?" *Kenya Historical Review* 5, no. 1 (1977): 123–33.

Loos, Tamara. "Transnational Histories of Sexualities in Asia." *American Historical Review* 114, no. 5 (2009): 1309–24.

Lyons, Tanya. "Guerrilla Girls and Women in the Zimbabwean National Liberation Struggle." In *Women in African Colonial Histories*, edited by Jean Allman, Susan Geiger, and Nakanyike Musisi, 305–26. Bloomington: Indiana University Press, 2002.

Mabogunje, Akin L. "Urban Planning and the Post-Colonial State in Africa: A Research Overview." *African Studies Review* 33, no. 2 (1990): 121–203.

Macmillan, Hugh. "The Historiography of Transition on the Zambian Copperbelt—Another View." *Journal of Southern African Studies* 19, no. 4 (1993): 681–712.

Macmillan, Hugh. "Return to the Malungwana Drift—Max Gluckman, the Zulu Nation and the Common Society." *African Affairs* 94, no. 374 (1995): 39–65.

Macmillan, Hugh, and Shula Marks, eds. *Africa and the Empire: W. M. Macmillan, Historian and Social Critic*. London: Aldershot, 1989.

Macmillan, William M. 1929. *Bantu, Boer, and Briton: The Making of the South African Native Problem*. Oxford: Clarendon Press of Oxford University Press, 1963.

Macmillan, William M. *The Cape Colour Question: A Historical Survey*. London: Faber and Gwyer, 1927.

Mafeje, Archie. "Anthropology and Independent Africans: Suicide or End of an Era?" *African Sociological Review* 2, no. 1 (1998): 1–43.

Mafeje, Archie. "The Ideology of 'Tribalism.'" *Journal of Modern African Studies* 9, no. 2 (1971): 253–61.

Magubane, Bernard. "Pluralism and Conflict Situation in Africa: A New Look." *African Social Research* 7 (June 1969): 529–54.

Malkki, Liisa. "National Geographic: The Rooting of Peoples and the Territorialization of National Identity among Scholars and Refugees." *Cultural Anthropology* 7, no. 1 (1992): 24–44.

Mamdani, Mahmood. "Beyond Settler and Native as Political Identities: Overcoming the Political Legacy of Colonialism." *Comparative Studies in Society and History* 43, no. 4 (2001): 651–64.

Mamdani, Mahmood. *Citizen and Subject: Contemporary Africa and the Legacy of Late Colonialism.* Princeton, NJ: Princeton University Press, 1996.

Mamdani, Mahmood. *Define and Rule: Native as Political Identity.* Cambridge, MA: Harvard University Press, 2012.

Mamdani, Mahmood. *When Victims Become Killers: Colonialism, Nativism, and the Genocide in Rwanda.* Princeton, NJ: Princeton University Press, 2001.

Mandala, Elias C. "Capitalism, Kinship and Gender in the Lower Tchiri (Shire) Valley of Malawi, 1860–1960: An Alternative Theoretical Framework." *African Economic History* 13 (1984): 137–69.

Mandala, Elias C. *Work and Control in a Peasant Economy: A History of the Lower Tchiri Valley in Malawi, 1859–1960.* Madison: University of Wisconsin Press, 1990.

Mandaza, Ibbo. *Race, Colour, and Class in Southern Africa: A Study of the Coloured Question in the Context of an Analysis of the Colonial and White Settler Racial Ideology and African Nationalism in Twentieth Century Zimbabwe, Zambia and Malawi.* Harare: SAPES, 1997.

Mangat, J. S. *A History of the Asians in East Africa, c. 1886 to 1945.* Oxford: Oxford University Press, 1969.

Mann, Gregory. *Native Sons: West African Veterans and France in the Twentieth Century.* Durham, NC: Duke University Press, 2006.

Mapanje, Jack. "The Orality of Dictatorship: In Defense of My Country." In *A Democracy of Chameleons: Politics and Culture in the New Malawi*, edited by Harri Englund, 178–87. Stockholm: Elanders Gotab, 2002.

Marais, J. S. *The Cape Coloured People, 1652–1937.* London: Longmans, 1939.

Marcus, George E. *Ethnography through Thick and Thin.* Princeton, NJ: Princeton University Press, 1998.

Marcus, George E., and Michael M. J. Fischer. *Anthropology as Cultural Critique: An Experimental Moment in the Human Sciences.* Chicago: University of Chicago Press, 1986.

Mark, Peter. *"Portuguese" Style and Luso-African Identity: Precolonial Senegambia, Sixteenth–Nineteenth Centuries.* Bloomington: Indiana University Press, 2002.

Marks, Shula. "Changing History, Changing Histories: Separations and Connections in the Lives of South African Women." *Journal of African Cultural Studies* 13, no. 1 (2000): 94–106.

Marks, Shula, ed. *"Not Either an Experimental Doll": The Separate Worlds of Three South African Women.* Bloomington: Indiana University Press, 1987.

Marks, Shula, and Stanley Trapido, eds. *The Politics of Race, Class, and Nationalism in Twentieth-Century South Africa.* New York: Longman, 1987.

Martin, William G. "Region Formation under Crisis Conditions: South vs. Southern

Africa in the Interwar Period." *Journal of Southern African Studies* 16, no. 1 (1990): 112–38.

Marx, Anthony W. *Making Race and Nation: A Comparison of South Africa, the United States, and Brazil.* New York: Cambridge University Press, 1998.

Mbembe, Achille. "African Modes of Self-Writing." *Public Culture* 14, no. 1 (2002): 239–73.

Mbembe, Achille. "Necropolitics." *Public Culture* 15, no. 1 (2003): 11–40.

Mbembe, Achille. *On the Postcolony.* Berkeley: University of California Press, 2001.

Mbembe, Achille. "On the Power of the False." *Public Culture* 14, no. 3 (2002): 629–41.

Mbembe, Achille. "Ways of Seeing: Beyond the New Nativism." *African Studies Review* 44, no. 2 (2001): 1–14.

McClintock, Ann. *Imperial Leather: Race, Gender, and Sexuality in the Colonial Contest.* New York: Routledge, 1995.

McCracken, John. "The Ambiguities of Nationalism: Flax Musopole and the Northern Factor in Malawian Politics, c. 1956–1966." *Journal of Southern African Studies* 28, no. 1 (2002): 67–87.

McCracken, John. "Economics and Ethnicity: The Italian Community in Malawi." *Journal of African History* 32, no. 2 (1991): 313–32.

McCracken, John. *A History of Malawi, 1859–1966.* London: James Currey, 2012.

McCracken, John. "'Marginal Men': The Colonial Experience in Malawi." *Journal of Southern African Studies* 15, no. 4 (1989): 537–64.

McCracken, John. "The Nineteenth Century in Malawi." In *Aspects of Central African History*, edited by T. O. Ranger, 97–111. London: Heinemann, 1968.

McCracken, John. "Planters, Peasants and the Colonial State: The Impact of the Native Tobacco Board in the Central Province of Malawi." *Journal of Southern African Studies* 9, no. 2 (1983): 172–92.

McCracken, John. *Politics and Christianity in Malawi, 1875–1940: The Impact of the Livingstonia Mission in the Northern Province.* Cambridge: Cambridge University Press, 1977.

McCulloch, Jock. *Black Peril, White Virtue: Sexual Crime in Southern Rhodesia, 1902–1935.* Bloomington: Indiana University Press, 2000.

McKinnon, Susan. "Domestic Exceptions: Evans-Pritchard and the Creation of Nuer Patrilineality and Equality." *Cultural Anthropology* 15, no. 1 (2000): 35–83.

Mehta, Uday Singh. *Liberalism and Empire: A Study in Nineteenth-Century British Liberal Thought.* Chicago: University of Chicago Press, 1999.

Michaels, Walter Benn. "The No-Drop Rule." *Critical Inquiry* 20, no. 4 (1994): 758–69.

Michaels, Walter Benn. "Race into Culture: A Critical Genealogy of Cultural Identity." *Critical Inquiry* 18 (1992): 655–85.

Miescher, Stephan F. *Making Men in Ghana.* Bloomington: Indiana University Press, 2005.

Mignolo, Walter. *Local Histories/Global Designs: Coloniality, Subaltern Knowledges, and Border Thinking.* Princeton, NJ: Princeton University Press, 2012.

Miles, Robert, and Malcolm Brown. *Racism.* 2nd ed. New York: Routledge, 2003.

Mill, Charles W. *The Racial Contract.* Ithaca, NY: Cornell University Press, 1999.

Millin, Sarah Gertrude. *God's Stepchildren.* New York: Boni and Liveright, 1924.

Milner-Thornton, Juliette. "Absent White Fathers: Coloured Identity in Zambia." In *Burdened by Race: Coloured Identities in Southern Africa*, edited by Mohamed Adhikari, 185–207. Cape Town: UCT Press, 2009.

Milner-Thornton, Juliette. *The Long Shadow of the British Empire: The Ongoing Legacies of Race and Class in Zambia*. London: Palgrave Macmillan, 2012.

Mitchell, J. Clyde. *Cities, Society, and Social Perception: A Central African Perspective*. Oxford: Clarendon Press of Oxford University Press, 1987.

Mitchell, J. Clyde. Foreword to Jaap van Velsen, *The Politics of Kinship: A Study in Social Manipulation among the Lakeside Tonga of Nyasaland*, v–xiv. Manchester, UK: Manchester University Press, 1964.

Mitchell, J. Clyde. *The Yao Village: A Study in the Social Structure of a Nyasaland Tribe*. Manchester, UK: Manchester University Press, 1956.

Mitchell, Timothy. *Colonising Egypt*. Cambridge: Cambridge University Press, 1988.

Moore, Sally Falk. *Social Facts and Fabrications: "Customary" Law on Kilimanjaro, 1880–1980*. Cambridge: Cambridge University Press, 1986.

Morris, Brian. "The Ivory Trade and Chiefdoms in Pre-Colonial Malawi." *Society of Malawi Journal* 59, no. 2 (2006): 6–23.

Mudimbe, V. Y. *The Invention of Africa: Gnosis, Philosophy, and the Order of Knowledge*. Bloomington: Indiana University Press, 1988.

Munro, William A. *The Moral Economy of the State: Conservation, Community Development, and State-Making in Zimbabwe*. Athens: Ohio University Press, 1998.

Murphy, Philip. "'Government by Blackmail': The Origins of the Central African Federation Reconsidered." In *The British Empire in the 1950s: Retreat or Revival?*, edited by Martin Lynn, 53–76. New York: Palgrave, 2006.

Murray, S. S. *A Handbook of Nyasaland*. Zomba, Malawi: Government Printer, 1932.

Muzondidya, James. "Race, Ethnicity and the Politics of Positioning: The Making of Coloured Identity in Colonial Zimbabwe, 1890–1980." In *Burdened by Race: Coloured Identities in Southern Africa*, edited by Mohamed Adhikari, 156–84. Cape Town: UCT Press, 2009.

Muzondidya, James. *Walking a Tightrope: Towards a Social History of the Coloured Community of Zimbabwe*. Trenton, NJ: Africa World, 2005.

Mwase, George Simeon. *Strike a Blow and Die, a Narrative of Race Relations in Colonial Africa*. Edited by Robert I. Rotberg. Cambridge, MA: Harvard University Press, 1967.

Nasson, Bill. *Abraham Esau's War: A Black South African War in the Cape, 1899–1902*. Cambridge: Cambridge University Press, 1991.

Ndlovu-Gatsheni, Sabelo J. "Nativism and the Debate on African Public Sphere in Postcolonial Africa: Reflections on a Problematic 'Reverse-Discourse.'" Paper presented at the Twelfth General Assembly, Council for the Development of Social Science Research in Africa, Yaoundé, Cameroon, December 7–11, 2008.

Ndlovu-Gatsheni, Sabelo J. "Tracking the Historical Roots of Post-Apartheid Citizenship Problems: The Native Club, Restless Natives, Panicking Settlers and the Politics of Nativism in South Africa." Leiden, the Netherlands: African Studies Centre, 2007.

Newell, Jonathan. "'A Moment of Truth'? The Church and Political Change in Malawi, 1992." *Journal of Modern African Studies* 33, no. 2 (1995): 243–62.

Newell, Stephanie. *The Power to Name: A History of Anonymity in Colonial West Africa.* Athens: Ohio University Press, 2013.

Ngai, Mae M. *Impossible Subjects: Illegal Aliens and the Making of Modern America.* Princeton, NJ: Princeton University Press, 2003.

Ng'ong'ola, Clement. "The State, Settlers, and Indigenes in the Evolution of Land Law and Policy in Colonial Malawi." *International Journal of African Historical Studies* 23, no. 1 (1990): 27–58.

Ngũgĩ wa Thiong'o. *Decolonising the Mind: The Politics of Language in African Literature.* 1986. London: James Currey, 2011.

Northrup, Nancy. "The Migrations of Yao and Kololo into Southern Malawi: Aspects of Nineteenth Century Africa." *International Journal of African Historical Studies* 19, no. 1 (1986): 59–75.

Nuttall, Sarah. *Entanglement: Literary and Cultural Reflections on Post-Apartheid.* Johannesburg: Wits University Press, 2009.

Nyamnjoh, Francis B. "Blinded by Sight: Divining the Future of Anthropology in Africa." *Africa Spectrum* 47, nos. 2–3 (2012): 63–92.

Nyamnjoh, Francis B. "From Quibbles to Substance: A Response to Responses." *Africa Spectrum* 48, no. 2 (2013): 127–39.

Ojiaku, Mazi Okoro. "European Tribalism and African Nationalism." *Civilisations* 22, no. 3 (1972): 387–404.

Ong, Aihwa. *Flexible Citizenship: The Cultural Logics of Transnationality.* Durham, NC: Duke University Press, 1999.

Ortner, Sherry B. "Resistance and the Problem of Ethnographic Refusal." *Comparative Studies in Society and History* 37, no. 1 (1995): 173–93.

Page, Melvin E. *The Chiwaya War: Malawians and the First World War.* Boulder, CO: Westview, 2000.

Painter, Nell Irvin. *The History of White People.* New York: W. W. Norton, 2011.

Palmer, Robin H. *Land and Racial Domination in Rhodesia.* Berkeley: University of California Press, 1977.

Pape, John. "Black and White: The 'Perils of Sex' in Colonial Zimbabwe." *Journal of Southern African Studies* 16, no. 4 (1990): 699–720.

Parpart, Jane L. *Labor and Capital on the African Copperbelt.* Philadelphia: Temple University Press, 1983.

Pascoe, Peggy. *What Comes Naturally: Miscegenation Law and the Making of Race in America.* New York: Oxford University Press, 2010.

Patterson, Sheila. *Colour and Culture in South Africa: A Study of the Status of the Cape Coloured People within the Social Structure of the Union of South Africa.* London: Routledge and Kegan Paul, 1953.

Pedersen, Jean Elisabeth. "'Special Customs': Paternity Suits and Citizenship in France and the Colonies, 1870–1912." In *Domesticating the Empire: Race, Gender, and Family Life in French and Dutch Colonialism,* edited by Julia Clancy-Smith and Frances Gouda, 43–64. Charlottesville: University of Virginia Press, 1998.

Peel, J. D. Y. *Religious Encounter and the Making of the Yoruba.* Bloomington: Indiana University Press, 2000.

Pels, Peter. "The Anthropology of Colonialism: Culture, History, and the Emergence of Western Governmentality." *Annual Review of Anthropology* 26 (1997): 163–83.

Penvenne, Jeanne. *African Workers and Colonial Racism: Mozambican Strategies and Struggles in Lourenço Marques, 1877–1962*. Portsmouth, NH: Heinemann, 1995.

Penvenne, Jeanne. "João dos Santos Albasini (1876–1922): The Contradictions of Politics and Identity in Colonial Mozambique." *Journal of African History* 37, no. 3 (1996): 419–64.

Penvenne, Jeanne. "'We Are All Portuguese!': Challenging the Political Economy of Assimilation: Lourenço Marques, 1870–1933." In *The Creation of Tribalism in Southern Africa*, edited by Leroy Vail, 255–88. Berkeley: University of California Press, 1989.

Peters, Pauline E. "Against the Odds: Matriliny, Land and Gender in the Shire Highlands of Malawi." *Critique of Anthropology* 17, no. 2 (1997): 189–210.

Peterson, Derek R. *Creative Writing: Translation, Bookkeeping, and the Work of Imagination in Colonial Kenya*. Portsmouth, NH: Heinemann, 2004.

Peterson, Derek R. *Ethnic Patriotism and the East African Revival: A History of Dissent, c. 1935–1972*. New York: Cambridge University Press, 2012.

Peterson, Derek R., and Giacomo Macola, eds. *Recasting the Past: History Writing and Political Work in Modern Africa*. Athens: Ohio University Press, 2009.

Phiri, Kings M. "Some Changes in the Matrilineal Family System among the Chewa of Malawi since the Nineteenth Century." *Journal of African History* 24, no. 2 (1983): 257–74.

Phiri, Kings M., and Kenneth R. Ross, eds. *Democratization in Malawi: A Stocktaking*. Zomba, Malawi: Kachere, 1998.

Pierre, Jemima. *The Predicament of Blackness: Postcolonial Ghana and the Politics of Race*. Chicago: University of Chicago Press, 2012.

Piot, Charles. *Remotely Global: Village Modernity in West Africa*. Chicago: University of Chicago Press, 1999.

Pitts, Jennifer. *A Turn to Empire: The Rise of Imperial Liberalism in Britain and France*. Princeton, NJ: Princeton University Press, 2005.

Plaatje, Solomon. "The Mote and the Beam: An Epic on Sex-Relationship 'Twixt White and Black in British South Africa (1921)." *English in Africa* 3, no. 2 (1976): 85–92.

Posel, Deborah. *The Making of Apartheid, 1948–1961: Conflict and Compromise*. Oxford: Clarendon Press, 1991.

Posel, Deborah. "Race as Common Sense: Racial Classification in Twentieth-Century South Africa." *African Studies Review* 44, no. 2 (2001): 87–113.

Posel, Deborah, Jonathan Hyslop, and Noor Nieftagodien, "Editorial: Debating 'Race' in South African Scholarship." *Transformation* 47 (2001): i–xviii.

Posner, Daniel N. "Malawi's New Dawn." *Journal of Democracy* 6, no. 1 (1995): 131–45.

Povinelli, Elizabeth A. *The Empire of Love: Toward a Theory of Intimacy, Genealogy, and Carnality*. Durham, NC: Duke University Press, 2006.

Powdermaker, Hortense. *Copper Town: Changing Africa—The Human Situation on the Rhodesian Copperbelt*. New York: Harper and Row, 1962.

Power, Joey. "'Eating the Property': Gender Roles and Economic Change in Urban Malawi, Blantyre-Limbe, 1907–1953." *Canadian Journal of African Studies* 29, no. 1 (1995): 79–109.

Power, Joey. "Marrying on the Margins: Church, State and Marriage Law in Colonial Malawi." In *Communities at the Margin: Studies in Rural Society and Migration in Southern Africa, 1890–1980*, edited by Alan H. Jeeves and Owen J. M. Kalinga, 59–79. Pretoria: UNISA Press, 2002.

Power, Joey. *Political Culture and Nationalism in Malawi: Building Kwacha*. Rochester, NY: University of Rochester Press, 2010.

Power, Joey. "Race, Class, Ethnicity, and Anglo-Indian Trade Rivalry in Colonial Malawi, 1910–1945." *International Journal of African Historical Studies* 26, no. 3 (1993): 575–607.

Power, Joey. "Remembering Du: An Episode in the Development of Malawian Political Culture." *African Affairs* 97, no. 388 (1998): 369–96.

Prakash, Gyan. "Writing Post Orientalist Histories of the Third World: Perspectives from Indian Historiography." *Comparative Studies in Society and History* 32, no. 2 (1990): 383–408.

Quayson, Ato. "Obverse Denominations: Africa?" *Public Culture* 14, no. 3 (2002): 585–88.

Rafael, Vicente L. "Regionalism, Area Studies, and the Accidents of Agency." *American Historical Review* 104, no. 4 (1999): 1208–20.

Raftopoulos, Brian, and Tsuneo Yoshikuni, eds. *Sites of Struggle: Essays in Zimbabwe's Urban History*. Harare: Weaver, 2001.

Ranger, Terence. *Are We Not Also Men? The Samkange Family and African Politics in Zimbabwe, 1920–1964*. Portsmouth, NH: Heinemann, 1995.

Ranger, Terence. *Bulawayo Burning: The Social History of a Southern African City, 1893–1960*. London: James Currey, 2010.

Ranger, Terence. "The Invention of Tradition in Colonial Africa." In *The Invention of Tradition*, edited by Eric Hobsbawm and Terence Ranger, 211–62. Cambridge: Cambridge University Press, 1983.

Ranger, Terence. "The Invention of Tradition Revisited: The Case of Africa." In *Legitimacy and the State in Twentieth Century Africa: Essays in Honour of A. H. M. Kirk-Greene*, edited by Terence Ranger and Olufemi Vaughan, 62–111. London: Macmillan, 1993.

Ranger, Terence. "Nationalist Historiography, Patriotic History and the History of the Nation: The Struggle over the Past in Zimbabwe." *Journal of Southern African Studies* 30, no. 2 (2004): 215–34.

Ray, Carina E. "Decrying White Peril: Interracial Sex and the Rise of Anticolonial Nationalism in the Gold Coast." *American Historical Review* 119, no. 1 (2014): 78–110.

Ray, Carina E. "Interracial Sex and the Making of Empire." In *A Companion to Diaspora and Transnationalism*, edited by Ato Quayson and Girish Daswani, 190–211. Malden, MA: Blackwell, 2013.

Read, Margaret. *Children of Their Fathers: Growing Up among the Ngoni of Nyasaland*. London: Methuen, 1959.

Read, Margaret. "The Ngoni and Western Education." In *Colonialism in Africa, 1870–1960*, vol. 3: *Profiles of Change: African Society and Colonial Rule*, edited by Victor Turner, 346–92. Cambridge: Cambridge University Press, 1971.

Read, Margaret. *The Ngoni of Nyasaland*. London: Oxford University Press, 1956.

Redfield, Robert. *The Little Community and Peasant Society and Culture*. Chicago: University of Chicago Press, 1960.

Rich, Jeremy. "Torture, Homosexuality, and Masculinities in French Central Africa: The Faucher-d'Alexis Affair of 1884." *Historical Reflections* 36, no. 2 (2010): 7–23.

Rich, Jeremy. " 'Une Babylone Noire': Interracial Unions in Colonial Libreville, c. 1860–1914." *French Colonial History* 4 (2003): 145–69.

Richards, Audrey I. "A Problem of Anthropological Approach." *Bantu Studies* 15, no. 1 (1941): 45–52.

Robinson, R. E. "The Administration of African Customary Law." *Journal of African Administration* 1, no. 4 (1949): 158–76.

Rodney, Walter. *A History of the Upper Guinea Coast, 1545–1800*. Oxford: Clarendon Press of Oxford University Press, 1970.

Roediger, David R. *Colored White: Transcending the Racial Past*. Berkeley: University of California Press, 2002.

Roediger, David R. *The Wages of Whiteness: Race and the Making of the American Working Class*. New edition. London: Verso, 2007.

Root, Maria P. P., ed. *The Multiracial Experience: Racial Borders as the New Frontier*. Thousand Oaks, CA: Sage, 1995.

Rosaldo, Renato. "Imperialist Nostalgia." *Representations* 26 (Spring 1989): 107–22.

Rose, Sonya O. "Cultural Analysis and Moral Discourses: Episodes, Continuities, and Transformations." In *Beyond the Cultural Turn: New Directions in the Study of Society and Culture*, edited by Victoria E. Bonnell and Lynn Hunt, 217–38. Berkeley: University of California Press, 1999.

Ross, Andrew C. *Blantyre Mission and the Making of Modern Malawi*. Blantyre, Malawi: Kachere Press, 1996.

Ross, Robert. *Adam Kok's Griquas: A Study in the Development of Stratification in South Africa*. Cambridge: Cambridge University Press, 1976.

Ross, Robert. *Status and Respectability in the Cape Colony, 1750–1870: A Tragedy of Manners*. Cambridge: Cambridge University Press, 1999.

Rotberg, Robert I. "The African Population of Malawi: An Analysis of the Censuses between 1901 and 1966 by G. Coleman, *The Society of Malawi Journal*, Volume 27, No. 1, 1974." *Society of Malawi Journal* 53, no. 1/2 (2000): 108–22.

Rotberg, Robert I. *The Rise of Nationalism in Central Africa: The Making of Malawi and Zambia, 1873–1964*. Cambridge, MA: Harvard University Press, 1965.

Saada, Emmanuelle. *Empire's Children: Race, Filiation, and Citizenship in the French Colonies*. Translated by Arthur Goldhammer. Chicago: University of Chicago Press, 2012.

Said, Edward W. *Culture and Imperialism*. New York: Knopf, 1993.

Said, Edward W. *Orientalism*. New York: Vintage, 1978.

Sales, Jane M. *Mission Stations and the Coloured Communities of the Eastern Cape, 1800–1852*. Cape Town: Balkema, 1974.

Sarkar, Sumit. "The Kalki-Avatar of Bikrampur: A Village Scandal in Early Twentieth Century Bengal." In *Subaltern Studies: Writings on South Asian History and Society*, edited Ranajit Guha, 6:1–53. New Delhi: Oxford University Press, 1989.

Scarnecchia, Timothy. *The Urban Roots of Democracy and Political Violence in Zimbabwe: Harare and Highfield, 1940–1964. Rochester, NY: University of Rochester Press, 2008.

Schmidt, Elizabeth. "'Emancipate Your Husbands!' Women and Nationalism in Guinea, 1953-1958." In *Women in African Colonial Histories*, edited by Jean Allman, Susan Geiger, and Nakanyike Musisi, 282–304. Bloomington: Indiana University Press, 2002.

Schmidt, Elizabeth. *Peasants, Traders, and Wives: Shona Women in the History of Zimbabwe, 1870–1939*. Portsmouth, NH: Heinemann, 1992.

Schmidt, Heike Ingeborg. "Colonial Intimacy: The Rechenberg Scandal and Homosexuality in German East Africa." *Journal of the History of Sexuality* 17, no. 1 (2008): 25–59.

Schneider, David M. *A Critique of the Study of Kinship*. Ann Arbor: University of Michigan Press, 1984.

Schoenbrun, David L. "Conjuring the Modern in Africa: Durability and Rupture in Histories of Public Healing between the Great Lakes of East Africa." *American Historical Review* 111, no. 5 (2006): 1403–39.

Schoffeleers, J. Matthew. *River of Blood: The Genesis of a Martyr Cult in Southern Malawi, c. A.D. 1600*. Madison: University of Wisconsin Press, 1992.

Schumaker, Lyn. *Africanizing Anthropology: Fieldwork, Networks, and the Making of Cultural Knowledge in Central Africa*. Durham, NC: Duke University Press, 2001.

Scott, David. "Colonial Governmentality." *Social Text* 43 (Fall 1995): 191–220.

Scott, James C. *Domination and the Arts of Resistance: Hidden Transcripts*. New Haven, CT: Yale University Press, 1992.

Scott, James C. *The Moral Economy of the Peasant: Rebellion and Subsistence in Southeast Asia*. New Haven, CT: Yale University Press, 1976.

Scott, James C. *Seeing Like a State: How Certain Schemes to Improve the Human Condition Have Failed*. New Haven, CT: Yale University Press, 1998.

Scott, James C. *Weapons of the Weak: Everyday Forms of Peasant Resistance*. New Haven, CT: Yale University Press, 1985.

Scott, Joan W. "The Evidence of Experience." *Critical Inquiry* 17, no. 4 (1991): 773–97.

Seirlis, Julia Katherine. "Islands and Autochthons: Coloureds, Space and Belonging in Rhodesia and Zimbabwe, Part 1." *Journal of Social Archaeology* 4, no. 3 (2004): 405–26.

Sexton, Jared. *Amalgamation Schemes: Antiblackness and the Critique of Multiracialism*. Minneapolis: University of Minnesota Press, 2008.

Shepperson, George, and Thomas Price. *Independent African: John Chilembwe and the Nyasaland Rising of 1915*. Edinburgh: Edinburgh University Press, 1958.

Shohat, Ella. "Area Studies, Gender Studies, and the Cartographies of Knowledge." *Social Text* 20, no. 3 (2002): 67–78.

Short, Philip. *Banda*. London: Routledge and Kegan Paul, 1974.

Shryock, Andrew. *Nationalism and the Genealogical Imagination: Oral History and Textual Authority in Tribal Jordan*. Berkeley: University of California Press, 1997.

Shutt, Allison K. "'I Told Him I Was Lennox Njokweni': Honor and Racial Etiquette in Southern Rhodesia." *Journal of African History* 51, no. 3 (2010): 323–41.

Shutt, Allison K. "'The Natives Are Getting out of Hand': Legislating Manners, Insolence and Contemptuous Behaviour in Southern Rhodesia, c. 1910–1963." *Journal of Southern African Studies* 33, no. 3 (2007): 653–72.

Shutt, Allison K., and Tony King. "Imperial Rhodesians: The 1953 Rhodes Centenary Exhibition in Southern Rhodesia." *Journal of Southern African Studies* 31, no. 2 (2005): 357–79.

Simone, AbdouMaliq. *For the City Yet to Come: Changing African Life in Four Cities.* Durham, NC: Duke University Press, 2004.

Smedley, Audrey, and Brian D. Smedley. "Race as Biology Is Fiction, Racism as a Social Problem Is Real: Anthropological and Historical Perspectives on the Social Construction of Race." *American Psychologist* 60, no. 1 (2005): 16–26.

Smith, Mary F. *Baba of Karo: A Woman of the Muslim Hausa.* 1954. New Haven, CT: Yale University Press, 1981.

Smith, Rogers M. *Stories of Peoplehood: The Politics and Morals of Political Membership.* Cambridge: Cambridge University Press, 2003.

Southall, Aidan W. "The Illusion of Tribe." *Journal of Asian and African Studies* 5, nos. 1–2 (1970): 28–50.

Spear, Thomas. "Neo-Traditionalism and the Limits of Invention in British Colonial Africa." *Journal of African History* 44, no. 1 (2003): 3–27.

Spear, Thomas, and Richard Waller, eds. *Being Maasai: Ethnicity and Identity in East Africa.* Athens: Ohio University Press, 1993.

Spitzer, Leo. *Lives in Between: Assimilation and Marginality in Austria, Brazil, and West Africa, 1780–1945.* New York: Cambridge University Press, 1990.

Spivak, Gayatri Chakravorty. "Can the Subaltern Speak?" In *Marxism and the Interpretation of Culture*, edited by Cary Nelson and Lawrence Grossberg, 271–313. Champaign: University of Illinois Press, 1988.

Spivak, Gayatri Chakravorty. "The Rani of Sirmur: An Essay in Reading the Archives." *History and Theory* 24, no. 3 (1985): 247–72.

Stedman Jones, Gareth. *Languages of Class: Studies in English Working Class History, 1832–1982.* Cambridge: Cambridge University Press, 1983.

Steedman, Carolyn. *Dust: The Archive and Cultural History.* New Brunswick, NJ: Rutgers University Press, 2002.

Steinmetz, George. *The Devil's Handwriting: Precoloniality and the German Colonial State in Qingdao, Samoa, and Southwest Africa.* Chicago: University of Chicago Press, 2007.

Stocking, George, ed. *Colonial Situations: Essays on the Contextualization of Ethnographic Knowledge.* Madison: University of Wisconsin Press, 2001.

Stoler, Ann Laura. *Along the Archival Grain: Epistemic Anxieties and Colonial Common Sense.* Princeton, NJ: Princeton University Press 2009.

Stoler, Ann Laura. *Carnal Knowledge and Imperial Power: Race and the Intimate in Colonial Rule.* Berkeley: University of California Press, 2002.

Stoler, Ann Laura, ed. *Haunted by Empire: Geographies of Intimacy in North American History.* Durham, NC: Duke University Press, 2006.

Stoler, Ann Laura. "Imperial Debris: Reflections on Ruins and Ruination." *Cultural Anthropology* 23, no. 2 (2008): 191–219.

Stoler, Ann Laura. "'In Cold Blood': Hierarchies of Credibility and the Politics of Colonial Narratives." *Representations* 37 (Winter 1992): 151–89.

Stoler, Ann Laura. "Making Empire Respectable: The Politics of Race and Sexual Morality in Twentieth-Century Colonial Cultures." *American Ethnologist* 16, no. 4 (1989): 634–60.

Stoler, Ann Laura. *Race and the Education of Desire: Foucault's History of Sexuality and the Colonial Order of Things*. Durham, NC: Duke University Press, 1995.

Stoler, Ann Laura. "Racial Histories and Their Regimes of Truth." *Political Power and Social Theory* 11 (1997): 183–206.

Stoler, Ann Laura. "Tense and Tender Ties: The Politics of Comparison in North American History and (Post) Colonial Studies." In *Haunted by Empire: Geographies of Intimacy in North American History*, edited by Ann Laura Stoler, 23–69. Durham, NC: Duke University Press, 2006.

Stoler, Ann Laura, and Frederick Cooper. "Between Metropole and Colony: Rethinking a Research Agenda." In *Tensions of Empire: Colonial Cultures in a Bourgeois World*, edited by Frederick Cooper and Ann Laura Stoler, 1–56. Berkeley: University of California Press, 1997.

Strathern, Marilyn. *After Nature: English Kinship in the Late Twentieth Century*. Cambridge: Cambridge University Press, 1992.

Summers, Carol. *From Civilization to Segregation: Social Ideals and Social Control in Southern Rhodesia, 1890–1934*. Athens: Ohio University Press, 1994.

Swann, Alfred J. *Fighting the Slave-Hunters in Central Africa: A Record of Twenty-Six Years of Travel and Adventure Round the Great Lakes*. 2nd ed. Edited by Robert I. Rotberg. London: Frank Cass, 1969.

Tangri, Roger. "Inter-War 'Native Associations' and the Formation of the Nyasaland African Congress." *Transafrican Journal of History* 1, no. 1 (1971): 84–102.

Tew, Mary. *Peoples of the Lake Nyasa Region*. London: Oxford University Press, 1950.

Thomas, Lynn M. "Modernity's Failings, Political Claims, and Intermediate Concepts." *American Historical Review* 116, no. 3 (2011): 727–40.

Thomas, Lynn M. *Politics of the Womb: Women, Reproduction, and the State in Kenya*. Berkeley: University of California Press, 2003.

Thompson, E. P. "The Crime of Anonymity." In *Albion's Fatal Tree: Crime and Society in Eighteenth-Century England*, edited by Douglas Hay et al., 255–308. New York: Pantheon, 1975.

Thompson, E. P. *The Making of the English Working Class*. New York: Vintage, 1966.

Thompson, E. P. "The Moral Economy of the English Crowd in the Eighteenth Century." *Past and Present* 50, no. 1 (1971): 76–136.

Thornton, Robert. "The Rhetoric of Ethnographic Holism." *Cultural Anthropology* 3, no. 3 (1988): 285–303.

Tilley, Helen. *Africa as a Living Laboratory: Empire, Development, and the Problem of Scientific Knowledge, 1870–1950*. Chicago: University of Chicago Press, 2011.

Trouillot, Michel-Rolph. *Silencing the Past: Power and the Production of History*. Boston: Beacon, 1997.

Tsing, Anna Lowenhaupt. *In the Realm of the Diamond Queen: Marginality in an Out-of-the-Way Place*. Princeton, NJ: Princeton University Press, 1993.

Turner, Victor. *Schism and Continuity in an African Society: A Study of Ndembu Village Life*. Manchester, UK: Manchester University Press, 1957.

Vail, Leroy, ed. *The Creation of Tribalism in Southern Africa*. Berkeley: University of California Press, 1989.

Vail, Leroy. "Introduction: Ethnicity in Southern African History." In *The Creation of Tribalism in Southern Africa*, edited by Leroy Vail, 1–19. Berkeley: University of California Press, 1989.

Vail, Leroy, and Landeg White. "Tribalism in the Political History of Malawi." In *The Creation of Tribalism in Southern Africa*, edited by Leroy Vail, 151–92. Berkeley: University of California Press, 1989.

Van den Berghe, Pierre L. "Pluralism and Conflict Situations in Africa: A Reply to B. Magubane." *African Social Research* 9 (June 1970): 681–89.

Van der Ross, R. E. *The Rise and Decline of Apartheid: A Study of Political Movements among the Coloured People of South Africa, 1880–1985*. Cape Town: Tafelberg, 1986.

Van Onselen, Charles. *Chibaro: African Mine Labor in Southern Rhodesia, 1900–1933*. London: Pluto, 1976.

Van Onselen, Charles. *New Babylon, New Ninevah: Everyday Life on the Witwatersrand, 1886–1914*. 2nd ed. Johannesburg: Jonathan Ball, 2001.

Van Onselen, Charles. "Race and Class in the South African Countryside: Cultural Osmosis and Social Relations in the Sharecropping Economy of the South-Western Transvaal, 1900–1950." *American Historical Review* 95, no. 1 (1990): 99–123.

Van Onselen, Charles. *The Seed Is Mine: The Life of Kas Maine, a South African Sharecropper, 1894–1985*. New York: Hill and Wang, 1996.

Vansina, Jan. *How Societies Are Born: Governance in West Central Africa before 1600*. Charlottesville: University of Virginia Press, 2004.

Vansina, Jan. *Paths in the Rainforests: Toward a History of Political Tradition in Equatorial Africa*. Madison: University of Wisconsin Press, 1990.

Van Velsen, Jaap. *The Politics of Kinship: A Study in Social Manipulation among the Lakeside Tonga of Nyasaland*. Manchester, UK: Manchester University Press, 1964.

Van Velsen, Jaap. "Some Early Pressure Groups in Malawi." In *The Zambesian Past: Studies in Central African History*, edited by Eric Stokes and Richard Brown, 376–412. Manchester, UK: Manchester University Press, 1966.

Vaughan, Megan. *Curing Their Ills: Colonial Power and African Illness*. Stanford, CA: Stanford University Press, 1991.

Vaughan, Megan. "Mr. Mdala Writes to the Governor: Negotiating Colonial Rule in Nyasaland." *History Workshop Journal* 60, no. 1 (2005): 171–88.

Vaughan, Megan. "Reported Speech and Other Kinds of Testimony." In *African Words, African Voices: Critical Practices in Oral History*, edited by Luise White, David William Cohen, and Stephan F. Miescher, 53–77. Bloomington: Indiana University Press, 2001.

Vaughan, Megan. *The Story of an African Famine: Gender and Famine in Twentieth-Century Malawi*. Cambridge: Cambridge University Press, 1987.

Vaughan, Megan. "Which Family? Problems in the Reconstruction of the History of the Family as an Economic and Cultural Unit." *Journal of African History* 24, no. 2 (1983): 275–83.

Vaughan, Megan, and Henrietta L. Moore. *Cutting Down Trees: Gender, Nutrition, and Agricultural Change in the Northern Province of Zambia, 1890–1990*. Portsmouth, NH: Heinemann, 1994.

Vergès, Françoise. *Monsters and Revolutionaries: Colonial Family Romance and Métissage*. Durham, NC: Duke University Press, 1999.

Visweswaran, Kamala. *Un/common Cultures: Racism and the Rearticulation of Cultural Difference*. Durham, NC: Duke University Press, 2010.

Wacquant, Loïc. "For an Analytic of Racial Domination." *Political Power and Social Theory* 11 (1997): 221–34.

Waldman, Linda. *The Griqua Conundrum: Political and Socio-Cultural Identity in the Northern Cape, South Africa*. Oxford: Peter Lang, 2007.

Watts, Michael. "Space for Everything (A Commentary)." *Cultural Anthropology* 7, no. 1 (1992): 115–29.

Weber, Max. *From Max Weber: Essays in Sociology*. Edited by H. H. Gerth and C. Wright Mills. Oxford: Oxford University Press, 1958.

Weinbaum, Alys Eve, et al., eds. *The Modern Girl Around the World: Consumption, Modernity, and Globalization*. Durham, NC: Duke University Press, 2008.

West, Michael O. *The Rise of an African Middle Class: Colonial Zimbabwe, 1898–1965*. Bloomington: Indiana University Press, 2002.

Western, John. *Outcast Cape Town*. 1981. Berkeley: University of California Press, 1996.

Western, John. "Undoing the Colonial City?" *Geographical Review* 75, no. 3 (1985): 335–57.

Wheeldon, P. D. "The Operation of Voluntary Associations and Personal Networks in the Political Processes of an Inter-Ethnic Community." In *Social Networks in Urban Situations: Analyses of Personal Relationships in Central African Towns*, edited by J. Clyde Mitchell, 128–80. Manchester, UK: Manchester University Press, 1969.

White, Landeg. *Magomero: Portrait of an African Village*. Cambridge: Cambridge University Press, 1987.

White, Landeg. "'Tribes' and the Aftermath of the Chilembwe Rising." *African Affairs* 83, no. 333 (1984): 511–41.

White, Luise. "Civic Virtue, Young Men, and the Family: Conscription in Rhodesia, 1974–1980." *International Journal of African Historical Studies* 37, no. 1 (2004): 103–21.

White, Luise. *The Comforts of Home: Prostitution in Colonial Nairobi*. Chicago: University of Chicago Press, 1990.

White, Luise. *Speaking with Vampires: Rumor and History in Colonial Africa*. Berkeley: University of California Press, 2000.

White, Luise. "Telling More: Lies, Secrets, and History." *History and Theory* 39, no. 4 (2000): 11–22.

White, Luise. "The Traffic in Heads: Bodies, Borders and the Articulation of Regional Histories." *Journal of Southern African Studies* 23, no. 2 (1997): 325–38.

White, Owen. *Children of the French Empire: Miscegenation and Colonial Society in French West Africa, 1895–1960*. New York: Oxford University Press, 1999.

White, Richard. *The Middle Ground: Indians, Empires, and Republics in the Great Lakes Region, 1650–1815*. Cambridge: Cambridge University Press, 1991.

Wilder, Gary. "Colonial Ethnology and Political Rationality in French West Africa." *History and Anthropology* 14, no. 3 (2003): 219–52.

Williams, G. J., ed. *Lusaka and Its Environs: A Geographical Study of a Planned Capital City in Tropical Africa*. Lusaka: Zambia Geographical Association, 1986.

Williams, Raymond. *The Country and the City*. New York: Oxford, 1973.

Williams, Raymond. *Marxism and Literature*. New York: Oxford University Press, 1978.

Williams, Vernon J., Jr. *Rethinking Race: Franz Boas and His Contemporaries*. Lexington: University Press of Kentucky, 1996.

Wills, Walter H., and R. J. Barrett, eds. *The Anglo-African Who's Who and Biographical Sketch-Book*. London: Routledge, 1905.

Wilmsen, Edwin N. *Land Filled with Flies: A Political Economy of the Kalahari*. Chicago: University of Chicago Press, 1989.

Winant, Howard. *The World Is a Ghetto: Race and Democracy since World War II*. New York: Basic, 2001.

Wolf, Eric R. *Europe and the People without History*. Berkeley: University of California Press, 1982.

Wolfe, Patrick. "Land, Labor, and Difference: Elementary Structures of Race." *American Historical Review* 106, no. 3 (2001): 866–905.

Wright, Marcia. *Strategies of Slaves and Women: Life-Stories from East/Central Africa*. London: James Currey, 1993.

Yoshikuni, Tsuneo. *African Urban Experiences in Colonial Zimbabwe: A Social History of Harare before 1925*. Harare: Weaver, 2007.

Young, Crawford. *The Politics of Cultural Pluralism*. Madison: University of Wisconsin Press, 1979.

Young, Robert J. C. *Colonial Desire: Hybridity in Theory, Culture and Race*. New York: Routledge, 1995.

Young, T. Cullen. "Tribal Intermixture in Northern Nyasaland." *Journal of the Royal Anthropological Institute of Great Britain and Ireland* 63 (January–June 1933): 1–18.

Zachernuk, Philip S. *Colonial Subjects: An African Intelligentsia and Atlantic Ideas*. Charlottesville: University of Virginia Press, 2000.

Zachernuk, Philip S. "Of Origins and Colonial Order: Southern Nigerian Historians and the 'Hamitic Hypothesis' c. 1870–1970." *Journal of African History* 35, no. 3 (1994): 427–55.

INDEX

∷

Note: Page numbers in italics indicate figures.

Omani communities, 11, 12

Onselen, Charles van, 152

ontologies of intimacy, use of term, 24, 28, 51, 52, 144

oral histories, 44–51, 53, 73, 147–48, 154–55, 157–58, 171, 174, 245–46

Order in Council (Nyasaland, 1892), 37

Passfield, Lord (Sidney James Webb), 101–2, 104–5

patrilineal customs. *See* cultural practices, agnatic

Plaatje, Solomon, 58

politics of birth, 89, 91, 170, 183

poor theory, 155

postcolonialism/postcolonial period: African nationalism and, 3, 4, 7, 12–13, 44, 53–54, 236, 246; nativism and, 8, 10, 11, 12–13, 19, 24, 234, 239, 241, 242, 245, 253n43; scholarship, 4, 8, 10, 13, 14, 15, 20–21, 24, 29, 33, 234–35, 238–39, 240–41, 243, 244, 246; as time period, 3, 4, 13–14, 20–21, 28, 32, 33, 45, 51–52, 148, 242, 244

postnational research agenda, 10, 239

poverty in Lusaka, 209–16

Povinelli, Elizabeth, 144

Price, Leonard W. S., 203

prostitution, 38, 58

Providence Industrial Mission (Nyasaland), 151

Public Services Inquiry Commission (Southern Rhodesia, 1945), 124

race: aptitude and, 5, 126; as colonial reason, 7, 239–40, 242; defined, 5; identity by, 14, 15, 18, 21, 34, 49, 71, 96–97, 99–108, 118, 138, 156, 183–84, 217; as marker, 5; vs. nation, 6–7; privilege, 149–50, 156–65; racial minorities, 5, 10–12, 243; racial state model, 97–99; as schema, 5; as socio-historical construction, 5, 99, 103, 112, 113, 138; subject races, 13, 92; terminology, 13–16, 45, 113, 138; typologies, 9. *See also* nativism; non-nativism; *specific groups*

racism: antiracism, 5–6, 246–47; colonialism and, 4, 5–6, 17, 56, 57, 97, 98, 150–52, 243; conflict vs. connections, 17;

defined, 5–6; in documentation, 36–37; genealogical imagination and, 206; in imperial politics, 20; legislative, 37, 57–58; marginality and, 156; vs. nativism, 18, 239–40, 242; oppression and, 4; scientific, 57; status and, 127, 142, 150, 205, 230, 235. *See also* apartheid; segregation

Radcliffe-Brown, A. R., 9

Raftopoulos, Gerald, 235

Ranger, Terence, 176

Ravenor, Thomas, 157

Reed, Haythorne/Reed ruling, 96–97, 99–104, 109–10, 116, 138, 149, 162–63, 166, 185, 202

Report of the Committee Appointed by the Government of Southern Rhodesia to Enquire into Questions Concerning the Education of Coloured and Half-Caste Children in the Colony (Foggin Commission), 115–16, 169

Report of the Committee to Inquire into the African and Eurafrican Housing Position in Lusaka, 216–17

Report of the Committee to Inquire into the Status and Welfare of Coloured Persons in Northern Rhodesia (Kreft Commission), 130, 212, 217

Representative Committee of Northern Province Native Associations (Nyasaland), 153

research imagination, use of term, 243, 244

Rhodes, Cecil, 202, 203, 204

Rhodesia Cape Afrikander Association of Bulawayo (Southern Rhodesia), 100, 115, 176

Rhodesia Coloured Society (Southern Rhodesia), 115, 182

Rhodesia Eurafrican Vigilance Association (Southern Rhodesia), 100, 115, 176

Rhodesia National Association (Southern Rhodesia), 235

Rhodesian Front (Southern Rhodesia and Rhodesia), 1, 235

Rhodesian Railways, 123, 124

Rhodesian Tribune (newspaper), 28, 175–76, 178–83, 179, 184–206, 197

Rhodesian Tribune Foundation (Southern Rhodesia), 195

CPI Antony Rowe
Eastbourne, UK
October 23, 2014